FRANK LLOYD WRIGHT AND LE CORBUSIER

For Mildred Leon Etlin

and in memory of Ben Etlin

RICHARD A. ETLIN

Frank Lloyd Wright and Le Corbusier
The romantic legacy

Manchester University Press
Manchester and New York

distributed exclusively in the USA and Canada by St. Martin's Press

Copyright © Richard A. Etlin 1994

Published by Manchester University Press
Oxford Road, Manchester M13 9PL, UK
and Room 400, 175 Fifth Avenue, New York, NY 10010, USA
Distributed exclusively in the USA and Canada
by St. Martin's Press, Inc., 175 Fifth Avenue, New York, NY 10010, USA
British Library Cataloguing-in-Publication Data
A catalogue record for this book is available from the British Library
Library of Congress Cataloging-in-Publication Data
Etlin, Richard A.
    Frank Lloyd Wright and Le Corbusier : the romantic legacy /
Richard Etlin.
       p.   cm.
    ISBN 0–7190–4060–4
    1. Wright, Frank Lloyd, 1867–1959—Aesthetics. 2. Le Corbusier,
1887–1965—Aesthetics. 3. Architecture, Modern—19th century–
–Influence. I. Title.
NA737.W7E84   1994
720′.92—dc20   93–12796
                                                   CIP

ISBN 0 7190 4060 4 *hardback*

Designed by Max Nettleton

Photoset in Linotron ITC Garamond by
Northern Phototypesetting Co. Ltd., Bolton

Printed in Great Britain
by Redwood Books, Trowbridge

CONTENTS

List of colour plates   vi

List of figures   vii

Preface   xi

List of acknowledgements   xviii

1   *The architectural system*   1

2   *The picturesque*   76

3   *Eclecticism and modern architecture*   150

4   *The spirit of the age*   165

Notes   201

Index   219

COLOUR PLATES

1 Le Corbusier and Pierre Jeanneret. Swiss Dormitory. South facade

2 Le Corbusier. Villa Shodhan. South-west facade and swimming-pool

3 Le Corbusier. Jaoul Houses. Interior   *between pp. 14 & 15*

4 Le Corbusier. Pilgrimage chapel of Notre-Dame-du-Haut, Ronchamp. View of the east facade

5 Frank Lloyd Wright. Johnson Wax Company Administration Building. Mezzanine

6 Frank Lloyd Wright. Johnson Wax Company Administration Building. Exterior

7 Frank Lloyd Wright. Johnson Wax Company Administration Building. Detail

8 Frank Lloyd Wright. Unity Temple

9 Frank Lloyd Wright. Unity Temple. Interior of the sanctuary   *between pp. 30 & 31*

10 Frank Lloyd Wright. Frederick C. Robie House. Detail

11 Frank Lloyd Wright. Guggenheim Museum

12 Frank Lloyd Wright. William H. Winslow House

13 Frank Lloyd Wright. Arthur Heurtley House   *between pp. 46 & 47*

14 Frank Lloyd Wright. Frank Thomas House

15 Frank Lloyd Wright. Second Herbert Jacobs House. The solar hemicycle

16 Frank Lloyd Wright. 'Hollyhock' House

17 Frank Lloyd Wright. 'Fallingwater'

18 Frank Lloyd Wright. John C. Pew House

19 Frank Lloyd Wright. Pew House. View to the living room

20 Frank Lloyd Wright. Pew House. Living room with view to dining alcove

21 Frank Lloyd Wright. Pew House. View from the dining alcove toward the living room

22 Le Corbusier. Monastery of La Tourette. Detail of the cloister

23 Le Corbusier. Monastery of La Tourette. Detail of the chapel   *between pp. 142 & 143*

FIGURES

1.1   The Acropolis, Athens (an analytical drawing from Auguste Choisy, *Histoire de l'architecture*, 1899, in Le Corbusier's *Vers une Architecture*, 1923)   *page* 10

1.2   Le Corbusier. 'Dom-ino' project, shown with a traditional house in Flanders   15

1.3   Le Corbusier. 'Five Points for a New Architecture,' 1926 (from his *Précisions sur un état de l'architecture et de l'urbanisme*, 1930)   16

1.4   Le Corbusier and Pierre Jeanneret. Maison Cook. Front facade   18

1.5   Le Corbusier and Pierre Jeanneret. Maison Cook. Floor plans   19

1.6   Le Corbusier and Pierre Jeanneret. Villa Stein. Front facade   20

1.7   Le Corbusier and Pierre Jeanneret. Villa Stein. Floor plans   20

1.8   Le Corbusier and Pierre Jeanneret. Villa Savoye   21

1.9   Le Corbusier and Pierre Jeanneret. Villa Savoye. Entrance hall   21

1.10 Le Corbusier and Pierre Jeanneret. Villa Savoye. Ground floor plan   21

1.11 Le Corbusier and Pierre Jeanneret. Swiss Dormitory. View under the elevated dormitory block   22

1.12 Le Corbusier and Pierre Jeanneret. Swiss Dormitory. North facade, detail   22

1.13 Le Corbusier and Pierre Jeanneret. Swiss Dormitory. Ground floor plan   22

1.14 Le Corbusier. Dr Currutchet's House   24

1.15 Le Corbusier. Dr Currutchet's House. Ramp   24

1.16 Le Corbusier. Dr Currutchet's House. Sections   24

1.17 Le Corbusier. Dr Currutchet's House. Floor plans   24

1.18 Le Corbusier. Carpenter Center for the Visual Arts   25

1.19 Le Corbusier. Carpenter Center for the Visual Arts. Second floor plan   25

1.20 Le Corbusier. Villa Shodhan, Ahmedabad. Floor plans   26

1.21 Le Corbusier and Pierre Jeanneret. Weekend house, La Celle Saint-Cloud   28

1.22 Le Corbusier and Pierre Jeanneret. Weekend house, La Celle Saint-Cloud. Interior   28

1.23 Le Corbusier. Jaoul Houses. West facade of house A   29

1.24 Le Corbusier and Pierre Jeanneret. Vacation house, Les Mathes   29

1.25 Le Corbusier. Pilgrimage chapel of Notre-Dame-du-Haut, Ronchamp. Interior view   30

1.26 Japanese Ho-o-Den (from the *Inland Architect*, October 1893)   31

1.27 Frank Lloyd Wright. Frederick C. Robie House   31

1.28 Frank Lloyd Wright. Darwin D. Martin House   32

1.29 'Navy Yard,' in the 'Driftless Area', Wisconsin   33

1.30 Frank Lloyd Wright. Robie House. Ground and first floor plans   35

1.31 Frank Lloyd Wright. Larkin Company Administration Building   36

1.32 Frank Lloyd Wright. Larkin Company Administration Building. Interior   36

1.33 Frank Lloyd Wright. Larkin Company Administration Building. Ground and second floor plans   37

1.34 Frank Lloyd Wright. Johnson Wax Administration Building. Main work space   38

1.35 Frank Lloyd Wright. Johnson Wax Administration Building. Plan   38

1.36 Frank Lloyd Wright. Guggenheim Museum. Entrance   40

1.37 Frank Lloyd Wright. Guggenheim Museum. Main gallery   41

1.38 Frank Lloyd Wright. Second Herbert Jacobs House. Rear facade   41

1.39 Frank Lloyd Wright. William H. Winslow House. Reception hall   42

1.40 Frank Lloyd Wright. Warren R. Hickox House. East elevation and wall section   43

1.41 Frank Lloyd Wright. Hickox House. Plan   43

1.42 Frank Lloyd Wright. H. Harley Bradley House   44

1.43 Frank Lloyd Wright. Bradley House. Plan   44

1.44 Frank Lloyd Wright. Ward W. Willits House — *page* 45

1.45 Frank Lloyd Wright. Willits House. Plan — 45

1.46 Frank Lloyd Wright. Alice Millard House ('La Miniatura') — 46

1.47 Frank Lloyd Wright. 'La Miniatura.' Fireplace — 46

1.48 Frank Lloyd Wright. Wall construction for 'Usonian Automatic' concrete block houses — 49

1.49 Frank Lloyd Wright. Samuel Freeman House — 49

1.50 Frank Lloyd Wright. Wellington and Ralph Cudney House (project) — 50

1.51 Frank Lloyd Wright. Owen D. Young House (project) — 50

1.52 Frank Lloyd Wright. Richard Lloyd Jones House — 52

1.53 Frank Lloyd Wright. Edgar J. Kaufmann House ('Fallingwater'). Living room — 54

1.54 Frank Lloyd Wright. Imperial Hotel, Tokyo — 56

1.55 Frank Lloyd Wright. Robie House. View from the dining room — 57

1.56 Frank Lloyd Wright. Arthur Heurtley House. Living room — 58

1.57 Frank Lloyd Wright. Willits House. Dining room — 59

1.58 Frank Lloyd Wright. Johnson Wax Company Research Tower — 62

1.59 Frank Lloyd Wright. Price Company Tower — 63

1.60 Frank Lloyd Wright. Beth Sholom Synagogue — 64

1.61 Frank Lloyd Wright. Beth Sholom Synagogue, in construction — 65

1.62 Frank Lloyd Wright. First Jacobs House. Front view — 66

1.63 Frank Lloyd Wright. First Jacobs House. Rear view — 67

1.64 Frank Lloyd Wright. First Jacobs House. Plan — 67

1.65 Le Corbusier. Cover of the second edition of *Une Petite maison* (1968). — 69

1.66 Le Corbusier. Opening in the garden wall (from his *Une Petite maison*, 1954) — 69

1.67 Le Corbusier. Drawing of the house on the site (from his *Une Petite maison*, 1954) — 69

1.68 Le Corbusier. Project for the 'Open Hand' — 72

1.69 Le Corbusier. 'The Place of all measures' (from his *Précisions sur un état de l'architecture et de l'urbanisme*, 1930) — 74

1.70 Le Corbusier. 'An authentic "architectural event" ' (from his *Une Petite maison*, 1954) — 74

2.1 'Old English Mansion' (from Augustus Welby Pugin, *The True Principles of Pointed or Christian Architecture*, 1841) — 80

2.2 Augustus Welby Pugin. Saint Oswald's, Liverpool (from his *The Present State of Ecclesiastical Architecture*, 1843) — 80

2.3 Types of composition (from Andrew Jackson Downing, *Cottage residences*, 1842) — 81

2.4 Castle in the landscape (from Eugène-Emmanuel Viollet-le-Duc, *Entretiens sur l'architecture*, 1863) — 82

2.5 City hall (from Eugène-Emmanuel Viollet-le-Duc, *Entretiens sur l'architecture*, 1863) — 82

2.6 Jacques Tetaz. Drawing of the Erechtheion, Athens — 84

2.7 Philippe Titeux and Louis Chaudet. Drawing of the Propylaia, Athens — 84

2.8 'Architecture. Pure création de l'esprit' (from Le Corbusier, *Vers une Architecture*, 1923) — 84

2.9 Temple compound on the island of Philae (from James Fergusson, *An Historical Inquiry into the True Principles of Beauty in Art*, 1849, and *The Illustrated Handbook of Architecture*, 1859) — 91

2.10 Pyramids at Meroë (from James Fergusson, *An Historical Inquiry into the True Principles of Beauty in Art*, 1849, and *The Illustrated Handbook of Architecture*, 1859) — 91

2.11 Analysis of the Caryatid tribune of the Erechtheion, Athens. (from Eugène-Emmanuel Viollet-le-Duc, *Entretiens d'architecture*, 1863) — 96

2.12 Analytical drawing. View in front of the Propylaia, Athens (from Auguste Choisy, *Histoire de l'architecture*, 1899) — 98

2.13 Analytical drawing. View of the Parthenon, Athens (from Auguste Choisy, *Histoire de l'architecture*, 1899) — 98

2.14 Analytical drawing. View of the Erechtheion, Athens (from Auguste Choisy, *Histoire de l'architecture*, 1899) — 98

2.15 Analytical drawing. Curvature of steps bounding the western side of the platform of the Parthenon, Athens (from Auguste Choisy, *Histoire de l'architecture*, 1899) — 100

2.16 The principles of Egyptian architecture (an analytical drawing from Auguste Choisy, *Histoire de l'architecture*, 1899, in Le Corbusier's *Vers une Architecture*, 1923) — 103

2.17 The principles of Hindu architecture (an analytical drawing from Auguste Choisy, *Histoire de l'architecture*, 1899, in Le Corbusier's *Vers une Architecture*, 1923)   *page* 103

2.18 Sequencing of spaces in King Sargon's summer palace in Khorsabad (from Auguste Choisy, *Histoire de l'architecture*, 1899)   104

2.19 Sequencing of spaces in the Baths of Caracalla, Rome (from Auguste Choisy, *Histoire de l'architecture*, 1899)   104

2.20 The Acropolis, Athens (from Auguste Choisy, *Histoire de l'architecture*, 1899)   106

2.21 Analytical drawing, 'that public squares should be enclosed entities' (from Camillo Sitte, *Der Städte-Bau nach seinen künstlerischen Grundsätzen*, 1889)   108

2.22 Analytical drawings. The turbine plaza (from Camillo Sitte, *Der Städte-Bau nach seinen künstlerischen Grundsätzen*, 1889)   108

2.23 Historical example showing appropriate street design (from the French edition of Camillo Sitte, *Der Städte-Bau nach seinen künstlerischen Grundsätzen*)   109

2.24 Karl Henrici. 'Langweilige und kurzweilige Strassen' (from the *Deutsche Bauzeitung*, 3 June 1893)   111

2.25 Charles-Edouard Jeanneret. Street designs (from the unpublished manuscript *La Construction des villes, c. 1910*)   112

2.26 Le Corbusier and Pierre Jeanneret, La Roche-Jeanneret Houses. Project   117

2.27 Le Corbusier and Pierre Jeanneret, La Roche-Jeanneret Houses. First floor plan (analytical drawing from Kurt Forster, 'Antiquity and Modernity in the La Roche-Jeanneret Houses of 1923,' *Oppositions* nos. 15/16, Winter/Spring 1979)   117

2.28 Le Corbusier and Pierre Jeanneret, La Roche-Jeanneret Houses. Triple-height entrance hall of the La Roche House   117

2.29 Hermann Muthesius. Villa Neuhaus. Entrance hall   118

2.30 Juan Gris. *Harlequin*   118

2.31 Le Corbusier and Pierre Jeanneret. Villa Stein. Living room   119

2.32 Robert Mallet-Stevens. Hôtel Collinet. Front and rear facades   120

2.33 Le Corbusier and Pierre Jeanneret. Maison Cook. Living room   122

2.34 Raymond Duchamp-Villon. Maison Cubiste (Salon d'Automne, Paris, 1912)   124

2.35 Jean Aubert and Jacques Gabriel. Hôtel du Maine (analytical plan showing sequencing of space, from Auguste Choisy, *Histoire de l'architecture*, 1899)   125

2.36 Santa Maria in Cosmedin, Rome (from Le Corbusier, *Vers une Architecture*, 1923)   126

2.37 Le Corbusier. Millowners' Association Building, Ahmedabad. West facade   128

2.38 Frank Lloyd Wright. Susan Lawrence Dana House. View across the gallery   131

2.39 Frank Lloyd Wright. Avery Coonley House. Living room   131

2.40 Alexander Jackson Davis. Rotch House   132

2.41 Bruce Price. William Kent House   133

2.42 Frank Lloyd Wright. Isabel Roberts House. Living room   135

2.43 Frank Lloyd Wright. John C. Pew House. Plans   138

2.44 Frank Lloyd Wright. John C. Pew House. Early project, elevation and plan   141

2.45 Frank Lloyd Wright. John C. Pew House. Sections   143

2.46 Le Corbusier and Pierre Jeanneret. Mass-produced artisans' houses (project)   146

2.47 Le Corbusier. Secretariat, Chandigarh   147

2.48 Le Corbusier. Unité d'Habitation, Marseille   148

2.49 Le Corbusier. Monastery of La Tourette   148

3.1 The 'grammar' of Frank Lloyd Wright's architecture (from a letter of 13 May 1904 by Charles E. White, Jr)   159

3.2 The Great Gallery of Aké (from Désiré Charnay, *The Ancient Cities of the New World*, 1887)   161

3.3 Egyptian pylon temple (from Auguste Choisy, *Histoire de l'architecture*, 1899)   162

4.1 'Eyes That Do Not See.' ' "Air Express" Goliath Farman' (from Le Corbusier, *Vers une Architecture*, 1923)   184

4.2 'Eyes That Do Not See.' Architectural monuments compared in size to the ocean liner Aquitania (from Le Corbusier, *Vers une Architecture*, 1923)   184

4.3 'Mass-produced houses' (from Le Corbusier, *Vers une Architecture*, 3rd edn, 1928)   185

4.4 'The Goliath Farman, Paris–Prague in six hours. Paris–Warsaw in nine hours' (from Le Corbusier, *Vers une Architecture*, 1923)   185

4.5   Sample page spread from Otto Wagner, *Moderne Architektur* (2nd edn, 1898)   *page* 188

4.6   A page from Hendrik Petrus Berlage, *L'Art et la société*, 1913–14, 2nd edn, 1921   190

4.7   A page from Hendrik Petrus Berlage, *L'Art et la société*, 1913–14, 2nd edn, 1921   191

4.8   'Eyes That Do Not See. I. Ocean Liners' (from Le Corbusier, *Vers une Architecture*, 1923)   193

4.9   Le Corbusier and Pierre Jeanneret. Maison Cook. 'One enters under the house'   195

4.10   Le Corbusier and Pierre Jeanneret. Villa Stein. 'Entrance to the property'   195

4.11   The *Aquitania* (from Le Corbusier, *Vers une Architecture*, 1923)   197

4.12   'Architectural promenade.' Le Corbusier and Pierre Jeanneret. Villa Savoye   197

PREFACE

All artists bear the imprint of their times, but the great artists are those in whom this is most profoundly marked.

Henri Matisse, *Notes of a Painter* (1908)[1]

Frank Lloyd Wright and Le Corbusier are widely considered the two greatest architects of the twentieth century. The beauty and originality of their buildings, the profundity and complexity of their artistic endeavors, and the variety of their stylistic achievements constitute an extraordinary accomplishment. Whereas the work of these two architects rises above that of most if not all of their contemporaries, it also strongly confirms Matisse's observation that the greatest artists are most deeply marked by their times.

Although the major buildings by Frank Lloyd Wright and Le Corbusier date from this century, the architectural world to which they belong extends back to the Romantic revolution of the early nineteenth century when major changes in cultural attitudes displaced the dominant outlook of the Enlightenment. From the 1820s onward, a new set of ideas and principles, directed now toward the creation of an appropriate contemporary architecture, dominated architectural discourse until World War II, when its authority began to weaken. By the 1960s, the ideology and stylistic concerns of post-modernism began to challenge the assumptions of the previous era to the point where its hegemony over architectural culture was irrevocably fractured. Many of the fundamental principles of the Romantic age, which had been repeatedly articulated by successive generations over the course of a century, now had become vaguely understood, often misrepresented, and at times simply forgotten.

This book is at once a study of the new set of principles articulated in the nineteenth century to guide the creation of a modern architecture and a demonstration of their fundamental importance to the architecture of Frank Lloyd Wright and Le Corbusier. In a period dominated by the revival of historical styles, no nineteenth-century architect was truly successful in realizing the progressive vision of the age in a sustained manner. Frank Lloyd Wright and Le Corbusier were the first and perhaps the only architects of the era to achieve this goal. Paradoxically, their artistic achievements, milestones in twentieth-century culture, were fundamentally guided by this nineteenth-century progressive vision. Their genius largely consisted in understanding how to translate a challenging set of abstract ideas into original and compelling buildings.

This study is organized around the key terms and concepts of the nineteenth-century progressive tradition – the 'architectural system,' the 'picturesque,' 'eclecticism,' 'representative architecture,' the engineer's aesthetic, and the 'spirit of the age.' I concur with the Reverend John Louis Petit who in 1854 prefaced his search for 'true architectural principles' useful to promoting the creation of a contemporary architecture by observing, 'I am far from thinking that nomenclature is a remedy for every defect in art or science: still I cannot but feel that confusion of terms generally springs from, and always leads to, confusion of ideas.'[2] Whereas some of these concepts have been studied in recent histories of this period, others have been only partially explored or even ignored.[3] My goal is to provide a more complete and balanced account, while demonstrating that the architecture of Frank Lloyd Wright and Le Corbusier was guided by this nineteenth-century reform tradition.

The design principles and cultural values studied in this book constitute the main elements of the Romantic legacy. From the onset of the Renaissance in the early fifteenth century through the Neoclassical period of the late eighteenth century, Western architecture was dominated by the classical architecture of the Greco-Roman tradition. Generation after generation of architects saw itself as participating in an ongoing creative endeavor that worked with what the French simply called 'la bonne architecture,' that is, good architecture. After a hiatus of several hundred years in which it was now deemed that architecture had degenerated into a barbarous 'gothic' style, architecture had returned to the true principles of regularity and symmetry, consecrated by the divinely created form of the human body, and to the true canon of beauty, as found in the classical language of architecture and in the grammar that regulated the combination of its parts.

The hegemony of classical architecture was broken in the early nineteenth century by a series of related changes in cultural attitudes that since that time have been identified with the term 'Romanticism.' I am using the term 'Romantic revolution' to refer to the broad cultural phenomenon that, as Ludovic Vitet observed in 1825, transcended the various movements that adopted or were given the label of Romanticism. Extending beyond new literary and artistic movements, Romanticism reflected a major shift in cultural attitudes, and has been characterized as a new cultural relativism that replaced the Enlightenment's emphasis on the definition of universal man and its application of a single set of standards to different peoples.[4] This new cultural relativism focused attention on the contributions to civilization made by different national and ethnic cultures, many of which were outside the Western tradition. A new awareness and acceptance of the plurality of architectural styles as found across the globe and over time resulted, as is well known, in a century of historicism, dominated by various revivals of past artistic styles.

Yet there also arose a new cultural imperative as a corollary to the new interest in different societies. From the 1820s onward, it was widely held that every major civilization had its own architecture, which embodied its highest achievements or expressed its most typical aspects. As a consequence of this understanding, a challenge emerged in the Romantic era, a need to create an architecture expressive of contemporary culture. As John Summerson astutely observed in the 1940s, 'no other century but the nineteenth' would have felt compelled to create a style expressive of the times.[5] Actually, this quest would dominate the culture of Western architecture until World War II. Summerson's reflections at that time about this 'curious' task signal the beginning of its demise.

The concept of the 'spirit of the age' was central to this Romantic quest for a modern architecture. Progressive architects and critics interested in realizing this new cultural imperative of creating a modern style, expressive of the most significant or highest manifestations of contemporary life, used three new conceptual tools to translate their interest in the 'spirit of the age' into architectural form — eclecticism, picturesque architecture and urbanism, and the 'architectural system.' All three were integral components of the Romantic legacy.

Eclecticism was a Romantic rather than an Enlightenment phenomenon. The challenge posed by the plurality of historical styles was rapidly turned into an asset by theorists who argued that the principles rather than the forms of past styles provided the key to creating a new, modern architecture. The picturesque was a relatively new aesthetic category that had become important in the second half of the eighteenth century, where it had been applied primarily to landscape appreciation, garden design, and minor buildings. In the Romantic era, it now entered the realm first of architecture and then of urbanism as a major force that challenged the principles of classical harmony which had dominated the West over the previous four centuries. Finally, the notion of the 'architectural system' arose from the Romantic conviction that each culture – Egyptian, Assyrian, Greek, Roman, Byzantine, and so forth – had its characteristic architecture grounded in a new and distinctive way of building. Each historical style was understood as an organic development of a particular manner of building that used contemporary materials and methods of construction and that responded to current sensibilities. To describe this complex phenomenon architects and critics developed a new concept called the 'architectural system,' which was seen as composed of three sub-systems – construction, form, and decoration. This term, one of the most powerful analytic tools in the vocabulary of architecture, has virtually been forgotten today. Its mention in architectural histories of the nineteenth and early twentieth centuries has been casual, without an attempt to trace the history of its use.

Chapter one sketches the history of the term – the architectural system – and then explores how Frank Lloyd Wright and Le Corbusier were guided by this concept. Le Corbusier himself discussed the term in his *Almanach d'architecture moderne* (1925) and began to realize its potential when in 1926 he formulated the 'Five Points for a New Architecture,' which would direct his work through the remainder of his long career. Frank Lloyd Wright's Prairie houses were informed, in part, by this notion of the architectural system, but more importantly by Gottfried Semper's alternative definition of the 'symbolic' architectural system – hearth, protecting roof, building erected upon a base, and screen walls. Beginning with the textile block houses of the 1920s, Wright integrated these two concepts of the architectural system even more fully. The remainder of his career was marked by innovative applications of the architectural system in which a building's form and decoration were derived from a modern and generally innovative system of construction – Fallingwater, Johnson Wax Company Administration Building and Research Tower, Beth Sholom Synagogue, Guggenheim Museum, etc.

Chapter two studies the concept of the picturesque, a major aesthetic category in the nineteenth century. It was felt that asymmetrical picturesque design, as opposed to formal symmetry, imparted life to a building as well as enabling it to respond more sensibly to conditions of program and siting. I trace the history of the picturesque in this period through the new genre of the history of world architecture and through the rise of a French Hellenism stimulated by the creation of the Ecole Française d'Athènes in 1846. This chapter explores the rules for asymmetrical design devised by Viollet-le-Duc and Auguste Choisy in response to these trends and compares them with those formulated by Andrew Jackson Downing. It also explains W. Burgh's concept of the 'picturesque principle,' Dugald Stewart's of 'sufficient reason,' and considers the notion of the reasoned picturesque. Furthermore, the urban design principles of Camillo Sitte and his followers are related to the ongoing development of the concept of the picturesque. Frank Lloyd Wright's and Le Corbusier's debt to this tradition is explored with particular emphasis on the reasoned picturesque and the sequencing of spaces, which Viollet-le-Duc called the *mise en scène*, and Le Corbusier, the 'architectural promenade.'

Chapter three treats the concept of eclecticism. The nineteenth century saw itself as an eclectic age. Stylistic eclecticism certainly dominated architectural design. At the same time, though, progressives developed what might be termed a 'philosophical eclecticism' to guide the creation of a new architecture. This entailed extracting principles, as opposed to stylistic features, from the history of world architecture that could be used to inform a modern style. When in 1945 Frank Lloyd Wright explained to the press that his design for the Guggenheim Museum had been inspired by the Assyrian ziggurat, he was giving one specific instance from a long career during which he had taken design principles from other eras and given them new and modern forms. The same is true of Le Corbusier who applied his 'Five Points for a New Architecture' in a way that combined the lessons of Egyptian and Greek architecture, which he then transfused with a Cubist aesthetic.

In the literature of art and architectural history the fundamental Romantic concept of the 'spirit of the age' has generally been limited to the German idealistic notion of the *Zeitgeist*. In chapter four, I explore the different meanings given to the phrase in a number of Western cultures to show its importance as a principle for guiding architectural expression. I also argue that the German idealist meaning constituted a rare and isolated use of the term within the culture of architecture, which usually grounded it in an empirical approach.

Interest in investing architecture with the 'spirit of the age' was directed toward what was called 'representative architecture.' Ever since the construction of the first monumental palaces and temples, there has been what nineteenth-century theorists termed 'representative architecture.' In the nineteenth century, though, representative architecture was redefined to mean not the seat of power and authority but rather the building type most characteristic of a particular culture – the Greek temple, the Roman baths, the Gothic castle or cathedral, and so on. Now, in what was seen as the age of industrialization and the crowd, it was argued that there were new representative building types that had replaced the temple and the palace in cultural importance – railroad stations, factories, power stations, department stores, office buildings, and most importantly, housing for the masses. For both Frank Lloyd Wright and Le Corbusier, the task of investing architecture, especially these buildings types, with an aspect appropriate to their status as representative buildings of the age was a guiding principle.

One of the most important lessons for the creation of a representative architecture was the engineer's aesthetic. Whereas the use of historical styles seemed to progressives a dead and empty practice, the new engineering marvels of the day – railroad bridges and train stations, world's fair exhibition halls, factories and grain silos, and ocean liners, automobiles, and airplanes – became a source of inspiration. Their combination of technological achievement and graceful form offered a model that architects sought to emulate in the domain of building. The works of civil and mechanical engineering were even elevated to the status of iconic images to be integrated into the new architecture. Chapter four traces the development of this attitude and then explores the degree to which the engineer's aesthetic informed the architecture of Frank Lloyd Wright and Le Corbusier.

All of these concepts came together in the illustrated architectural treatise written to expound the principles of modern architecture. The most famous, Le Corbusier's *Vers une Architecture* (1923), has never been systematically studied in light of its predecessors. In this final chapter, I trace the development of this genre in the pioneering and influential works by Otto Wagner, Hendrik Petrus Berlage, and finally Le Corbusier.

The major premise behind this book was determined inductively. In the early 1980s, after having devoted a decade to French architecture and urbanism of the Enlightenment, I began a study of modern Italian architecture in the first half of the twentieth century. I was struck by the quest for a modern architecture grounded in a new way of building that so obsessed the architects of this era. It was a compulsion generally absent from the eighteenth-century Enlightenment. Tracing this notion back in time, I began to discover and to explore systematically a complex of ideas that seemed to originate and coalesce as a driving intellectual force with the Romantic revolution of the 1820s. At each stage of my research, I found myself exclaiming that these were the informing principles behind the architecture of Frank Lloyd Wright and Le Corbusier.

Le Corbusier has been a major source of interest since the late 1960s when I wrote an undergraduate senior thesis at Princeton University entitled 'Le Corbusier: A Mediterranean Dialectic.' My attention to Wright's architecture followed several years later when I began to teach in 1975. At that time I joined my previous interest in Gaston Bachelard's study of the 'poetics of space' and the 'material imagination,' which I had been exploring in Le Corbusier's *Une Petite maison* (1954), with Wright's *The Natural House* (1954).

To a great degree, this book presents two parallel stories – one on nineteenth-century theory, the other on the ways in which Frank Lloyd Wright and Le Corbusier used these principles to guide the creation of a modern architecture. To present these stories, I begin each chapter with a lengthy consideration of the principal concepts of nineteenth-century progressive architectural thought. In the latter part of each chapter, I then explain how both Frank Lloyd Wright and Le Corbusier used them to guide their vision of a modern architecture. Given the current state of knowledge about all the subjects treated here, there is an inherent difference between these two parts. Whereas the first section of each chapter discusses in detail the four main concepts – the architectural system, the picturesque, eclecticism, and the spirit of the age – with an abundance of sources that will probably be new to most readers, the second section of each chapter largely addresses the well-known and extensively studied characteristics of Wright's and Le Corbusier's architecture in an attempt to cast them in a new light. I beg the indulgence of those readers already familiar with the basic features reviewed in the second part of each chapter. These sections should be useful not only for newcomers to the field but also to determine whether more advanced readers and I are in agreement as to what the main principles and aspects of Wright's and Le Corbusier's architecture actually are.

In developing the two parts of each chapter according to what I see as their differing inner needs, I have allowed a certain independence to remain between them. The discussions of nineteenth-century theory are not limited to the particular sources that Wright and Le Corbusier were likely to have read, but rather are broadened in an attempt to show how widespread these ideas were throughout the West during the Romantic era. In fact, this part of the book on nineteenth-century progressive theory can be seen as a prelude to further studies of twentieth-century modern architecture beyond the work of Wright and Le Corbusier. In this book, I have chosen their work for the second part of each chapter, in part as a demonstration of the importance of the Romantic legacy, but also because it uses this legacy most completely.

In preparing this book, I have incurred debts of gratitude that I am pleased to acknowledge here. The most important is to the General Research Board of Graduate Studies and Research of the University of Maryland, which granted me a 1989–90 Academic Year Research Award. During this period I prepared a final draft of my manuscript, which I had written in rough form principally in 1985–86. I am grateful to Peter Buchanan, guest editor of the January 1987 issue of *The Architectural Record*, and to Richard E. Spear, Editor-in-Chief of *The Art Bulletin* (June 1987), for having published two articles on Le Corbusier that adapted portions of this manuscript. These articles, in turn, put into print the material from academic papers delivered at the 1985 annual meeting of the Society of Architectural Historians and the 1986 annual meetings of the Society for French Historical Studies and of the Western Society for French History. Selections from chapter one were read at the annual conference of the Association of Collegiate Schools of Architecture, Northeast Region, on 24 October 1986, at the New Jersey Institute of Technology, under the title 'The Architectural System from Quatremère de Quincy to Frank Lloyd Wright and Le Corbusier.' My ideas about the relationship between Le Corbusier and Auguste Choisy were presented in a public lecture series that I gave in conjunction with a graduate seminar at the School of Architecture of the University of Virginia in the fall, 1981. I cherish the memories of the hospitality extended me as a visiting faculty member by Robert Dripps and Dean Jaquelin T. Robertson. Finally, I thank Douglas Graf, who had resuscitated *Connections*, a student publication of the Harvard Graduate School of Design, for publishing my first article when I was a graduate student in architecture school. The subject matter of this youthful piece, entitled 'At The Still Point of the Turning World,' which appeared in the 1971 issue, has found its place in altered form at the end of chapter one.

Archival research on Le Corbusier and Frank Lloyd Wright was a pleasure thanks to the directors and staff of the respective collections. In particular, I am grateful to the assitance provided at the Fondation Le Corbusier by Evelyne Tréhin, Délégué Général, and by Martine Lasson and Holy Raveloarisoa, and at The Frank Lloyd Wright Foundation by Bruce Brooks Pfeiffer, Director of Archives, Oscar Munoz, Administrator of Archives and Photographic Collection, and Margot Stipe, Assistant to the Director. Among the owners of Frank Lloyd Wright houses who faciliated my research, I am particularly grateful to Dr John and Cindy Edwards and to James and Nancy Dennis for their interest in my work and for their hospitality.

This book went into production while I was spending the year as the Paul Mellon Senior Fellow at the Center for Advanced Study in the Visual Arts (CASVA), National Gallery of Art, Washington, D.C. This fellowship allowed me uninterrupted time to address the final phase of this project. I benefited from the assistance of the staff both at CASVA and at the Library of the National Gallery of Art.

In translating texts from several languages I have consulted various friends and colleagues. I wish in particular to thank Kurt Günther for his assistance with the German texts. Responsibility, of course, for all the translations is my own. Permission to quote the longer passages from Frank Lloyd Wright, *An Autobiography* and *The Natural House*, has been granted courtesy of The Frank Lloyd Wright Foundation. Finally, a generous grant from the Graham Foundation for Advanced Studies in the Fine Arts has made it possible to provide the black and white illustrations that accompany the text.

Since I wrote this book in tandem with *Modernism in Italian Architecture, 1890–1940* (The MIT Press, 1991), switching back and forth from drafts of one manuscript to the other, the reader will find that these two books are complementary. The book on Italian architecture, which is a study of the changing and pluralistic notion of modernism in this crucial fifty-year period, is a case study of the dilemma that arose with the Romantic revolution of how to create a contemporary architecture at once national in character and modern in aspect. The concepts of the architectural system, philosophical eclecticism, the spirit of the age, and the engineer's aesthetic are briefly introduced in relation to the relevant aspects of the various modern movements in Italian architecture. The book presented here on Frank Lloyd Wright and Le Corbusier explores these concepts more fully and seeks to demonstrate their fundamental importance to the work of these two geniuses. Whereas much of the research undertaken today concerning these two architects traces the development of their buildings through a minute study of archival documents to reconstruct the evolution of the design and the history of its patronage and of its construction, I have chosen to concentrate on the ideals and principles publicly proclaimed by the two architects and generally accepted by historians, and to relate this public artistic persona to the nineteenth-century Romantic reform tradition.

In many respects the preparation of this book has been an intellectual odyssey that covers the expanding interests of over twenty years of association with the field of architecture. Whereas I write this book as a document of history, I find myself considering it as a statement of faith. If two great minds and artistic temperaments so utterly different as Frank Lloyd Wright and Le Corbusier saw in these principles a way to create great architecture, then surely they have enduring validity beyond any fashions of the day.

ACKNOWLEDGEMENTS

Figures 1.1–1.25, 1.65, 1.67–1.69, 2.8. 2.16. 2.17, 2.25, 2.26. 2.28, 2.30–2.33, 2.36, 2.37, 2.46–2.49, 4.1–4.4, 4.8–4.12
  © 1993 ARS, New York/SPADEM, Paris

Figures 1.28, 1.30–1.36, 1.39–1.52, 1.54–1.61, 1.64, 2.38, 2.39, 2.42–2.45
  © 1993 The Frank Lloyd Wright Archives

Figure 1.27   Photo: Hedrich-Blessing Photo, HB-19312 A
Figure 1.53   Photo: Hedrich-Blessing Photo, HB-04414 U2
  Hedrich-Blessing photos courtesy Chicago Historical Society

Figure 1.29   Photo: Henry Hamilton/H. H. Bennett Studio Foundation

Figure 1.37   Photo: Robert E. Mates © The Solomon R. Guggenheim Foundation, New York

Figure 1.38   Photo: Ezra Stoller © Esto

Figures 1.62, 1.63   Photos: © 1993 Paul Rocheleau Photographer

Figures 1.66, 1.70   Photos: Melle Péter © 1993 ARS, New York/SPADEM, Paris

Figures 2.6, 2.7   Ecole nationale supérieure des Beaux-Arts, Paris

Figures 2.21–2.23 © 1986 Rizzoli International Publications, Inc.

Figure 2.27   Analytical drawing by Kurt Forster over floor plan by Le Corbusier and Pierre Jeanneret
  © 1993 ARS, New York/SPADEM, Paris

Figure 2.34   Association André Mare, Paris. © 1993 ARS, New York/SPADEM, Paris

Figures 2.40, 2.41   Drawings: Peter Noonan

Figure 3.1 © Charles E. White, Jr.

Figures 4.6, 4.7 © Editions Tekhné, Brussels

Colour plates 2, 22   Photos: © 1993 Steven W. Hurtt

Colour plates 4, 23   Photos: © 1993 Lauren Goldberg

Colour plates 3, 5–21   Photos: © 1993 Richard A. Etlin

Extracts from Frank Lloyd Wright's *An Autobiography* and *The Natural House* quoted courtesy of The Frank Lloyd Wright Foundation

CHAPTER 1

The architectural system

The search for a modern architecture was guided by the universal conviction that architecture was grounded in the art of building. Reformers soon had a powerful conceptual tool to assist them through the introduction of a new concept, the 'architectural system.' The phrase 'architectural system' generally designated the integral co-ordination of structure, form, and decoration, such that architecture was grounded in construction, but ultimately refined by aesthetics. Yet construction and art were indispensable to each other. Just as structure could not determine the form, aesthetics could not ignore the fabric of building. Each component of the architectural system had an inalienable contribution to offer to the final product.

By comparing the definitions of architectural style and architectural system, it becomes evident that 'system' served a purpose that 'style' could not satisfy. Style referred to *'le trait caractéristique,'* the general aspect or look.[1] Its reach was global. System, in contrast, was analytical. It permitted a dissection of architecture into its constituent parts, which, in turn, had to be considered in their totality. Either the term 'architectural system' or the concept that it represents dominated the architectural discourse of the nineteenth and early twentieth centuries.

In defense of Gothic architecture

It was Quatremère de Quincy, an influential figure in the art world, who in the 1820s and 1830s brought the phrase into the mainstream of architectural thought in an attempt to maintain the hegemony of classical architecture at a moment when it was being seriously challenged for the first time since the Renaissance.[2] This inveterate classicist hoped to counter the nascent enthusiasm for national styles, such as the Gothic and its related Romanesque, as well as a growing cultural relativism, which admitted a multiplicity of architectural styles into the pantheon of cultural achievements. Although Quatremère de Quincy conceded that there were numerous architectural systems, none, he believed, was as satisfactorily developed as that of Greek architecture.[3]

Quatremère de Quincy lost no opportunity to criticize Gothic architecture as the fruit of chaotic fantasy. When Quatremère de Quincy looked at the Gothic, he saw only the absence of coherent systems of construction, form, and decoration. History seemed to confirm his aesthetic judgement, for the Gothic style had been 'born of so many heterogeneous elements and in the time of such confusion.' In short, Gothic architecture conveyed 'only the idea of *disorder*.'[4]

The terms of Quatremère de Quincy's denigration of Gothic architecture were repeated again in 1846 by Raoul-Rochette, speaking for the prestigious Académie Royale des Beaux-Arts in his capacity as Secrétaire Perpétuel.[5] Each of these attacks provoked a spirited response. Ludovic Vitet, former first Inspector General of Historical Monuments, answered Quatremère de Quincy in his study of Notre-

Dame de Noyon (1844), 'the first monograph of a medieval French cathedral treated as an historical source.'[6] This was followed by another defense in 'De l'art et de l'archéologie' (1845) by Jean-Baptiste-Antoine Lassus, restorer of the Sainte Chapelle (begun 1838) and, since 1844, collaborator with Viollet-le-Duc on the restoration of Notre Dame Cathedral in Paris.[7] Raoul-Rochette's paper was then answered by Viollet-le-Duc in his article, 'Du Style Gothique au XIXe siècle' ('On the Gothic Style in the Nineteenth Century') (1846).

So compelling had the definition of the 'architectural system' become that Vitet, Lassus, and Viollet-le-Duc responded by attempting to demonstrate that indeed Gothic architecture did enjoy all the features of a true architectural system. 'In a word,' wrote Vitet,

to reduce to precise terms the opinion of the illustrious writer [i.e., Quatremère de Quincy], he believes that it is totally impossible to discern in this supposed architecture the basis either of a system of proportion, a system of construction, or a system of ornamentation, three things without which an architecture does not exist. The question is clearly posed. We accept the terms. To our mind, the architecture of the thirteenth and fourteenth centuries possesses a system of proportion, a system of construction, and a system of ornamentation; systems that are its own, that constitute its originality, and that make it profoundly different not only from classical architecture, but also from all other ways of building used successively in other periods of the Middle Ages.

In addition to explaining the systematic nature of Gothic proportions, structure, and ornamentation, Vitet also argued that the Gothic had undergone three successive evolutionary phases – from primitive heaviness to perfectly balanced harmony and then to exaggerated lightness and mannered aspect – which, as he had written earlier, had characterized the cycle of Greek art.[8]

Viollet-le-Duc, quoting from Vitet and Lassus, adduced additional arguments to demonstrate the originality and coherent order of Gothic architecture that made it worthy of consideration as an architectural system.[9] Thus, by the mid-1840s, the concept of the architectural system had become central to architectural discourse in France. Indeed, the notion of the architectural system was the touchstone by which the aesthetic integrity and worth of Gothic architecture were re-established in that country.

The concept of the architectural system was useful not only to defend Gothic architecture against attacks from champions of classicism; it also helped clarify the issue of historical origins. The English architect Thomas Hope, for example, who used the term 'architectural system' in one of the first histories of world architecture, written toward 1831, stressed the systematic and coherent integration of all of architecture's constituent parts. This can be seen most clearly in Hope's discussion of Gothic architecture, referred to as the 'pointed style,' at a time when the nomenclature of historical periods and styles was virtually being pioneered. 'But the mere question,' explained Hope, ' "Who invented the pointed arch?" taken thus separately, and out of its combination with the other modifications of the pointed style, is in itself a subject' of little significance.[10] What did it matter, wrote Vitet, that several elements of Gothic architecture, perhaps including the pointed arch itself, came from the Orient? One should not conclude that herein resided 'the true origin of the system, because a system is one thing and the scattered and incoherent elements of which it is constituted is another.'[11] The historical evolution of the architectural systems of Gothic and Greek architecture furnished a major subject for the *Rudimentary Treatise on the Principles of Design in Architecture as Deductible from Nature and Exemplified in the Works of the Greek and*

Gothic Architects by the architect Edward Lacy Garbett. First published in London in 1850, this book was in its third edition by 1867 and continued into a ninth edition of 1906. Garbett's extensive use of the term and concept of the 'architectural system' helped to familiarize the English-speaking world with this idea.[12]

The three-part definition of the architectural system popularized by Quatremère de Quincy, while comprehensive in regard to the creation of form, was obviously deficient from the point of view of the professional architect who had to address the user's needs. It lacked the important eighteenth-century notion of *la distribution*, which referred to the functional arrangement of spaces in a building. This inadequacy was corrected by the French engineer, Léonce Reynaud. In the entry 'Architecture' for Charles Gosselin's *Encyclopédie Nouvelle* (1836), Reynaud added the category of *la distribution* to construction, form, and decoration, in his definition of the architectural system. For Reynaud, if architecture was to reflect the essential characteristics of a particular culture, it would have to be what he called a 'complete architectural system':

Thus, if *la distribution* conforms with current needs, if the methods of construction are those indicated by science, if the proportions and the methods of decoration issue naturally from the feelings and taste of the times, the architectural system that will result from this will have the privilege of representing society in all of its aspects.[13]

The system of construction

The system of construction was universally seen as the basis for the systems of form and decoration. So common was this perception that the repeated lament about the nineteenth century not having its own characteristic architecture was often phrased in these terms. Thus, Vitet, writing in 1838, explained:

I do not believe that it is possible to expect our century to have its own architecture, that is to say, an entirely new, special, and individual system of construction that distinguishes itself from all others that preceded it. Architecture is an art that reproduces too faithfully contemporary mores and social conditions for a distinctive identity to issue forth from our bland and undistinguished era.[14]

In 1902, to choose an example from the early twentieth century, the Italian art critic Ugo Ojetti addressed the outpouring of excitement about the creation of a new art – Art Nouveau – occasioned by the Prima Esposizione Internazionale d'Arte Decorativa Moderna (First International Exposition of Modern Decorative Art), which was being held in Turin, by wondering whether the success in the decorative arts had found a counterpart in architecture: 'Is there yet a new constructive style, a new architecture . . .?'[15] Ojetti's choice of words – *un nuovo stile costruttivo* – is instructive because it conveyed the sense of an architectural system developing out of a system of construction and to which it would remain intimately tied in all of its aesthetic aspects.

Over the course of the nineteenth and early twentieth centuries, one finds repeated assertions about the primacy of construction as the guiding force in the creation of 'an architecture' or an architectural style. A brief sampling of quotations taken from different times during this period and from different countries will illustrate the universality of this conviction. Sometimes this notion was presented as a self-evident principle; other times it was invoked with the lessons of history as witness to its truth. John Claudius Loudon, writing in *The Architectural Magazine* (1834), of which he was the editor, explained: 'The architecture of all ages and countries may be reduced to two primitive elements; viz., the roof and the prop by which it is supported.'[16] In 1852 the leading English Gothic revivalist, George Edmund Street, expressed this notion directly in his 'True Principles of Architecture': 'In all architecture, the first principles are most eminently constructional.'[17] After reviewing the development of Romanesque, Byzantine, and Gothic churches in his *Elementary Lectures on Christian Architecture* (1879), Richard Popplewell Pullan concluded, 'thus each change in style was produced by the introduction of what were thought to be improvements in construction.'[18] In the United States at the turn of the twentieth century, an article in the American journal *The Craftsman* (1906), when discussing the expressive potential of a certain approach to skyscraper design, observed: 'It already has the first essential of a new style, a new principle of construction.'[19] As the eminent German critic Karl Scheffler expressed it in 1907: 'Technics has always been the mother of stylistic ideas.'[20] 'It is not at all a discredit,' he later wrote in 'The New Style,' 'to the styles of building, as ingenious creations of mankind, when one proves their dependence upon constructive principles . . . . No new living style of building can take form and continue to be effective if it is not based on a powerful constructive idea born out of the creative instinct of the time.'[21] Likewise, in 1927 Le Corbusier expressed an analogous thought: 'How can one speak about current or future architecture if not always by keeping in mind the past, tradition? . . . The past shows us architectures that are all based upon systems of structure.' Paraphrasing Viollet-le-Duc, Le Corbusier went on to explain: 'These systems of structure = the totality of available technical means.'[22]

Sometimes this thought was accompanied by reflections on the passing from the first principles of construction to fully mature architectural forms. This was certainly the case with observers of the new tall office buildings of the late nineteenth century in Chicago. The distinguished American architectural critic Montgomery Schuyler wrote of transforming construction into 'artistic expression,' or as the American architect Henry Van Brunt put it: 'the frank conversion of practical building into architectural building without affectations or mannerisms . . . . It is based on a sleepless inventiveness in structure; on an honest and vigorous recognition of the part which structure should play in making a building fitting and beautiful; on an intelligent adaptation of form to the available building materials,' and so forth.[23]

Viollet-le-Duc, in his *Entretiens sur l'architecture* (1863), had expressed this notion in an aphorism about Greek architecture that echoed through three-quarters of a century in various forms. Greek architecture, which Viollet-le-Duc termed the 'most absolute and most perfect type that realizes the principles to which I will repeatedly have occasion to direct the reader's attention,' was 'la construction faite l'art,' 'construction transformed into art.'[24] The Viennese Otto Wagner echoed this principle in his *Moderne Architektur*: 'One can affirm with certainty: every architectural form is born from construction and then is transformed into art.'[25] Similarly, the Italian architect Angiolo Mazzoni recalled that when he saw Josef Hoffmann's Austrian pavilion at the International Exposition of 1911 in Rome, he learned a basic lesson about the nature of architecture: 'It revealed to me how architecture should be: construction become poetry.'[26]

This concord of form and decoration with structure and materials, with the former being inspired by and derived from the latter, was the leitmotif of early twentieth-century theory as well. Thus, in 1911 the German architect Hans Poelzig complained about the architect who 'avoided descending into the laws that inform construction and who forgets that from these needs issue the norms on which to base the character and beauty of the construction.'[27] In a similar vein, the French architect and teacher Anatole de Baudot reminded his readers in 1916 that the 'main principle that dominates and emerges incontestably from the analysis of truly creative works is the reasoned and judicious use of materials and their concordance with the forms that should be the consequence of their use.'[28]

Over the course of the nineteenth century, there had been a series of studies that had stressed the primacy of construction in historical architecture, while reinforcing the notion that each true architectural system had its own original system of construction. At mid-century in France, there appeared a remarkable set of independent, specialized studies that extended these ideas to a variety of historical architectures with both depth and detail to a degree generally not found before: Albert Lenoir on Byzantine architecture (1840), Viollet-le-Duc on Gothic architecture (1844–46), Paul-Emile Botta on the newly discovered Assyrian architecture (1849–50), Jules Quicherat on Romanesque architecture (1851), Charles-Edouard Isabelle on ancient domed buildings (1855), and Anatole de Baudot on French medieval vernacular architecture (1867).[29] These were followed by Auguste Choisy's masterful *L'Art de bâtir chez les Romains* (1873) and *L'Art de bâtir chez les Byzantins* (1883). The first volume of Viollet-le-Duc's *Entretiens sur l'architecture* (1863), written as a thematic and analytical history of world architecture, as opposed to the customary chronological approach, placed this concept before an even broader audience while offering a consideration of different historical architectures. In 1899, Choisy published his two-volume *Histoire de l'architecture*, which offered the most complete history of world architecture conceived according to the parameters of the architectural system in which architecture was understood as the art of building elevated to the highest level of aesthetic perfection.

In a century obsessed with ascertaining the true nature of each historical culture – understood as the complex of customs, mores, beliefs, institutions, and technics of a society – both Viollet-le-Duc and Choisy found the art of building to offer a privileged point of entry for the inquisitive historian. In the opening passage of the second volume of his *Entretiens* (1872), Viollet-le-Duc would maintain: 'In the times of Classical Antiquity, as also during the Middle Ages, there was perhaps no product of human intelligence which more clearly indicated the social condition and aptitudes of a people than their method of building.'[30] Whereas some of Viollet-le-Duc's generalizations about past cultures may seem suspect today, albeit no more so than those by Taine, Guizot, Michelet, and the other great nineteenth-century cultural historians, Choisy's careful philologico-archaeological studies of Greek building practice, in particular, still remain invaluable today, not only for their insights into building practice itself, but also into the values, institutions, and social structure of Greek society.[31]

Structure was not merely the basis of the development of an architectural style, it was also for many writers the *raison d'être* for aesthetic expression. This aesthetic imperative goes beyond Augustus Welby Pugin's admiration for the honest expression of structure in Gothic architecture that he and many others advocated as a basic principle for contemporary architecture. When Pugin was still a child, the German philosopher Arthur Schopenhauer had set forth a broader principle in *The World as Will and Idea* (1818). For Schopenhauer, the expression of the forces of gravity that any construction had to accommodate was the aesthetic basis of all architectural expression: '. . . for properly speaking the conflict between gravity and rigidity is the sole aesthetic material of architecture; its problem is to make this conflict appear with perfect distinctness in a multitude of different ways.'[32] 'The sole theme of architecture,' he reiterated, is 'burden and support.'[33] Greek architecture, for Schopenhauer, had achieved the highest resolution of this problem. It was 'complete and perfect in essential matters' and 'not susceptible of any important enrichment.'[34]

Although Schopenhauer wrote eloquently about Gothic architecture, he saw its accomplishment as of a lesser nature. 'Its mysterious and hyperphysical character . . . principally arises . . . from . . . the effect of the groin vaulting born by slender, crystalline, aspiring pillars, raised high aloft, and all burden having disappeared, promising eternal security. . . .' The problem with this magic was precisely that it was unreal, 'a mere appearance, a fiction accredited by illusion.' Thus, Gothic architecture was 'the negative pole of architecture,' counterbalancing the Greek whose aesthetic expression was based on 'an actual and true conflict in nature.'[35]

Garbett, in his popular *Rudimentary Treatise on the Principles of Design in Architecture*, expounded a similar idea. He used the term 'constructive unity' to refer to the consistency with which the 'various *pressures* be perceived.' To Garbett, 'constructive unity,' along with 'constructive truth,' were the 'two most important principles to be borne in mind, in tracing the history of architecture.' Only Greek and Gothic architecture, these 'perfected architectural systems,' had succeeded in displaying true 'constructive unity.' The challenge to the future was to create a new 'system of architecture' with 'constructive unity' different from the Greek and Gothic, which were 'past and dead.'[36]

Karl Boetticher, a German architect and classical archaeologist, as well as teacher at the Bauakademie in Berlin since 1839, also used the example of Greek and Gothic architecture to discuss the concept of the architectural system. In his 'The Principles of Hellenic and Germanic Ways of Building with Regard to Their Application to Our Present Way of Building' (1846), Boetticher envisaged the 'architectural system' as consisting of a 'structural system' that was used to create 'spatial forms,' which in turn were decorated through painting and sculpture with 'art-forms' that, when successful, expressed the workings of the structural system.[37] Boetticher gave a Hegelian twist to his ideas, which he extended beyond the realm of architecture, in his highly influential *Die Tektonik der Hellenen*, whose first volume appeared in 1844, followed by a complete edition in 1852 and a revised edition in 1874. Here Boetticher argued that the only basis for aesthetic expression in the making of objects on any scale, from utensils to buildings, was the 'visualizing of the material, static achievement' of the 'tectonic body.' For Boetticher, Greek architects had succeeded eminently at this task by beginning with an 'Idea' that was given a *Kernform* (core-form) or *Werkform* (work-form), which in turn was completed as a *Kunstform* (art-form). Examples of the 'art-form' include the swelling of the columnar shaft and the flaring of the capital. These features, argued Boetticher, had no static purpose but rather visualized through artistic expression the workings of the tectonic system.[38]

Finally, Gottfried Semper's influential *Der Stil in den technischen Künsten* (1860–63) reinforced in German-speaking countries the primacy of the constructive process. The nature of its influence might be gauged by turning to one of its most avid readers, the leading Dutch architect Hendrik Petrus Berlage, who reported on Semper's ideas in 1903 to a meeting of the Amsterdam architectural association, Architectura et Amicitia. Berlage was particularly impressed by Semper's 'extremely subtle' suggestions that perhaps the word *Naht* (sewing) was etymologically related to *Not* (need),

such that the famous saying, 'Aus der Not eine Tugend machen' (Make a virtue of necessity) could become: 'Aus der Naht eine Tugend machen' (Make a virtue of sewing). In other words, he is inviting us not to camouflage the constructive framework – and here it is a question of textiles – the necessary sewing, but rather to make a virtue of it, that is to say, an element of decoration. He demonstrates how primitive peoples, with their innate artistic sense, had also proceeded in this way.[39]

Progressively minded architects found Semper's studies of textiles a source of suggestive analogies for developing an architecture that visually celebrated the constructive process.

By the time that Berlage was lecturing his colleagues on such ideas, the fundamental tenets of the architectural system had become widely accepted even by important elements of the establishment. The Sixth International Congress of Architects held in 1904 in Madrid had two themes for discussion directly related to the theme of new art and new construction: 'Theme 1: Art Nouveau in Architecture,' 'Theme 4: The Influence of Modern Procedures of Construction on Artistic Form.' In Madrid, the assembled architects adopted the following resolutions on this latter subject:

1 Decoration must celebrate a building's materials and structure.
2 To be beautiful, these forms must be in harmony with the qualities of the material.
3 Of all the modern means of construction, reinforced concrete is one of those that unites the most constructive conditions that respond the most to the greatest number of uses. But we have not yet found the artistic form corresponding to the use of this method of construction.
4 A good and beautiful architecture can be obtained only to the extent that, given a particular material, the artistic form is a consequence of the properties of this material, adopted for the end for which this material has been used.
5 To obtain a new style, there must be a new generating principle of construction and a new application of this principle.
6 Reasoning and feeling in architecture are perfectly compatible. Every artistic form must be logical.[40]

This last item, linking reason and poetry, was not an afterthought, but rather was integral to the general understanding of the relationship of aesthetics to construction during this period and hence deserves special attention.

Poetry and symbols

It would be a mistake to attribute the widespread emphasis on construction, structure, and materials in nineteenth- and early twentieth-century architectural thought to a denial of the importance of intuition, poetry, feeling, and all manner of aesthetic refinement. This issue was explicitly addressed by the most important writers on the architectural system. In the same article in which he defined the 'complete architectural system,' the engineer Reynaud, for example, stressed that structural considerations 'do not completely determine either the shape of the building or the form of its parts. They only give approximations; they only pose limits.' It was left to the domain of 'art' to 'establish between all the parts of the building that rhythm and harmony which exist for architecture just as much as for music and for all the other arts.' Although harmony in architecture, as in music, follows natural laws, it cannot be 'determined *a priori* by rules or formulas; because although it exists . . . it must also always vary. And it is precisely because it can only be felt and not expressed by words that architecture, which is based upon this, is an art.'[41] Reynaud reiterated this sentiment at greater length in his popular *Traité d'architecture*.[42]

Just as the German language lent itself to coining a word such as *Konstruktionsstil*, used by Semper to express the grounding of an architecture in the system of construction, so too did it furnish a term that suggested the complex and reciprocal importance of aesthetics and construction, what the German architect and theorist Hermann Muthesius called the *ästhetisch-tektonische Anschauung* (the aesthetic-tectonic outlook).[43] Or, as Fritz Stahl expressed it in an article of 1919 discussing Hans Poelzig's architecture: 'A contradiction between fantasy and functionality exists only in the minds of romantics estranged from real life. . . .'[44]

Viollet-le-Duc and Auguste Choisy, who accorded the greatest cultural significance to construction and who expended the most effort to explain the constructive systems of historical architecture, were also among the greatest champions of what Viollet-le-Duc called the 'poetry' of architecture. Ironically, both Viollet-le-Duc and Choisy have been miscast by historians who have labeled them as 'structural rationalists,' which designates a position that sees all decisions about form and decoration as having issued from reasons of structure and construction.

Viollet-le-Duc's sensitivity to the aesthetic dimension of architecture is evident from his letters to his father written during his trip to Italy in 1836–37. His frustration, in spite of his considerable skill at sketching, at his inability to draw satisfactorily the Temple of Concord at Agrigento, which he attributed to an ineffable harmony that the architect had achieved and that he could only perceive but not capture on paper, reveals his appreciation of the type of beauty about which Reynaud was then writing.[45]

Although Viollet-le-Duc's ideas evolved over time, their constant theme was that great historical architecture was a profoundly reasoned creation. Confronted with the academic assault on Gothic architecture that Quatremère de Quincy and Raoul-Rochette had dismissed as capricious and disordered, Viollet-le-Duc responded by demonstrating the reasonableness and order in Gothic construction as well as in its proportions and decoration. Responding to the new interest in the restoration of French medieval buildings, Viollet-le-Duc saw a need to explain the method of construction adopted by each period of the Middle Ages to promote an accurate reconstruction.

The full breadth of Viollet-le-Duc's understanding of the complex nature of architecture was revealed in the first volume of the *Entretiens*. His discussion of the sensitive siting of Greek temples in the landscape; of the *mise en scène*, which was a variation of what Le Corbusier would call the 'architectural promenade'; of the aesthetic logic behind the 'ponderation' or balancing of asymmetrical buildings; of the orientation and subtle inclination of the Caryatids of the Erechtheion; and so forth, all contradict the popular image today of Viollet-le-Duc as a structural rationalist. In his complex and fully balanced appreciation of all aspects of the architectural system that he found in the Erechtheion, Viollet-le-Duc even took a position diametrically opposed to that of structural rationalism. Commenting on the decision to use Caryatids rather than piers at the corners of the tribune, Viollet-le-Duc remarked that if piers had been employed by the architect, 'certainly he would have done something sensible, even irreproachable from the point of view of construction, but he would have obtained only a banal silhouette. . . .' For Viollet-le-Duc, everything in architecture had to be submitted to reason, 'not to the dry and pedantic reason of the geometrician, but rather to reason guided by the senses and by the observation of natural laws.'[46]

Choisy had a knack not merely for explaining structural systems, but also cultural values. In a single paragraph, he could convey not only a culture's basic structural principles, but also an entire philosophy concerning the use of materials and the way of building.[47] Choisy's *Histoire de l'architecture* presented a balanced consideration of the architectural system for each historical culture. He not only followed the commonly accepted tripartite division of the architectural system into interrelated systems of construction, form and proportion, and decoration, he also related these features to the nature of the social order and to the more intangible aspects of thought, with particular emphasis on the cultural value of representative building types.

Choisy also explicitly rejected the position that today is called structural rationalism. In a work dedicated to explaining the ingenuity of Byzantine construction, Choisy expressed his disagreement with the Byzantine belief that the most knowledgeable builder would be the best architect:

To build, in the eyes of Justinian and his contemporaries, such was the essential role of the architect. . . . Public opinion designated at that time the most knowledgeable builder as the best architect: certainly an exaggerated emphasis, but nonetheless characteristic of a period in which the sensitivity to nuances had given way to grand ideas and in which the refined sense of form had ceded to ingenious and at times subtle investigations into the art of building.[48]

Choisy was as much a master of explaining aesthetic refinements as he was of methods of construction. He believed, for example, that the horizontal curves of the Greek temples were aesthetic adjustments not merely to rectify disagreeable optical illusions, but also to impart life to the form through a sense of elasticity. Whenever possible he commented on these types of aesthetic refinements, noting, for example, John Pennethorne's discovery of curved lines in Egyptian architecture. Choisy's youthful analysis of the picturesque architectural promenade at the Periclean Acropolis is probably the most complex discussion of asymmetrical and picturesque design ever written.[49] It was also to be the most influential, for it provided the foundation of Le Corbusier's own description of the architectural promenade in *Vers une Architecture*, as well as his application of the concept to his avant-garde architecture (figure 1.1).

The same is true of Choisy's analysis of the subtle and progressive refinements to the profile of the Doric capital to optimize the effect of clear contrasts of light and shadow.[50] This analysis found a profound echo once again in Le Corbusier who made it the basis of the most lyrical chapter of *Vers une Architecture* – 'Architecture, pure création de l'esprit' ('Architecture, pure creation of the mind and spirit').[51] This attention to the subtle modeling of lines and form in architecture constituted, according to Le Corbusier, an entire aesthetic category, called *la modénature*, a term which was relatively 'unknown.' Yet why should this be, Le Corbusier wondered?

The word can be found throughout the pages of Auguste Choisy, that admirable retired

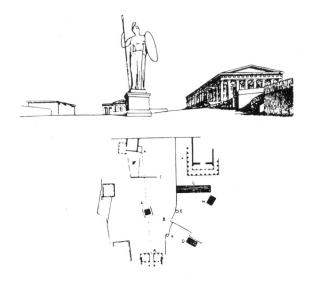

1.1
Auguste Choisy. Drawing of the
Acropolis, Athens, from Le Corbusier,
Vers une Architecture (1923)

Inspector General of the Ponts and Chaussées, author of the most worthy book there ever was on architecture [i.e., the *Histoire de l'architecture*]. . . . I wrote in *Vers une Architecture*: 'La modénature is the architect's touchstone . . La modénature is a pure creation of the mind and spirit; it calls for the plastic artist.[52]

Viollet-le-Duc's *Entretiens* and Choisy's *Histoire* are filled with disdain for anything that is dry, lifeless, or pedantic in architecture. Both books required the conjunction between form and construction to be reasoned and reasonable, the arrangement of forms artistically dynamic and programmatically meaningful, and the refinement of ornamentation consistent with structure and fully harmonious to the eye.

Baukunst, nicht Stilarchitektur

Coexisting comfortably at first with the word 'style,' the concept of the 'architectural system,' by the end of the nineteenth century, came to represent a way of approaching architecture that was diametrically opposed to the use of past architectural styles. The revival of historical styles in the nineteenth century was subjected to a double assault by those who believed both in the architectural system and in the correspondence of each architecture to a particular culture. At mid-century, James Fergusson repeatedly mocked what he called the 'monkey styles of modern Europe,' which he saw as beginning with the Renaissance and continuing until the current day, or, in other words, 'from the time when men first began to copy, instead of thinking, till the present time, when they have ceased to think, and can only copy. . . .'[53] Just as the period from the Renaissance to the end of the eighteenth century was a time of 'copying classical forms and details,' the nineteenth century had degenerated 'towards a more servile imitation of another style [i.e., the Gothic], which — whether better or worse in itself — was not a style of our age, nor suited to our wants or feelings.'[54]

Repeating this criticism about four hundred years of copying, Montgomery Schuyler in 1891 emphasized the other problem with revivals: the disregard for methods of construction and materials that were being employed or that should have been employed. Until the Renaissance, except for the 'classical period in Rome,' explained Schuyler, 'the architect was himself a builder.' Thus, before the Renaissance,

. . . everything had been a simple development of the construction and the material of the building, and since that [time], men have thought they perceived that architecture was one thing and building was another, and they have gone on to design buildings without any sort of reference to the materials of which they were composed, or the manner in which they were put together. That is the origin of the exclusively modern practice of working in architectural styles, as it is called.[55]

This opposition between *Baukunst*, the art of building, and *Stilarchitektur*, designing with historical styles, furnished both the title and subject matter for Hermann Muthesius's book *Stilarchitektur und Baukunst* (1902). Otto Wagner was so taken with this argument that he changed the title of his *Moderne Architektur* in the fourth edition (1914) to *Die Baukunst unserer Zeit* (The Art of Building of Our Time). In the preface, Wagner thanked Muthesius for having inspired him to discover the title that truly fitted the message of his book. Wagner's enthusiasm was so great that he transcribed Muthesius's title in a mistaken but revealing way as *Baukunst, nicht Stilarchitektur*.

The opposition between the architectural system and style or between *Baukunst* and *Stilarchitektur* was accompanied by reflections about the emptiness of historical revivals. Although this was to be a popular theme in the early twentieth century, one can find previous instances as well. The noted French thinker Ernest Renan, for example, in his travel notes made during a tour through Italy in 1849 observed, 'Things that no longer have meaning did then. A small sculpture on an architrave, immeasurable worth, because it was spontaneous; today, it would be an imitation, following a rule.'[56] By the early twentieth century, this thought was repeatedly expressed as a contrast between an art that was living and one that was dead. Thus the French architect Charles Plumet, writing on 'Le Mensonge de l'architecture contemporaine' ('The Lie of Contemporary Architecture') in the first issue of Gabriel Mourey's progressive journal, *Les Arts de la Vie* (January 1904), objected to the 'copyists of these dead styles' and mused,

Until the Renaissance, the artist, aided by the elements at his disposition, transcribed the mores and customs of his contemporaries into beauty. Why, since that time, have the inventive qualities of the race, nourished by wit, clarity, truth, and logic, given way to a gift of immediate assimilation based on the copying of motifs created by other peoples in other ages? . . . This art of life becomes an art of death.'[57]

Berlage, in *Grundlagen und Entwicklung der Architektur* (Foundations and

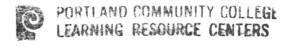

Development of Architecture) (1908) lamented in a similar manner, 'We copy these forms, which are no longer alive to us, in regard to the known proportions of the columns and entablatures, but we work completely arbitrarily, as far as the facades of the building are concerned, because we have no norms for that.'[58] Perhaps the most famous formulation of this thought comes from Le Corbusier's *Vers une Architecture*, where he charged, 'The "styles" are a lie.' Later in this book he explained, 'Architecture has nothing to do with styles. The styles of Louis XIV, Louis XV, Louis XVI, or the Gothic are to architecture what a feather is on a woman's head: it is sometimes pretty, but not always and never anything more.'[59] In his third lecture in Buenos Aires, given during his tour of 1929, Le Corbusier sketched a few classical motifs and then canceled them out with a large red 'X': 'This is not architecture; these are styles. Once living and magnificent, today they are no more than cadavers.'[60] As Frank Lloyd Wright, in his article, 'What "Styles" Mean to the Architect,' had written in the previous year, 'A few examples may serve to show "architecture" a corpse, like sticking a pin into some member of a cadaver. Such architectural members for instance as the cornice – pilasters and architraves – the facade and a whole brain-load of other instances of the moribund.'[61]

New materials and methods of construction

The emphasis on building – materials and methods of construction – as the way in which a modern architecture characteristic of the times would begin, found widespread expression, among the eminent and the unknown, over the course of the nineteenth and early twentieth centuries. A certain H. Toler Booraem was voicing a common conviction when in his article, 'Architectural Expression in a New Material: Practical and Ethical Problems of Design in Reinforced Concrete' (1908), he asserted, 'A new material, revolutionary in certain constructive principles, must in the end produce a complete system of design, a pronounced architectural style.'[62] At first, iron seemed to be this new material. Fergusson had expressed the hope of progressive thinkers when he cited the Crystal Palace at Sydenham as offering the promise of a new style: 'No material is used in it which is not the best for its purpose, no constructive expedient employed which was not absolutely essential, and it depends wholly for its effect on the arrangement of its parts and the display of its construction.'[63] Léonce Reynaud introduced the second edition of his *Traité d'architecture* (1860) by explaining,

… finally, I have entered more than I had been able previously into the details of these constructions in iron, these constructions characteristic of our age, which become more extensive every day and which alone would suffice to demonstrate that Architecture cannot remain stationary while everything around it grows and renews itself with a prodigious rapidity.[64]

Although utilitarian in purpose and hence not traditionally accorded the status of architecture, the new iron buildings, because they were both specific to the times and built out of the new material, seemed to have become representative cultural icons of the age. 'We can see what modern architecture will be,' wrote the critic Joris-Karl Huysmans in 1879:

The monuments are already there. The architects and engineers who built the Gare du Nord, les Halles, the cattle market of la Villette, and the new Hippodrome have created a new art, just as noble as the old, a fully contemporary art, suited to the needs of our times, which, transformed from top to bottom, almost does away with stone, wood, and the raw materials supplied by the earth to take from factories and foundries the power and lightness of their furnaces.[65]

Like the Great Exhibition of 1851 in Hyde Park, London, the Exposition Universelle of 1889 in Paris marked a new epoch in the development of iron architecture. The French architectural journal, *Encyclopédie d'Architecture*, for example, sponsored a competition for the design of a contemporary architecture based on the example of the iron structures at this world's fair, the most notable of which were the giant Galerie des Machines and the Eiffel Tower.[66]

Although iron and steel were seen as the principal nineteenth-century materials, others were accorded attention and respect when they were used in ways that might generate a new architecture. Montgomery Schuyler was quick to praise all efforts in this direction, whether Kimball and Wisedell's Casino Theater (1880–82) in New York City – 'It is a building in baked clay; there isn't a feature in it in brick or in terra cotta which could be translated into any other material without loss. It is a beautiful, adequate, modern performance' – or Louis Sullivan's Transportation Building at the 1893 World's Columbian Exposition in Chicago – 'It is the most ambitious of all the great buildings, for it is nothing less than an attempt to make a plaster architecture.'[67] One finds studies of various building materials undertaken in this spirit toward the turn of the century. Borrmann in *Die Keramik der Baukunst* (1897) referred to 'der konstruktive Organismus des Ziegelbaues' (the constructive organism of brick building). Walter Curt Behrendt, in 'Backstein als Baumaterial' ('Brick as Building Material') (1908), praised contemporary brick buildings that were pointing the way 'toward a new, thoroughly modern use of brick . . .,' just as Alfred Gotthold Meyer in *Eisenbauten* (1907) had done for iron, 'which is capable of becoming an objectively style-forming force.'[68]

Toward this time, concrete excited a similar interest. As Booraem explained in 1908: 'Concrete, it would appear, should certainly provide the long-hoped for medium for creative design, untrammeled by convention, as, on the contrary, all work must be which is confined to materials that have been so exhaustively worked over.'[69] In this same year in Paris, the young Swiss architect Charles-Edouard Jeanneret, not yet Le Corbusier, mused, 'On the Perrets' building site, I saw what concrete is, what revolutionary forms it *requires*.'[70]

Le Corbusier and the architectural system

The concept of the architectural system was of paramount importance to Le Corbusier. Before he built his avant-garde villas of the late 1920s he based his most important polemical writings on the cluster of ideas associated with the archi-tectural system. With his revolutionary architecture he then embarked on a life-long career of putting them into practice.

All the themes discussed in this chapter – the primacy of the system of construc-tion, the importance of poetry to the architectural system, the rejection of histori-cal revivals in favor of *Baukunst*, the opportunities afforded by new materials and new ways of building – are among the principal themes of Le Corbusier's polemical treatise *Vers une Architecture* (1923). The very title of the book actually reflects the totality of these concerns.

The cultural relativism ushered in by the Romantic revolution, whereby every civilization was seen as having had its distinguishing architecture, created a need for a word that could designate this phenomenon. Although awkward to the ear of

English-language speakers, 'an architecture' was a common way for Europeans in this period to refer to the architecture of each country and era. *Une architecture*, to use the French version, became a shorthand to designate the totality of a culture's architectural system. This equivalence was established by Quatremère de Quincy in his *Encyclopédie Méthodique. Architecture* (1820) and his *Dictionnaire historique d'architecture* (1832) under the heading 'Gothic Architecture.' Here Quatremère de Quincy used the term *une architecture* in the same way as an 'architectural system': 'To respond to these questions, one must begin by considering the entire complex of notions relative to the formation of what is properly called an architecture, as constituting an ensemble of its own characteristic forms, a method of construction based on a real need, and a system of ornamentation in relationship to local ideas and particular customs.'[71] This equivalence between *un système d'architecture* and *une architecture* would endure throughout the nineteenth and early twentieth centuries.

We know from Le Corbusier's *Almanach d'architecture moderne* (1925) that he was conversant with this equivalency. In this book, Le Corbusier defined both the 'architectural system' and 'an architecture' in a way that reiterated the meanings that they had carried through the course of the nineteenth and early twentieth centuries:

Using materials native to a region, a way of building consonant with the technics of an age, a way of thinking belonging to a period of civilization, architecture creates coherent systems of organization. . . . Over the course of time, architecture has left pure systems. These pure systems constitute the diverse architectures of history. . . . Every time that an age has not brought a system to fruition, the architectural moment will not have been produced. This system requires the rigorous solution of statics: to each architecture is attached a method of *structure*. This system requires the creation of a harmonious play of forms that realize a total plastic phenomenon. . . . The 'styles' then have nothing to do with architecture.[72]

In this text, Le Corbusier insisted upon the dual nature of the architectural system grounded in a system of construction and brought to fruition as a plastic system of form, 'provoking a profound physiological and spiritual emotion.' Such a 'pure system' would also be in harmony with the technics and ways of thought and feeling of the times.[73]

The choice of title for Le Corbusier's immensely influential book, *Vers une Architecture*, was neither casual nor immediate. Its translation in 1927 as *Towards a New Architecture* by Frederick Etchells has helped to obscure the full import of the title by emphasizing only one aspect of its meaning. In effect, Le Corbusier had actually considered giving his book a similar title. His contract with the publisher signed and dated 21 December 1922 lists the title as *L'Architecture Nouvelle* (The New Architecture).[74] On the other hand, Le Corbusier also prepared a cover for the book identical to the one that was published but with the title *Architecture ou Révolution* (Architecture or Revolution), which made reference to the last chapter.[75] In the end, Le Corbusier selected the term – *une architecture* – that had a long association with both the concept of the architectural system and the idea of architecture as expressive of a particular culture. *Vers une Architecture*, toward an architecture, refers to the challenge of creating a new and modern architectural system that would respond to contemporary sensibilities and needs and symbolize contemporary culture, just the way each historical architecture had done in previous times.

Le Corbusier developed an architectural system, which he used to create a modern architecture in his avant-garde houses of the late 1920s. These buildings,

Le Corbusier and Pierre Jeanneret. Swiss Dormitory. South facade

Le Corbusier. Villa Shodhan. South-west facade and swimming-pool

Le Corbusier. Jaoul Houses. Interior

the Maison Cook (Boulogne-sur-Seine, 1926), the Villa Stein (Garches, 1927), and the Villa Savoye (Poissy, 1928–31), were all designed according to his 'Five Points for a New Architecture' (1926).[76] These buildings, which have become canonical works in the history of modern architecture, are grounded in a system of construction, with systems of form and decoration developed in conjunction with it.

1.2
Le Corbusier. 'Dom-ino' project (right) shown with a traditional house in Flanders (left), whose largely glazed facade helped inspire this modern system of building

The premises for Le Corbusier's new system of construction date from the architect's proposal for the rapid erection of new housing in response to the devastation in Flanders caused in 1914 at the onset of World War I (figure 1.2). At that time, Le Corbusier envisaged a 'pure and complete concept of a system of construction,' fashioned from mass-produced, standardized components of reinforced concrete assembled into a structural skeleton.[77] The basic structure used six thin reinforced concrete columns to hold up the floors, which would extend slightly beyond the vertical supports in the form of a cantilever. Le Corbusier called the building system the 'Dom-ino' house both because the floor plan resembled a domino game piece and because the units could be aligned in a series, like dominoes, to make row houses of different patterns. Not only were the combinations of units flexible, so too were the floor plans. With structural walls eliminated and the exterior facade totally open, the 'Dom-ino' frame provided the user with flexibility to arrange the interior as desired and to flood the house with light and natural ventilation.

Looking back upon this concept in 1929, Le Corbusier reflected that the full aesthetic potential of the 'Dom-ino' system of construction had not been apparent to him when he developed the initial idea in 1914.[78] This came later in 1926 with the 'Five Points for a New Architecture' (figure 1.3). These five features are:

1 Using stilts called *pilotis* to raise the building off the ground. This frees the ground level for additional outdoor use as well as the visual pleasure of an uninterrupted view. At the same time it eliminates the basement, which Le Corbusier, like Frank Lloyd Wright, saw as a dark and damp inconvenience.

2 Using the flat roof to create a roof garden. Once again this increases outdoor use of the same area covered by the house for the pleasures of catching breezes, sunbathing, protected play areas, privacy, and panoramic views.

3 Using the open floor area afforded by the columnar structure to create what Le Corbusier called the 'free plan.' Every floor can be subdivided with non-structural walls independent of those on the other floors.

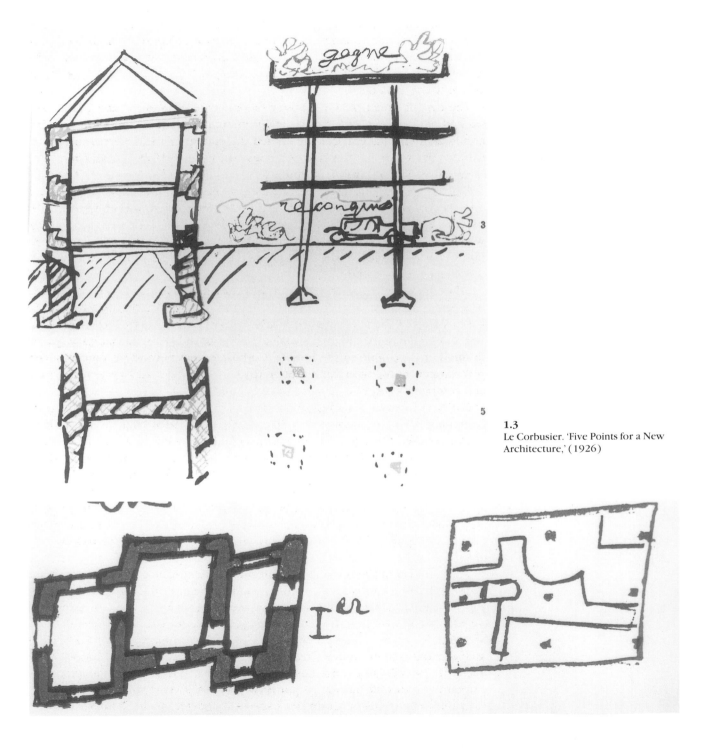

1.3
Le Corbusier. 'Five Points for a New Architecture,' (1926)

4 Using the totally unobstructed surface of the exterior to create the 'free facade,' which can be left entirely open to face a terrace or glazed extensively for maximum light and ventilation.
5 Using a long horizontal window, *la fenêtre en longueur*, for even and abundant illumination.

Taken by themselves, the 'Five Points for a New Architecture' furnished a system of form developed from a modern system of construction that used modern materials and equipment, such as reinforced concrete, sliding glass windows, and asbestos and cement 'eternit' roofing. The system of decoration consisted in the beauty of the metal, wood, linoleum, and so on, used as finishing materials, as well as the architectural polychromy derived from painting adjacent surfaces and neighboring volumes different colors.

The overall aspect of Le Corbusier's avant-garde villas of the late 1920s, considered as members of a broad family of similar modern buildings by other architects from this era, quickly earned the epithet of the 'International Style.' Generations not only of architects but also the general public have learned from Henry-Russell Hitchcock and Philip Johnson's book of this title, or from the numerous histories that use its nomenclature, that modern buildings appearing as cubical prisms which emphasize surface and volume, often painted white on the exterior, generally devoid of applied surface ornamentation, furnished with large windows, and provided with flat roofs which were sometimes fashioned into outdoor terraces, constituted the avant-garde trend of Western 'architecture since 1922' (the book's subtitle).[79]

While accurate in identifying the features of this modern 'style,' Hitchcock and Johnson's title obscures the fuller and more profound intentions behind Le Corbusier's buildings. They are realizations not merely of a 'style,' but rather of an 'architecture' based upon a new 'architectural system.' With this notion of system in mind, it is possible to see how Le Corbusier went beyond his contemporary practitioners of the International Style to give his architectural system a richness and complexity generally absent from other buildings.

This Le Corbusier achieved by the way in which he developed the free plan. Beginning with the avant-garde villas of the late 1920s (figures 1.4–10), Le Corbusier used the grid of free-standing columns as a foil to walls, which stand apart from these vertical supports. Sometimes straight, sometimes curved, these walls become sculptural entities placed within the gridded space of the columnar structure. The result is a dynamic architectural ballet in which the moving spectator feels his own body space become engaged in a dialogue of ever-changing relationships within a sculptural field of forms created by walls and columns. In this way, Le Corbusier made the structural system an integral component of the system of form.

The architectural system that Le Corbusier developed in the Maison Cook, the Villa Stein, and the Villa Savoie would dominate the remainder of his long professional career. But he was constantly exploring new variations of all three subsystems of construction, form, and decoration within the overall framework of the architectural system. Every decade saw new developments in Le Corbusier's architectural system. In the 1920s, the avant-garde villas reflected his optimism about the wonders of a machine civilization that not only was bringing new amenities to daily life but was also providing a visual identity for modern culture.

In the early 1930s Le Corbusier expressed concern about the dehumanizing

1.4
Le Corbusier and Pierre Jeanneret.
Maison Cook, Boulogne-sur-Seine,
1926. Front facade

aspects of the machine and declared the birth of a 'second period of machine civilization' in which new efforts would be made to counter these negative tendencies.[80] At this time he made two substantial changes to the basic components of his architectural system. First, Le Corbusier introduced rustic elements into his buildings. Second, he altered the basic relationship between the columnar grid and the walls. No longer fixed with regularly gridded spacing, now the columns moved as if in dialogue with the walls.[81]

The most dramatic instance of this change can be found in the Pavillion Suisse (Paris, 1930–32), which is the Swiss student dormitory at the Cité Universitaire. The entire building reads as a metaphor of the relationship between nature and a machine civilization (colour plate 1, figures 1.11–1.13). To one side rises the block of identical student rooms, lifted off the ground by *pilotis* and faced with a glass facade whose elegant detailing contributes to the effect of a light and airy membrane characteristic of the machine world. To the other side of the building a curved, low rubble stone wall forms the back to the students' common room. The

Note
Throughout this book, 'first floor' has been used, following the British convention, to refer to the floor immediately above the ground floor (and other floors accordingly)

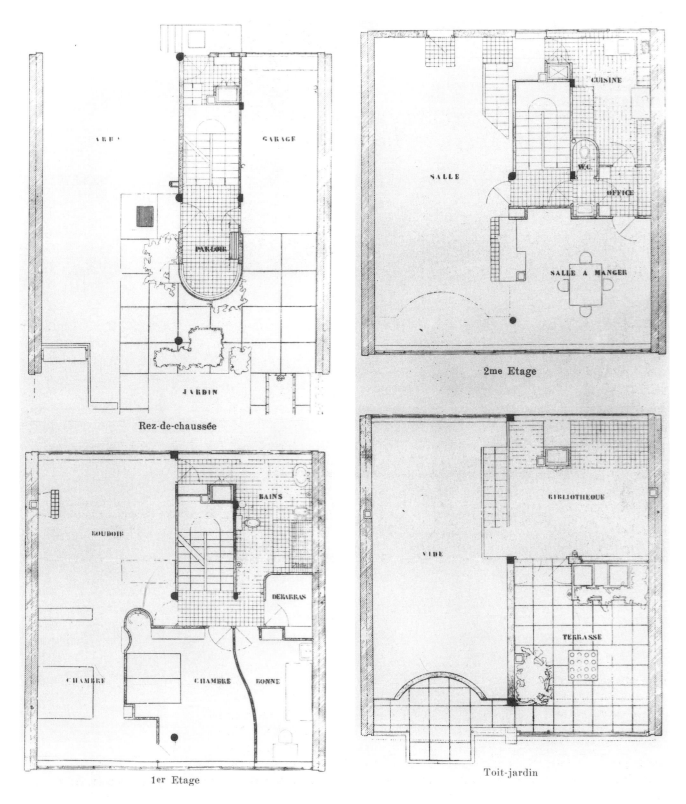

Rez-de-chaussée

2me Etage

1er Etage

Toit-jardin

1.5
Le Corbusier and Pierre Jeanneret. Maison Cook, Boulogne-sur-Seine,
1926. Ground and first floors (left), second and third floors (right)

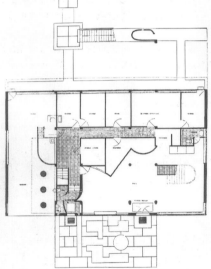

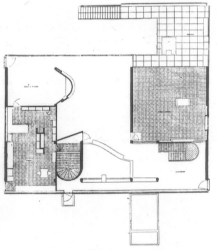

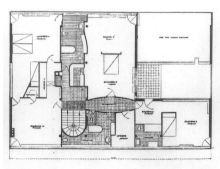

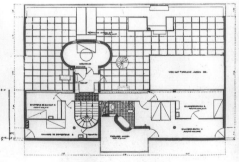

Rez-de-chaussée
Entrée et grand hall, garage, chambres de domestique, buanderie et repassage,
vestiaires, etc.

Premier étage
Grand living-room, bibliothèque, salle à manger, cuisine et
terrasse-jardin couverte

2e étage
Deux chambres à coucher avec boudoirs et salles de bains,
chambres d'amis, lingerie, etc.

Toit-jardin
Deux chambres d'amis, chambres de domestique, débarras
et la grande terrasse-jardin

1.6, 1.7
Le Corbusier and Pierre Jeanneret.
Villa Stein, Garches, 1927

Front facade

Floor plans

facade here is given one of the most rustic treatments imaginable, for the mortar between the irregularly shaped stones is not flush with the surface but rather pushes outward like old roots winding their way across the ground. One could not imagine a more striking contrast between the image of machine precision and simple nature.

Inside the building, the columns in the entrance hall and the common room give the impression of having been arranged in regular rows that then warp in response to the curvature of the far rubble wall. Even the stairs, which begin beside the sculptural ventilation shaft, participate in this concerted twisting of columnar grid and walls. Outside, the *pilotis* have changed form. Now thick and sculptural, reminiscent of organic forms like bones, they are made of reinforced concrete with a rough finish. These *pilotis*, images of organic nature, support a rough concrete substructure upon which the machine-like block of repetitive cells of dormitory rooms rises. One could continue with a discussion of the refinements within this building, like the kinesthetic effect of the double curvature of the first steps of the stairs, which provides a vitalizing experience similar to that of Le Corbusier and Charlotte Perriand's *chaise-longue* or lounge chair, or like the subtle ways in which the architect uses gravel and paving to define the separate domains of nature and architecture around the entrance.[82] Such matters, though, would take us beyond the purpose of sketching the major outlines of Le Corbusier's architectural system.

When in the 1940s Le Corbusier replaced what appeared to be the thin skin of the 'free facade' of his first avant-garde villas with the deep, three-dimensional

1.8, 1.9, 1.10
Le Corbusier and Pierre Jeanneret.
Villa Savoye, Poissy, 1928–31

Entrance hall

Ground floor plan

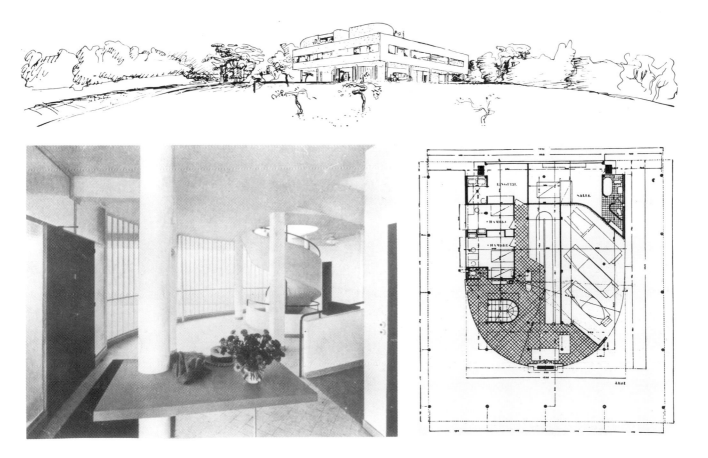

facade of the *brise-soleil*, the sun break, he made another major change in his use of the 'Five Points for a New Architecture.' The *brise-soleil*, applied most effectively in buildings ranging from Dr Currutchet's House (La Plata, Argentina, 1949) (figures 1.14–1.17), through the Carpenter Center for the Visual Arts (Harvard University, 1960–63) (figures 1.18–1.19), also altered the relationship between interior and exterior. The closed prisms of the 1920s yielded to assemblages of volumes whereby even the facade is a deep space that can be physically occupied and at times inhabited, as in the sunbreaks of the Villa Shodhan (Ahmedabad, India, 1952–1956) (colour plate 2, figure 1.20). Whereas the spacing of the columnar grid and the shapes of the columns or piers in this later period were simpler and more regular than in the late 1920s and 1930s, the volumetric nature of the facade as well as the sculptural quality of the entire form, along with the introduction of a ramp that reached between or beyond major spatial elements, gave new meaning

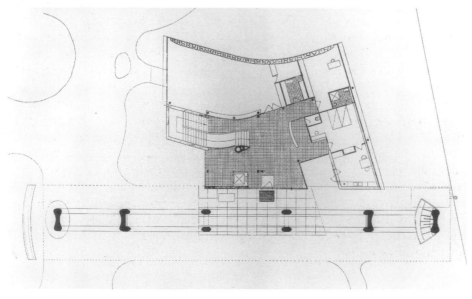

1.11, 1.12, 1.13
Le Corbusier and Pierre Jeanneret. Swiss Dormitory, Paris, 1930–32

View under the elevated dormitory block

North facade, detail

Ground floor plan

to Le Corbusier's aphorism in *Vers une Architecture*: 'Architecture is the skillful, accurate, and magnificent play of volumes seen in light.'[83]

In following the course of Le Corbusier's career, then, certain themes emerge as he altered the character of the architectural system. First, there was the evolution from closed prism with thin exterior membrane walls to the sculptural assemblage of volumes, including the volumetric sun-break. Second, along with this change came the abandonment of the smooth surfaces that appeared to have a machine finish in favor of rough concrete textures that either showed the wood used for the form-work into which the concrete had been poured or were covered with large pebbles. Complex patterns of windows and sun-breaks often accompanied these items. Third, as we have seen, the organic shapes of the late 1920s villas were joined in the 1930s with images of a rusticated natural world. Fourth, from the late 1920s onward, the columnar grid changed character both in its spacing and in the shapes of the supports themselves. This last subject will be discussed in greater detail in chapter two on the picturesque.

From the 1930s Le Corbusier developed a secondary type of architectural system that reflected his new interest in rough natural forms. Unlike the architectural system developed for the 'Five Points for a New Architecture,' which he used more often, this other system employed vaulted ceilings with bearing walls in ways that combined traditional and modern construction. From the weekend house outside Paris at La Celle Saint-Cloud (1935) (figures 1.21, 1.22) to the Jaoul Houses in Neuilly (1954–56) (figure 1.23, colour plate 3) these buildings created an almost cave-like atmosphere.[84]

Even when Le Corbusier's buildings departed from these two models, they were still conceived according to some architectural system. The vacation house at Les Mathes (1935) (figure 1.24), for example, used stone bearing walls with a secondary carpentry frame and a tertiary system of glass and asbestos sheeting infill panels conceived and articulated as a system of construction made into systems of form and decoration. Similarly, the free-form Philips Pavilion (1957–58) at the International Exposition in Brussels used the rigor of a hyperbolic-paraboloid to generate its structure and form.[85]

Even the sculptural forms of the pilgrimage chapel of Notre-Dame-du-Haut at Ronchamp (1950–55) (colour plate 4, figure 1.25) joined the various components of the architectural system together. The splayed south wall, punctured in so many places with funnel-like window openings filled with colored glass and surfaced with a whitewashed sprayed cement, is easily understood as a modern structure, a hollow wall with transverse reinforced-concrete fins and surface framed with steel reinforcing bars and covered with wire mesh. The curved roof, made of rough-shuttered reinforced concrete, hovers over the chapel in a manner that contributes to the strong, otherworldly atmosphere there. The thin slot of space between the walls and roof, with its magical sliver of light entering below the weighty curve above the pilgrim's head, also demonstrates that the walls are not load-bearing structures. Vertical piers emerge from the walls to reveal the nature of support for the roof.

All of these examples testify to Le Corbusier's understanding of architecture as an architectural system. For nearly a half century the forms used in his architecture changed and the style evolved. Yet throughout the work ran the constant theme of the architectural system.

1.14, 1.15, 1.16, 1.17

Le Corbusier. Dr Currutchet's House, La Plata, Argentina, 1949

Ramp from the street to the entrance of the house and then up again to the doctor's office, which faces the street

Sections. Double-height living-room and roof-terrace with canopy (above). Ramp from the street to the house and then back to the doctor's office (below)

Floor plans

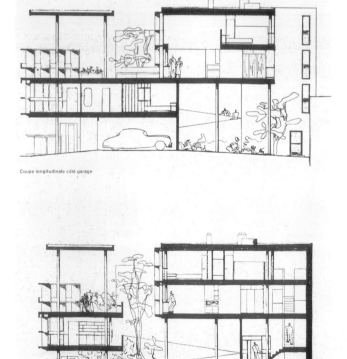

Coupe longitudinale côté garage

Coupe longitudinale côté rampe

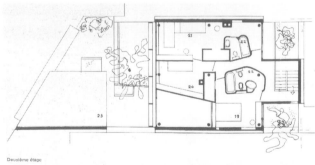

Deuxième étage

12 Palier d'entrée
13, 14, 15 Salle commune (en pointillé double hauteur sous plafond)
16 Cuisine
17 Débarras
18 Terrasse (en pointillé partie couverte)
19 20 21 Chambres
22 Salles de bain
23 Salle de couverture

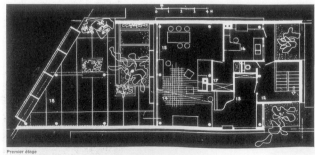

Premier étage

Frank Lloyd Wright and the architectural system

The concept of the architectural system was as fundamental to Frank Lloyd Wright as it was to Le Corbusier. Just as Le Corbusier developed his own approach to architecture through the avant-garde Parisian houses of the 1920s, Frank Lloyd Wright formulated a new architecture according to the parameters of the architectural system with his 'Prairie houses.' Wright's Prairie houses, though, combined

1.18, 1.19
Le Corbusier. Carpenter Center for the Visual Arts, Harvard University, 1960–63

Second floor plan

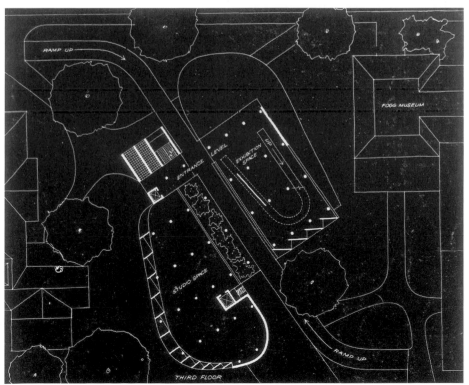

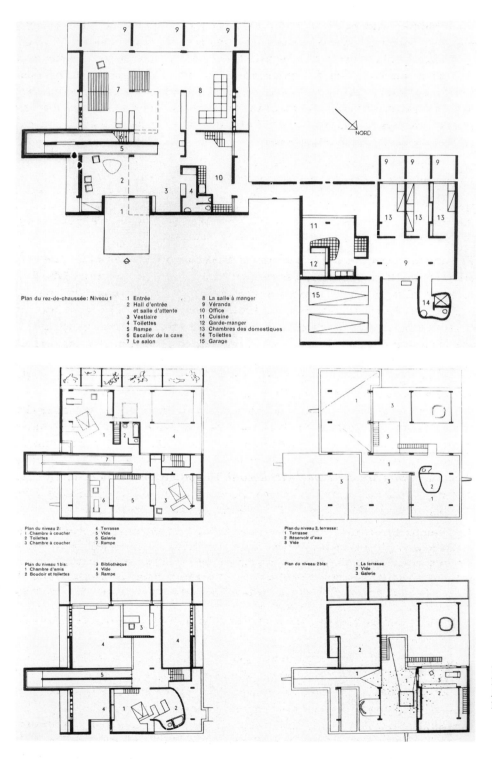

Plan du rez-de-chaussée: Niveau 1

1 Entrée	8 La salle à manger
2 Hall d'entrée	9 Véranda
et salle d'attente	10 Office
3 Vestiaire	11 Cuisine
4 Toilettes	12 Garde-manger
5 Rampe	13 Chambres des domestiques
6 Escalier de la cave	14 Toilettes
7 Le salon	15 Garage

Plan du niveau 2:
1 Chambre à coucher
2 Toilettes
3 Chambre à coucher
4 Terrasse
5 Vide
6 Galerie
7 Rampe

Plan du niveau 1bis:
1 Chambre d'amis
2 Boudoir et toilettes
3 Bibliothèque
4 Vide
5 Rampe

Plan du niveau 3, terrasse:
1 Terrasse
2 Réservoir d'eau
3 Vide

Plan du niveau 2bis:
1 La terrasse
2 Vide
3 Galerie

1.20
Le Corbusier. Villa Shodhan,
Ahmedabad, India, 1952–56.
Floor plans

the customary understanding of the architectural system with a symbolic architectural system explained by the German architect and theorist Gottfried Semper.

Whereas Viollet-le-Duc and Auguste Choisy demonstrated how aesthetically rich an architectural system grounded in the art of building could become, Gottfried Semper explained how mythically suggestive *der architektonischen Systeme* had become in various historical cultures. Semper believed that the primary impetus behind historical architectures had been the creation of a shelter around the central focus of the hearth.

The hearth is the first embryo of the social settlement. Around this hearth the first family groups gathered. It was here that the first treaties were made and the first religious rites practised. The hearth is the holy center and the focus to which the different parts of a settlement were directed during all the periods of development of society. Even today it is the center of our domestic life and in its higher meaning as an altar, the center of our religious institutions. It is the symbol of civilization and religion.[86]

The hearth, stressed Semper, 'is the first and most important, the *moral* element of architecture.' It was the primary feature and focus of what Semper termed the 'four elements of architecture': 'Around it were grouped the three other elements: the *roof*, the *enclosure*, and the *mound*, the protecting negations or defenders of the hearth's flame against the three hostile elements of nature.' Semper stressed that the enclosure developed historically from weaving: 'Wickerwork, the original space divider, retained the full importance of its earlier meaning, actually or ideally, when the light mat walls were transformed into clay tile, brick, or stone walls. Wickerwork was the *essence of the wall*.'[87]

Semper's ideas were part of the intellectual fare in Chicago architectural circles when Wright first arrived in that city. The German-born Chicago architect Frederick Baumann seems to have lost no opportunity to introduce them into his public lectures and comments in public forums, some of which were recorded in the local *Inland Architect and News Record*. This progressive architectural journal at the same time published Semper's 'Ueber Baustyle' in a translation by John Wellborn Root and Fritz Wagner. Here Chicago architects could read:

The domestic hearth of the wandering nomad, with its sheltering primitive roof-covering, remained through all times the sacred symbol of civilization, and retained its bright consecration as altar and as temple-cell. It was the fundamental form of the concealed Egyptian sekos, the Chaldaic Assyrian pyramidal superstructure and the Jewish tabernacle, through all phases of culture to the Holy Kaaba and the Christian Tabernacle, added to this separating inclosure and the hearth-protecting lower structure. We will find all the inventions of architecture expressed in those few primitive motives borrowed, we might say, from the first couple in Eden.[88]

Several years after the publication of Semper's ideas about the four elements of architecture in the *Inland Architect*, 'all the progressives of the young Chicago school of architects (and there were many)'[89] were impressed by a building that presented the constituent parts of Semper's symbolic architectural system in the form of the Ho-o-Den (figure 1.26), the secular modification of a Japanese temple erected at the World's Columbian Exposition of 1893 in Chicago. The basic elements of this Japanese structure were its shrine, which corresponded to Semper's hearth; its platform; its non-structural, sliding screen walls, which were analogous to Semper's wickerwork walls; and its broad, spreading roof.

In the Prairie houses (figure 1.27) Frank Lloyd Wright articulated what he called the 'grammar' of his architecture in a way that closely approximates Semper's four elements and its equivalent in the Japanese Ho-o-den. The constituent parts of the

Prairie house were its fireplace, treated like a domestic altar and furnished with a prominent chimney; the broad, spreading roof; the low base from which the building rose; and the walls, conceived as space-enclosing screens, which rose from this base until they reached the line of windows below the roof. These windows, often a continuous series, allowed the roof to float visually above the walls, thereby articulating each element.

The example of Japanese architecture reinforced not only the lesson of Semper's

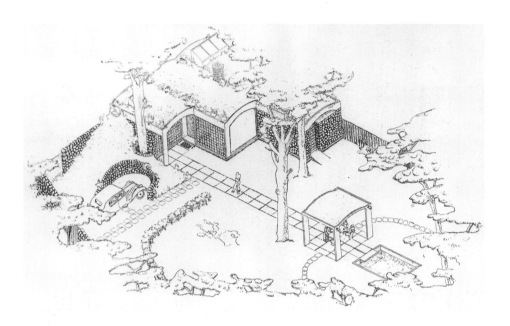

1.21, 1.22
Le Corbusier and Pierre Jeanneret.
Weekend house, La Celle Saint-Cloud,
1935

Interior

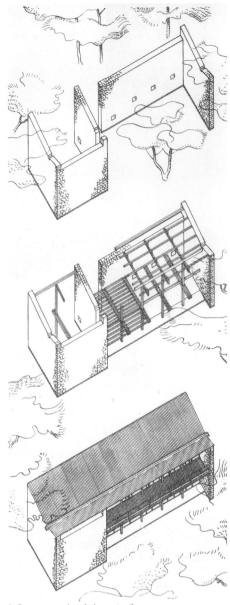

1.23, 1.24

Le Corbusier. Jaoul Houses, Neuilly, 1954–56. West facade of house A

Le Corbusier and Pierre Jeanneret. Vacation house, Les Mathes, 1935. Successive phases of construction

1. Etappes successives de la construction

writings about the symbolic architectural system, it also demonstrated a way to realize the goal of securing a psychological sense of shelter in domestic architecture according to the terms popularized in Chicago by the architect Irving K. Pond, future president of the American Institute of Architects. Echoing John Ruskin in an article entitled 'The Home,' Pond explained how one could achieve a 'quiet repose' in domestic architecture in terms that Wright would soon make his own:

From the time when man first began to feel, broad, low masses and horizontal lines have carried to his mind the suggestion of strength and repose, because of their sympathy with the earth which was to him the highest external expression of these attributes. . . . Thus, a house with a long low roof line and a broad, low treatment of the parts seems to be a thing of the earth and as such it appeals strongly to man a creature of the earth.[90]

1.25
Le Corbusier. Pilgrimage chapel of
Notre-Dame-du-Haut, Ronchamp,
1950–55. Interior view focusing on the
east end with statue of Mary and the
altar

Frank Lloyd Wright's Prairie houses are famous world-wide for the strong sense of comforting shelter that they afford. Perhaps more than any other architect Frank Lloyd Wright was able to tap the primal needs and satisfactions that this type of architecture can provide. Wright invested each of the four elements of Semper's symbolic architectural system with qualities that sustained the sense of shelter. For a platform, Wright set the house upon a 'projecting base course' that made the house '*look* as though it began there *at* the ground.' The exterior walls were made to seem as if they emerged organically from the earth. As Wright put it, they 'started at the ground' upon this base course to rise as a 'screen' uninterrupted until they came just below the roof where they opened into a 'continuous window series below' the 'low spreading roof, flat or hipped or low gabled, with generously projecting eaves over the whole' to impart 'the essential look' of '*shelter*.'[91] Finally, Wright developed what he called the '*integral* fireplace' (figure 1.28), an architecturally impressive opening encased within a broad expanse of masonry, which 'justified the great size of this chimney outside':

The big fireplace in the house below [a 'broad generous' roof] became now a place for a real fire. A real fireplace at that time was extraordinary. There were mantels instead. A mantel was a marble frame for a few coals in a grate. Or it was a piece of wooden furniture with tiles stuck in it around a grate, the whole set slam up against the plastered, papered wall. Insult to comfort. So the *integral* fireplace became an important part of the building itself in the houses I was allowed to build out there on the prairie. It comforted me to see the fire burning deep in the solid masonry of the house itself. A feeling that came to stay.[92]

Whatever Wright's familiarity with Ruskin's writings or Pond's essay, his observation that this image of the house 'seems to be my own'[93] was essentially correct.

Le Corbusier. Pilgrimage chapel of
Notre-Dame-du-Haut, Ronchamp.
View of the east facade

Frank Lloyd Wright. Johnson Wax
Company Administration Building.
Mezzanine

Frank Lloyd Wright. Johnson Wax
Company Administration Building

Exterior

Detail

Frank Lloyd Wright. Unity Temple
Interior of the sanctuary

1.26, 1.27

Japanese Ho-o-Den, World's
Columbian Exposition, Chicago, 1893.
Detail of the south pavilion

Frank Lloyd Wright. Frederick C. Robie
House, Chicago, 1909

Not only had Wright created a new and original architecture, but the sense of shelter that it conveyed was obviously a reflection of deep personal feeling. As Wright explained, the idea of shelter is 'probably rooted deep in racial instinct.'[94]

Through his Prairie houses Wright conveyed a primal sense of shelter that combined what the French philosopher Gaston Bachelard has termed the 'material imagination' and the 'poetics of space.' The importance of these concepts for understanding the nature of Wright's use of the architectural system, and thus for understanding his architecture, merits a brief consideration of Bachelard's account of the creative mind. Between 1949 and 1957, Bachelard published a series of books arguing that many great poets grounded their work on reveries about the four classic elements – air, water, fire, and earth – or about space itself. The material imagination refers to reveries that are clustered around one of the four material elements; the poetics of space involves feelings of cozy shelter, conveyed through certain spatial configurations such as miniatures, nests, corners, and the movement from cellar to attic, as well as the dialectical counterpart to coziness, which is the sentiment of expansive freedom. [95]

Readers of the anthropologist Edward T. Hall are used to the concept of the personal space 'bubble' that each person has around his or her body, a 'bubble' that expands or contracts according to the degree of formality or intimacy in a relationship. Hall has identified four zones of this spatial sense of self – from intimate to personal to social and then to public.[96] Once one is aware of Hall's observations about the spatial component of this human sense of territoriality, then it becomes easier to understand Bachelard's insight that the spatial sense of self, what he termed the 'poetics of space,' is also a fundamental component of the imagination. To illustrate the poetics of space, Bachelard recounted Charles Baudelaire's observation that a fire indoors feels so much cozier when it is snowing outside.

1.28
Frank Lloyd Wright. Darwin D. Martin House, Buffalo, N.Y., 1904. Reception room

Baudelaire has his fictional character 'each year [hope] for as much snow, hail, and frost as possible. He hoped for a Canadian winter, a Russian winter. His nest would be so much warmer, so much sweeter, so much more loved.' In this example, the home imagined as a 'nest' provides a sense of shelter, which is augmented by contrast with the cold and inhospitable weather outside.[97] In Wright's Prairie houses, the four elements of Semper's symbolic architectural system are developed to create this comforting sense of shelter through the poetics of space.[98]

The poetics of space alone, though, will not explain Wright's use of Semper's symbolic architectural system. Wright's 'material imagination' must be considered as well. As has been argued, Wright's homes are related to the earth according to what might be called a 'geological imagination.'[99] Wright gives ample evidence, through his buildings and his writings, that he conceived of his houses as extensions of the earth. For Wright, the earth itself presented a natural architecture that grew upward from the ground: 'The long, low lines of colorful, windswept terrain, the ineffable dotted line, the richly textured plain, great striated, stratified masses lying noble and quiet or rising with majesty above the vegetation of the desert floor: nature-masonry is piled up into ranges upon ranges of mountains that seem to utter a form-language of their own.'[100] The earth's 'form-language' was to be the basis for humankind's architecture:

Read the grammar of the Earth in a particle of stone! Stone is the frame on which the Earth is modeled, and wherever it crops out – there the architect may sit and learn. . . . For in the stony bone-work of the Earth, the principles that shaped stone as it lies, or as it rises and remains to be sculpted by winds and tides – there sleep forms and styles enough for all the ages for all of Man.[101]

In responding to the lessons of the earth, the architect was to create forms that, through varying degrees of imitation and abstraction, seemed to belong to the

1.29
'Navy Yard,' in the 'Driftless Area,' Wisconsin

earth. This is what Wright called an 'earth-architecture.' Such had been the achievement of 'primitive American architecture – Toltec, Aztec, Mayan, Incan – . . . mighty, primitive abstractions of man's nature . . . all earth-architectures. . . .' This architecture had 'stirred [his] wonder, excited [his] wishful admiration' as a boy.[102] Such was the task that Wright set for himself.

Numerous writers have emphasized the importance of the particular geology of the Wisconsin valleys in which Wright's family had lived for three generations and to which it had become so attached (figure 1.29). The Lloyd-Joneses, explains Grant Carpenter Manson, 'identified themselves so quickly and thriftily with Iowa County, Wisconsin, that they convey[ed] the impression of having lived there for centuries.' This land, continued Manson, 'consists of small, level valleys opening southward from the Wisconsin River and bounded by low, round hills from the summits of which outcroppings of yellow ledgestone jut forth in curiously weathered shapes.'[103] These outcroppings were part of a special geological zone known as the 'Driftless Area,' a region, explains Thomas Beeby, that 'miraculously was saved from glacial destruction and residual drift':

It is a region of dissected tableland with broad ridges of limestone separated widely by poorly drained valley floors. These deep and winding spaces are sharply delineated by exposed rock escarpments. Alternate layers of limestone and sandstone are eroded differentially, creating figural rock formations with deep overhangs, projecting ledges, and shallow caves. Erosion by water exposes the stratification or structure of the earth.[104]

We know from the biographical sketch published by Wright's daughter, Iovanna Lloyd Wright, that the youthful Frank Lloyd Wright, growing up on his uncle's farm, was deeply impressed by this geology: 'Sometimes, too tired to sleep after a day's work, he would rise at night in the full of the moon and walk over the stony ridges to his favorite hill. . . . He thought of the rock stratas that were built into the hills. And in all the marvels and miracles he had learned of he began to see a plan.'[105] Along the river banks and in the hills of his beloved Wisconsin valleys, Wright, then, had direct experiences with what he would later call an earth-architecture.

At first, in the Prairie houses and related buildings, Wright adhered to the geometric conventions of Western architecture as he explored ways to make the house appear to grow from the earth through the regular courses of brick or horizontal wood siding. Then, in the textile block houses, Wright was able to make the houses seem as if they were crystalline structures growing out of the earth. In the meantime, at Taliesin, Wright had the stone walls constructed in imitation of the natural strata of the region's rock, with stones projecting forward so as to suggest an uneven and irregular stratification. Through the remainder of his life, Wright would continue to design houses that seemed to belong to and emerge out of the earth through varying degrees of these types of imitation and abstraction.

It is true that, at least from the Prairie houses onward, 'there is a single intention that runs through all of Wright's work,' which was an 'imitation of nature.' It is not, though, an imitation of nature according to any 'classical meaning' of 'architecture as an art of representation.'[106] Rather, it was a deeply felt imaginative process that saw architecture as belonging to and growing out of the earth. Wright's use of Semper's symbolic architectural system followed the logic of the 'material imagination' and of the 'poetics of space.'

In an important study of Wright's Prairie houses, Grant Hildebrand has shown

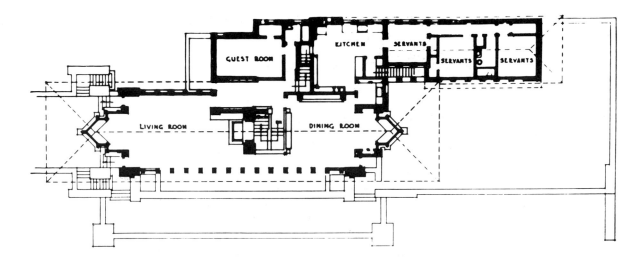

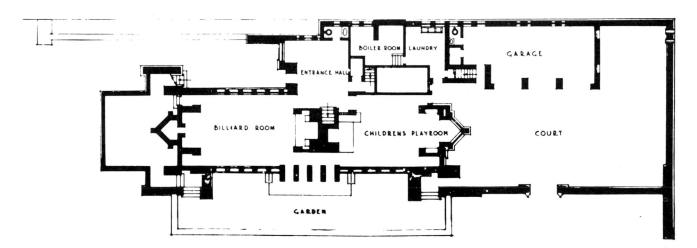

1.30
Frank Lloyd Wright. Frederick C. Robie
House, Chicago, 1909. Ground and first
floor plans

that the architect's use of the fireplace, roof, and walls created ideal settings for the
fulfillment of what Jay Appleton, in *The Experience of Landscape* (1975), outlined
as the 'prospect–refuge theory': 'By prospect he means the unimpeded opportunity
to see, thus the broad vista across land or water or both. Refuge is the opportunity
to hide while at the same time being able to view the access to prospect, thus the
sheltering grove, the cave, or the hill-pocketed ravine.'[107] Bachelard explored the
paired concepts of prospect and refuge in his chapters on 'house and universe' and
'intimate immensity' in *The Poetics of Space* as well as in his earlier discussion of the
grotto in *Le Terre et les rêveries du repos*.[108] This is a fundamental characteristic of
the imagination that Wright applied to his architecture and that he acknowledged
when he explained that the horizontal line was both the line of shelter, which
associated the building with the ground, and the line of freedom, which extended
unbounded into the landscape.[109]

In the end, to understand Wright's use of the symbolic architectural system, it
will be necessary to consider the logic of the 'material imagination' and the 'poetics

1.31, 1.32, 1.33 [*facing*]
Frank Lloyd Wright. Larkin Company
Administration Building, Buffalo, N.Y.,
1904

Interior

Ground and second floor plans

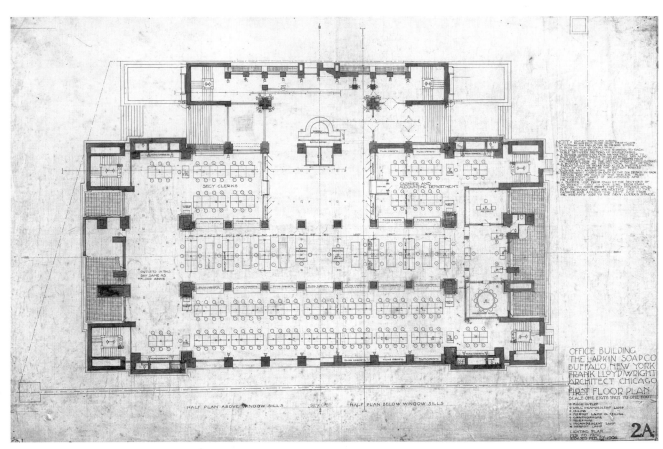

HALF PLAN ABOVE WINDOW SILLS   HALF PLAN BELOW WINDOW SILLS

OFFICE BUILDING
THE LARKIN SOAP CO
BUFFALO NEW YORK
FRANK LLOYD WRIGHT
ARCHITECT CHICAGO
FIRST FLOOR PLAN

2A

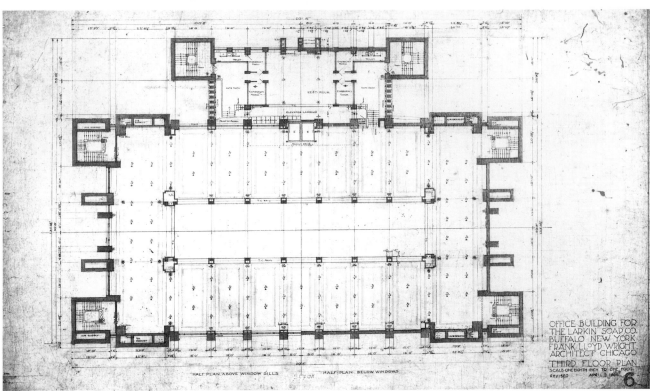

HALF PLAN ABOVE WINDOW SILLS   HALF PLAN BELOW WINDOWS

OFFICE BUILDING FOR
THE LARKIN SOAP CO.
BUFFALO NEW YORK
FRANK LLOYD WRIGHT
ARCHITECT CHICAGO
THIRD FLOOR PLAN
SCALE ONE EIGHTH INCH TO ONE FOOT
REVISED   APRIL 2 190

6

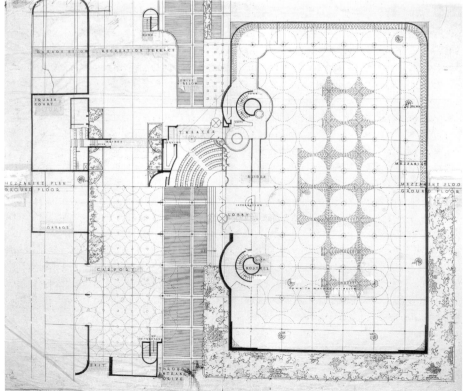

1.34, 1.35
Frank Lloyd Wright. Johnson Wax
Administration Building, Racine, Wis.,
1936

Main work space

Plan

of space' that researchers and philosophers such as Appleton and Bachelard have studied. The key can be found in Bachelard's definition of the dialectical opposition between two contrary values that mutually reinforce each other through their simultaneous presence. Appleton's pairing of prospect and refuge is a fundamental instance of this phenomenon.

In Wright's architecture, this dialectical pairing of poetic elements became the basis for ordering the design. The Prairie houses, as well as all later homes that partake of their formal logic, exploit the bipolar directionality of the chimney-stack, which seems to root the house into the earth while reaching upward into the sky . These images are reinforced by the enclosing walls, which seem to grow out of the earth, and by the extended roof, which suggests vectors of energy flying through space but also anchored to the chimney stack (figures 1.27, 1.30, colour plate 10). In both instances, the main poetic elements are earth and air, mediated by fire.

At the same time that Wright was developing his Prairie houses, which, in the architect's own terms, exploded the 'box' inside and out, he reaffirmed the 'box' in the inward-looking instititutional buildings of the Larkin Administration Building (figures 1.31–1.33. and Unity Temple (colour plates 8, 9). In these edifices and then in the major institutional works that followed, such as the Johnson Wax Administration Building (colour plates 5–7, figures 1.34, 1.35) and the Guggenheim Museum (colour plate 11, figures 1.36, 1.37), Wright developed an architecture in which the importance of sunlight, which entered from above to fill the volume with a golden glow, became the dominant theme. Whereas the warmth, both actual and poetic, from the fireplace at ground level dominated Wright's domestic architecture, the warmth from the sun, descending from the sky above, dominated his important institutional buildings. Just as the houses united earth and air in their poetics, so too these institutional buildings brought together sun and water. This latter pairing became clear in the Johnson Wax Administration Building, the experience of which observers have often likened to being under water and looking up toward the sunfilled sky.[110] The Guggenheim Museum literally conjoins the elements of sun and water by having the spiraling ramp that defines the sunfilled interior volume issue from a pond. The union of the pool of water, half inside and half outside, with the symbolically curved glass facade of the solar hemicycle house, first built as the second Jacobs House (figure 1.38, colour plate 15), shows how Wright could make the poetics of sun and water an integral aspect of his domestic architecture as well.

The essential features of Wright's grammar were already in place with the Winslow House (River Forest, Illinois, 1893) (colour plate 12). The building rises from a low, projecting base with brick walls that continue to the level of the second-story windows. The Roman brick used for these walls, because it is thinner than standard American brick, provides a compactness to its aspect as well as a horizontal feel, which at the time was the best that Wright could achieve with his goal of making the building seem as if it grew out of the ground. The double-hung windows of the first* floor are set within a richly ornamented terracotta band that has a tendency to dissolve the solid appearance of this part of the wall, thereby emphasizing the widely projecting roof above. A substantial chimney rises above the roofline along the central approach axis. Upon opening the door, the visitor enters into a reception hall (figure 1.39) where several steps lead up to a niche that contains the fireplace set within a broad brick wall, the 'integral fireplace.' A delicate wooden screen, reminiscent of a rood screen in a church that separates the

* Throughout this book, 'first floor' has been used, following the British convention, to refer to the floor immediately above the ground floor (and other floors accordingly)

1.36, 1.37 [*facing, at head*]
Frank Lloyd Wright. Solomon R.
Guggenheim Museum, New York City,
1956

Entrance

Main gallery

elevated chancel from the nave, completes the sacred aspect of this domestic altar.[111]

From this point onward, one can see how Wright developed the base, the walls, the windows, the roof, and the fireplace to make his buildings seem as if they participate more intimately with the earth. At the River Forest Golf Club (1898) the horizontal wood sheathing with its raised batten above each board took the unit of the projecting base and repeated it successively to make the walls.[112] Continuous bands of casement windows were more successful in making the spreading roof seem to hover as a psychological element of shelter. The Warren R. Hickox House (figures 1.40, 1.41) and the B. Harley Bradley House (figures 1.42, 1.43), both built in Kankakee, Illinois, in 1900, repeated the dark line of the projecting base at various levels so that the house seems to be horizontally layered with stacked units that begin with the base level joined to the ground. The Frank Thomas House (Oak Park, 1901) (colour plate 14) and the Ward W. Willitts House (Highland Park, 1902) (figures 1.44, 1.45) further develop this idea by consistently repeating these horizontal lines in the projecting forms of the roof. The most

1.38 [*facing, at foot*]
Frank Lloyd Wright. Second Herbert
Jacobs House, Middleton, Wis., 1943.
View of the rear facade with earth berm

complete instance of this technique occurs with the Robie House (Chicago, 1909) (figures 1.27, 1.30, colour plate 10), universally recognized as the masterpiece of Wright's Prairie houses.

At the Robie House the drama of the low walls that seem to grow from the ground, only to be repeated as a horizontal plane that hovers in mid-air under the daring projections of cantilevered roofs, is complete. These features, which create a strong sense of shelter, are combined with a dynamic sense of forces moving through the air, as found in the roof forms, which are pinned by the massive chimney stack. Earth and sky thus are joined around the central element of fire. Each of these elements calls forth its own reveries in this architecture of the material imagination.

We know how hard Wright worked to achieve the desired effect. He was no longer satisfied simply with the low profile of the Roman brick that he had used in the Winslow House. He had experimented with raised courses of brick at the Heurtley House (Oak Park, 1902) (colour plate 13) to create the effect of a horizontal striation growing out of the ground, similar to what he had achieved with powerful effect in wood at the River Forest Golf Club. Now, though, at the Robie House, he increased both the force and subtlety of the horizontal lines by using Roman brick with red mortar in the vertical joints only, so that each brick course would read as a continuous, thin horizontal band. In this way, Wright achieved further unity between the horizontal sweep of the base, the low walls, the stone copings, and the roof.

At the Robie House, the hidden entrance, placed not along the front or side, but rather at the rear, made the house seem to emanate outward from the massive chimney-stack. This was a true inner sanctum, the ultimate expression of secure

1.39
Frank Lloyd Wright.
William H. Winslow House,
River Forest, Ill., 1893.
Reception hall

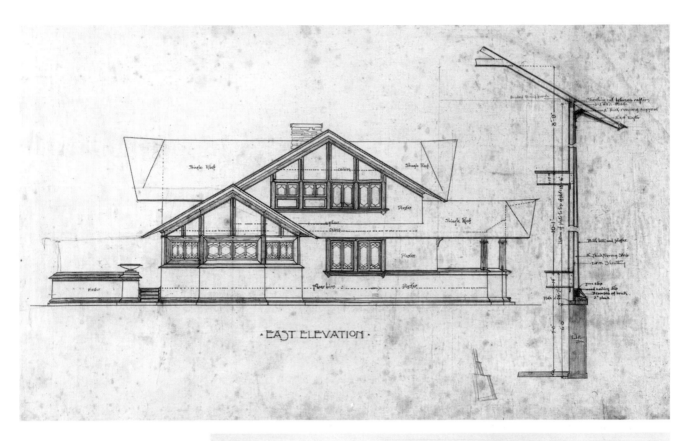

· EAST ELEVATION ·

1.40, 1.41
Frank Lloyd Wright. Warren R. Hickox
House, Kankakee, Ill., 1900

East elevation and wall section
showing the inclination of the exterior
surface of the outside walls

Plan

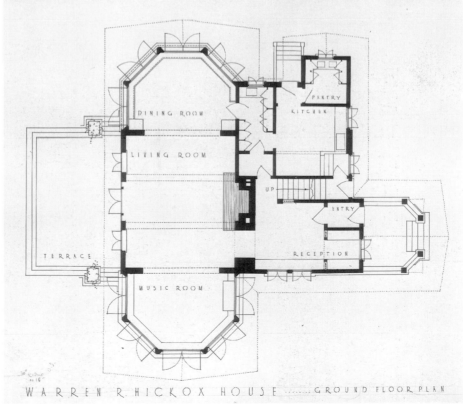

WARREN R HICKOX HOUSE ······ GROUND FLOOR PLAN

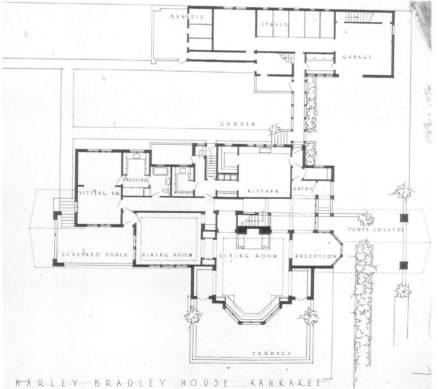

1.42, 1.43
Frank Lloyd Wright. B. Harley Bradley
House, Kankakee, Ill., 1900

Plan

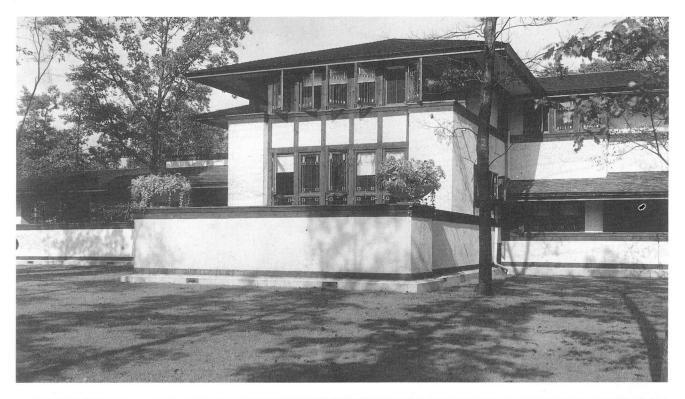

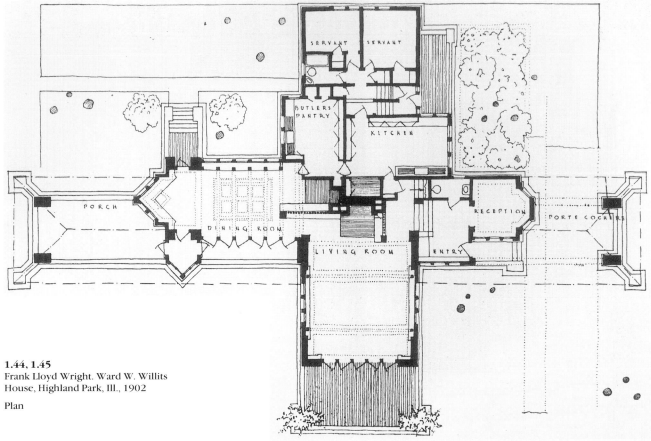

1.44, 1.45
Frank Lloyd Wright. Ward W. Willits
House, Highland Park, Ill., 1902

Plan

1.46, 1.47
Frank Lloyd Wright. Alice Millard
House ('La Miniatura'), Pasadena,
1923

Detail of fireplace in the living-room

Frank Lloyd Wright. Frederick C. Robie
House. Detail

Frank Lloyd Wright. Guggenheim
Museum

Frank Lloyd Wright. William H. Winslow House

Frank Lloyd Wright. Arthur Heurtley House

shelter. We can trace the evolution of Wright's thought about the relationship of the entrance to the fireplace and chimney from the frontal and axial alignment at the Winslow House onward. The Hickox and Bradley houses, for example, situate the entry to the side under the projecting roof of a porte-cochère. In these houses, the main volumes appear as extensions of the central chimney. On the other hand, the Thomas and Heurtley houses celebrate the entrance once again, but do not align it with the chimney. At the latter house, a low wall reminiscent of a fortified bastion partially obscures the entry. Finally, the Robie House removes the entrance entirely from view in favor of focusing attention on the chimney-shaft, which rises prominently above the roofline from within the heart of the house.

One could continue this type of review of Wright's use of Semper's four elements of the architectural system according to the dynamics of the 'material imagination' and the 'poetics of space' on a building by building basis for the rest of Wright's work. Before considering, though, the other major applications in his domestic and institutional architecture, it would be helpful to explore the degree to which Wright was also designing according to the architectural system championed by Quatremère de Quincy, Viollet-le-Duc, Auguste Choisy, and others.

We know that Wright was fully aware of the notion of the architectural system as grounded in a system of construction. This was the constant theme of Viollet-le-Duc's *Discourses on Architecture*, a book so important to Wright that he later gave a copy to his architect son John Lloyd Wright with the recommendation: 'In these volumes you will find all the architectural schooling you will ever need.'[113] From Wright's autobiographical account of the design of Unity Temple, it is clear that he was thinking in these terms at least as early as 1904 (colour plates 8, 9). Although the relevant passage is too long to quote in its entirety, a representative sampling will demonstrate the degree to which the systems of construction, form, proportions, decoration, heating and ventilating, and functional planning were integrated around the primacy of the structure, materials, and methods of building:

The first idea was to keep a noble room for worship in mind, and let that sense of the great room shape the whole edifice. Let the room inside be the architecture outside.

What shape? Well, the answer lay in the material. There was only one material to choose – as the church funds were [meager]. Concrete was cheap.

Why not make the wooden boxes or forms so the concrete could be cast in them as separate blocks and masses, these grouped about an interior space in some such way as to preserve this sense of the interior space, the great room, in the appearance of the whole building? . . .

What roof? What had concrete to offer as a cover shelter? The concrete slab – of course. The reinforced slab. Nothing else if the building was to be thoroughbred, meaning built in character out of one material.

Too monumental, all this? Too forthright for my committee, I feared. . . . But the flat slab was cheap and direct. It would be nobly simple. The wooden forms or molds in which concrete buildings must at that time be cast were always the chief item of expense, so to repeat the use of a single form as often as possible was necessary. Therefore a building, all four sides alike, looked like the thing. This, reduced to simplest terms, meant a building square in plan. That would make their temple a cube – a noble form in masonry.

. . . The site was noisy. . . . Therefore it seemed best to keep the building closed on three front sides. . . . And why not put the pulpit at the entrance side at the rear of the square Temple, and bring the congregation into the room at the sides on a lower level so those entering would be imperceptible to the audience? . . . Out of that thought came the depressed foyer. . . .

The room itself – size determined by comfortable seats with legroom for four hundred people – was built with four interior free-standing posts to carry the overhead structure.

These concrete posts were hollow and became free-standing ducts to insure economic and uniform distribution of heat. The large supporting posts were so set in plan as to form a double tier of alcoves on four sides of the room. I flooded these side-alcoves with light from above to get a sense of a happy cloudless day into the room. And with this feeling for light the center ceiling between the four great posts became skylight, daylight sifting through between the intersecting concrete beams, filtering through amber glass ceiling lights. . . . This scheme of lighting was integral, gave diffusion and kept the room-space clear.

Now for proportion – for the concrete expression of concrete in this natural arrangement – the ideal of an organic whole well in mind.[114]

Not only is this a perfect account of the architectural system as explained by Viollet-le-Duc, it also reflects the terms of the passage that John Lloyd Wright quoted from the *Discourses* in his book on his father. After relating Frank Lloyd Wright's words about the importance of Viollet-le-Duc's book, the son could see no better way to explain the French writer's influence on his father than to reproduce Viollet-le-Duc's discussion of organic architecture for the entirety of his chapter.

As is well known, Frank Lloyd Wright used the term 'organic architecture' so often that it became his hallmark. Yet, there was a dual meaning to the phrase. On the one hand, Wright's organic architecture harmonized with nature and even seemed a part of its realm. On the other hand, as Wright's description of Unity Temple reveals, organic architecture meant the complete integration of parts and the reasonable character of all actions to achieve the same type of fitness and wholeness found in the flora and fauna of the natural world. What this meant in architecture was building according to the definition of the architectural system. In that sense, organic architecture, as used by Frank Lloyd Wright and Viollet-le-Duc, was synonymous with the architectural system.

The two notions of organic architecture came together in Wright's next major achievements in domestic building through the creation of what Wright called the 'textile' concrete block houses.[115] Small concrete blocks were stacked together to make the walls. After the first realization of this system at the Alice Millard House (Pasadena, 1923), called 'La Miniatura' (figures 1.46, 1.47), Wright added thin steel reinforcing bars, which were placed into the grooved edges of the blocks before a cement grout was poured in to make the wall into a monolithic whole. After World War II, he applied this system of building to the lower cost homes that he was designing for the average American family. This he called the 'Usonian Automatic' house (figure 1.48).[116]

Wright did not invent the concrete block method. According to Pamela H. Simpson, concrete blocks were 'enormously popular' in the United States between 1905 and 1930 when 'thousands of concrete block buildings were constructed.'[117] Yet Wright gave a complete development to the building technique that was generally absent in the work of his predecessors and competitors. By using the block to make his typically dynamic architectural forms and by impressing the blocks with decorative patterns, he made a mere system of construction into a true architectural system. Not only was the ornamental character established simultaneously with the fabrication of each block, but the use of the block as a finished surface both inside and out created a further unity between construction and architectural form. The textile block houses, then, represent a major realization of the architectural system as defined by Quatremère de Quincy and those who followed.[118]

At the same time, though, Wright continued to center the home around the hearth. In this sense, the symbolic architectural system defined by Semper also

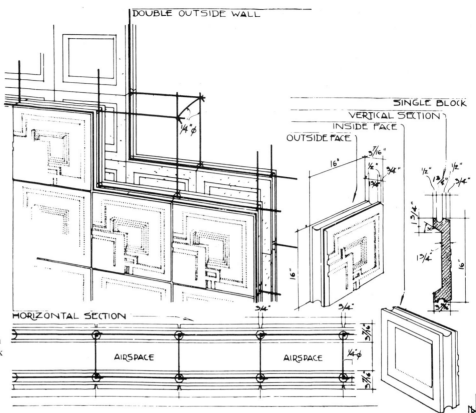

1.48, 1.49

Frank Lloyd Wright. Wall construction for 'Usonian Automatic' concrete block houses

Frank Lloyd Wright. Samuel Freeman House, Los Angeles, 1924

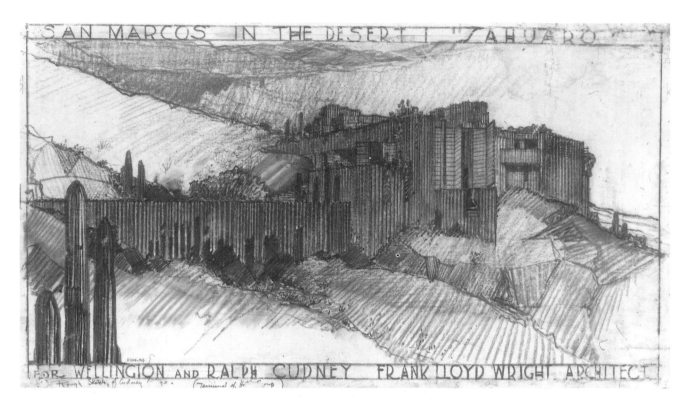

1.50
Frank Lloyd Wright. Wellington and Ralph Cudney House (project), San-Marcos-in-the-Desert, Arizona, 1927

1.51
Frank Lloyd Wright. Owen D. Young House (project), San-Marcos-in-the-Desert, Arizona, 1927

appears to have informed the textile block buildings. Even the name itself is significant, for the building's enclosure, Semper had explained, had originated in woven mats. All later forms of more solid walls were said to have been derived from these primitive origins. In effect, Wright referred to himself as 'the Weaver' when describing the Millard House: 'Yes, argued the Weaver – is anyone smiling? – have not all great ideas in art had an origin as humble as this? Or more so? At last: a real building-method beginning in this little house; here at last was a weaving in building that could go on forever and not go wrong for anyone.'[119] Using steel rods, Wright 'wove' together the concrete blocks, some plain, others ornamental, in a patterned wall such that the overall effect is like a 'masonry fabric.'[120]

If Wright was following Semper here, then he was modifying Semper's symbolic system in two significant ways. First, at times, Wright eliminated the appearance of a sheltering roof. Second, he altered, and in places even abolished, the projecting base. The result was to make the house seem as if it grew out of the ground with a directness not present in the earlier Prairie houses. As Wright explained about the Millard House,

The house would rise tall out of the ravine gardens between the two eucalyptus trees. . . . And the appropriate but expensive garden terraces, balconies and roof gardens that had come to join the original inexpensive programme of interior rooms made the whole so naturally a part of that ravine that no one could even think of that building anywhere else or regret what the additional features cost.[121]

Even the blocks themselves appear as man-made analogs to stones. The effect is to make the building seem as if it were a geological outcrop. This is further evidence of Wright's material imagination, of his 'geological' imagination in particular.

Wright enhanced this effect through the siting of the building, as well as through the overall massing. For the Millard House, he explained, 'Meantime we had rejected the treeless lot originally purchased, as my eyes had fallen upon a ravishing ravine near by, in which stood two beautiful eucalyptus trees. . . . No one would ever want to build down in a ravine out there. . . . The house would rise tall out of these ravine gardens between the two eucalyptus trees.'[122] The reason that nobody would want to build in the ravine, explains Brendan Gill, is that what to Wright was a romantic setting was actually an 'arroyo,' a dry gully that carries off 'large quantities of floodwater in the rainy season and [is] much more dangerous to live by than the comparatively harmless ravines of [Wright's] Illinois. . . . Flying in the face of conventional prudence, Wright and [Mrs. Millard] decided to build at the very bottom of the arroyo, where a small pool would be dug to reflect the house.'[123]

There had to be a compelling reason, then, to place the house at the bottom of the arroyo. Its location there certainly accords with Wright's desire to make the home appear as if it were wedded to the ground. At the Millard House, he achieved this effect to such an extent that the building seems as if it had grown out of the earth. He would repeat this effect often in his textile block and other houses. The Freeman House (Los Angeles, 1924) (figure 1.49.) appears to grow out of the crest of a hill overlooking Hollywood. His project for the Wellington and Ralph Cudney House (San-Marcos-in-the-Desert, Arizona, 1927) (figure 1.50) seems to grow out of the rocks in the desert. Here the shape of the block, which Wright explains was patterned after the Saguaro cactus, also appears as a faceted geological form.[124] The related project for the Owen D. Young House (figure 1.51) uses diamond-shaped blocks and masses that even more forcefully convey the sense of natural crystalline forms emerging from the earth. On the plains of Tulsa, Oklahoma, in 1929, Wright

1.52
Frank Lloyd Wright. Richard Lloyd
Jones House, Tulsa, Okla., 1929

built the Richard Lloyd Jones House (figure 1.52) where alternating vertical bands of stacked blocks or glass rise from the flat earth, once again, with the appearance of a natural outcrop well suited to the site.

The Richard Lloyd Jones House, as well as the Benjamin Adelman House, this a 'Usonian Automatic,' show a fuller integration of the architectural system than the earlier textile block houses. Here the integration of solid and void, wall and window, block forms and interior partitions, shelves, and cabinets achieved a high level of integrated unity. As usual, Wright was thinking in terms of the architectural system.

The most famous examples of Wright's houses growing out of the ground are his headquarters, named 'Taliesin,' in Spring Green, Wisconsin, and the Kaufmann vacation house, 'Fallingwater' at Bear Run, Pennsylvania. Wright explains that he named his house and studio complex 'Taliesin,' the Welsh word meaning 'shining brow.' The buildings, dating from 1911, but rebuilt in 1914 and later years, belonged to the landscape:

I knew well that no house should ever be *on* a hill or *on* anything. It should be *of* the hill. Belonging to it. . . . Now I wanted a *natural* house to live in myself. I scanned the hills of the region where the rock came cropping out in strata to suggest buildings. How quiet and strong the rock-ledge masses looked with the dark red cedars and white birches, there, above the green slopes.[125]

If Bachelard had used statements from architects as well as poets and novelists in his study of the material imagination, he certainly would have chosen passages like these from Frank Lloyd Wright.

Wright's successful building with rock masses emerging from the earth at Bear Run gave him a house that undoubtedly rivals all others as the most famous and most visited in the world. Perched over a waterfall (colour plate 17), the Kaufmann residence, known as 'Fallingwater' (1935), seems to grow out of the landscape.[126] The dramatic cantilevered terraces echo the flagstone ledges, which jut out from the earth below. The massive flagstone chimney-stack appears to grow out of the ground. Indeed, the fireplace inside the house is literally built upon exposed bedrock (figure 1.53). Local flagstone was used for the interior walls; the floors were surfaced with irregular flagstone slabs. In both the walls and the chimney-stack, Wright had the masons lay the stone with projecting thin bands interspersed among the thicker ones. This created a rougher look more akin to nature than to a smooth wall. At the same time, it gave the impression of density to the wall as if it had arisen stone course by stone course from the bedrock. We have seen how Wright had experimented with Roman brick, projecting brick courses, horizontal wooden trim, and even projecting stone to achieve this effect in the past. The stacking of concrete blocks in the textile block houses also had this appearance in mind. Nowhere was Wright as successful in achieving this effect as in Fallingwater. Here, then, was a perfect realization of the geological imagination, a house truly belonging to the realm of the earth.

Semper, as we have seen, had argued that historically the mound, the enclosure, and the roof had clustered around the hearth to protect the fire from the other three elements. At Fallingwater, the architecture makes a celebration of the four elements, with fire, in the form of the hearth, at the symbolic core. Through the walls, the chimney-stack, and even the cantilevered terraces, the earth pervades the house in actual and metaphorical ways. As with the rooflines of the earlier Prairie houses, the cantilevered terraces, crossing above each other at right angles, give the impression of dynamic forces of the wind crystallized into built form. Not only is the house built over the waterfall, but the waxed flagstone floor gives the impression of water rushing over a stream bed, like the water of Bear Run outside. This similarity is made forcefully apparent when looking through the glass-covered 'hatch,' which leads from the living room down to the stream: 'A glance through the hatch could reveal how the house took its place above the stream. The waxed flags of the living-room floor had the same color and the same texture as the glistening bedrock of the stream.'[127] Even irregular forms of the flagstone floor slabs are made to cross the thresholds between rooms to ensure the feeling of a continuous flow.[128]

For all its poetic meaning, though, Fallingwater is also an instance of the architectural system grounded in the system of construction. Fallingwater is designed around the principle of the cantilever. In this house, Wright pushed modern concrete cantilever construction to new structural limits, while supplying novel architectural forms. As was often the case with Wright's unaccustomed structural experiments, both engineering authorities and the builder were reluctant to follow Wright's instructions. There were dire predictions of structural disaster, which never occurred. In chronicling the disagreements, tensions, and subterfuges related to the building's construction, Donald Hoffmann tells the now famous story of the stone wall that the builder extended, upon the engineers' recommendation, to reduce the span of the principal cantilever from twelve to eight feet:

[T]he terrace was test-loaded two days later, and the engineers were satisfied. Wright, when he discovered it later, was not. No one had asked him about the wall, so he did not tell anyone when he ordered [his assistant] Mosher to take out the top course of stones. Edgar Kaufmann, Jr., recalls his father finally confessing to Wright: 'If you've not noticed it . . . there can't be anything very bad about it, architecturally.' Wright then walked with Kaufmann to below the terrace. 'When I was here last month,' he said, 'I ordered the top layers of stone removed. Now, the terrace has shown no sign of falling. Shall we take down the extra four feet of wall?'[129]

Fallingwater is just one instance of Wright's repeated realizations of the nineteenth-century goal of creating a modern architecture from a new architectural system, based upon a new system of construction, using modern materials and methods of construction. When one considers his most famous buildings, they are usually

1.53
Frank Lloyd Wright. Edgar J. Kaufmann
House ('Fallingwater'), Bear Run, Pa.,
1935. Partial view of living-room with
fireplace on the exposed bedrock

instances in which he pioneered new architectural forms with modern methods of construction. Wright explicitly explained the relationship between structure and aesthetics, which he likened to the workings of the natural world:

Every true aesthetic is an implication of nature, so it was inevitable that this aesthetic ideal should be found to enter into the actual building of the building itself as a principle of construction. But later on I found that in the effort to actually eliminate the post and beam in favor of structural continuity, that is to say, making the two things one instead of two separate things, I could get no help at all from regular engineers. . . . Walls made one with floors and ceilings, merging together yet reacting upon each other, the engineer had never met. And the engineer has not yet enough scientific formulas to enable him to calculate for continuity. Floor slabs stiffened and extended as cantilevers over centered supports, as a waiter's tray rests upon his upturned fingers, such as I now began to use in order to get planes parallel to the earth to emphasize the third dimension, were new, as I used them, especially in the Imperial Hotel [1915, figure 1.54]. But the engineer soon mastered the element of continuity in floor slabs with such formulas as he had. The cantilever thus became a new feature of design in architecture. As used in the Imperial Hotel at Tokyo it was the most important of the features of construction that insured the life of that building in the terrific tremblor of 1922. So, not only a new aesthetic but proving the aesthetic as scientifically sound, a great new economic 'stability,' derived from steel in tension, was able now to enter into building construction.[130]

We can trace not only the cantilever but also the concept of the architectural system grounded in a way of building back to Wright's Prairie houses. These buildings obviously do not exhibit an architectural system in same evident manner as Wright's later textile block houses or Le Corbusier's buildings designed according to the 'Five Points for a New Architecture.' Both of these types, it should be noted, date from the 1920s and onward. Yet, at the turn of the century, Wright was certainly thinking in terms of the architectural system that Quatremère de Quincy and others had popularized from the 1830s onward.

Wright, in the first of his articles 'In the Cause of Architecture,' published in *The Architectural Record* (March 1908), revealed that he was thinking in terms of the architectural system grounded in a system of construction:

The old structural forms which up to the present time, have spelled 'architecture' are decayed. Their life went from them long ago and new conditions industrially, steel and concrete and terra cotta in particular, are prophesying a more plastic art wherein as the flesh is to our bones so will the covering be to the structure, but more truly and beautifully expressive than ever.

To create such an architecture would require a radical break from current trends in American architecture: 'So what might be termed the democratic character of the exteriors [of my buildings] is their first undefined offense – the lack, wholly, of what the professional critic would deem architecture; in fact, most of the critic's architecture has been left out.'[131] In his following article, published in May 1914, Wright, in reviewing his pioneering Prairie houses, further explained that he had had to 'break ground and make the forms I needed, alone – absolutely alone. These forms were the result of a conscientious study of materials and of the machine which is the real tool, whether we like it or not, that we must use to give shape to our ideals.'[132]

Wright even used the term 'an architecture' while summarizing his achievement, which he saw as effective for one man but obviously not sufficient to make an architecture for an entire age: 'There are enough types and forms in my work to characterize the work of an architect, but certainly not enough to characterize an architecture.'[133] In his next installment, published in May 1927, Wright reiterated the common nineteenth-century notion, 'Every age and period has had its technique. The technique of the age or period was always a matter of its industrial system and tools, or the systems and tools were a matter of its technique. It doesn't matter which. And this is just as true to-day.'[134] Wright, then, was thinking in terms of the architectural system grounded in a way of building, which would yield forms expressive of the times, forms that in their totality would constitute 'an architecture.'

In his articles published in 1927–28, Wright organized his discussion primarily around materials – steel, reinforced concrete, wood, clay, stone, and glass. Yet, we should not be misled by the very apt title of Henry-Russell Hitchcock's important book, *In the Nature of Materials: The Buildings of Frank Lloyd Wright, 1887-1914* (1942), to think that it was the nature of the materials alone that was the driving force to Wright's thought.[135] Rather, as Wright's articles amply show, it was the relationship of the material to the architectural system. Hence the great lesson of steel and reinforced concrete, according to Wright, was the new forms of construction that they permitted and then the new architectural forms that could be created with them:

1.54
Frank Lloyd Wright. Imperial Hotel,
Tokyo, 1915

And again, easier to comprehend are the new forms brought to hand by reinforced concrete. First among them is the slab – next the cantilever – then the splay. . . . the economic structural principle of the cantilever. A new stability as well as a new economy. The most romantic of all structural possibilities is here. And last, there is the splay or sloping wall, used as a slide from wall into projections or from floors into walls or used in connection with the cantilever slab. It may be used as an expression of form in itself for protection or light. For economy it may be useful as support in both cases and enhance the plastic effect of the whole.[136]

In these articles, Wright's selection of illustrations with their accompanying captions shows the full extent of his application of the architectural system, with views of long, unsupported spans made possible by steel or reinforced concrete, surfaced with brick screens, either solid or perforated, with carved lava-stone, or with molded terra cotta.[137] Throughout these articles Wright demonstrates how he created new forms from the materials used in construction, which he then decorated with an integral ornamentation.

This type of thinking, i.e., according to the architectural system, also informed Wright's article of January 1928, entitled 'The Logic of the Plan.' For Wright, the logic of the plan was not primarily the Beaux-Arts logic of the axial and hierarchical organization of spaces, but rather the nature of the plan, and hence the volumes, enclosures, and openings, conceived according to the material used. Each material suggested a different type of architecture:

A wood plan is slender: light in texture, narrower spacing.
A stone or brick plan is heavy: black in masses, wider in spacing.
Combination of materials: lightness combined with massiveness.
A cast-block building: such massing as is felt to be adequate to the sense of block and box and slab; more freedom in spacing.[138]

Wright then illustrated these principles with the wood plan of the Coonley House, the cast-block and slab plan of Unity Temple, the brick plan of the Martin House in Buffalo and of the Ullman House in Oak Park, and the pre-cast block plan of the Ennis House in Hollywood. In Wright's mind then, the Prairie houses were designed according to the strictures of the architectural system just as his later buildings were.

When we turn to contemporary accounts, we find that the Prairie architecture of Wright and his admirers was seen in these terms as well. An article in *The Architectural Record* in 1904, for example, praised the house by a follower of Frank Lloyd Wright for its 'manifest seeking for structural honesty. The architect is evidently thinking in terms of masses, surfaces, and of light and shade.'[139] Turning to Wright's own buildings and proceeding beyond the 'logic of the plan' to consider the other ways in which Wright applied the notion of the architectural system, we find three types of consideration: the use of new materials and ways of building to create modern forms; the use of molding to signal the system of construction, and the creation of a total environmental system from the formal elements of the new architecture.

The Robie House is the best example of all three themes. Here is a building whose forms are developed out of the possibilities of steel construction. Whereas Wright in his earlier Prairie houses had made dramatic use of the broadly extended roof, it was in the Robie House that he used steel construction not only for the daring cantilever of the roof but also for what appears to be the long unsupported span of the front terrace.[140] These were the elements that later architects, such as the Italian Rationalists of the Gruppo 7, would identify as the absolutes of modern architecture, having the same importance as the column and the arch in ancient architecture.[141]

Inside the Robie House (figure 1.55), as well as the other Prairie houses,

1.55
Frank Lloyd Wright. Frederick C. Robie House, Chicago, 1909. View from the dining-room toward the living-room to the far side of the fireplace

Wright, as he himself explained, arranged the decorative woodwork with straight lines that were both produced by and indicative of modern machine production.[142] Thus, the ornamentation in the Prairie houses was harmonious with the modern system of construction. Edward R. Ford has argued that there was even a closer fit between construction and decoration in these buildings. In architecture, molding was traditionally used to hide joints and to cover residual spaces between two surfaces, as when a window is set in a wall. 'In the mature Prairie Houses,' however, explains Ford, 'Wright used the trim to create an analogous structural system – an ornamental system of trim that describes the structure it conceals.' For example, the

Bradley house has dropped beams in the entry hall, but the ceilings of the living and dining rooms – formed of plaster and thin wood strips – parallel the ceiling joists above. . . . The ceiling of the Heurtley house is more complex, since here there are no rooms above the living [figure 1.56] and dining rooms and the ceilings may project into the attic space. The living and dining rooms have ceilings that imitate in miniature the hip roof outside. . . . Like the Heurtley house, the Willits house uses trim to create a structure analogous to the real structure which it clads. . . . [In] the Martin house [in Buffalo, figure 1.28], there are several systems of trim and ornament, and they delineate precisely which portions are concrete and which are wood. These ornamental systems express Wright's interpretations of the nature of the structural systems they clad. . . . In the early Prairie Houses, moldings are used to make transitions and cover joints. Thus, the junctions of wall and floor, of wall and ceiling, and of column and beam are all locations for elaborations. In the Robie house, trim is used for one dominant purpose: to delineate structure. Other uses for moldings are eliminated or minimized.

Wright's use of trim here is a perfect example of the role of decoration in the architectural system in which the forms used and the ornament applied are

1.56
Frank Lloyd Wright. Arthur Heurtley House, Oak Park, Ill., 1902. Living room

1.57
Frank Lloyd Wright. Ward W. Willits
House, Highland Park, Ill., 1902.
Dining-room

consonant with the structural system. As Ford explains, at this time, it 'never
occurred to Wright to expose any of these structural systems, any more than it
occurred to Sullivan. They are all expressions of his flesh-and-bones concept of
structure and form. . . . The ornament and trim were what Wright called the
'efflorescence' which expressed the nature of that structure.'[143]

Yet, in some cases, where Wright opens the ceiling for skylights, as in the
dining room of the Ward Willits House (1902, figure 1.57), the pattern of
decorative trim also coincides with the actual framing of the glazed openings. This
means of expression soon afterward became the basis for the ceilings of the Larkin
Administration Building (1904, figure 1.32) and Unity Temple (colour plate 9).
What had been an incident in the Ward Willits House became a major theme in
these later buildings.

Finally, as Reyner Banham has discovered, the Robie House presents a complete
system of natural ventilation that is inseparable from the distinguishing architectural elements of the design (figure 1.55). In the hot Chicago summer, the broad
overhanging roof to either side of the house gathers pockets of cool, shaded air. The
battery of French doors to one side and casement windows to the other can be
opened to allow this refreshing air to pass directly through the house. Furthermore,
even the lighting fixtures and the chimney contribute to the summer cooling.
Banham has noted that Wright pioneered the decorative use of electric lighting by
exploiting a potential not possible with gas and oil flames. He recessed the electric
bulbs behind decorative wooden screens along each side of the main living level.
Placed within a row of decorative globes, other bulbs appear as accents at the end
of the ornamental ceiling bands and run parallel to the recessed lights on each side.
All of these electric lamps give off heat that creates a convection current, thereby
creating a natural breeze which draws the cool air inside and upward, where it is

vented out of the house through a duct at the main chimney.[144] This confluence of the mechanical system with the systems of structure, form, and decoration is a perfect example of a successful architectural system.

Beginning with the textile block houses, Wright applied himself even more vigorously to create true architectural systems based on a way of building. As Ford explains, the Prairie houses, although structurally innovative at times with non-traditional formats of structure, were still variants of conventional methods of construction. The Robie House, 'with load-bearing brick walls, wood-frame floors, and standard balloon framing . . . stretched these systems to their limits, but it did not go outside them.' From the textile block houses onward, each major change in Wright's aesthetic derived from a new realization of the architectural system grounded in a new system of construction.

The Johnson Wax Administration Building (Racine, Wisconsin, 1936) presents another famous example of novel architectural form developed from modern means of cantilevered construction (colour plates 5, 7, figures 1.34, 1.35). Here Wright used lily-pad reinforced concrete columns that provided structure as well as part of the roofing. In an unprecedented move that pushed beyond the technical capabilities of the time (as far as creating waterproof seams was concerned), Pyrex glass tubes were used for the roof spaces between the concrete pads, for clerestory lighting at the top of the perimeter walls, and for glass surfaces (colour plate 7) inside the building.[145] Together, the lily-pad columns, the Pyrex glass tubing, and the innovative sandwich brick walls made a powerful and original architectural space.

Kenneth Frampton, in his introduction to Jonathan Lipman's *Frank Lloyd Wright and the Johnson Wax Buildings* (1986), has argued that 'Wright's Administration Building for Johnson Wax is not only the greatest piece of twentieth-century architecture realized in the United States to date but also, possibly, the most profound work of art that America has ever produced.' Frampton's reasoning is highly instructive, for he effectively praises Wright for having created a masterful architectural system. 'The grounds for such an assertion,' Frampton continues,

lie primarily in the fact that in this singular masterwork the sixty-seven-year-old Wright was to push himself to the very limits of his architectonic creativity, thereby producing a building that was not only suavely composed and brilliantly organized, but also one that employed a totally unprecedented structural device. It was a concept, in fact, that introduced a new tectonic and spatial discourse into twentieth-century architecture. . . . Wright's architectonic invention of a top-lit hypostyle hall, made up of sixty reinforced-concrete, hollow, tapering, 'lily-pad' mushroom columns, projects the Johnson Wax buildings into another historical class, comparable one might say, to Brunelleschi's building of the dome over Santa Maria dei Fiore in Florence in 1434 or, at the very least, to Henri Labrouste's building of a lightweight cast- and wrought-iron infrastructure over the reading room of the Bibliothèque Nationale in Paris between 1854 and 1875.[146]

Jonathan Lipman himself introduced the marvel of Wright's Johnson Wax buildings to his readers in analogous terms. 'I was first struck,' begins Lipman,

by the inner logic of Frank Lloyd Wright's Johnson Wax buildings, and their utterly original solutions to the design of the workplace. . . . Wright orchestrated every element in them; virtually all of the components – the delicate mushroom columns, wall system, glazing, detailing, and furniture – were newly invented. Sunlight is so transformed by the skylights and by its interaction with the curving shapes of the buiding that it also seems to be a newly created element.[147]

Time and again we will find observers of Wright's innovative architecture describing his success as a function of what throughout the nineteenth and early twentieth centuries was termed the architectural system, deemed the guiding principle of all past ages with great architecture and the ultimate ideal of the contemporary designer.

Historians have emphasized that the pioneering Swiss engineer Robert Maillart had been working with mushroom-shaped reinforced concrete columns in previous years.[148] As with the textile block houses, Wright took an advanced structural form and made it distinctly his own, in this case transforming the solid mushroom column into a dramatic, elongated lily-pad version with hollow core and steel-mesh reinforcing. As with Fallingwater, Wright had to convince outside authorities of the structural safety of his design. Henry-Russell Hitchcock explains: 'But so novel were the hollow tapered piers, reinforced by tissues of expanded metal lath and supporting only their own lily-pad-like tops, that a building permit was not issued until the following spring.'[149] Jonathan Lipman relates that when Wright was required to erect a lily-pad column to test whether it could carry the appropriate load, Wright insisted on pushing the test to the limit:

At twelve tons the state inspectors were satisfied. Wright, however, was not, and he continued the test. There was a break for lunch. . . . At thirty tons, enjoying the drama, Wright directed the loading crew, 'Keep piling.' . . . By late afternoon there was no more room at the top of the column. Wright scrutinized the concrete shaft through binoculars, searching for cracks. His creation was carrying sixty tons, five times the load required by the state, and was only now displaying slight cracks at the calyx. 'Well, I guess that's enough. Pull the column down,' Wright ordered as sunset approached. The crane jerked out one of the timber braces. The column snapped cleanly at the calyx and fell. . . . The slender shaft of the column, however, remained intact. [150]

The magical quality of the interior space at the Johnson Wax Administration Building has impressed itself upon countless users and visitors. Eminent architectural historians have repeatedly likened this space to an underwater realm. Henry- Russell Hitchcock, recently seconded by Kenneth Frampton, has written:

For the interior space is here entirely cut off from the outside. The light, coming straight down from the open spaces between the lily-pad pier tops, and entering also in bands below the surrounding balcony and at the top of the wall, is extraordinarily even. Perhaps because of its points of origin, perhaps because of the Pyrex glass tubes which fill the openings, the light has a very special quality. With the special forms of the piers, there is a certain illusion of sky seen from the bottom of an aquarium.[151]

Vincent Scully has described this space as an aquatic realm preceded by a cave-like antechamber:

Therefore the exterior walls are expressed as non-bearing, i.e., as purely for enclosure, and they rush in strong curves toward the low, dark entrance, where the columns are compressed, as at the entrance to a cave. Beyond this dark place, however, the shafts rise up swelling to their full height and receive the light which filters down through the glass tubing above them. They thus stand as if growing and floating in the quietest place of all, a deep and limpid pool.[152]

From the Larkin Administration Building to Unity Temple to the Johnson Administration Building to the Guggenheim Museum, Wright was always adducing some functional justification to create a centralized great space with interior balconies that was closed off from the exterior world. One senses, though, in visiting his institutional buildings, that the truly compelling reason to shut out the exterior world was to create an interior with a spiritual aura. In many, if not all of these buildings, the poetics of sun and water dominate. Whereas Wright's domestic architecture is grounded in the poetic imagery of earth, fire, and air, his institutional architecture primarily exploits the realm of water. This is not a question of symbols or metaphors, but of what the French call 'lived space,' that is, of the workings of the material imagination.

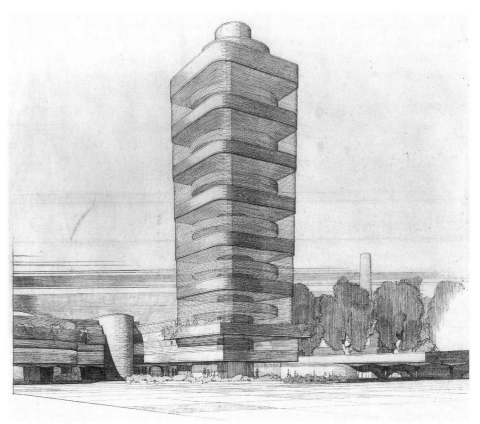

1.58
Frank Lloyd Wright. Johnson Wax Company Research Tower, Racine, Wis., 1944

The Johnson Wax Administration Building was soon joined by a Research Tower (1944) built according to the parameters of the architectural system (figure 1.58). Rather than follow the customary manner of skeletal frame construction with a cage of structural supports, Wright designed a building around the principle of the cantilever off a central core, much like the branches extending out from a tree trunk. As is well known, Wright had proposed this system of construction for residential towers in his Saint Marks in the Bowery project of 1929. A variation of this tower was erected in the form of a combined office and apartment building as the Price Company Tower (1952, figure 1.59) in Bartlesville, Oklahoma. In all cases, including the unbuilt Crystal Heights project of 1940 for Washington, D.C., which links a series of residential towers together, Wright developed integrated systems of spatial planning, form, and decoration to suit the new system of construction.[153] The Price Company Tower, for example, includes single-height office floors as well as apartments with double-height living rooms. Vertical copper louvers around the apartment side and horizontal copper louvers for the offices provide protection from the sun as well as decoration for the facade. Wright's own

1.59
Frank Lloyd Wright. Price Company
Tower, Bartlesville, Okla., 1952. View
from the south

description of the Crystal Heights project reveals the ways in which he understood
the systems of spatial planning, form, and decoration working together:

The scheme for the Hotel is ideal from a practical standpoint, as any portion of it may be
apartments of any one of the classes you mentioned. There is no break between Hotel and
apartment. ... And this is to suggest that you change [the name] Temple Heights to
CRYSTAL HEIGHTS because of the crystalline character of the whole edifice. It will be an
iridescent fabric with every surface showing of the finest quality. There are no accommodations in Washington or any other city so luxurious and spacious in effect. Crystal is the
word when you see the buildings.

I have assumed that you wanted the last word which is also the first word in all this and we
have it – the apotheosis of GLASS.

... The Dining Room Banquet Hall and all Private Support Rooms are all sunlit overlooking
garden terraces – gleaming crystal palaces. Versailles is no more.[154]

Two more examples from Wright's late work should suffice to demonstrate the degree to which he was constantly thinking in terms of the architectural system. The form of the Beth Sholom Synagogue (1954–59) in Elkins Park, Pennsylvania, is developed from the steel-framed tripod, clad in aluminum, which, in turn, is embossed with decorative patterns (figures 1.60, 1.61). Sheets of fiberglass enclose the sanctuary, thereby making it into another of Wright's inward-looking structures. This time the building becomes a 'mountain of light,' thereby satisfying the rabbi's desire for a building in the form of a 'traveling Mount Sinai.'[155] Similarly, the reinforced concrete used to construct the dramatic spiral with its sweeping cantilevers at the Guggenheim Museum (1956, colour plate 11, figures 1.36, 1.37) in New York City is, as Vincent Scully has observed, 'so structurally suited to the form.'[156] The Guggenheim Museum, moreover, like many other buildings by Wright, not only matches form, plan arrangement, and decoration with structure, it has a further internal consistency derived by designing everything, from the decoration in the sidewalk to the tokens deposited for entry in the turnstile, to the

ramped galleries, and to the auditorium below and skylight above according to the discipline of the circle placed within the rectilinear grid of Manhattan.

At the same time that Wright was exploring innovative applications of the architectural system to institutional buildings, he was also developing houses for ordinary Americans according to still other types of architectural systems. We have seen how the textile block houses first built in the early 1920s were developed into the Usonian Automatic houses after World War II. In the interim, Wright created still another architectural system for the Usonian House.

Wright's first Usonian house was built in 1937 for the journalist Herbert Jacobs, his wife Katherine, and their young daughter (figures 1.62–1.64). The architect gives the cost as five thousand five hundred dollars. Everything about Wright's description of this building reads like an explanation of the architectural system. The economies in design and construction also yielded integrated systems of structure, form, and decoration: 'Inside and outside should be complete in one operation, the house finished inside as it is completed outside.' To this end, Wright

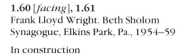

1.60 [*facing*], **1.61**
Frank Lloyd Wright. Beth Sholom
Synagogue, Elkins Park, Pa., 1954–59

In construction

developed a special sandwich wall consisting of 'three thicknesses of boards with paper [i.e., a damp-proof membrane] placed between them, the boards fastened together with screws.' Wright extolled the additional benefits of this approach:

These slab walls of boards – a kind of plywood construction on a large scale, can be high in insulation value, vermin-proof, and practically fireproof. These walls like the fenestration may be prefabricated on the floor, with any degree of insulation we can afford, and raised into place, or they may be made at the mill and shipped to the site in sections. The roof can be built first on props and these walls shoved into place under them.

There was, then, a harmony and concordance between materials used, methods of construction, and architectural form. The same was true of the finishings: 'No painting at all. Wood best preserves itself. A coating of clear resinous oil would be enough.' Furthermore, ornamentation was derived from the patterns created by the very construction of the wall: 'We must also use a vertical-unit system which will be the width of the boards and batten bands themselves, interlocking with the brick courses.' In the Usonian houses Wright also used what he called his 'horizontal-unit system of construction,' which consisted in gridding the concrete floor slab to guide the builder in the placement of walls and doors. The grid, permanently incised into the floor itself, provided scale, rhythm, and ornamentation. As for the surface, the 'floor mat of concrete squares' would be waxed to provide a functional and aesthetic finish. The roof could not be 'complicated.' The flat roof cantilevering far beyond the house to provide shade and even a carport harmonized in construction and form with the walls that supported it.[157]

1.62 [*facing*], **1.63, 1.64**
Frank Lloyd Wright. First Herbert
Jacobs House, Madison, Wis., 1937

View of the front with carport at the left

View of the rear with patio, yard, and
garden

Plan

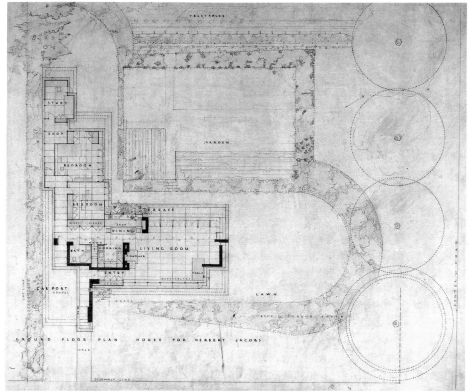

Doors and windows were also conceived as systems of construction that contributed to the systems of form and decoration:

The way the windows are used is naturally a most useful resource to achieve the new characteristic sense of space. All this fenestration can be made ready at the factory and set up as the walls. But there is no longer sense in speaking of doors and windows. These walls are largely a system of fenestration having its own part in the building scheme – the system being as much a part of the design as eyes are part of the face.

The extensive use of built-in furnishings strengthened the unity and completeness of the architectural system. 'Furniture, pictures, and bric-a-brac are unnecessary because the walls can be made to include them or *be* them.' Even the lighting was conceived as a system of form and decoration derived from the system of construction: 'We can make the wiring system itself be the light fixture, throwing light upon and down the ceiling. Light will thus be indirect, except for a few outlets for floor lamps.'[158] Rarely have the systems of structure and construction, form, and decoration been so fully integrated.

The functional arrangement of space was also integrated with the other aspects of the architectural system. In the Jacobs House and the subsequent Usonian houses of similar and related plan forms, Wright used the economically designed unit of kitchen with adjacent bathroom as a buffer between the living–dining area and the bedrooms. In that way the bathroom was accessible both to the public and the private spaces. The kitchen, 'take[n] away from outside walls and [turned] up into overhead space within the chimney' has an 'immediate' connection with the dining space without losing 'outside wall space . . . to the principal rooms.' The greater height given to the kitchen, its location next to the fireplace, and its venting into the chimney meant that a 'natural current of air is thus set up toward the kitchen' such that 'no cooking odors' would escape 'back into the house.'[159]

As with Wright's concrete block houses, the Usonian houses used the architectural system to give a satisfying sense of shelter and to make the building seem part of the earth. Wright explained that the broadly extending flat roof imparted a 'shelter gratifying to the sense of shelter because of the generous eaves.' The unique heating system used also furthered this end. Wright's discovery in 1914 of an Oriental method that sent heated air through cavities below the floor gave him the means to strengthen the type of reverie which had inspired him to declare that it warmed his heart to see the fire burning deep in the masonry of the house. In the Usonian house, Wright placed steam or hot water pipes under the concrete floor slab. He had wanted to use these in the Johnson Administration Building, 'but all the professional heating contractors except one (Westerlin & Campbell) scoffed, refusing to have anything to do with the idea.' First realized, then, in the Jacobs House, this system provided '*gravity heat* – heating coming up from beneath as naturally as heat rises. . . . There is no other "ideal" heat. Not even the heat of the sun.' No longer would the user simply dream about the heat from the '*integral* fireplace' spreading throughout the fabric of the house. He or she could actually feel the heat coming from the floor so as to wrap the home in a blanket of heat that was as comforting psychologically as physically.[160]

Even the nature of the foundations contributed to this reverie. According to Wright, in 1902 he learned from an old Welsh stone mason a method of 'dry wall footing' that consisted in setting a building directly on the ground over a bed of large broken stones. Thus, the basement could be eliminated. In using this method for his Usonian houses, Wright was literally able to achieve the effect which he had been seeking aesthetically since the Prairie houses, of marrying his building to the ground.[161]

Finally, in Wright's mind, the foundation, heating, flooring, walls, doors and fenestration, and roofing were one physical and conceptual system: 'The old-fashioned basement, except for a fuel and heater space, was always a plague spot. A

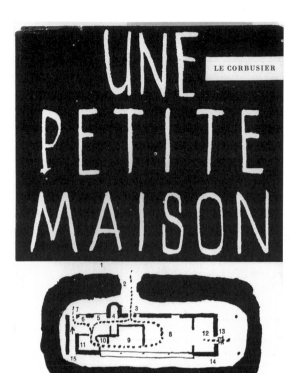

1.65, 1.66, 1.67
Le Corbusier. *Une Petite maison*

Cover of the second edition (1968). The illustration at the bottom of the page also appears in the text both here and in the first edition (1954)

Opening in the garden wall facing the lake and mountains, labeled 'To give human scale'

Drawing of the house on the site. Note the transformation of the mountains to the right into an open hand reaching upward to the sky

steam-warmed concrete mat four inches thick laid directly on the ground over gravel filling, the walls set upon that, is better.' Just as all of the components worked together to satisfy reveries of shelter, they also provided its complementary suggestion of expansive freedom as had the Prairie houses: 'A modest house, this Usonian house, a dwelling place that has no feeling at all for the "grand" except as the house extends itself in the flat parallel to the ground. It will be a companion to the horizon. . . . There is freedom of movement, and a privacy too, afforded by the general arrangement here that is unknown to the current "boxment." '[162]

Perhaps the final developments in Wright's architectural system that enhanced even more the sense of shelter and the reveries of the building belonging to the earth came in those houses where he placed a mound of earth along one or more sides of the house (figure 1.38) and then even on the roof, which could be planted with grass. Writing about the roof covered with earth, Wright observed, 'Always I like the feeling you have when beneath it.'[163]

'Oh "excuse-me," Vignola!'

My discussion to this point has emphasized the degree to which Frank Lloyd Wright synthesized what might be termed the reasoned and poetic versions of the architectural system. It would be a mistake, though, to think that Le Corbusier's architecture did not reflect the poetry of the material imagination. The sense of body-space engagement with the rich field of columns and architectural forms that he presented to the user in his buildings certainly works on the psyche in this manner. Perhaps it operates more within the realm of what Bachelard called the 'poetics of space' than in reveries on the elements of water, fire, earth, and air. Whenever considering the effects of the buildings designed by Le Corbusier according to the reasoned architectural system, it would be helpful to keep in mind the degree to which his spaces and forms were developed to respond to this poetics of space. Fortunately, Le Corbusier himself published a book with this as its main subject.

In 1922–23 Le Corbusier traveled throughout Europe with a project in his pocket for a house for his aging parents, a plan awaiting its site. Finally Le Corbusier discovered the right property – a lot facing Lake Léman with a view across to the mountains that seem to rise precipitously from the placid waters. Anyone who has seen this spectacle can easily understand when Le Corbusier writes that his father, who lived there only one year before his death, was in awe of the location: 'Ce paysage le comblait.'[164]

In 1954 Le Corbusier published a book, *Une Petite maison* (figure 1.65), that describes this building and its site. The most remarkable thing about the house is its extreme modesty. In effect, it is not a piece of distinguished high-style architecture. Rather, it is an essay in the poetics of space, in which no special architectural features detract from the simple immediacy of its effects.

Une Petite maison is about the act of dwelling. As Bachelard explains, 'the act of dwelling arises almost infallibly as soon as one has the impression of being sheltered.'[165] Le Corbusier's book is a series of lessons on the poetics of shelter. They begin with the title and cover. 'Une petite maison' means not simply a quantitatively small house but especially a qualitatively little house. We sleep more soundly, observes Bachelard, in a 'little house' than in a large one.[166] The 'little house' calls for reveries of coziness associated with miniatures. This cozy seclusion is even suggested on the cover where Le Corbusier has drawn a broad black band around the floor plan, thereby placing the image in its own sheltered nest.

Before entering the house, Le Corbusier takes the reader through an architectural genesis that begins with the delimitation of outdoor space by erecting a garden wall. In the beginning, all is landscape:

> The *raison d'être* of the enclosing wall that you see here is to shut out the view to the north, to the east, in part to the south, and to the west: the landscape, omnipresent on all sides, omnipotent, becomes fatiguing. Have you noticed that in such conditions 'you' no longer 'look' at it? In order to make the countryside count, it must be delimited, dimensioned by a radical decision: block out the horizon by raising walls and revealing it by opening the wall only at strategic points. This rule has been followed here. The walls. . . have made of it [i.e., the garden] a room of greenery – an interior.[167]

The theme of the overpowering landscape has been explored by various twentieth-century writers. In stressing the tiring aspects of an unlimited vista, Le Corbusier appears to have experienced a milder version of a sensitivity to vast spaces that threatened to become a veritable living nightmare in the imaginations of writers such as Jules Supervielle and Henri Bosco. Their more exaggerated experiences help us to understand the general psychological phenomenon that Le Corbusier is addressing.

In an autobiographical essay, Supervielle explained the paradox of limitless space that is felt as a confining prison: 'I found myself for several days in the countryside, and I remember very well in spite of the horse and the freedom – because even of an excess of horse and freedom – because of this horizon, unalterable in spite of desperate galloping, the pampas acquired for me the aspect of a prison, hardly any larger than others.'[168] This paradox of limitless space becoming a confining prison Supervielle succinctly formulated in a reflection upon a child's orientation to the world: 'Too much space suffocates us much more than if there had not been enough.'[169]

Through a fictional character, Henri Bosco also expressed the feeling of a psychic dissolution in the expansive landscape. A flatlands facilitates 'this internal dispersion by which I vanish. I have no hold there upon myself and I lose the wondrous sense of my own presence, I am forever elsewhere, a floating, fluid elsewhere.'[170] Readers familiar with the reflections on wide open spaces by the eighteenth-century Neoclassical architect Etienne-Louis Boullée will recognize here a similar concern and an analogous response.[171]

On the subject of the dwelling, Supervielle had one of his fictional protagonists proclaim: 'Here are the walls of my home, the ceiling of my home, the floor of my home. We do not reflect enough about these things that protect us so humbly but so surely from the infinity that surrounds us.'[172] The vulnerability that a Supervielle or a Bosco felt derives from the overwhelming sense of dispersion or suffocation engendered by an unmediated contact with a vast exterior space. When Le Corbusier opens the wall in the garden, he offers a secure perch from which to view the dramatic spectacle (figure 1.66). 'To give human scale' – Le Corbusier repeats this caption for two photographs of the aperture in the southern wall that permits a view to the lake and mountains beyond. The ledge, table, benches, jug, and the very size and proportions of the opening in the wall all contribute not only to the human scale but also to the feeling of a human presence at this first breach in the enclosure. The shade of the paulownia tree, which envelops this space within a protective realm, reinforces the sense of security. The branches fall outside the wall to cover the opening partially, thereby obliging the viewer to peer through the foliage, which further encloses this sheltered space. Such a 'curtain of foliage,' explains Bachelard, can be effective in creating a sense of a grotto, a space of refuge and tranquility.[173]

After this controlled contact with the expansive landscape, Le Corbusier is ready to remove the wall: 'Suddenly, the wall ends and the spectacle surges: light, space, the water and the mountains. . . . There, the game is played!' At this point in the narrative Le Corbusier directs his reader's attention both to the banal metallic post that supports the porch and to the low wall by the lake. The architect stresses that these modest objects, close at hand and at human scale, cross 'at a right angle – the co-ordinates of the waters and the mountains.'[174]

To the rationalist mentality, Le Corbusier's text at this point certainly presents one of the most obscure enigmas of architectural literature. In order to ascertain the meaning, once again Bachelard's study of the poetic imagination is helpful. In his essay, 'Les nymphéas ou les surprises d'une aube d'été' (Water Lilies or the Surprises of a Dawn in Summer), Bachelard reflects upon the iris and water lilies in a painting by Monet: 'the dialectic of the straight leaf and of the leaf calmly, obediently, heavily resting on the water. Is this not the dialectic of the water plant: one wants to surge animated in some manner of revolt against the native element, the other is faithful to its element.'[175] When Le Corbusier considered the spectacle at Lake Léman, he appears to have identified with the immense spreading calm of the horizontal waters and the grand surging verticality of the mountains that seem to rise directly from the water across the lake. The crossing of the porch support and the low wall by the lake are the mediating elements at human scale that take the viewer safely outward into the immensity of this dialectical space of the imagination in which nature becomes the vehicle for the two poles of interior human cosmic feeling. Toward the end of the book, Le Corbusier conveys this feeling pictorially when he shows the house in perspective recession that joins the line of the mountains (figure 1.67). As the eye follows the mountain range to the right it discovers that the last peaks have been fashioned into a giant hand reaching upward

1.68
Le Corbusier. Project for the 'Open Hand' as part of the site composition composed with the High Court Building and the Himalaya Mountains at the capital city of Chandigarh, India, 1952

La Haute Cour dans le paysage. L'esplanade du Capitol, les bassins à reflets, au fond la «main ouverte»

to the sky. The drawing dates from 1945. Several years later at the capital of Chandigarh, India, Le Corbusier would use the statue of a similar giant 'Open Hand' reaching up to the sky erected against the backdrop of the Himalaya Mountains as the symbol for the human condition (figure 1.68).[176]

When delving into the realm of the material imagination we are privileged when the artist, in this case the architect, actually voices his deepest response to such elemental configurations as the crossing of the right angle. In Le Corbusier's third lecture at Buenos Aires in October 1929, he told his audience about this type of experience, which he entitled 'the place of all measures' (figure 1.69):

I want to lead you to the point where you will feel something sublime, by which man, at the apogee [of his powers], has shown his mastery. I call it '*the place of all measures.*' Here it is:

I am in Brittany; this pure line is where the ocean meets the sky; a vast horizontal surface stretches out toward me. Its majestic rest fills me like a voluptuousness. Here are several rocks to the right. The sinuosity of the sand beach enchants me like a very soft modulation of the horizontal surface. I am walking. Suddenly I stop. Between the horizon and my eyes a sensational event occurs: a vertical rock, a granite stone is standing there, like a menhir; its vertical makes with the horizon of the sea a right angle. Crystallization, fixing the site. Here is a place where man stops, because there is a total symphony, magnificence of relationships, nobility. The vertical fixes the sense of the horizontal. One lives because of the other. That is the power of synthesis.

I reflect. Why am I so moved? Why has this emotion come to me in other circumstances and in other forms throughout my life?[177]

In *La Petite maison*, Le Corbusier explores those other circumstances that produce this type of emotion, in all its nuances from secure refuge to exhilaration. In the process he mocks the grandiose architectural traditions that have been enshrined by the academy, because, in the realm of the poetics of space, true architecture is not a question of style or of elaborate decor. Rather it issues from the primordial depths of the human psyche, which are evoked by distinctions between the dark cellar and the roof-top.

Hence Le Corbusier publishes photographs (figure 1.70) of a low bench in front of a plain wall punctured by three low windows and ennobles it with the seemingly paradoxical caption, 'An authentic "architectural event," ' and then simply, 'Architecture.' The accompanying text reads: 'However, at the end [of the facade] is an authentic "architectural event" (oh "excuse me" Vignola!). A board serves as bench and, behind, three little horizontal windows light the cellar. That is enough to give happiness (if you don't agree, simply forget it!).'

A subsequent photograph, captioned 'one climbs,' shows a narrow stair that leads to the roof:

One climbs to the roof. A pleasure that belonged to certain civilizations in certain epochs. Reinforced concrete brings the roof-terrace and, with fifteen or twenty centimeters of earth, the 'roof-garden.' . . . Leaning against the hand-rail of a ship. . . Leaning against the edge of the roof. . . Beatitude that until now has been reserved only for those cats called alley cats.[178]

Le Corbusier accompanies this suggestive text with an expansive view over the lake to a distant shore. To understand further the psychological mechanism at play here it would be helpful to consider a text by Marcel Proust where in *Jean Santeuil* the narrator turns to the reader to ask:

And you, reader, older than Jean, from the boundary of a garden situated on an eminence did you not sometimes have the sensation that these were not simply other fields, other trees that spread out before you, but a certain country under its special sky? The several trees that came up to the boundary where you were leaning, these were like the real trees of the foreground of a panorama, they served as a transition between what you knew, the garden you had come to visit, and this unreal, mysterious thing, a country that spread out before you under the appearance of plains, developing richly into valleys, letting the sun that stopped there at this moment play upon it, and that, from its own sky, had sent it luminous and puffy clouds.[179]

Each of these spatial situations – the *petite maison*, the drama of the garden wall, the contrast between the cellar windows and the climb to the roof, and the view of the landscape from the roof garden – figure among the principles themes in Bachelard's *La Poétique de l'espace*, where he studied them in chapters entitled: 'The House, from Cellar to Attic,' 'House and Universe,' 'The Nest,' 'The Miniature,' and 'The Dialectic of Outside and Inside.' If Bachelard had studied Le Corbusier's architecture he might have added still another theme, the dialectic of small and large. Le Corbusier used the paired experiences of concentration and expansion through the combination of single- and double-height spaces not only throughout his avant-garde architecture but also as the basis of the apartment unit in his urban plans.

Le Corbusier's commitment to the combination of single- and double-height spaces can be gauged not only from their central role in his private town houses and suburban villas but also through his adamant stance in the modernist debate about minimum housing standards. Repudiating the 'minimum lodging' current in Germany, Czechoslovakia, Poland, and Russia as 'destructive, inhuman,' in short, 'a cage,' Le Corbusier called for 'the *maximum* living room,' for 'life . . . has a need for space.' To the living room Le Corbusier assigned the height of 4.5 meters; to the other spaces, 2.2 meters, which is the height of a person six feet tall reaching

1.69, 1.70

Le Corbusier. 'The Place of All Measures'

Le Corbusier. 'An authentic "architectural event" '

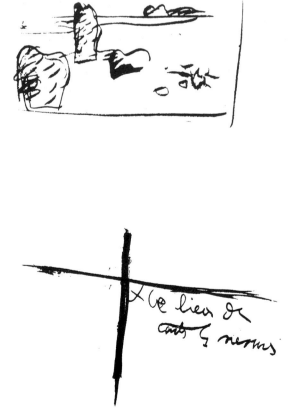

Un authentique «fait d'architecture»

upward with arm and hand extended. The place of social intercourse is thereby given an expansive dimension, while places of work, solitude, intimacy, and rest, a contrasting modest dimension. Presenting photographs of an interior with this combination of double- and single-height rooms, Le Corbusier asks rhetorically, 'Why this large breath . . . and this intimacy?'[180]

For Le Corbusier, the height of 2.2 meters, considered as a human dimension, was confirmed through repeated experience. 'In the course of my constant travels, I observed how this rule was maintained through the centuries.'[181] Now the wisdom of tradition had been put to the test of modern functional planning, for this was also 'the height applied in ocean liners to all that is dwelling space: simple cabins or luxury apartments.'[182] Finally, in Paris Le Corbusier discovered that boutique design, from Louis XV to the Restoration, had incorporated a space of 4.5 meters toward the street and two spaces half this height at the rear.[183] 'So many confirmations, so many incitements.'[184] Beginning in the private houses and the idealized urban schemes of the 1920s, Le Corbusier would almost invariably use combinations of single- and double-height spaces in designing his architecture. They offered an integral component to the spatial poetics by which he gave form to his new architectural system.[185]

In conclusion, then, both Frank Lloyd Wright and Le Corbusier grounded their architecture in the notion of the architectural system. For Wright, the dual concepts of a reasoned and a poetic architectural system offered the basis for creating a satisfying architecture. Le Corbusier, on the other hand, joined the notion of a reasoned architectural system with a sensitivity to the poetics of space. Having provided a compelling definition of the nature of architecture for successive generations over the course of the nineteenth century, the concept of the architectural system was finally given rich and varied substance in the work of these two great creative artists. While it is certainly possible to appreciate the magnitude of their achievement without reference to the architectural system, it is not possible to understand their motivations without this concept. Throughout their mature work, both architects were guided by the idea of the architectural system, which gave them the essential framework for the creation of an original and complete architecture.

CHAPTER 2

The picturesque

Nineteenth-century architectural thought was revolutionized by the widespread significance given to the notion of the picturesque. Just as classical architecture had dominated the field since the Renaissance, so too had the concept of bilateral symmetry as the natural means of achieving order in architectural design. The picturesque, associated in the eighteenth century with the new landscape garden as well as with minor buildings, such as small country cottages, became a major aesthetic category in architecture with the Romantic revolution. The picturesque now displaced the formality of classical design as the reflection of natural order and became allied with the wisdom of human reason.

In progressive architectural literature, the picturesque complemented the equally new idea of the architectural system. Although the concept of the architectural system taught designers the importance of deriving their forms and ornamentation from the system of construction, it did not guide them in the choice of a particular aesthetic orientation or in the resolution of functional issues. The nineteenth-century understanding of the picturesque served this dual purpose.

Whereas the virtues of picturesque design reached Frank Lloyd Wright and Le Corbusier from the general culture of architecture, they were also fundamental themes in the writings that these two architects most admired, Viollet-le-Duc's *Discourses on Architecture* (1863–72) for Wright and Auguste Choisy's *Histoire de l'architecture* (1899) for Le Corbusier. Both of these works belonged to the new nineteenth-century genre of the history of world architecture, a genre prompted by the cultural relativism ushered in by the Romantic revolution. Nearly everywhere a person looked in the nineteenth century, the picturesque was being adduced as a guiding principle. Not only was it championed by advocates of the Gothic revival, it was also seen as informing ancient Greek architecture, which was only first becoming known at this time. Furthermore, writers of the world or universal history of architecture found that it had been a fundamental principle in many previous societies. Viollet-le-Duc and Choisy's universal histories synthesized these cultural forces while adding their own original observations in ways that became compelling for Frank Lloyd Wright and Le Corbusier.

The picturesque principle

The notion of the picturesque has undergone almost as many definitions as the word Romanticism with which it is associated in this study. On the one hand, it designated opposing schools of landscape garden design, such as 'Capability' Brown's rolling lawns punctuated by isolated clumps of trees or Richard Payne Knight's denser patterns of shrubs and ground cover. In the 1795 edition of *The Landscape, A Didactic Poem*, Knight felt justified in affirming, 'It is now, I believe, generally admitted that the system of picturesque improvement, employed by the late Mr. Brown and his followers, is the very reverse of picturesque.'[1] Picturesque also meant in the manner of a picture as found in the landscape scenes of Claude Lorrain, Gaspard Poussin, Nicolas Poussin, and Salvator Rosa.[2] As John Claudius Loudon explained in 1806, the phrase 'picturesque beauty' 'seems to have been originally applied to such objects or scenes as were best suited for producing a good effect when painted. It is now applied more generally, and is characterized by roughness, abruptness, and irregularity, either in the outline, form, disposition, or colour.'[3]

Just as Ludovic Vitet formulated the concept of 'philosophical romanticism,' which cut across all the individual variations of the different romantic movements, so too a certain William Burgh has left an explanation of what he termed the 'picturesque principle' that cuts across the various permutations of the word's meaning.[4] In his commentary to the 1783 edition of William Mason's *The English Garden: A Poem*, Burgh codified two of the distinguishing features of the landscape garden, 'variety' and the 'path,' as the components of what he called the 'picturesque principle.'

Variety, for Burgh, referred to asymmetrical design. The irregular ordering that constituted variety was becoming so important that John Claudius Loudon would feel justified in defining the word 'harmony' not with the usual emphasis on symmetry but rather as the realization of the picturesque. 'Harmony, in the general form,' explained Loudon, 'is produced by the introduction of masses and towers of different forms and sizes, and placing them at different distances from each other.'[5]

For Burgh, the path referred to the sequence of asymmetrical 'pictures' or views that one encountered while moving through a landscape garden along a winding way and over an irregular terrain. Burgh stressed the sequence of changing foreground scenes that continuously redefined the stroller's relationship to the entire view, which also included middle ground and background elements.[6] Of course, the successive 'pictures' that one encountered were the asymmetrical landscape scenes composed after the manner of the painters listed above in the opening paragraph of this section.

In the course of the nineteenth century, the concept of the path was to be transferred to the arrangement of site plans that married architecture and landscape, to the layout of urban streets, and even to the design of buildings themselves. Loudon himself, anticipating John Nash's plan for Regent Street (1811) and anteceding Camillo Sitte's influential publication of 1889 on city design 'according to its artistic principles,' turned classical precepts upside down by advocating winding streets for the main thoroughfares of a town, 'especially if any natural circumstances favor that idea, as a river, inequality of surface, the irregular side of a hill, or perhaps some established road already existing.' For straight streets, Loudon suggested using projections from buildings to impart variety to the scene. In either case, the viewer would be presented with a continuous sequence of changing and varied views, generally asymmetrical in character.[7]

Sufficient reason

Whereas Burgh's concept of the 'picturesque principle' defined the two main features of picturesque design, the notion of 'sufficient reason,' articulated in 1810 by the Scottish philosopher Dugald Stewart, linked the concept of reasonableness to classical and picturesque design, while favoring the latter. Stewart's 'sufficient reason' was an elaboration of a thought that Knight had succinctly voiced in *The Landscape, A Didactic Poem*:

For, as the principle of taste is sense,
Whatever is void of meaning gives offence.

In this passage, Knight was referring to the shape of a garden path that had to seem natural in its meanderings:

Then let your easy path spontaneous flow;
With no affected turn or artful bend,
To lead you round still farther from the end.[8]

To explain such a thought, Stewart applied Leibnitz's philosophical notion of 'sufficient reason' to the realm of aesthetics.[9] Stewart's definition of sufficient reason, like Burgh's notion of the picturesque principle, redirected the axis of thought by shifting concern from specific aesthetic features to general aesthetic principles.

At the same time, Stewart attacked the validity of customary definitions of beauty and the picturesque. According to authorities such as Edmund Burke and Uvedale Price, smooth lines were associated with beauty; and sharp angles, rough forms, and irregular shapes, with the picturesque. Yet the 'brilliant cut in diamonds and . . . the numberless angular forms (so contrary to Mr. Burke's theory) in ornaments of cut crystal' are beautiful, whereas 'smoothness and trim regularity . . . on the surface, for example, of a sheep-walk, or of a deer-park' are not agreeable at all.[10]

The real issue, though, was not the specific characteristics of beautiful and picturesque things or scenes but rather the reasonableness of what was being viewed. 'Sufficient reason' required that the visual properties seem reasonable rather than arbitrary. Aesthetic pleasure was conditioned in large part by satisfying this need of the heart and the mind.

First considering objects with no utilitarian purpose, Stewart explained that 'regular forms' and 'uniform arrangements' were more pleasing than irregular ones since in the latter case 'no circumstance can be imagined which should have decided the choice of the artist in favor of that particular figure which he has selected.' All of this changes, though, once 'fitness and utility' come into play. Then 'regularity and uniformity' are agreeable only if they 'do not interfere with purposes of utility.'[11] Stewart gave examples from landscape and architectural design to illustrate his point:

The beauty of a winding approach to a house, when the easy deviations from the straight line are all accounted for by the shape of the ground, or by the position of trees, is universally acknowledged; but what more ridiculous than a road meandering through a plain, perfectly level and open? In this last case, I am inclined to refer the disagreeable effect to the principle of *the Sufficient Reason* already mentioned. The slightest apology for *a sweep* satisfies the taste at once.[12]

In a house, which is completely detached from all other buildings, and which stands on a perfectly level foundation, why are we offended when the door is not placed exactly in the middle; or when there is a window on one side of the door, and none corresponding to it on the other? Is it not that we are at a loss to conceive how the choice of the architect could be thus determined, where all circumstances appear to be so exactly alike? This disagreeable affect is, in a great measure, removed, the moment any purpose of utility is discovered; or even when the contiguity of other houses, or some peculiarity in the shape of ground, allows us to imagine, that some reasonable motive may have existed in the artist's mind, though we may be unable to trace it. An irregular castellated edifice, set down on a dead flat, conveys an idea of whim or of folly in the designer. . . . The same, or yet greater irregularity, would not only satisfy, but delight the eye, in an ancient citadel, whose ground-work and elevations followed the rugged surface and fantastic projections of the rock on which it is built.[13]

Thus, in explaining the principle of 'sufficient reason,' Stewart firmly linked the idea of reasonableness to aesthetic pleasure when common sense or appropriateness could be found in picturesque design. As he further explained, irregularity was to be expected in Nature as a mark of divinity.

The remarks which have now been made apply, as is obvious, to the works of Man alone. In those of Nature, impressed, as they are everywhere, with the signatures of Almighty Power, and of Unfathomable Design, we do not look for that obvious uniformity of plan which we expect to find in the productions of beings endowed with the same faculties, and actuated by the same motives as ourselves. A deviation from uniformity, on the contrary, in the grand outlines sketched by *her* hand, appears perfectly suited to that *infinity* which is associated, in our conceptions, with all her operations; while it enhances, to an astonishing degree, the delight arising from the regularity which, in her minuter details, she everywhere scatters in such inexhaustible profusion.[14]

Stewart's *Philosophical Essays* enjoyed two subsequent editions, published in 1816 and 1818. His influence on architects and landscape designers was greatly enhanced by the inclusion of the passage on sufficient reason with the example of the 'irregular castellated edifice' in the immensely popular *Encyclopedia of Cottage, Farm, and Villa Architecture and Furniture* by Loudon, who, as we have seen, was a champion of the picturesque.[15] Stewart's reasoning was subsequently taken up by two of the most influential writers of the nineteenth century, Augustus Welby Pugin and Viollet-le-Duc.

Augustus Welby Pugin's publications of the early 1840s helped to popularize the picturesque while making important distinctions that later architects, critics, and historians would keep in mind. Pugin's eminence as publicist and as Gothic revival architect, whose accomplishments included the decoration for Charles Barry's winning entry to the Houses of Parliament competition (1835), gave special prominence to his writings.[16] To Pugin the picturesque was a natural aesthetic based upon reason and confirmed by the history of ecclesiastical architecture. He dismissed the 'senseless uniformity of modern design': 'The idea of everything being exactly alike on both sides, has created an unreal style of buildings which was quite unknown to our ancestors. . . . When once the trammels and bondage of this regularity system are broken through, and people are taught not to consider a portico and two uniform wings the perfection of design, we may expect vast improvements.'[17] Not all picturesque design, though, was admissible. Here Pugin distinguished between a natural and an artificial use of the picturesque:

The picturesque effect of the ancient buildings results from the ingenious methods by which the old builders overcame local and constructive difficulties. An edifice which is arranged with the principal view of looking picturesque is sure to resemble an artificial waterfall or a made-up rock, which are generally so *unnaturally natural* as to appear ridiculous. An architect should exhibit his skill by turning the difficulties which occur in raising an elevation from *a convenient plan* into so many *picturesque beauties*. . . . But all these [modern] inconsistencies have arisen from this great error, – *the plans of buildings are designed to suit the elevation, instead of the elevation being made subservient to the plan.*[18]

Both in built churches and in didactic designs for institutional and domestic architecture, Pugin proceeded according to the reasoned picturesque by which he made his elevations suit his plans. This meant articulating each area with a volume

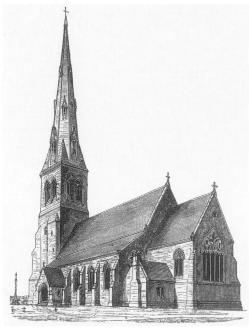

whose position and size corresponded to functional and symbolic purpose. Writing about the 'old English Catholic mansions' (figure 2.1), Pugin explained,

Each part of these buildings indicated its particular destination: the turreted gate-house and porter's lodging, the entrance porch, the high-crested roof and Louvred hall, with its capacious chimney, the guest chambers, the vast kitchens and offices, all formed distinct and beautiful features, not *masked or concealed under one monotonous front*, but by their variety in form and outline increasing the effect of the building, and presenting a standing illustration of good old English hospitality.[19]

Similarly, in viewing a church by Pugin (figure 2.2.), for example, it is easy to identify the entry, tower, nave, side aisles, presbytery, and chancel. While arguing that he was adhering to medieval custom developed according to Church canon, Pugin obviously derived aesthetic pleasure from picturesque design.[20] Moreover, the idea expressed in the quotation above that difficult circumstances of site and construction had spurred architects to invent ingenious picturesque solutions was to become a leitmotif of architectural literature on the picturesque over the succeeding decades.

Whereas the tenets of the reasoned picturesque articulated by Pugin gave general guidance to the architect, those cases that did not involve relationships established by Church canon could prove perplexing to the designer. As the architect Francis Goodwin observed in 1835, although the picturesque presented exciting opportunities, it also left the architect 'totally unfettered by any positive rules' and hence 'deprived of their guidance.'[21] How could the architect be certain of creating harmony in an asymmetrical design? Viollet-le-Duc, in his elaboration of the concept of sufficient reason attempted a response. This effort, rare in the literature on the picturesque, had its counterpart in the popular writings of the American Andrew Jackson Downing, whose ideas will also be considered here.

2.1, 2.2

'Old English Mansion'

Augustus Welby Pugin. Saint Oswald's, Liverpool, 1840

'Ponderation' and 'irregular symmetry'

Andrew Jackson Downing, who was familiar with Goodwin's *Rural Architecture* (1835) and hence with the lament about the absence of rules for asymmetrical design, formulated specific principles that were widely disseminated in his *Cottage Residences* (1842) and *The Architecture of Country Houses* (1850). Building on Loudon's association of harmony with the picturesque, Downing argued that picturesque design was actually a form of symmetry. '[I]n all irregular compositions entirely satisfactory,' he explained, 'it will generally be found that there is a kind of hidden proportion which one half of the whole bears to the other, and it is this balance which constitutes symmetry.'[22] Symmetry, then, did not necessarily mean the placement of identical features to either side of a center line. In *Cottage Residences*, Downing demoted this type of symmetry to the lesser category of 'uniformity' (figure 2.3).[23]

FIG. 1.

2.3
Andrew Jackson Downing. Types of composition: 'symmetry' ('Fig. 1'), 'uniformity' ('Fig. 2'). In 1850 Downing would revise his terminology to 'irregular symmetry' and 'regular symmetry' respectively

FIG. 2.

In his subsequent consideration of the subject in *The Architecture of Country Houses*, Downing modified his terminology. Symmetry was now defined as the balancing masses to either side of a central body: 'Symmetry is that quality of beauty in material objects which may be defined, that balance of *opposite parts* necessary to form an agreeable whole.' Thus, if a building had only one mass, which had identical features to either side of the center line, it was not symmetrical but merely 'regular.' If all facades were identical, then it exhibited 'uniformity.' 'Symmetry,' explained Downing, 'involves something more. It asks for a central part, which shall connect the two other parts into a whole, and thereby make something involving a more complete idea than regularity and uniformity.' There were, then, two types of symmetry. If the masses to either side were identical, then this constituted 'regular symmetry.' If they were dissimilar, then the entire asymmetrical composition was an example of 'irregular symmetry.'[24] The latter offered a superior type of beauty.[25]

In his *Entretiens sur l'architecture*, which were translated as *Discourses on Architecture*, Viollet-le-Duc was constantly inveighing against the 'banal rules of symmetry.'[26] His main objection to symmetry was that it made 'architecture into a type of recipe applicable to every object, to every program, a banal formula that anybody could employ, without having any need to engage in reasoning.'[27] As for the historical evidence, Viollet-le-Duc affirmed,

> In truth, I do not know how, since the sixteenth century, people came to attach these ideas of symmetry to ancient domestic architecture, because I find no trace of it either in the buildings or in the texts. At Pompeii, there is not a single house with its plans or elevations submitted to the rules of symmetry. Cicero and Pliny, in their letters, write much about orientation, about the particular arrangement of each room in their country houses; but about symmetry, they speak not a word. From this, [we can see that] their houses were a juxtaposition of rooms, porticoes, bedrooms, galleries, etc., placed in response to daylight, wind, sun, shade, and view, all conditions that excluded symmetry.[28]

Asymmetry, then, was a natural aesthetic because it issued from the workings of reason in response to the constraints and opportunities of the program and the site.

To guide the architect in asymmetrical design, Viollet-le-Duc, like Downing, postulated rules based on the concept of balancing masses, which the French theorist termed 'ponderation.' Through the 'skillful . . . ponderation of masses' the architect could achieve a 'subtle system of harmony.'[29] To demonstrate this principle he adduced two examples. In one (figure 2.4) the architect must place a single tower on a square castle located on sloping land. Viollet-le-Duc explained that a modern architect would locate the tower in the middle of the facade. Yet to achieve a harmonious balance of 'ponderation' would require placing the tower at

2.4, 2.5

Castle in the landscape. An example of ponderation

City hall. An example of ponderation

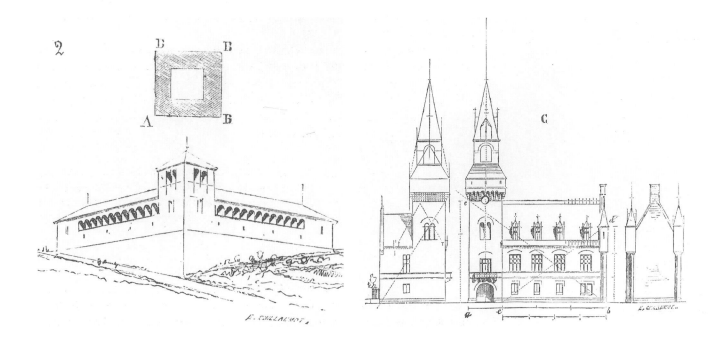

the corner where the land falls away. Viollet-le-Duc's design for a city hall (figure 2.5) illustrated another way of balancing unequal masses. Here the larger rectangle of the building's mass, which is anchored by the tall corner tower (triangle a-b-c), is 'ponderated' by a smaller form of comparable configuration that faces the other way (triangle b-d-e).

Whereas Viollet-le-Duc's two illustrative examples were intended as adaptations of French medieval and Renaissance architecture, they stand out as infrequent native illustrations of picturesque design in a book largely devoted to the discussion of ancient Greek architecture. Viollet-le-Duc's most sustained and extensive arguments about the relationship of poetry and reason in architectural design, as well as the functional suitability and aesthetic beauty of the picturesque, were developed here through a highly laudatory study of Greek architecture. In effect, Viollet-le-Duc's *Discourses* synthesize an entire body of literature, written mostly by the architects and classical scholars of the new Ecole Française d'Athènes, who saw both a natural and ingenious order within the apparent disorder of the architecture of the Athenian Acropolis. Not only were Viollet-le-Duc's elaborations on this theme highly important to many later architects, including Frank Lloyd Wright and Le Corbusier, but the stimulus that this entire body of French thought provided to a young engineering student named Auguste Choisy was profoundly to affect Le Corbusier's understanding of the underlying nature of architecture.

Romantic Hellenism

The cultural relativism of the Romantic era presented a seeming paradox. Just as the hegemony of Renaissance classicism was being broken in favor of a pluralism of architectural styles and of the ascendancy of the Gothic, ancient Greek architecture achieved a status at least equal to the Gothic. This paradox quickly dissolves when one considers that the classicism which had reigned for four centuries had been grounded in a knowledge and admiration of ancient Roman architecture. Serious interest in ancient Greek architecture, which dates from the late eighteenth century, was seen as a challenge to accepted wisdom concerning the classical tradition.

The archaeological study of Greek architecture was not possible until after the liberation of Greece from the Turks in 1833. At that time, the first sustained look at Greek architecture revealed a world of picturesque design that turned received ideas about classicism upside down. Typical of the texts published in this period was the polemical stance taken by Ernest Beulé, former member of the Ecole Française d'Athènes and future Secrétaire Perpétuel of the Académie des Beaux-Arts:

We often hear about the irregularity of the Erechtheion [figure 2.6]. I confess that I do not understand this any better than that of the irregularity of the Propylaia [figure 2.7]; unless, by irregularity, is meant the absence of that symmetry that the moderns love and that the Greeks seemed to have disdained in their ensembles, that is to say, in buildings composed of several blocks.[30]

Beulé's *L'Acropole d'Athènes* (1853–54; second edition in 1862) presented to the educated public his own experiences and discoveries in Athens as well as those of other French classicists and architects who were publishing articles in journals such as the *Revue Archéologique*, *Archives des Missions Scientifiques et Littéraires*, *Journal des Savants*, and *Revue des Deux Mondes*. These French texts

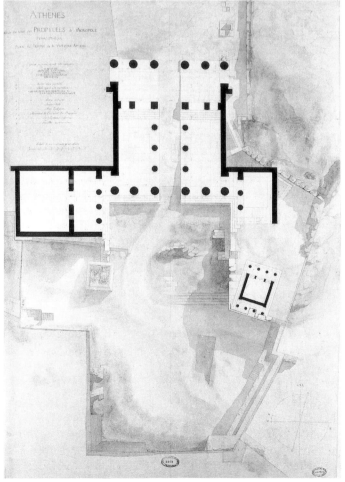

2.6, 2.7, 2.8

Jacques Tetaz. Drawing of the Erechtheion, Athens, as it was in 1847–48

Philippe Titeux and Louis Chaudet. Drawing of the Propylaia, Athens, as it was in 1846

'Architecture. Pure création de l'esprit'

PARTHÉNON.

ARCHITECTURE

III

PURE CRÉATION DE L'ESPRIT

were the third generation, so to speak, of observations about a generally unexpected type of classicism, the initial discoveries concerning which had largely been made by the British.

Stuart and Revett's *The Antiquities of Athens*, whose first volume appeared in 1762, was received as a threat to champions of the accepted classical canon. Sir William Chambers attacked 'Attic deformity' in the 1791 edition of *A Treatise on the Decorative Part of Civil Architecture*. When volume three of *The Antiquities of Athens* appeared in 1794, after Stuart's death, it contained a defense of Greek architecture by Willey Reveley written in response to Chambers's hostility. Reveley's nuanced appreciation of Greek architecture was followed by William Leake's *Topography of Athens* (1821 second edition, 1841) and John Papworth's 'An Essay on the Principles of Design in Architecture,' published as the preface to the 1826 posthumous edition of Chambers' *Treatise*, a book that had become a 'necessary appendage to the office of every architect.'[31]

These works, which might be considered the first generation of Romantic Hellenism in architecture, concentrated on the awe-inspiring aspect and subtle harmonies found especially at the Acropolis in Athens. Subsequent studies of this same architecture, which concentrated on the picturesque, should be seen not only as a reflection of the importance of the concept by mid-century, but also as a further refinement of these earlier published observations. Since the reflections by all three generations of Romantic Hellenists were to furnish essential material to Le Corbusier's *Vers une Architecture*, they will be briefly considered here.

Reveley's appreciation of the sublimity of the Parthenon is especially important because it conveys the powerful effect that the building would have on successive generations of visitors (figure 2.8). It forms the substratum of feeling that made the subtle refinements and complex picturesque strategies discussed by other architects and classicists worth describing in such detail. 'Sublimity,' Charles Blanc would write in the *Grammaire des arts du dessin* (1867), 'is like the sudden encounter with infinity.' Unlike beauty, which is man's 'domain,' sublimity places the observer 'beyond and above us.'[32] From Reveley to Le Corbusier, this was the response of the Romantic Hellenists who visited the Parthenon. As Reveley put it:

> The awful dignity and grandeur in this kind of temple, arising from the perfect agreement of its various parts, strikes the beholder with a sensation, which he may look for in vain in buildings of any other description. ... In the species of temple we are here considering, the causes of the sublime may easily be perceived. ... There is a certain appearance of eternal duration ... that gives a solemn and majestic feeling, while every part is perceived to contribute its share to this character of durability.[33]

In part, this experience was due to the character of the Doric order used here. It exhibited a 'masculine boldness and dignity ... the grandeur of whose effect ... can scarcely be understood by those who have never seen it. ...' At the same time the expression of grandeur and durability was joined with ineffable grace: 'The columns rise with considerable diminution in the most graceful, sweeping lines, and from the top of the shaft, projects a capital of a style at once bold, massive, and simple.' But it was not merely the characteristics of the parts, but also the effect of utter simplicity and unity of the whole that impressed Reveley and those who followed.[34]

In this first Romantic generation of observations on ancient Greek architecture, writers closely analyzed the design components that made the Parthenon such an extraordinary building. Leake, for example, considered the evolution of the Doric temple with respect to type of portico, sculpture, and material. Built as an octastyle temple, that is with eight columns in the portico, the Parthenon overcame the problems inherent in the customary six-column or hexastyle temple, such as the Panhellenion at Aigina and the Hephaisteion (Theseion) in Athens. Making the temple bigger or smaller would create an entablature either too heavy in appearance for the pediment or too light for a 'lofty' and 'majestic' effect. The choice of eight columns to carry the pediment brilliantly solved this dilemma: 'the multiplicity of columns alone gave elegance and splendour to the edifice, rendering it fit for any decoration which the upper parts of the building could receive, and even requiring such ornament.' The larger pediment given to this building also received the finest sculpture of any Doric temple, as Europeans familiar with the Elgin marbles now knew.[35]

Reviewing as well the evolution of the placement of sculpture in the Doric temple, which culminated in the Parthenon, Leake then considered the effect of Pentelic marble. This was a stone with 'as fine a surface, and presenting as beautiful a colour, as ivory, with a still sharper edge.' Comparing the 'common limestone' of the Temple of Zeus at Olympia with the Pentelic marble of the Parthenon, Leake concluded that the latter 'invited and demanded a much more elaborate and finished workmanship in all the details.' Leake felt justified, then, in concluding that the Parthenon, 'by its united excellencies of materials, design, and decorations, was the most perfect [building] ever executed.'[36]

The architect John Papworth gave further precision to Leake's observations concerning the Parthenon. He systematically considered the interrelationship between large and small parts; horizontal, vertical, and diagonal lines; the architectural function of sculpture and the sculptural quality of the architecture with respect to light and shadow; and the visual properties of Pentelic marble. For Papworth the utter 'unity' in the design enabled it to 'obtain an effect of sublimity not dependent on actual magnitude.' 'On a first view of a temple,' he explained, 'the mind is engrossed by the edifice, as a magnificent whole; on the second, by the relation and harmony of its parts, and at length by the richness produced by its sculpture and its shadows.' Harmony was achieved through the mediating elements that joined horizontal with vertical, flat plane with deep space, and front surface with rear. Thus, the play of 'sloping and curved shadows' over the fluted columns made them harmonize with the sculpture. Similarly, the light and shadow of the statuary in the pediment conveyed a sense of depth to the pediment, which visually joined with the deep portico below. Then too, the high relief of the metopes broke the bold shadow projected by the cornice, thereby preventing this shadow from dividing the entablature in two. The effect, rather, was to create an 'undulating edge of shadow.' On the frieze around the cella inside the peristyle, the bas-reliefs 'enrich the broad shadow by their varied forms and softly reflected lights,' without competing with the exterior sculpture, while, at the same time, unifying front and rear planes. Finally, the diagonal lines of the moldings combined with those of the shadows as a tertiary set of forms that tied the dominant horizontals and secondary verticals into a unified whole. Unlike the later Romans, observed Papworth, the Greeks restricted the use of the diagonal in their moldings in order 'to preserve . . . broad quantities of light, relieved by striking depths of shadow and sparkling lights.' Roman molding, in contrast, with its more pronounced diagonals, more numerous divisions, and circular curves, as opposed to the conical sections used by the Greeks, did not achieve such striking contrasts of light and shadow. Finally, the 'perfection of the chiaroscuro of the composition' was possible only through the use of Pentelic marble, which was capable of being highly polished.[37]

Papworth also reflected upon the entasis or outward swelling of the Doric column, which had been discovered in the first years of the nineteenth century. This was one of the numerous subtle design features intended to perfect the visual harmony of the temple. In this case, the convex curvature of the columnar shaft obviated the disturbing appearance of thinness at the center that results when a column has a perfectly straight outline. In a similar way, the expedient of moving the outermost corner columns inward and increasing their thickness countered the visual weakening of the end columns seen at the edge of the portico and against the sky.[38]

Curved lines and inclined planes

The second wave of Romantic Hellenism in architecture further refined this understanding and appreciation of ancient Greek building through the discovery toward 1836–38 by German and English architects that the Parthenon had virtually no straight lines and no plumb surfaces. Now, after the liberation of Greece had enabled observers to make careful measurements of the Parthenon, architects discovered that all the columns and walls leaned inward so as to form a pyramid whose lines, if extended, would meet high above the temple. In addition, it was learned that the horizontal surfaces of the stylobate, entablature, and pediment were slightly curved in a convex manner according to regular conic sections. Thus, the entasis given to the columns and the irregular spacing and sizing occasioned by adjustments to the end columns were not isolated features, but rather were aspects of a carefully reasoned and closely observed composition.

As a result of this new knowledge, the Greek temple, which had previously been considered the epitome of classical regularity and symmetry, now seemed to have greater affinity with the picturesque. Like the picturesque, the Greek Doric temple was actually irregular in its features. Furthermore, each departure from the rules of regularity and symmetry in this architecture was a carefully reasoned decision undertaken to achieve the most ineffable beauty and awe-inspiring sublimity.

Under Greece's new king, the Bavarian Prince Otto, the Acropolis was transformed from a fortified citadel into an archaeological precinct. The scholarly Ludwig Ross, appointed Conservator of Antiquities, and Joseph Hoffer, official architect for the Greek kingdom, guided the initial dismantling of the citadel, the clearing away of debris from the monuments, and the appropriate restorations.[39] It appears that Hoffer, while directing the removal of rubbish from the platform of the Parthenon in 1836, was the first to notice a curvature not only of the newly excavated steps that formed the base of the Parthenon, but also in the other horizontal lines of the temple. The German Edward Schaubert, who had assisted in the reconstruction of the Temple of Athena Nike after the liberation of Greece, seems to have made his own independent discovery of this phenomenon in 1837, as did John Pennethorne, a young English architect visiting Athens in that year. The public reports made by these three architects were soon joined by publications by another English observer, Francis Cranmer Penrose, whose *An Investigation of the Principles of Athenian Architecture* (1851, 2nd expanded edition 1888) became a standard reference work.[40]

In the Parthenon, observed Pennethorne, 'all apparently horizontal and straight lines are curved lines' and all 'general surfaces' are not planes but curves.[41] Taking wax casts of architectural details, Pennethorne confirmed earlier observations that the curved surfaces on the columns and in the moldings were all arcs of conic sections.[42] Likewise, Penrose determined that the steps on the north and south sides of the Parthenon 'closely' followed the curve of 'analogous' parabolas. The steps along the temple's flank as well as the horizontal lines of the entablature followed curves with less rise. Finally, the 'entasis of the columns is exactly the same both in amount and nature of curvature' as the horizontal lines.[43]

For most observers who believed in the intentional nature of the horizontal curves, these visual adjustments had two purposes. Pennethorne, Penrose, Hoffer, and others believed that the gently rising horizontal curves were intended to prevent an optical impression of drooping lines that would have resulted if the lines had actually been straight. In that sense they were similar to the entasis that kept the columns from appearing pinched at the center. Yet the horizontal curvature was also slightly perceptible. In other words, it exceeded the bend merely necessary to make lines appear straight. Different theories were proposed to explain this phenomenon.

To Penrose, the entablature had been given a noticeable horizontal curvature 'to obviate a disagreeable effect produced by the contrast' of a straight line with the diagonals of the pediment. In order for the steps to harmonize with the entablature, they too had to be curved. Penrose held that the curved lines imparted the 'feeling of a greater appearance of strength' and a 'beauty inherent in a curved line.' Similarly, the subtle inward inclination of the vertical surfaces had the 'effect of giving generally to the entire structure, the pyramidal appearance so essential to the idea of the repose of strength, whilst they do not differ sufficiently from the perpendicular to impair the expression of energy.'[44] Unlike Pennethorne, who saw the curves only as a means to restore the appearance of straight lines, Penrose understood the Greek temple to be a visually elastic organism, expressing strength and stability as well as graceful beauty in a way that the straight-line copies of so 'dry' a character in contemporary England failed to convey.[45] Like the other architects and archaeologists of this second wave of Romantic Hellenists and like their predecessors of the first wave, Penrose concluded that from the point of view of design, the Parthenon was 'humanly speaking, perfect.'[46]

Among the first discoverers of the curved lines, Joseph Hoffer offered the most lyrical interpretation. The 'system of curved lines,' which exhibited a 'perfect logic,' had enabled Greek architects 'to infuse the lifeless forms of art with a breath of living Nature,' for 'Nature avoids the rectilinear and develops its most attractive forms in swelling curves.' Hoffer's explanation entered into the mainstream of German architectural history. Franz Kugler, in his important universal history of architecture, *Geschichte der Baukunst* (1856), remarked that the horizontal curves of the platform of the Parthenon gave the effect of 'breathing life.' Similarly, Carl Schnaase, in his encyclopedic eight-volume *Geschichte der Bildenden Künste* (1843–79), observed that through the horizontal curvatures and the entasis of the columns 'a feeling of life inspired the whole building, dispelling its mathematical rigidity.'[47]

This was the state of knowledge and enthusiasm for ancient Greek architecture when the third generation of Romantic Hellenists, the architects and classical scholars of the Ecole Française d'Athènes, arrived to consider still other aspects of the Greek achievement. Rediscovering for themselves the knowledge gained by their predecessors, they added still another dimension to the contemporary appreciation of Greek architecture by ascertaining the highly sophisticated use of picturesque design principles. In the process of determining rules for the creation of order within an apparent disorder, they also advanced the current understanding of the potential functional and aesthetic uses of the picturesque.

The order of disorder

Until 1845, the Ecole des Beaux-Arts and the Académie des Beaux-Arts had frowned on the study of classical architecture other than from the Roman past. When the Prix-de-Rome architect Henri Labrouste broke with precedent in 1829 to submit the first restoration of a Greek site, as his fourth-year *envoi* sent from the Académie de France in Rome, he was severely criticized.[48] In 1845, in the process of founding the Ecole Française d'Athènes, official policy changed. The Académie des Beaux-Arts voted on 22 February 1845 to permit Prix-de-Rome architects in their third year at the Académie de France to spend four months in Greece. Three Prix-de-Rome architects immediately took advantage of the new opportunity to study Greek architecture in Athens.[49] With the establishment of the Ecole Française d'Athènes on 11 September 1846, Prix-de-Rome architects would be assigned on a regular basis to the Ecole, where they engaged in a fruitful collaboration with the classical scholars there.[50] The result was the creation of a body of literature that challenged the premises of French Academic architecture, with its emphasis on symmetry and axiality, its lack of concern with the specifics of a locale, and its fondness for rhetorical gestures in the shaping of space and the decoration of form.

The French architects and classicists in Athens provided a new perspective not only on Greek architecture but also on the picturesque. The nature of their accomplishment can be best seen not only in comparison with the work of the two earlier generations of Romantic Hellenists, but also in light of the roughly contemporaneous publications by James Fergusson that stressed the importance of the picturesque as a universal design principle common to many cultures. Fergusson's experience living in India provided him with a special perspective on the architectural debates in Europe. His exposure to 'Hindoo' architecture taught him that the Gothic, so popular in England at that time, was not the only picturesque style. Both presented 'the same irregularity' of architectural form.[51] Whether in the interiors of temples where Fergusson marveled at the 'infinite variety and complexity of perspective' or to the exterior where a grouping of buildings in different sizes furnished an impressive 'architectural panorama,'[52] Indian architecture inspired Fergusson to look at other cultures as well for comparable effects.

These he found and documented in his popular history of world architecture whose first three editions appeared in 1849, 1855, and 1859.[53] Fergusson understood the picturesque as providing a lively variety, which he greatly admired. Fergusson's books, in many respects, seconded John Ruskin's argument about a 'living architecture' in *The Seven Lamps of Architecture* (1848), which held 'in contempt . . . exact symmetry and measurement, which in dead architecture are the most painful necessities.'[54] Whereas Ruskin concentrated on small-scale irregularities in form and ornamentation, Fergusson addressed the broader issue of composition.

In reviewing various historical architectures, James Fergusson repeatedly stressed the pains that architects had taken to avoid symmetry and axiality in favor of the picturesque. Writing about ancient Egyptian architecture, Fergusson concentrated on the picturesque quality of the Ptolemaic and Roman periods, such as the non-axial alignment at the Temple of Mandulis at Kalabsha and the overall irregularity of the temple compound on the island of Philae (figure 2.9). At Philae,

no two buildings, scarcely two walls, are in the same axis or parallel to one another. No Gothic architect in his wildest moments ever played so freely with his lines or dimensions, and none, it must be added, ever produced anything so beautifully picturesque as this. It contains all the play of light and shade, all the variety of Gothic art, with the massiveness and grandeur of the Egyptian style.

Similarly, the pyramids at Meroë (figure 2.10) he described as 'being grouped with the most picturesque irregularity,' which derived largely from 'no two being ever placed, except by accident, at the same angle to the meridian.'[55] Fergusson found that ancient Persian architecture at Persepolis was designed according to a similar understanding of picturesque principles:

[O]ne of the most pleasing features in the whole is the taste with which the architects have availed themselves of the irregularities of the surface to group their buildings on different levels, taking especial care that no two should be alike or symmetrical – nor placed on the same axis: so that every building or apartment is a separate design and tells its own tale, while the whole taken together group themselves into one pleasing and picturesque whole. This, however, is not peculiar to Persepolis, but to all true styles of art, and was as essentially a characteristic of the Grecian and Gothic as of Persian architecture.[56]

In discussing Greek architecture, Fergusson made an observation that would resonate throughout the texts of the French architects and classicists in Athens: the symmetry of individual Greek buildings assembled into asymmetrical groupings. Here Fergusson argued that the 'commonly assumed [notion that] symmetrical regularity is a property of Greek architecture . . . only exists in the imagination of the moderns, for no style is freer from its absurdities than that of the Greeks.' Nor were the Greeks alone in combining symmetrical design of the parts with picturesque grouping of the whole, for this was 'one of the fundamental laws of true architecture in every part of the globe.'[57]

Fergusson illustrated this principle with discussions of the Propylaia and the Erechtheion at the Athenian Acropolis. With the Propylaia he marveled at the articulation of the two side wings, which were 'studiously separated from the main design, and one wing made unlike the other.' In front to one side stood the diminutive Temple of Athena Nike, 'at a most incongruous angle'; to the other side rose a pedestal 'whose axis was, of course, different from that of every other part.' The entire grouping, moreover, 'was placed so as to be as unsymmetrical with the Parthenon, or with any other building, as was possible.'[58] For the Erechtheion, Fergusson's rapture knew no bounds: 'no Gothic architect in his wildest moments could have conceived anything more picturesquely irregular.'[59] Like the previous generations of Romantic Hellenists, Fergusson found Greek architecture to be the most perfect. Yet now the assessment was based on its accomplishments in the realm of the picturesque. By combining 'the greatest harmony with the greatest variety' in the Erechtheion, the Greeks, wrote Fergusson, achieved a level of composition not found in any other civilization.[60]

Variety in picturesque design was especially important to Fergusson who emphasized the meaningful relationship of forms articulated as distinct but related units. Such visual differentiation was necessary, so that each part of a building or each building in an ensemble could 'express separately each its own story.'[61] To obscure these differences was to create a 'vicious' falsehood, for 'the fundamental canon of true art in architecture, is that the exterior of a building shall in every part

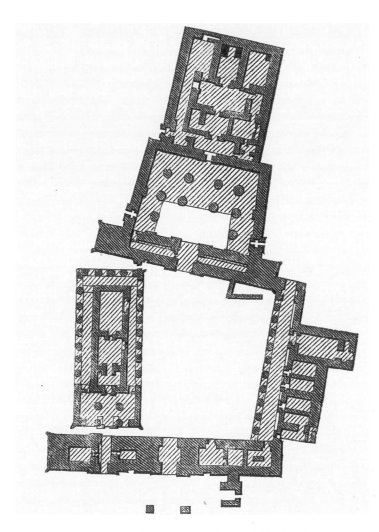

2.9, 2.10

Temple compound on the island of
Philae

Pyramids at Meroë

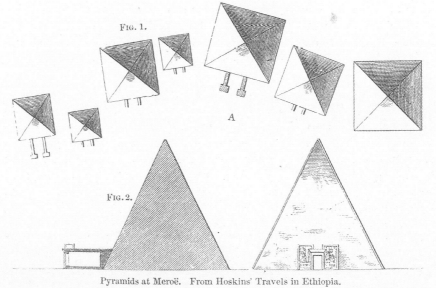

Pyramids at Meroë.   From Hoskins' Travels in Ethiopia.

FIG. 1.—Plan of Principal Group.   Scale 100 ft.
to 1 inch.

FIG. 2.—Section and Elevation of that marked A.
Scale 50 ft. to 1 inch.

and every detail express the interior as correctly as it is possible.'[62] There is no determinism in Fergusson's position. To design a fully differentiated but harmonious composition required great skill and application. Repeatedly Fergusson remarked about 'what pains' the architect took to achieve this end.[63]

Whereas Fergusson stressed the purposeful avoidance of regularity in his universal history of architecture, the French Hellenists directed their attention to discovering the visual logic behind the apparent disorder of Greek architecture. To this end, they concentrated, like Fergusson, on the Propylaia and the Erechtheion. In 1821 Leake had approvingly reminded his contemporaries that ancient Greek authors, with whom he agreed, had accorded the Propylaia a status at least equal to that of the Parthenon. The Propylaia, he had written, was the 'greatest production of civil architecture in Athens, which equalled the Parthenon in felicity of execution, and surpassed it in boldness and originality of design.'[64]

In considering the Propylaia and the Erechtheion, the constant theme of the French Hellenists was how the ancient Greek architects, when confronted with seemingly intractable site conditions and complex building programs, had used these constraints as a stimulus to create brilliant picturesque buildings. As Beulé expressed it, 'All these difficulties became a source for new beauties.'[65] We have already seen that Pugin had uttered this thought in connection with Gothic architecture. It is likely, though, that Beulé appropriated this concept for himself from the classicist Emile Burnouf and the architect Jacques-Martin Tetaz, who had preceded him in Athens. Burnouf, in turn, had taken this formulation from Quatremère de Quincy's discussion of the Propylaia.[66]

For the sake of brevity, rather than trace the evolution of the French analysis of the picturesque qualities of the Propylaia and Erechtheion, I will use Beulé's synthesis, which appeared in book form, as opposed to the earlier articles in scholarly journals by Burnouf on the Propylaia and by Tetaz on the Erechtheion. Beulé's book has the dual virtue of incorporating these earlier ideas with his own and of presenting them in a public forum where they would be consulted by other influential figures, such as Ernest Renan, whose 'Prière sur l'Acropole' was ardently sought by Charles-Edouard Jeanneret (not yet Le Corbusier) just before his first visit to the Acropolis. Finally, when considering the analyses made by these young Frenchmen of the Ecole Française d'Athènes, it is important to keep in mind the fragmentary character of the buildings that they were studying. Their ruinous state required an extraordinary degree of attentiveness and imagination.

The French Hellenists' studies of the Propylaia and the Erechtheion consisted of three parts: a description of the harmonious nature of the picturesque massing; a consideration of the ingenious, subtle, and beautiful design features of the buildings' components, and thanks to Beulé, a general theory about the underlying order within the apparent disorder of such singularly different edifices. We can begin with a brief consideration of the harmonious beauty, which astounded Beulé and his compatriots, of so irregular a building as the Propylaia. The main and central pavilion, with its majestic Doric frontispiece of columns and pediment, was flanked to either side by smaller and unequal wings that featured smaller Doric columns carrying only an entablature. The daring juxtaposition of the larger and smaller orders and the asymmetrical massing were remarkable in themselves. That they occurred in the same edifice, which also included an Ionic order within the porch, prompted even greater wonder.

The Ionic columns were understood to be a solution to the difficult problem of carrying the massive, twenty-foot-long marble architrave to either side of the central passageway. These columns had to be taller than those of the front and rear porticoes but could not rival them in importance. The more delicate and slender Ionic order provided the requisite height, while exhibiting a grace that deflected attention from the considerable load it carried. Another difficulty arose through the disparity in levels between the front and rear porticoes that straddled the sloping terrain. To hide this lack of vertical alignment, the architect introduced a wall across the porch near the rear, which prevented the simultaneous view of the two porticoes. Even the spacing of the large Doric columns in the porticoes departed from accepted practice. The two central columns were spread widely apart to signal the main passage. The two other columns to each side were then spaced with progressively narrower intervals between them. This arrangement was reflected in the wall between the two porticoes where five doors were arranged with descending height and width corresponding to the intercolumniation. 'Every-thing,' Beulé concluded, 'was innovation in the Propylaia, a great temerity for a people like the Greeks who were attached to the traditions of art.' The entire design, moreover, was conceived and executed with a 'genius that gave to each part of the edifice its most perfect proportion and to the ensemble an ideal harmony.'[67]

The Erechtheion, 'this building, which is irregular already because of the diversity of the columns of its facades, becomes even more so by its location on two different levels.'[68] Here the French Hellenists were especially impressed by the Caryatid tribune (figure 2.6). Beulé observed that the statues of the young maidens were not only masterpieces of sculpture but also design elements that harmonized with the 'lines and feeling of the entire building.' Their aspect was at once 'calm and firm' as they appeared to carry the entablature 'as easily' as a vase. This effect was achieved through the overall proportioning of the figures; the lines of the drapery; the seemingly effortless connection between the neck, head, and capital; and the shifted weight of the body that leaned contrapuntally to the diagonal line of the slightly bent knee. This attitude imparted a 'supple grace and ease' to the statue while it carried its load.[69]

Just as the columns and walls of the Erechtheion were inclined inward 'toward an imaginary center' to create a pyramidal form – 'the most perfect image of stability' – so too was the stance of the Caryatids arranged so as to harmonize with this effect. For the viewer facing the tribune, the three Caryatids to the left bend the left knee; the three to the right bend the right knee. As a result, all six figures incline inward toward the middle. 'This is what makes the opposing movements of the two groups into so logical and harmonious an ensemble.'[70]

Relying heavily now upon Tetaz's analysis, Beulé explained the reciprocal atten-tions of the architect and the sculptor. In order to avoid a direct comparison in size between the larger-than-life Caryatids and the spectators, the sculptural figures were removed from the viewers' immediate proximity by an 'uncustomarily high' stylobate. On the other hand, to insure an unobstructed view of the Caryatids who were seen from below, each was elevated slightly upon a plinth. The seeming ease with which the female figures carried their heavy loads was facilitated by modifying the traditional capital so as to marry it 'without effort to the human head.' Finally, in what Beulé considered to be 'assuredly the most audacious innovation,' the entablature was reduced in height and hence in actual and apparent weight by omission of the frieze, 'the sole occurrence in Greek architecture.'[71]

Yet even with such a complex analysis of two buildings so different in form and on such unequal terrain, Beulé believed that he had discovered the unifying design principle that informed the arrangement of both buildings. The Propylaia and the Erechtheion were each designed with two unequal wings attached to a central, dominant mass.[72] The similarity between this analysis of the underlying design principle for the two asymmetrical buildings of the Acropolis and Downing's analogous concept of irregular symmetry is noteworthy. Both the idea of intentional order within asymmetrical design and the perception of an irregular symmetry were to have profound implications for Auguste Choisy's revolutionary analysis of the underlying order among the different buildings of the Acropolis. Before proceeding to this subject, though, it will be necessary to consider the effect of the writings of the architects and classicists of the Ecole Française d'Athènes on Viollet-le-Duc. Although today commonly labeled a Gothicist and an advocate of structural rationalism, Viollet-le-Duc, in the first volume of his *Entretiens sur l'architecture* (Discourses on Architecture), proved to be an ardent champion of the lessons of the picturesque as found in ancient Greek architecture. Viollet-le-Duc's enthusiastic embrace of French Hellenism integrated the work of the Ecole Française d'Athènes into the mainstream of Western architectural literature where it had a profound effect on Frank Lloyd Wright and Le Corbusier.

Fusing poetry and reason

Even though for Viollet-le-Duc Gothic architecture constituted the French national heritage that would have to be renewed in a modern manner, he came to see Greek architecture as the highest achievement in world architecture. As he explained in his *Entretiens*, a book written to ascertain the 'development of the immutable principles of our art,' Greek architecture offered 'the most absolute and most perfect type that realizes the principles to which I will repeatedly have occasion to direct the reader's attention.'[73] The primacy Viollet-le-Duc accorded to Greek architecture in the *Entretiens* contrasts markedly with his earlier conviction of 1846 that thirteenth-century French Gothic architecture 'is the only architecture, in my opinion, that should be studied in France.' At that time Viollet-le-Duc had relegated Greek architecture to the minor status of '*archaeology*, in the true meaning of the word.'[74] The publications of the French Hellenists at the Ecole Française d'Athènes seem to have been responsible for this significant shift in Viollet-le-Duc's attitude.

Throughout his survey of different cultures in the *Entretiens*, Viollet-le-Duc privileged the lessons afforded by ancient Greek architecture in the area of the reasoned picturesque. Greek architecture, to Viollet-le-Duc, presented the most exquisite union of poetry and reason:

If we consider one by one all the parts of a Greek temple, if we study them by themselves and in their immediate relationship with the whole, we will always find the influence of those judicious and delicate observations which signal the presence of art, that exquisite sentiment that submits all forms to reason, not to the dry and pedantic reason of the geometrician, but to reason directed by the senses and by the observation of natural laws.[75]

This reasoning led the Greek architect to embrace the picturesque. The ancient Greek architects, affirmed Viollet-le-Duc, 'understood in a broad way what we call *the picturesque*.'[76] More specifically,

I have tried to explain the importance to the [ancient Greek architect] of the effect, how he sensitively observes the play of light and shadow over surfaces and the picturesque silhouette against the sky. The Greek artist is endowed with too delicate a sense to submit to a blind and imperious law. If he permits symmetry, it is rather through a balancing than through a geometric rule.[77]

This same poetic reason was applied to matters of building: 'I have said that with the Greeks, the exterior form of their architecture was none other than the result of reasoned construction, of the discrete observation of the effects produced by light and shadows, and of the feeling for proportion.'[78] Like the French Hellenists who preceded him, Viollet-le-Duc echoed the conviction that the picturesque wonders of Greek architecture were largely the result of an ingenious response to various difficulties: 'If we analyze the buildings of the Greeks . . . we always find this subtly perceptive spirit that knows how to turn any difficulty and every obstacle into an advantage for art, even down to the smallest details.'[79]

Although it would be inaccurate to conclude that the *Entretiens* 'did not offer a coherent theory of architecture,'[80] the clarity of Viollet-le-Duc's meaning at times suffered from a partial presentation of his ideas. Readers intent on finding evidence to support the widespread conviction that Viollet-le-Duc was a structural rationalist will find confirming statements only by a partial and selective reading of the text. In the second 'Entretien,' for example, while discussing the structure of a Greek temple, Viollet-le-Duc observed that since the corner columns carry a greater load than the others, as a measure of safety, the architect moved them inward toward the center and slightly increased their diameter. This was done, he explained, in response to a flexible reasoning that could, when necessary, violate the laws of symmetry, which would have decreed an equal spacing of columns of identical breadth.[81] In the fourth 'Entretien,' when the subject was a temple's visual appearance, Viollet-le-Duc remarked that the Greek architect altered the spacing of the triglyphs so that the last one would fall at the end of the frieze rather than in its customary location directly above the column. To maintain the appearance of harmonious spacing among all the triglyphs the architect diminished the interval between the last three columns to either side of the portico. In contrast, the Romans later applied an 'absolute symmetry' in this matter by keeping the inter-columniation equal and the triglyphs over the axis of each column.[82] Once again Viollet-le-Duc presented the Greek approach as one of reason, but of a reason both flexible and subtle in the solution of aesthetic problems. As he expressed it: 'The Greek knows no other rules than those of reason; but reason reasons, discusses, it is ungraspable.'[83]

If the reader considers only Viollet-le-Duc's text from the second 'Entretien,' then Viollet-le-Duc would seem to be a structural rationalist, attributing all formal decisions to a response to the requirements of structure and materials. If one uses only the text in the fourth 'Entretien,' then Viollet-le-Duc would appear as an aesthete. Taken together, these two texts reveal Viollet-le-Duc's true attitude, which seeks to find the harmony between structural integrity and aesthetic expression.

Viollet-le-Duc's discussion of the Erechtheion contrasts strongly with Fergusson's summary remarks, which were limited to marveling at the architect's efforts to distinguish between the assembled sanctuaries through picturesque design. In a complex analysis of this building in the second 'Entretien,' Viollet-le-Duc interwove an entire range of functional, structural, and aesthetic matters, ranging from the channeling of rain water off the roof to a delight in the play of light and shadows over sculpted forms, from a respect for sacred places that precluded altering the level of the uneven ground to the hierarchical expression of major and minor sanctuaries, from the reasoning behind selection of forms of various sizes and shapes to the desire not to obscure important views of the Acropolis from the city below. Here and elsewhere in his book, Viollet-le-Duc gave greater subtlety and precision to the three components of the picturesque that Fergusson had championed in his history of world architecture: the articulation of forms, the artificiality of symmetry, and the harmony between the building and the landscape.

So important were what Viollet-le-Duc called the 'poetic' aspects of architectural design, that he considered a building deficient if it merely satisfied the exigencies of structure.[84] Returning to the subject of the Erechtheion in the seventh 'Entretien,' Viollet-le-Duc remarked that the architect could well have used piers instead of human figures at the corners of the Caryatid tribune: 'certainly he would have done something sensible, even irreproachable from the point of view of construction; but he would have obtained only a banal silhouette.' The decision to use Caryatids not just in the middle, as in the facade of the Treasury of the Siphnians (*c.* 530 B.C.) in Delphi, but at the corners as well as was, to Viollet-le-Duc, virtually an act of genius – 'c'est une énormité.' Even the positions of these human figures evidenced the subtlest aesthetic sense:

An artist subjected to the banal laws that we take today to have been the classical tradition would never have dared to present the corner Caryatids in profile and especially not those in the second row. He would have turned the face of those at the corners diagonally outward and would not have missed rotating by ninety degrees the Caryatids in the rear such that they would always show their face to the exterior and their back toward the interior of the portico.

Elaborating upon a theme raised by Beulé, Viollet-le-Duc attempted to demonstrate that the Caryatids' stances were both consciously determined and naturally correct, just like the inward inclination of the corner columns of a typical temple. With paired illustrations (figure 2.11), Viollet-le-Duc contrasted the actual grouping with an alternative arrangement. Had the architect reversed the contrapuntal leaning motion of hip and torso of the end statues, as in the second illustration, then the human figures would not have seemed capable of supporting the entablature 'and the small edifice would have seemed ready to fall apart.'[85]

Viollet-le-Duc was particularly interested in the harmonious siting of Greek buildings in the landscape. His observations set the stage for Choisy's subsequent thoughts about the Acropolis, for they contradicted not only the tenets of Beaux-Arts design but also the express judgement about the Acropolis by the Prix-de-Rome architect Alexis Paccard. In the 'Mémoire' of 1845 that accompanied his hypothetical restoration of the Parthenon, a restoration that won a medal at the Exposition Universelle of 1855, Paccard conveyed his conclusions about his study of the Acropolis:

When one examines the overall aspect that the Acropolis of Athens presents, one is struck before all else by the contrast between the great magnificence that the buildings . . . must have presented with the extreme simplicity of arrangement and decoration that must have existed in the ascending paths leading to these buildings and in the spaces between them. In effect, it is the rock itself that serves today as the way that leads from the Propylaia to the temples situated on the most elevated part of the Acropolis. There is no doubt that this was the same in the past. . . . In addition, the principal temples rise either on a rude base whose stones are visible or on fragments of the rock, which are equally visible. . . . [O]ne can conclude that the Greeks did not accord much importance to this part of the decoration [of the site] and that they even neglected it on purpose, either to highlight better the beauty and richness of the buildings or perhaps even to preserve religiously the traces of previous

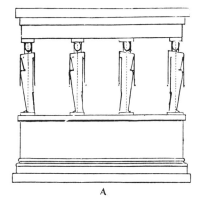

A

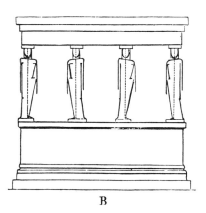

B

2.11
Analysis of the Caryatid tribune of the Erechtheion, Athens. 'A' depicts the actual building

constructions. In light of what I have just explained, it is certain that there never was a general aesthetic arrangement either to relate the buildings together or to arrive in a worthy manner at the different levels on which the temples were built.

Paccard had not only attempted with obvious failure to apply the Beaux-Arts principles of symmetry, axiality, and formal geometric terracing to a site at which they were conspicuously not present, he could not imagine that this absence was intentional. Without adducing any evidence, he nonetheless concluded that if only events had permitted, no doubt the architects would have provided the order and dignity that he found lacking: 'One can presume, however, that the Greek architects intended to create more grandeur and harmony among all the parts of the Acropolis, but that political reasons prevented them from carrying out this project.'[86]

Without considering the overall issue of the design of the Acropolis, Viollet-le-Duc nevertheless offered an alternative interpretation of Greek design principles that undermined Paccard's assumptions. Viollet-le-Duc insisted that the Greek architect had designed according to the picturesque and hence in harmony with the irregular, natural features of the landscape. 'The Greek architect,' explained Viollet-le-Duc,

does not level the rock that will serve as a base for his building; he decorates it and takes advantage of its unevenness with taste and as a consummate connoisseur of effects. Look at Athens, Corinth, and especially those old cities of Sicily – Agrigento, Selinunte, Segesta, and Syracuse. Who has not said to himself in seeing the remains of these cities: 'How fortunate, how happy people must have been to have lived with such a complete harmony between art and the beauties of nature?[87]

Reflecting upon the Greek ruins at Agrigento, Viollet-le-Duc concluded that 'Greek architects were skillful landscape designers and that this quality did not harm their art.' In designing Greek cities, considerations of 'art,' achieved through the picturesque siting of temples in the landscape, were an integral part of the planning process, not 'a decoration, a superfluous afterthought.' 'The Greek architect,' explained Viollet-le-Duc, 'faithful to his principle of working in harmony with nature and of assigning it a place of prominence in his artistic creations, examined with a rare wisdom the dispositions of the terrain on which he had to build.'[88]

Not only did Viollet-le-Duc believe that the Greek architects had purposefully located their temples in a picturesque manner in the landscape, he also offered a brief but suggestive discussion of Egyptian, Greek, Roman, and Oriental societies that stressed the purposeful arrangement of the approach to a temple in order to create a sense of anticipation and climax through 'skillfully managed transitions.' He termed this the *mise en scène*. As part of his discussion here he summarily remarked that ensembles of ancient buildings, including the Acropolis, eschewed 'symmetry, which is contrary to our spirit, which bores and tires us' in favor of the 'picturesque.'[89] It was left to Auguste Choisy to combine these thoughts together as the basis for understanding what appeared to have been the purposeful picturesque ordering of the Acropolis.

Auguste Choisy and the picturesque architectural promenade

On 24 November 1865 a twenty-four-year-old engineering student at the Ecole des Ponts et Chaussées, Auguste Choisy, read a paper, 'Note on the Dissymmetrical Curvature of the Steps that Border the Western Side of the Platform of the

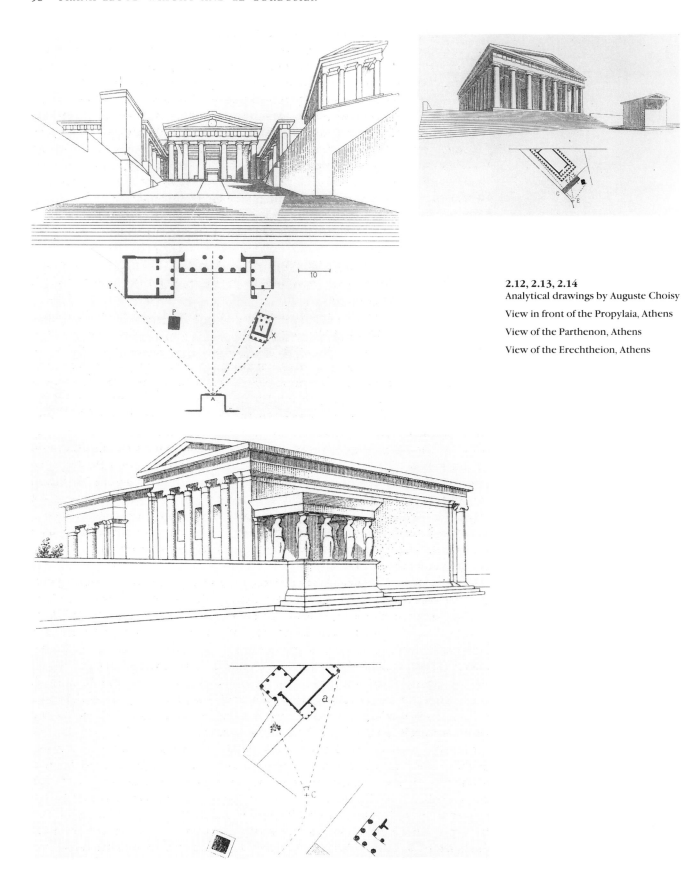

2.12, 2.13, 2.14
Analytical drawings by Auguste Choisy
View in front of the Propylaia, Athens
View of the Parthenon, Athens
View of the Erechtheion, Athens

Parthenon,' to the prestigious Académie des Inscriptions et Belles-Lettres and then again on 16 December to the Académie des Beaux-Arts.[90] Neither the youth of the author, nor his profession, nor the uninviting title should deceive, for this paper contained a radically new interpretation of Greek architecture that was to revolutionize twentieth-century modern architecture. Appearing again with illustrations in his *Histoire de l'architecture* (1899) as the culminating example of a world-wide phenomenon, the architectural promenade that Choisy had found at the Periclean Acropolis found a deep response in Charles-Edouard Jeanneret, who, under the pseudonym Le Corbusier, integrated Choisy's principles into his own polemical understanding of architecture expounded in the series of articles published between 1920 and 1922 in *L'Esprit Nouveau* and then gathered together in 1923 in the book entitled *Vers une Architecture*.

Choisy's paper effectively challenged Paccard's assertion that the Greeks had not considered the arrangement of the buildings on the Acropolis. To the contrary, Choisy found a subtly considered order based upon the picturesque principle whose two main attributes we have seen defined as asymmetrical 'variety' and the irregular, non-axial 'path.'

Apparently taking advantage of an opportunity to reach Greece because of an assignment that already put him in southern France, Choisy made his first visit to the Acropolis in the summer or early fall of 1865.[91] There he determined that the Greeks had actually established a 'system' by which they had given order to the Acropolis according to the two principles of 'dissymmetry' and 'displacement of axes.' Moreover, Choisy determined that the entire site had been arranged as a sequence of controlled views, a series of 'picturesque' scenes in which buildings and statues of different sizes and at different distances were asymmetrically balanced with respect to the central object, with the frontal view the exception and the oblique the rule. In each of the four major scenes – in front of the Propylaia (figure 2.12), just beyond the Propylaia (figure 1.1), approaching the Parthenon (figure 2.13), and, finally, approaching the Erechtheion (figure 2.14) – the points of major and minor focus had a thematic purpose related to their religious and civic significance. Perhaps there is no more fitting term for this aesthetic ordering than the one that Le Corbusier would later apply to his own new architecture, the architectural promenade.

Choisy carefully opened his discussion by addressing a seemingly obscure point of archaeology that actually had profound implications for his theory. In 1862 the German architect and archaeologist Karl Boetticher had discovered that the flight of steps in front of the western side of the platform preceding the Parthenon had a noticeable convex curvature. Boetticher, who did not believe that the horizontal curves of the temple itself had been intentional, cited the example of these curved steps as evidence for his argument. Since these steps were carved into the bedrock and had never carried a building, then what could their purpose possibly be? And if they had no aesthetic purpose, then the curved surfaces measured on the Parthenon itself could not have been intentional.[92]

Choisy, though, believed that he had not only discovered the aesthetic purpose of the curved lines to the platform, he also had found what seemed to be a mathematical proof of their intentionality. Determining that the summit of their curvature had been displaced 7.5 meters to the left of an imaginary axis leading to the center of the Parthenon's west front (figures 2.13, 2.15), Choisy explained that this asymmetrical condition was necessary for the steps to appear in harmony with the horizontally curved lines of the temple itself when viewed obliquely along the

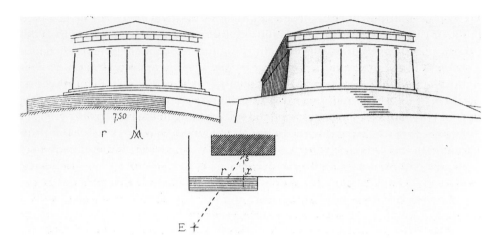

2.15
Analytical drawing by Choisy
(curvature of steps bounding the
western side of the platform of the
Parthenon, Athens)

approach from the Propylaia. Here Choisy may have been creatively applying the
observation by William Leake that, at the Acropolis of Athens, as well as 'at the
temple of Minerva at Sunium and Priene, and at the Panhellenium of Aegina,' the
temple was not on axis with the entrance to the sacred precinct but rather off to the
side so as to present 'a more imposing aspect' by offering simultaneously a front and
side view.[93] Thus, not only was the curvature of the steps along the western side of
the platform at the Acropolis intentional, it further confirmed the purposeful
aesthetic nature of the curved lines of the Parthenon itself. This issue, though, was
not Choisy's main subject. Rather it demonstrated the two principles of 'dissymmetry' and 'displacement of axes' by which the entire site was orchestrated
into an architectural promenade.

Choisy's first scene in the architectural promenade across the Acropolis began in
front of the Propylaia (figure 2.12). We have seen how Fergusson had stressed the
asymmetry and lack of parallelism among the buildings not only of the Acropolis as
a whole but especially of the monuments clustered together at the entrance. It is
important to note that Francis Cranmer Penrose, in an aside to his investigation of
the curved lines and inclined planes of the Parthenon, also briefly noted the
'remarkable absence of parallelism among the several buildings' of the Acropolis
that 'not only obviates the dry uniformity of too many parallel lines, but also
produces exquisite varieties of light and shade.' Penrose was especially taken with
the angular position of the two monuments to either side of the front portico of the
Propylaia – the Temple of Athena Nike to the right and the Agrippa pedestal to the
left – which remained in the shadows 'for a considerable time after the front of the
Propylaia has been lighted up.' Later, 'they gradually receive every variety of light,
until the sun is on the decline to shine nearly equally on all the western faces of the
entire group.' In short, Penrose admiringly concluded that 'this *asymmetria* is
productive of very great beauty' at the Acropolis.[94]

When Choisy considered this same scene, he went further than his predecessors
by explaining the principles by which the Periclean Acropolis was given order
within the apparent disorder of the site. The aesthetic rules that he applied to this
first scene were the same that he showed as governing the subsequent views across
the site as well. Emphasizing that each scene was revealed fully and suddenly to the
viewer so as to make a forceful and lasting initial impression, Choisy placed his
spectator at the newly discovered gateway to the forecourt in front of the

Propylaia, named the Beulé gate in honor of its discoverer. At this time, it was believed that the position and original architecture of the gate dated back to the classical Greek era.

From the Beulé gate the viewer was presented with a perfectly balanced asymmetrical view of the Propylaia. At the center rose the majestic Doric portico that preceded the deep entrance porch. The building's wings extended to either side, the larger Pinakotheke to the left and the smaller wing to the right. These unequal extensions were balanced by the placement of the Agrippa pedestal, once again considered to have been of the classical Greek period, in front of the Pinakotheke, and of the Temple of Athena Nike raised upon a high base to the right in front of the smaller wing. In his later discussion of the Acropolis, Choisy referred to the 'ponderation of masses' to describe the asymmetrical balance achieved in such a composition.

Turned at an angle to the entire scene and viewed obliquely against the sky, the diminutive Temple of Athena Nike, celebrating the Athenian victory over the Persians at Marathon in 490 B.C., was thereby given special importance in this scene. Choisy proceeded to explain that the right wing of the Propylaia was smaller than the left because it had been truncated so as not to obscure the view of the temple's silhouette against the sky. Here the geometry of the site not only offered confirmation of this interpretation but also showed how carefully the entire scene was ordered. If a center line were drawn along the central axis from Beulé's door (point A) through the middle of the central porch of the Propylaia, then the lines from point A to the outer corner of each side of the composition (lines AY and AX) presented identical angles. Furthermore, a line from Beulé's door (point A) to the inner edge of the Temple of Athena Nike would, when continued further, touch the outer edge of the right wing of the Propylaia, thereby signaling the exact point for the truncation. 'Nothing is in appearance more irregular than this plan,' Choisy would write in his *Histoire*, 'in fact, it is a balanced ensemble' of masses.[95]

Choisy's second scene occurs at the rear porch of the Propylaia (figure 1.1). Here the central figure is the towering statue of the warrior goddess Athena Promachos, whose pedestal is turned obliquely to the viewer for greater effect. Behind the goddess rises the partially obscured Erechtheion. The Parthenon is seen obliquely toward the rear on the right side; other buildings frame the view to the left. Once again the viewer is presented with an asymmetrically balanced composition.

The third scene (figure 2.13) is the diagonal approach to the Parthenon where the asymmetrical curvature of the steps in front of the platform from which the temple rises assures a harmonious view of the entire ensemble. Finally (figure 2.14), the visitor turns to view the Erechtheion, which also presents itself obliquely to reveal an asymmetrically balanced composition of masses. The Caryatid tribune, seen against the background of the long blank wall, is thrown into special focus. Choisy explains that it had been concealed by the base of the statue of Athena Promachos in the second scene because these smaller and more graceful figures, placed in the background, would have suffered by comparison. Now, with the 'menacing' statue of the warrior goddess only a 'memory,' these 'charming figures sculpted with the greatest delicacy and intended to be seen face to face at a close distance' became the center of interest.[96] Thus the element of memory entered into the architectural promenade.

When Choisy published his two-volume *Histoire de l'architecture* (1899), the architectural promenade across the Periclean Acropolis was presented as the culminating aesthetic example of the universal phenomenon of intentional sequencing of spaces found throughout the world. Choisy found this intentional sequencing to be most fully developed in the most representative building type for each culture: Egyptian, Assyrian, Hindu, Mycenaean, Greek, Roman, and eighteenth-century French. Before considering Choisy's treatment of this subject, it should be pointed out that the architectural promenade in different cultures had been addressed by other nineteenth-century writers in more summary and less systematic ways. Thomas Leverton Donaldson, Vice-President of the Royal Institute of British Architects, for example, outlined his course on the history of world architecture at the University College of London on 17 October 1842, with an appreciation of the effect upon a visitor to ancient Rome of the long sequence of tombs encountered along the ancient Appian Way; to a worshiper in ancient Egypt who proceeded down the avenue of sphinxes to the giant pylons that framed the entrance to a temple, which were followed by the courtyard lined with columns, then the darkened hypostyle hall, and finally after passing through somber vestibules, to 'the gloom' of the 'inmost sanctuary'; and to the visitor to the ancient Roman baths, who would find 'the vastness of their plans, the well-studied gradations of their several halls, courts, and chambers, the magical contrasts of the sections, and playful exuberance of the accompaniments, [which] captivate the attention, and lead in willing chains the enchanted imagination of the beholder.'[97] The British architect Charles Robert Cockerell made similar observations in his public lectures. He praised the partial concealment of the Parthenon by the Propylaia and the walls of the Acropolis, thereby leaving something 'to be imagined and discovered.' And he admired the Baths of Diocletian for the 'effect produced by the vistas' that 'excite a succession of new ideas.'[98]

In his universal history, Choisy used the work of nineteenth-century archaeologists whose excavations and studies vastly increased the knowledge of other civilizations. Applying his particular understanding of architecture to the newly acquired knowledge about these historical architectures, Choisy elucidated the relationship between the architectural promenade and its culture by explaining its purpose in the representative building type of each society. In addition, he also demonstrated that the architectural promenade provided the *raison d'être* for the coordination of structure, form, program, and aesthetics. Considered in conjunction with the architectural system, the architectural promenade furnished the guiding theme.

Beginning his study of historical periods with Egyptian architecture, Choisy found a clear reflection of its 'authoritarian' social order as well as the dominance of its 'theocracy' in the 'grandeur and mystery of its temples.' The basic principle of monumental Egyptian architecture (figure 2.16) was the 'repetition of the same motifs – *enfilade* of columns, rows of identical sphinxes or statues, . . . perhaps the most powerful means at architecture's disposal to create a striking impression.' These elements were carefully ordered to form a sequential architectural promenade with discrete features arranged from a beginning to an end. After passing down the *allée* of sphinxes, through the pylon gate, and across the courtyard, everything is then orchestrated to create an impression of 'mystery': 'In most of the temples, as one approaches the sanctuary, the floor rises, the ceilings are lowered, darkness increases, and the sacred symbol appears only when shrouded in a dim light.'[99] For Choisy, the Indian temple (figure 2.17) presented a variant on the Egyptian sense of order. Its concentric precincts 'recall by its formation and the effects of its pylons' Egyptian temple groups such as at Karnak.[100]

The discovery of Assyrian architecture in 1842 by the French consul in Mosul,

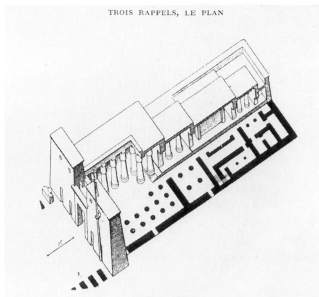

TROIS RAPPELS, LE PLAN

TEMPLE DE THÈBES. Le plan s'organise suivant l'axe d'arrivée : allée des sphinx, pylônes, cour avec péristyle, sanctuaire.

qu'une algébrisation aride au regard. Le travail du mathématicien reste tout de même l'une des plus hautes activités de l'esprit humain.

L'ordonnance, c'est un rythme saisissable qui réagit sur tout être humain, de même manière.

Le plan porte en lui-même un rythme primaire déterminé : l'œuvre se développe en étendue et en hauteur suivant ses prescriptions avec des conséquences s'étendant du plus simple au plus complexe sur la même loi. L'unité de la loi est la loi du bon plan : loi simple infiniment modulable.

Le rythme est un état d'équilibre procédant de symétries simples ou complexes ou procédant de compensations savantes. Le rythme est une équation : égalisation (symétrie, répétition) *(Temples égyptiens, hindous)*; compensation (mouvement des

5

TROIS RAPPELS, LE PLAN

L'architecture n'a rien à voir avec les « styles ».

Elle sollicite les facultés les plus élevées par son abstraction même. L'abstraction architecturale a cela de particulier et de magnifique que, se racinant dans le fait brutal, elle le spiritualise. Le fait brutal n'est possible d'idée que par l'ordre qu'on y projette.

Le volume et la surface sont les éléments par quoi se manifeste l'architecture. Le volume et la surface sont déterminés par le plan. C'est le plan qui est le générateur. Tant pis pour ceux à qui manque l'imagination!

TROISIÈME RAPPEL : LE PLAN

Le plan est le générateur.

L'œil du spectateur se meut dans un site fait de rues et de maisons. Il reçoit le choc des volumes qui se dressent à l'entour. Si ces volumes sont formels et non dégradés par des altérations

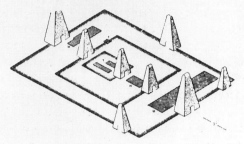

TYPE DU TEMPLE HINDOU. Les tours font une cadence dans l'espace.

intempestives, si l'ordonnance qui les groupe exprime un rythme clair, et non pas une agglomération incohérente, si les rapports des volumes et de l'espace sont faits de proportions justes, l'œil transmet au cerveau des sensations coordonnées et l'esprit en dégage des satisfactions d'un ordre élevé : c'est l'architecture.

2.16, 2.17

The principles of Egyptian architecture

The principles of Hindu architecture

(From Auguste Choisy, as reproduced in Le Corbusier, *Vers une Architecture*, 1923)

Paul-Emile Botta, and the subsequent work by his successor Victor Place and by the Englishman Austen Henry Layard, was possibly the most significant archaeological find of mid-century, for it revealed the material culture of a lost civilization. Utilizing the literature and drawings that resulted, Choisy directed his attention to the palace, which, 'englobing temples as annexes within its precinct,' reflected the dominance of a monarchy even over religion. In the architectural promenade at King Sargon's summer palace in Khorsabad (figure 2.18), Choisy found 'a model of skillful arrangement where the life of an Asiatic monarch seems written in entirety, with its refinements and its caution.'[101]

As both Botta and Place had recognized, Assyrian architecture presented an entire architectural system from the point of view of 'construction, materials, decoration, and layout,' one that differed radically from all others known by mid-nineteenth century. They were particularly struck by the system of adjacent rooms and courtyards with axial and cross-axial arrangements, at times closed off or shifted to create an enticing irregularity.[102] For Choisy, the primary element of this system was the architectural promenade arranged through the ceremonial rooms of the palace. Using Place's plan, Choisy traced the spatial sequence from the

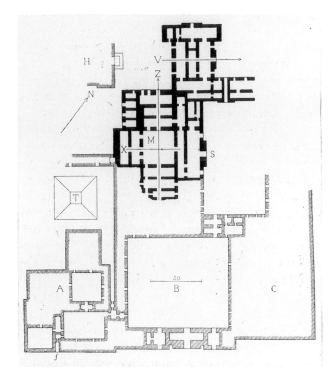

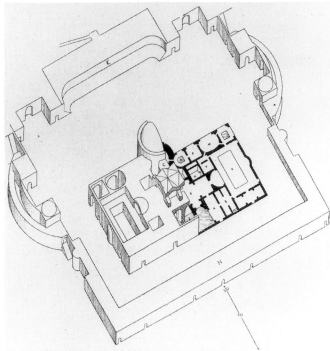

2.18, 2.19

Sequencing of spaces in King Sargon's summer palace in Khorsabad

Sequencing of spaces in the Baths of Caracalla, Rome

(From Auguste Choisy)

entry (S) to the large hall (M), which was reached by several lateral shifts and right-angle turns within the frontally layered space. After another right-angle turn in the large hall (M), the visitor proceeded along an axis through three successive rooms before encountering a courtyard where he or she was permitted 'only an oblique view' of the throne (H), before turning to exit along the *enfilade* labeled 'V.' 'Prudence and mystery,' concluded Choisy, 'could not be pushed any further.'[103]

In the architectural promenade of the ancient Roman bath (figure 2.19), 'the most clearly Roman building type,' Choisy found the epitome of varied effects within a framework of clear organization. Once again, there was unity between the structural, functional, and aesthetic order all orchestrated according to the architectural promenade. Using the hypothetical restoration of the Baths of Caracalla by Abel Blouet, Choisy pointed out that within the structural system of mutually abutting vaulted rooms, the principal services were clearly organized along a main axis according to a gradual and logical progression from cold to hot baths. Like Donaldson, Choisy was struck by the volumetric complexity of the architectural promenade here: 'Finally, from the point of view of the effects produced, one is struck by the variety of aspects: all the rooms differ: here an open rectangular basin with niches; there exedras; a gallery with groin vaults, a square room terminated by an apse; further on a round room, porticoes.' Yet this rich complexity was carefully kept under control, for 'nowhere will one find a more clearly or better ordered arrangement.' When filled with the Roman populace, 'alternately actor and spectator' in the various games and athletic contests, 'such a plan is a complete commentary on Roman life.'[104]

In the *Histoire*, Choisy preceded his discussion of the Periclean Acropolis by a consideration of Mycenaean culture and then of other Greek religious precincts to demonstrate a tradition of picturesque site planning that used a picturesque architectural promenade.[105] Using Schliemann and Dörpfeld's plan of the 'model Homeric citadel'[106] at Tiryns, Choisy traced a winding and shifting sequence of movement through successive courtyards and propylaea until reaching the innermost sanctum, the columnar hall with its central hearth. In this 'semi-royal, semi-patriarchal' setting for the Homeric epic, this building fully representative of 'primitive Greece,' Choisy found a skillfully arranged architectural promenade.[107]

Looking next at temple precincts, Choisy focused on the architectural setting deemed most representative of Greek architecture. This discussion, which culminated in a consideration of the Athenian Acropolis, was presented under the title 'The Picturesque in Greek Art: Dissymmetrical *Partis*, Ponderation of Masses.' Choisy's repeated references to the 'cold alignment,' 'cold regularity,' 'false regularity,' and 'monotony' of symmetrical design, as well as his disappointment with the ascendancy of the 'straight line' in Greek site planning toward the end of the fifth century B.C., clearly reveal the highly motivated nature of his text.[108] In other words, like Fergusson and Viollet-le-Duc, Choisy was using history to identify the universal principles capable of regenerating contemporary architecture. By the time the reader came to the end of the book, where Choisy reiterated the thought of an entire century that with the French Revolution 'a new society had been formed that wants a new art,' and where he expressed the optimism of *fin-de-siècle* architectural thought that with the new iron architecture a beginning had been made, he had left no doubt that the architectural promenade was an essential feature and that the picturesque was one of the highest principles to guide the rejuvenation of this art.[109]

Choisy began his discussion of the picturesque in Greek architecture by echoing Viollet-le-Duc's observations about the harmonious relationship between the landscape and the temple. Sounion, Kroton, Segesta, Selinunte, and Agrigento are all briefly considered. Then he proceeded to interpret the major temple sites that had recently been excavated by the Ecole Française d'Athènes (Delphi and Delos) and by the Germans (Olympia). The privileged nature of Olympia had been explained by the Prix-de-Rome architect Victor Laloux and the classical scholar Paul Monceaux in their hypothetical restoration of 1889:

Since religion mixed with every aspect of [Greek] life and thought, it is at the most celebrated sanctuary that the civilization of ancient Greece ought to have shown itself most brilliantly, in the astonishing variety of its original creations. Classical Olympia presents the most complete image of a great Greek religious site.

Laloux and Monceaux had found at the German excavations undertaken between 1875 and 1881 at Olympia an ordered disorder analogous to what Choisy had ascertained decades before at the Athenian Acropolis. 'One must not search there,' they admonished, 'for the regularity in composition of the Romans or moderns, boring in its cold monotony. The Greeks, as true artists, knew instinctively how to achieve unity within the boldness of contrasts. Sure of their taste, they dared to unleash their fantasy.'[110] In addition to explaining the picturesque arrangement of buildings and processional spaces at Olympia, Delos, and Delphi, Choisy also briefly mentioned the 'groupings no less ordered in their dissymmetry' at Eleusis, Epidauros, and Dodona.

All of this was a prelude to Choisy's discussion of the Acropolis, now undertaken in light of Kawerau and Dörpfeld's recent discoveries between 1885–91 of the pre-Periclean site as it existed in 480 B.C. when the invading Persians burned the

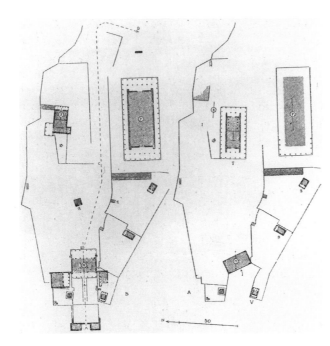

2.20
The Acropolis, Athens. Right: as it was in 480 B.C., before the Persian sack. Left: as rebuilt under the direction of Pericles

(From Auguste Choisy)

city (figure 2.20).[111] This earlier plan confirmed Choisy in his belief not only in the intentionality of the picturesque architectural promenade across the Acropolis but also of the inimitable superiority of the Periclean site with respect not only to other Greek architecture but also to the architecture of all times:

One sees that from one plan to the next only the details differ. But whereas one results from an agglomeration of buildings from different periods, the other is methodically conceived according to a comprehensive plan and adapted to a site freed by the fire. In this new Acropolis the apparent dissymmetries are now a means for creating a picturesque ensemble for the most skillfully ponderated group of buildings there ever was.[112]

Camillo Sitte and the picturesque in city design

The most influential book that would further the cause of picturesque design throughout the West toward the end of the century was the Viennese architect Camillo Sitte's *Der Städte-Bau nach seinen künstlerischen Grundsätzen* (City Design According to Its Artistic Principles). Published in Vienna in 1889, Sitte's *Der Städte-Bau* rapidly made its author one of the fathers of urban design. Its influence in Germany and Austria was immediate and extensive, where by 1893 there was a Sittesque school of urban design.[113] In France the book was translated in 1902 by the Swiss architect Camille Martin; in Italy, Sitte, along with the like-minded Belgian Charles Buls, burgomaster of Brussels and author of *Esthétique des villes* (1893), were the guiding lights through the first two decades of the twentieth century of the Associazione Artistica fra i Cultori di Architettura, founded in Rome with later subsidiaries in other cities.[114] In Switzerland, Charles-Edouard Jeanneret (not yet Le Corbusier), began his never-to-be-published book, *La Construction des villes* (The Building of Cities), toward 1910, which explored the precepts of the Sittesque school and even used its designs. Although the later Le Corbusier would reject the Sittesque approach of his youth for urban planning, it had a lasting effect on his development of the architectural promenade.

Sitte's book sets forth what its author believed were the universal principles that had governed urban design from antiquity to the Middle Ages and the Renaissance and then reaching across the Baroque era. Just as Choisy had contradicted the authority of Alexis Paccard's assessment of the absence of intentional planning principles in the Periclean Acropolis with a demonstration of picturesque principles, so too did Sitte offer an alternative to the judgement by the eminent 'theorist of modern city planning R[einhard] Baumeister (who) says in his book about city expansion, "... the various elements which produce a pleasing architectural impression [as regards plazas] *are hardly reducible to universal rules.*" '[115] Chapter by chapter Sitte outlined these universal principles which, in his mind, were synonymous with the picturesque.

In light of the most recent and influential scholarship on Sitte's book, it must be emphasized that Sitte's theme was the picturesque; it permeates the book. If one wishes to find explicit confirmation of its centrality, then one has only to turn to chapter ten, 'Artistic Limitations of Modern City Planning,' where the author repeatedly identifies artistic planning with '*malerisch* planning,' that is, the creation of 'pictorial' effects. The modern grid system of planning had caused the 'mass slaughter of the beauties of city planning.' 'These are the very beauties,' continued Sitte, 'which are designated by the word "pictorial" [*malerisch*].' In order to explain the 'essential ingredient in the charm of ancient and medieval designs,' Sitte began by focusing on the 'striking picturesqueness of Amalfi, for example.' Further on he introduced another argument in a similar manner: 'Assuming that in any new development the cityscape must be made as splendid and pictorial as possible.' Then he examined the extent to which the 'pictorial beauties' of previous 'artistic solutions' can be adapted to the exigencies of modern social, economic, and demographic urban life.[116] The idea that artistic city design meant picturesque design was so fundamental to Sitte that in his opening pages of chapter one he felt obliged to explain: 'In this investigation it is not our intention to recommend that every picturesque beauty of old towns be used for modern purposes, because especially in this area the saying applies: "necessity breaks iron." That which is essential for hygienic or other compelling reasons has to be carried out, even at the cost of any number of pictorial motifs.'[117]

Sitte's *Der Städte-Bau* was a reaction not only to contemporary gridiron planning but also to its recent application in Vienna's new Ringstrasse, where monumental buildings were set out within vast open spaces along the straight and wide thoroughfare that had been established along the former ramparts surrounding the old city. The architect began with a brief consideration of ancient planning where he especially praised the picturesque temple sites about which Choisy would also write ten years later. Like Choisy, Sitte shared the enthusiasm of the Romantic Hellenists.

The ultimate realization of [city design principles] is to be perceived, however, in the great temple precincts of Greek antiquity at Eleusis, Olympia, Delphi, and other places. There architecture, sculpture, and painting are united into an artistic synthesis that has the sublimity and grandeur of a great tragedy or a mighty symphony. The consummate example of this is offered by the Acropolis in Athens.[118]

Later Sitte would lament, 'In the field of city planning the limitations on artistry of arrangement have, to be sure, narrowed greatly in our day. Today such a masterpiece of city planning as the Acropolis of Athens is simply unthinkable.'[119]

Sitte's book, though, is not about the ancient city. As he explained in the

That Public Squares Should Be Enclosed Entities

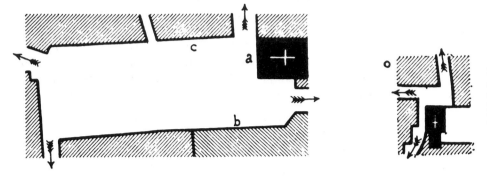

2.21
Analytical drawing, 'that public squares should be enclosed entities.' Piazza S. Pietro, Mantua (left), S. Clemente, Brescia (right)

introduction, he wished to articulate the universally valid principles of artistic city design by looking at examples closer 'in time and space' to contemporary Europeans.[120] Accordingly, he began by looking first at the medieval city, where the picturesque occurred with the greatest visual variety that irregular and asymmetrical arrangements could occasion. Although these cities exhibit important artistic principles, conditions such as greater population, higher cost of land, and modern traffic precluded their wholesale adoption, especially in their picturesque format with highly irregular spaces. Furthermore, the need to create new neighborhoods all at once on the drawing board would make irregular picturesque design seem artificial. To this end, Sitte then turned to Baroque planning, which demonstrated the possibility of a visually enticing, richly variegated solution to rectilinear planning. In addition, what Sitte termed the 'perspective' effects of Baroque urban complexes added further principles to the lessons of medieval cities, which, in turn, could be adapted to a Baroque-inspired format.

Der Städte-Bau nach seinen künstlerischen Grundsätzen is about the planning of urban plazas. It reflects Sitte's conviction at this point in time: 'Only freedom in the composition of plazas can instill life and movement into the total architecture of the city.'[121] Throughout the book Sitte's exposition of the logic behind the asymmetrical and irregular form of urban plazas repeatedly stressed the functional basis of the aesthetically dynamic arrangement. Sitte's artistic principles were conceived according to the reasoned picturesque. Using primarily Italian examples in chapters two through six, Sitte enunciated the basic artistic principles, some of which furnished the chapter's title: 'that the center of plazas be kept free,' 'that public squares should be enclosed entities' (figure 2.21), 'the size and shape of plazas' (small and cozy), 'the irregularities of old plazas,' 'plaza groupings.' Chapter

Improvements in the Modern System

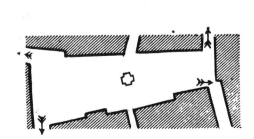

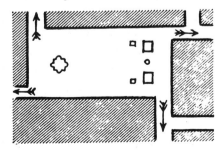

2.22
Analytical drawings. The Neuer Markt, Vienna, as a turbine plaza (left), proposed modern version of the turbine plaza (right)

seven addressed the variations in these principles in northern Europe before ending with a brief consideration of the Baroque.

The modern plaza, lamented Sitte, locates its buildings, fountains, and other monuments in the center. 'But this placement offers only disadvantages. . . . To start with, any lifelike organic integration with the site is ruled out.'[122] In contrast, the ancient, the medieval, and the Renaissance city placed them toward the side and away from the center. Sitte's example of the market fountain can be adduced to show how he employed the reasoned picturesque to explain an artistic principle:

It is precisely those market fountains which seem to stand on the oldest foundations that are most often found to be unsymmetrically situated on such islands in the square – and, as a matter of fact, usually next to the opening of a major street at the most important corner of the square. It may be that the watering of draft-animals in former times, etc., had a decisive influence on the choice of this spot.[123]

Similarly, the irregularity of old plazas joined picturesque aesthetic effect with functional purpose:

The reason for the quite typical irregularity of these old plazas lies in their gradual historical development. One can generally assume that there once was a practical basis for each of these odd curvatures, be it a water channel which has long since ceased to run, or a road, or a building of the shape in question. It is generally realized from personal experience that these irregularities do not have an unpleasant effect at all, but on the contrary, they enhance naturalness, they stimulate our interest, and, above all, they augment the picturesque quality of the tableau.[124]

Like Downing, Viollet-le-Duc, and Choisy before him, Sitte was particularly interested in the question of creating balance in asymmetrical picturesque design:

How unnecessary strict symmetry and geometric exactitude are to the creation of pictorial or architectonic effects has often been emphasized in the discussion of old castles. It has been pointed out that these buildings, in spite of all their irregularities, produce a harmonious effect because each motif is modeled in great clarity and each superstructure is given its counterpart, a balance being assured within the overall composition, albeit with great freedom of conception and a complex interrelationship of motifs. All this is true to an even greater degree in the building of cities, for the latter involves an even more intricate totality than the building of castles, and therefore can and should be treated with even greater freedom, since its motifs are ever so many and can all be combined without disturbing each other.[125]

Whereas contemporary exigencies precluded the wholesale creation of irregularly picturesque urban plans, many of the medieval configurations were susceptible to a modern adaptation according to Baroque principles. For example, the grouping of plazas around a single building, which Sitte celebrated as a means to present separate 'tableaux' all harmoniously related, could be repeated with a Baroque massing of variegated volumes and squares to afford not only a dynamic artistic grouping, but also a highly functional arrangement for the modern city. Similarly, the irregular plaza with intimate closure secured by streets that entered at different angles without continuing across the other side, could become the regular turbine plaza (figure 2.22). The predominance of straight-line planning, though, would not preclude the incorporation of curvilinear irregularities:

Irregularities of terrain, existing waterfalls, and roads should not be forcibly eliminated simply to achieve a banal rectangularity, but should instead be preserved as a welcome excuse for crooked streets and other diversities.[126]

Sitte's most influential immediate followers were extremely interested in these

2.23
Historical example showing appropriate street design

crooked streets and their relationship to urban squares. This issue represented the next logical development for Sitte's picturesque principles. When Camille Martin translated *Der Städte-Bau*, he even added a chapter on streets (figure 2.23), which he inserted after Sitte's chapter on plaza groupings. The Viennese architect's discussion of plaza groupings had stressed, as we have seen, the multiple, related 'tableaux' clustered around the central point of focus, one or more monumental buildings with squares on several sides. Sitte ended by stressing the dynamic sequence of scenes thus created: 'In conclusion, one should keep in mind the special effect that results from walking about from one plaza to another in such a cleverly grouped sequence. Visually our frame of reference changes constantly, creating ever new impressions.'[127] At this point, then, Sitte had considered that essential component of what Burgh had defined as the 'picturesque principle,' the 'path.' In the minds of Sitte's followers, the essential and unavoidable path in the city was to be found in its streets. Whereas the artistically designed plaza was certainly important, the city's more ubiquitous streets could be given artistic form, uniting picturesque 'variety' with the 'path' at every moment for the urban inhabitant and visitor. 'The ideal street,' explained Martin,

must form a completely enclosed unit! The more one's impressions are confined within it, the more perfect will be its tableau: one feels at ease in a space where the gaze cannot be lost in infinity. . . . Moreover, the winding character of the ancient streets kept sealing off perspective views in them while offering the eye a new aspect at each succeeding turn. These meanderings . . . often came about for very practical reasons.[128]

In the years following the publication of *Der Städte-Bau*, Sitte himself came to see the question of street design as the next area to be explored according to the subject of artistic design. The 'matter of street layout' is the principal subject of the prologue to the new periodical, *Der Städtebau*, that Sitte launched with Theodor Goecke in 1904. Written, according to George R. and Christiane Crasemann Collins, 'almost entirely' by Sitte, this prologue explains:

This careful attention to details also brings with it the consideration of a number of special topics which not too long ago one never dreamed of: such as the question of the most appropriate design for street intersections, that of street arrangement in hilly terrain, the layout of concavely or convexly curved streets, [etc.]. All this leads to the conviction that one must break radically with the traditional stereotype of geometric street layouts, that the greatest possible flexibility must be allowed in details, and that one ought not only to accept curvature in streets, but also diverse widths and asymmetrical cross-sections, as well as occasional irregularities in building-frontage lines and in the width of sidewalks, wherever there is a legitimate need for them. Nature and art, historical wisdom and a fresh effervescent life should always go hand in hand, so that dry tedious patterns may be dispensed with [etc.].[129]

These issues may have been considered new by Sitte, who had omitted streets from his book, but they had certainly had been of interest to his followers. Moreover, the aesthetics of street design analyzed by Martin and others presented marked analogies to those of Greek picturesque design that Choisy had discovered: 'displacing the axis' and 'breaking' the vista.[130] Examples of excellent street design, such as the Breitestrasse in Lübeck (figure 2.23) and the Rue des Pierres in Bruges, also demonstrated the principle of focusing each scene on a prominent monument in an asymmetrically balanced composition.

These were principles that especially interested Charles-Edouard Jeanneret, the future Le Corbusier, in his manuscript for *La Construction des villes*. From the title of the book to its outline, this was a thoroughly Sittesque affair. Jeanneret's title was a variation on the French title of Martin's translation – *L'Art de bâtir des villes* – as well as the original *Der Städte-Bau nach seinen künstlerischen Grundsätzen*. As the Collinses point out, *Städte-Bau* in Sitte's day 'still retained much of its literal meaning of "city building." '[131] The contents of Jeanneret's manuscript adhere to Sitte's format by opening with general considerations, followed by a chapter by chapter exposition of specific principles – the layout and parceling up of residential lots, streets, plazas, enclosing walls – and ending with a consideration of the means for implementing these principles, as well as a case study with suggested applications. Just as Sitte had used Vienna, Jeanneret took his home town of La Chaux-de-Fonds as his subject. H. Allen Brooks explains that Jeanneret was familiar with the work of Sitte's followers and that he used tracings of Sitte's plazas, including the two most important ones in *Der Städte-Bau*, the Acropolis of Athens and the Piazza San Marco in Venice.

Jeanneret's discussion of streets would be of considerable importance to his later notion of the architectural promenade as well as to the design of his first Cubist avant-garde Parisian villa, the La Roche-Jeanneret Houses (1923–24). 'This chapter,' the author explained, 'is the most important of all because it is from the design of streets that the impression of either charm or ugliness of a city is gained.'[132] Among the illustrations for this chapter Jeanneret used drawings that Karl Henrici, one of Sitte's most important followers,[133] had published in 'Langweilige und kurzweilige Strassen,' *Deutsche Bauzeitung* (3 June, 1893) (figure 2.24).[134] Here Henrici had addressed the issues that Sitte would later stress as important subjects for further attention – curved streets, concave streets, and the

2.24
Karl Henrici. 'Langweilige und kurzweilige Strassen'

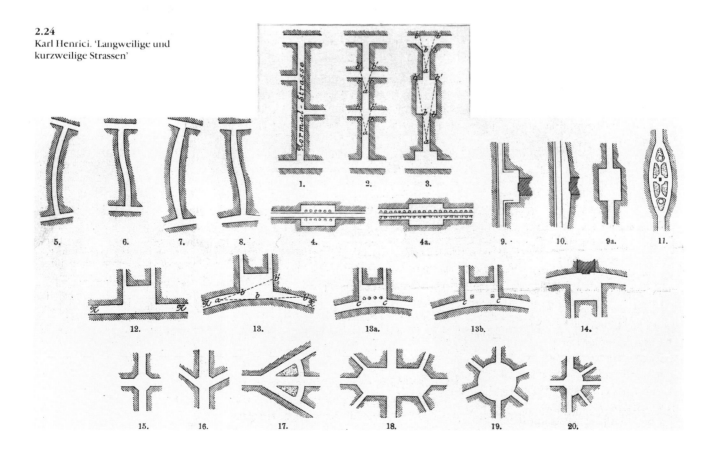

relationship of building massing to streets, along with considerations of perspective views.

Jeanneret was particularly impressed by a street configuration in which an object
of central focus moved into view from one side as the street curved away in the
other direction. Brooks explains that Jeanneret, in giving 'the curved and the
irregular street . . . almost unconditional praise[,] . . . singles out Neuhauserstrasse
in Munich as an example of how to close a view by projecting a building into the
line of sight along a straight stretch. . . .'[135] Jeanneret repeats this configuration and
gives a variant in a series of sketches that explore curving streets that ascend and
then descend (figure 2.25, items a and b). 'The beauty of this solution,' affirmed
Jeanneret, 'surpasses the need for commentary.'[136]

Jeanneret, though, would not share with the public his fascination with the
picturesque through his Sittesque account of city design but rather through a
conversion to the interests of Romantic Hellenism, crystallized by a visit to the
Acropolis and confirmed by a reading of Choisy's *Histoire de l'architecture*. His
vehicle would not be *La Construction des villes* but rather *Vers une Architecture*.
Once again the young architect would make the ideas of another thinker his own. It
is not a question here of plagiarism. Influence is too weak a term. First in Sitte and
then in Choisy, Jeanneret (Le Corbusier) found the revelation of a truth about
architecture whose deep resonance largely determined the course of his future
artistic life.

Le Corbusier defines the architectural promenade

In his 1942 lectures to students of architecture, Le Corbusier explained the
essential importance of the architectural promenade: 'Architecture can be
classified as dead or living by the degree to which the rule of *sequential movement*

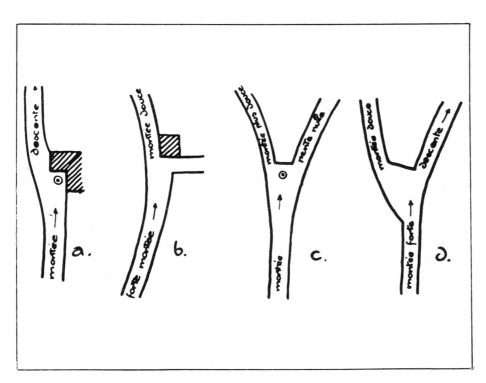

2.25
Charles-Edouard Jeanneret. Street
designs

has been ignored or, instead, brilliantly observed.'[137] From *La Construction des villes* to *Vers une Architecture*, we can trace the evolution of this understanding in the years that prepared Le Corbusier's creative persona for the revolutionary architecture that would follow. The principles of the architectural promenade were certainly closely related to the series of composed views acquired by moving through the Sittesque cityscapes that Le Corbusier had studied and imagined in his first (unpublished) book that he was writing toward 1910. Then in 1911 Jeanneret embarked on his journey to the East that took him through Asia Minor and to Italy and Greece, where he encountered repeated examples of aesthetically powerful sequences of spaces in buildings of various cultures. These experiences nearly reached the public in the form of a book-length manuscript, 'Le Voyage d'Orient,' scheduled to be published by the *Mercure de France* in 1914. The preface to the book that finally appeared in 1966 states that World War I interrupted this project.[138] These travel experiences, were, however, incorporated into *Vers une Architecture*, where they appear among the lessons about picturesque design and the architectural promenade gleaned from Choisy's world history.

Le Corbusier presented the architectural promenade to his readers in two chapters of *Vers une Architecture*: 'Trois rappels à Messieurs les architectes. III: Le Plan' (Three Reminders to Architects. Part III: The Plan) and 'Architecture. II: L'Illusion des plans' (Architecture. Part II: The Illusion of Plans). The first of these chapters uses as its title page the illustration of Choisy's second scene in the sequence of movement at the Periclean Acropolis (figure 1.1). Its presence is emblematic of the complete architectural promenade at the Acropolis as well as the entire phenomenon of the architectural promenade as an essential component in the history of world architecture.

In this chapter Le Corbusier reiterates the lessons of architectural design whereby several historical architectures are explained according to the sequence of spaces that its constituent elements had been organized to create. In every case, Le Corbusier uses Choisy's illustrations as well as his ideas. For ancient Egypt, Le Corbusier reproduces Choisy's axonometric drawing of the Temple of Khons, provided here with the caption (figure 2.16): 'Temple of Thebes. The plan is organized according to the axis of arrival: *allée* of sphinxes, pylons, courtyard with peristyle, sanctuary.' Echoing Choisy again in the text, Le Corbusier explains that Egyptian and Hindu temples used 'symmetry and repetition' as the basis for their architecture.[139] Choisy's axonometric drawing of the Hindu temple is reproduced to illustrate this point further (figure 2.17). As the caption explains, 'The towers create a cadence in space.' The lessons of Greek architecture present a marked contrast. Le Corbusier chooses as the principle of ancient Greek architecture the ponderation of masses in the picturesque scenes of the architectural promenade that Choisy had explained. Hence 'rhythm' in Greek architecture derives from 'compensation (movement of contraries) *(Acropolis of Athens)*.'[140] This is further explained in the captions to the title page illustration (figure 1.1) and to the plan of the Acropolis, also taken from Choisy's book. The first scene illustrates the picturesque principles of Greek composition. The second, with its dotted line showing a path of movement across the site, reveals the sequence of spaces that constitutes the architectural promenade.

The first caption combines Choisy's lessons with a reflection on the emotional impact of the site on the young Swiss architect at the time of his visit:

Acropolis of Athens. View of the Parthenon, Erechtheion, and the statue of Athena Promachos seen from behind the Propylaia. It should not be forgotten that the ground of the

Acropolis is very up and down, with considerable differences in level that have been used to establish imposing bases for the buildings. The whole being out of square provides richly varied vistas of a subtle kind; the asymmetrical masses of the buildings create an intense rhythm. The scene is massive, elastic, living, terribly keen, and dominating.

The second caption expands upon Choisy's analysis by placing the asymmetrical composition of the Acropolis within the wider context of the surrounding site: 'Acropolis of Athens. The apparent disorder of the plan could only deceive the unlearned. The balance of parts is in no way a paltry one. It is determined by the famous landscape that stretches from the Piraeus to Mount Pentelicus.'[141]

In the chapter on the illusion of plans, Le Corbusier argues that the true axis in architecture is not the straight central line of Beaux-Arts pedagogy and design but rather a mental organization that groups a sequence of spaces into a coherent composition related to a visitor's movement. When a straight line axis is used, it is important not to place the main elements along it but rather to dispose them to either side in a dynamically balanced composition. At times, the visitor should also be made to walk to either side and around this central line. Reproducing once again Choisy's second scene of the architectural promenade across the Acropolis, Le Corbusier completes his argument by recounting his own experience during his journey to the East with significant examples of such sequencing:

In Broussa in Asia Minor, at the Green Mosque, you enter by a little doorway of normal human height; a quite small vestibule produces in you the necessary change of scale so that you may appreciate, as against the dimensions of the street and the spot you came from, the dimensions with which it is intended to impress you. . . . You are in a great white marble space filled with light. Beyond you can see a second similar space of the same dimensions, but in half-light and raised on several steps (repetition in a minor key); on each side a still smaller space in subdued light; turning round, you have two very small spaces in shade. From full light to shade, a rhythm. Tiny doors and enormous bays. You are captured, you have lost the sense of common scale. You are enthralled by a sensorial rhythm, (light and volume). . . . What emotion, what faith! There you have motive and intention.

Casa del Noce, at Pompeii. Again the little vestibule which frees your mind from the street. And then you are in the Atrium; four columns in the middle (four *cylinders*) shoot up towards the shade of the roof, giving a feeling of force and a witness of potent methods; but at the far end is the brilliance of the garden seen through the peristyle which spreads out this light with a large gesture, distributes it and accentuates it, stretching widely from left to right, making a great space. . . . After twenty centuries, without any historical reference, you are conscious of Architecture, and we are speaking of what is in reality a very small house.

In actual fact a bird's-eye view such as is given by a plan on a drawing-board is not how axes are seen; they are seen from the ground, the beholder standing up and looking in front of him. The eye can reach a considerable distance and, like a clear lens, see everything beyond what is intended or wished. The axis of the Acropolis runs from the Piraeus to Pentelicus, from the sea to the mountain. The Propylaia are at right angles to the axis, in the distance on the horizon – the sea. . . . This is architecture of the highest order: the Acropolis extends its effects right to the horizon. The Propylaia in the other direction, the colossal statue of Athena on the axis, and Pentelicus in the distance. This is what counts. And because they are outside this forceful axis, the Parthenon to the right and the Erechtheion to the left, *you are enabled to get a three-quarter view of them*, in their full aspects. Architectural buildings should not be placed upon axes. . . .

And here in the House of the Tragic Poet we have the subtleties of a consummate art. Everything is on axis, but it would be difficult to apply a true line anywhere. The axis is in the intention, and the display afforded by the axis extends to the humbler things which it treats most skillfully (the corridors, the main passage, etc.) by optical illusions. The axis here is not an arid thing of theory; it links together the main volumes which are clearly stated and differentiated one from another. When you visit the House of the Tragic Poet, it is clear that everything is ordered. But the feeling it gives is a rich one. You then note clever distortions of the axis which give intensity to the volumes: the central motive of the pavement is set behind the middle of the room; the well at the entrance is at the side of the basin. The fountain at the far end is in the angle of the room. An object placed in the center of a room often spoils the room, for it hinders you from standing in the middle of the room and getting the axial view; a monument placed in the middle of a square often spoils the square and the buildings which surround it – often but not always; in this matter each case must be judged on its own merits.[142]

In Le Corbusier's mind, then, the lessons of sequential spaces and balanced picturesque compositions taught by Sitte and Choisy and confirmed by the experience of a trip to the East came together to establish the primacy of the architectural promenade while offering guidelines for its realization. This understanding informed the design of one of Le Corbusier's early avant-garde buildings, the contiguous La Roche-Jeanneret Houses of 1923–24 erected on a cul-de-sac in the Auteuil section of Paris. It would remain a constant feature of his architecture for the remainder of his life.

Le Corbusier applies the architectural promenade

The La Roche-Jeanneret Houses, Le Corbusier explained, presented a 'picturesque' composition (figures 2.26–2.28).[143] They also were designed around the notion of the architectural promenade. In the first volume of his *Oeuvre complète*, Le Corbusier discussed in great detail how especially in the house for the art collector Raoul La Roche he organized plan and volumes, arranged his doors and windows, and decided upon the colors of the walls to make an aesthetically compelling architectural promenade:

This second |of the two adjacent houses| will be then a little like an *architectural promenade*. You enter: the architectural spectacle offers itself successively to your view: you follow an itinerary and the perspectives develop with a great variety; we play with the afflux of light illuminating the walls or creating shadows. Window bays open views onto the exterior where you rediscover the architectural unity. To the interior, the first experiments with polychromy, based upon the specific effects of colors, permit an '*architectural camouflage*,' that is to say, the affirmation of certain volumes or, in contrast, their de-emphasis. The interior of the house should be *white*, but, *for this white to be appreciable requires the presence of a well ordered polychromy*: the walls in shadow will be blue, those in full light will be red: one makes a building efface itself by painting it in a shadowy earth color, and so forth.[144]

Whereas Le Corbusier has been describing the movement through the house that starts when one enters the central hall, which is a triple-height space with multiple views into other areas and complex plays of light and shadow, he could have begun his account of the architectural promenade from the very entrance into the site. As Kurt Forster has observed, 'Entrance into the [cul-de-sac] is also conceptual initiation into the sphere of Le Corbusier's architectural definition of space.'[145] To understand Le Corbusier's achievement here it is necessary to keep in mind his fascination with both Sittesque principles of street design and Choisy's analysis of the Periclean Acropolis.

The La Roche-Jeanneret Houses close the short cul-de-sac in a way remarkably similar to Le Corbusier's two favorite street designs that he had illustrated and discussed in his unpublished *La Construction des villes* (figure 2.25, a and b). In both streets, it will be remembered, a major focal point slides across the field of vision from the right to capture the attention of the approaching visitor as the space of the street slips away and beyond to the left. Furthermore, the central focal point is seen elevated against the sky by virtue of its position at the high point of the street, which then falls as it moves off the left. In the La-Roche Jeanneret Houses, the painting gallery, literally elevated off the ground and given a convex curve that pushes outward to greet the visitor, slides out from the rectangular mass of the building along the right to arrest the view, while the open space below lets the eye continue beyond and below this central focal point. Le Corbusier has effectively adapted his favorite street design to the volumetric placement of the building on the site. Moreover, the first scene in the sequence of carefully arranged views occurs here as one proceeds down the cul-de-sac on the way to the entrance to the La Roche House.

There is, though, no strident contrast between the exterior and interior scenes in this architectural promenade. As Forster has also observed, the space outside in the cul-de-sac has the quality of an interior just as the space inside the three-story hall gives the feeling of an exterior.[146] To understand Le Corbusier's intentions here it would be helpful to recall that Sitte had stressed that the 'essential ingredient in the charm of ancient and medieval designs' had been achieved by making exteriors seem as if they are at the same time interior so that the viewer would find himself 'at the same time inside a house and on the street.'[147] Le Corbusier, in turn, had devoted a section in the chapter on the illusion of plans in *Vers une Architecture* to a discussion of 'The Outside is Always an Inside.' As the text and drawings concerning ancient Greek and Roman sites reveal, Le Corbusier saw the architectural composition of walls, volumes, windows, doors, and columnar screens in this ancient architecture orchestrating interior architectural and exterior landscape features into a unified composition.

At the La Roche-Jeanneret Houses, Le Corbusier created an equivalency between the exterior cul-de-sac, with its enclosed feeling, and the triple-height hall, with its spacious volume connected visually to the exterior by a large window opening up the wall between them. Inside the hall the white surface of the exterior facade continues without interruption. A single-story bridge over the entrance brings the space down to human dimensions before it bursts open into an expansive volume reminiscent of the outdoor 'room' that one has just left.

Sitte had explained that the way classical and medieval designers had made the exterior seem to be an interior was through 'the external use of interior architectural elements (staircases, galleries, and so on).'[148] Le Corbusier has done the same here but in reverse. In the entrance hall, he has repeated the balcony that projects outward into the cul-de-sac at the far corner of the picture gallery. The double- or triple-height entrance hall, sometimes with a projecting balcony, had been an important feature in modern villa design in Europe and the United States since the last few decades of the nineteenth century (figure 2.29).[149] Le Corbusier's use of this theme in conjunction with the comparable balcony outside gave him the opportunity to interrelate interior and exterior scenes and to make their succession appear natural.

The complementary nature of the outdoor 'room' along the cul-de-sac and the entrance hall is reinforced by the disposition of the two balconies. As Kurt Forster has pointed out, these balconies, which are virtually in the same plane, are equidistant from a center line extended from the projecting volume at the front of the building (figure 2.27).[150] This is the type of geometric control that Choisy had found in the scene in front of the Propylaia (figure 2.12).

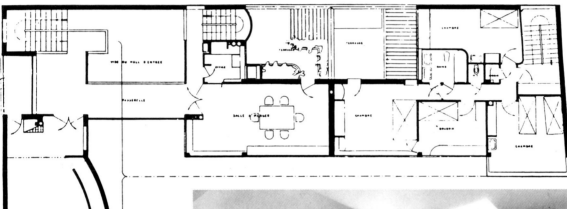

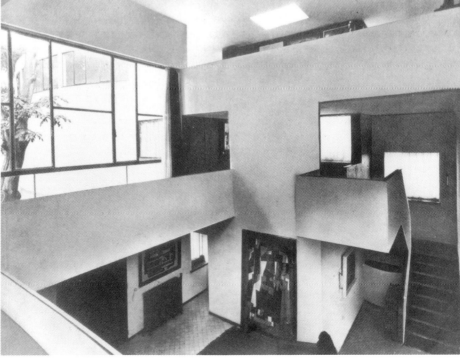

2.26, 2.27, 2.28
Le Corbusier and Pierre Jeanneret, La
Roche-Jeanneret Houses, Paris,
1923–24

Project. In the executed version the
balcony of La Roche House picture
gallery was shifted to the left corner
and the third house to the far right with
the three-story glass facade was not
built

First floor plan

Triple-height entrance hall of the La
Roche House

The peeling away of planes to create a dynamic composition of layered surfaces, with contrasts between solids and voids, and diagonal views across a frontally layered space in the La-Roche Jeanneret Houses present a marked parallel to the principles of synthetic Cubist painting. The next phase of Le Corbusier's development of the architectural promenade would address this issue directly.

2.29, 2.30
Hermann Muthesius. Villa Neuhaus, Berlin-Dahlem, 1906. Entrance hall

Juan Gris. *Harlequin*, June 1919. Oil on canvas, 39⅝″ × 25¼″

Cubism, the architectural system, and the architectural promenade

Cubism, to its contemporaries, was not merely a manner of painting, it was an aesthetic characteristic of the times. Cubist painting, affirmed Le Corbusier in 1924, had preceded the other arts in expressing the contemporary 'geometric spirit.' The 'ends that Cubism is pursuing,' he predicted, 'promise further changes in this direction.'[151] There already were Cubist poets.[152] Cubist architecture, affirmed Le Corbusier, would follow.[153] According to Le Corbusier and Ozenfant, synthetic Cubism, which they called 'crystalline' Cubism, was the second and more advanced form of the new aesthetic that had begun with analytical Cubism. Both artists were attempting to go beyond synthetic Cubism in their Purist paintings;[154] Le Corbusier was determined to adapt the lessons of synthetic Cubism to his avant-garde architecture.

In his next two significant avant-garde houses constructed in the Paris region – the Maison Cook (Boulogne-sur-Seine, 1926) and the Villa Stein (Garches, 1927) – Le Corbusier developed a three-dimensional equivalent to the two-dimensional synthetic Cubism of Juan Gris's paintings. Le Corbusier applied this Cubist aesthetic according to the principles of his architectural system, the 'Five Points for a New Architecture.' Furthermore, he organized the forms and spaces obtained with the Cubist aesthetic and the Five Points according to the picturesque architectural promenade.

The composition in Gris's synthetic Cubist paintings (figure 2.30) can be summarized as consisting of frontally layered planes which are given a counterpoint with diagonal movements and spaces that interpenetrate in S-shaped curves. These are also the basic aesthetic principles that inform the Maison Cook (figures 1.4, 1.5) and the Villa Stein (figures 1.6, 1.7), especially the latter where the S-shaped interpenetrating spaces are more fully developed (figures 2.31). Le Corbusier's technique of using rows of columns to convey the sense of parallel spatial planes has been well-known in the literature of modern architecture since Colin Rowe and Robert Slutzky published their essay in 1963 that defined this 'phenomenal' or conceptual transparency. The term refers to a conceptual as opposed to literal transparency whereby the viewer connects the columns to form a spatial plane that passes through any intervening objects.[155] Within the frontally gridded space created by the arrangement of columns, Le Corbusier places his walls, some straight, others curved, some defining edges, others making sculptural shapes.

As Kurt Forster has observed, Le Corbusier used curved forms to relate either to movement through the building or to 'equipment needed for comfort': 'Curvilinear enclosures invariably accommodate bathrooms, closets, smaller spaces such as the

2.31
Le Corbusier and Pierre Jeanneret. Villa Stein, Garches, 1927. The living-room

library cubicle in the Ozenfant house, toilets, and chimney flues. Tub and toilets, plumbing, fixtures, and lamps are always incorporated into the plans in such a way as to emphasize their compact, near-round bodies.'[156] These objects, when surrounded by curved walls, become metaphorical extensions of the body. They engage the user and visitor with a presence similar to the objects that Marcel Proust's narrator encountered in a hotel at which he was to pass the night. The narrator, it will be remembered, was strongly discomfited by strange rooms. Suddenly, though, he discovered a building in which the architecture and its furnishings exhilarate rather than threaten:

But I had been mistaken. I did not have the time to be dejected, because I was not for an instant alone. That is because there remained of the old palace an excess of luxury, unusable in a modern hotel, and that, removed from any pretense of practical use, had acquired in its lack of occupation a sort of life: corridors returning to their thresholds, from which one crossed at every moment comings and goings without destination, vestibules long like corridors and decorated like parlors, that had the air of living there rather than being part of the residence . . . [and] that immediately offered me their companionship. . . . In other words, the idea of a house, simple container of our present existence and only keeping us safe from the cold, from the sight of others, was totally inapplicable to this dwelling, ensemble of rooms, as real as a colony of people, with a silent life it is true, but that one was obliged to meet, avoid, and welcome when one returned.[157]

It was Le Corbusier's genius to create an architecture which in building after building imparted that dynamic sense of a living relationship between the user and the architectural forms which Proust had so vividly described. Through most of Le Corbusier's mature career, he achieved these effects by establishing a dialectical relationship between the free-standing columns and the walls, arranged as straight planes and as sculptural forms. Furthermore, these elements were often used in conjunction with adjacent single- and double-height spaces.

One can gauge how different Le Corbusier's architecture was from that of other practitioners of what is known as the International Style by comparing the Maison Cook with the adjacent Hôtel Collinet by Robert Mallet-Stevens (figure 2.32). Both buildings, which date from 1926, are of comparable size and program. Both feature unadorned cubical prisms, roof-garden, terraces, large windows, and double-

2.32
Robert Mallet-Stevens. Hôtel Collinet, Boulogne-sur-Seine, 1926. Front and rear facades

height living room with adjacent library and dining room to either side. Only the Maison Cook, though, uses a central row of columns that remain either free-standing, or, generally, as engaged columns whose rounded or square form is still visible. Within the narrow confines of these houses, which are bounded to either side by structural party walls, Le Corbusier chose to use a central row of structural columns, which are just enough to permit the rich dialectic between gridded space and organically shaped walls. In the Villa Stein, the larger area permitted a more complete application of this aesthetic.

Pure form and the mask of simplicity

The Maison Cook and the Hôtel Collinet also differ in another significant way. The massing of Mallet-Stevens's building follows the nineteenth-century tradition of the reasoned picturesque. Without either seeing the interior or knowing the plan, any observer can identify not only the entrance and the garage, but also the staircase and the living room and then distinguish between the bathroom and kitchen, on the one hand, and the library, dining room, and bedrooms, on the other hand. Each function is given the appropriate volume and window size, which are revealed to the exterior.

In contrast, the Maison Cook presents a mystery to the first-time visitor who approaches its facade. Le Corbusier has utilized his 'Five Points for a New Architecture' to present the viewer with what he termed a 'mask of simplicity.' This new attitude, which is a radical departure from the picturesque massing of the La Roche-Jeanneret Houses, enabled Le Corbusier to realize even further his goal of creating a Cubist architecture.

In an article of 1924 on Mallet-Stevens, Le Corbusier criticized the use of picturesque massing that he himself had embraced in the La Roche-Jeanneret Houses:

One can certainly say that [Mallet-Stevens] has a love of forms, and if one wanted to quibble a little, one could even say that he loves them so much that he uses too many. After this first flowering . . . of multiple forms pressing against each other, of irregular and agitated silhouettes . . . will come the recognition that light is more generous to a simple prism and that this complexity, this excessive wealth, this exuberance of forms will be disciplined under the aegis of the pure form. It will become evident that the whole is worth more than five or ten parts. This tendency toward the pure envelope that covers a richness with a mask of simplicity can only follow. We have time to wait.[158]

Le Corbusier pursued this critique of the 'artificial and illusory picturesque' in his letter of October 1925, which accompanied his second project for the unrealized Villa Meyer.[159] With the Maison Cook and the Villa Stein, Le Corbusier would create an interior of considerable 'richness,' which he concealed behind a 'mask of simplicity.'

The transformation of the facade into a mask of simplicity at the Maison Cook enabled Le Corbusier to translate into architecture the fundamental Cubist device of presenting a face in frontal view with an overlapping profile. In Cubist portraits, such as Gris's *Harlequin* (1919) (figure 2.30), this simultaneous presentation of frontal and side views of the subject's face provides the artist with a major organizational principle. The same is true of the composition of the Maison Cook.

Although the Maison Cook has a front facade, it paradoxically has no front door (figure 1.4). Entrance, as is pointed out in two captioned photographs in the *Oeuvre complète*, is through a door in the middle of a central cross-wall. On the

2.33
Le Corbusier and Pierre Jeanneret.
Maison Cook, Boulogne-sur-Seine,
1926. Living-room, occupying the left
half of the third and fourth floors. The
dining area is to the right at the front;
the library is to the upper right at the
rear

next two floors, the major activity spaces, which are grouped to the left of this wall, are entered through doors directly above this entrance door. A separate stairway to the top-level library varies this theme. Hence, although there is a central facade, the 'facade' through which one repeatedly enters and exits is the central cross-wall, which becomes the equivalent to the Cubist face rotated through ninety degrees.

This impression is reinforced by the volumetric arrangement of the interior. The double-height living room, bounded by this cross-wall, extends from front to rear (figure 2.33). Like the entrance hall of the La Roche-Jeanneret Houses, this living room presents the aspect of an 'exterior.' As a result, the cross-wall seen here appears as an interior 'facade' facing an interior 'outdoor' space.

The analogy between the actual facade and the cross-wall as rotated facade is strengthened by the parallel between the two balconies. In the La Roche-Jeanneret Houses, as we have seen, the balconies outside and over the hall are parallel, nearly aligned, and even equidistant from the projecting volume at the front of the house (figure 2.27). Similarly, the Maison Cook has paired balconies, each projecting outward just to the left of center on its respective 'facade.'

Finally, both exterior and interior 'facades' use Gris's characteristic Cubist four-part division of the face with tonal reversals to either side of the center line in the eyes above and the mouth below. In the *Harlequin*, for example, each side of the face is a different value: dark left, light right. The eye and mouth on each side is given the color and tonal value of the other side of the face: dark eye and mouth on the light right side, light eye and mouth on the dark left side. At the Maison Cook this four-part division is achieved through the contrasts between light and darkness or between deep and flat spaces in each 'facade.' The front facade, for example, presents on the top level a shallow concave space to the left and the deep space of the roof terrace to the right. This pattern is reversed on the ground level where the deep garden space is on the left and the convex entrance hall is recessed in a shallow space to the right. On the interior 'facade' the reversals are achieved through depth and flatness: deep left and shallow right above, shallow left and deep right below. As might be expected, these relationships are the reverse of those on the exterior facade.

The two facades at the Maison Cook are also important markers in the sequence of views and spaces of the architectural promenade. In each scene, whether frontal or diagonal, Le Corbusier achieves a balance of asymmetrically disposed elements in this Cubist composition. In 1912 Raymond Duchamp-Villon had exhibited at the Salon d'Automne a Maison Cubiste (figure 2.34), whose facade had been inspired by the first phase of Cubist painting, called analytical Cubism. Now Le Corbusier was offering not merely a facade but rather an entire building that translated the principles and themes of the second phase of Cubism, synthetic Cubism, into architectural design.

Duchamp-Villon's facade had depicted a traditional French town house or *hôtel*, dating from the last century of the *Ancien Régime*, in a Cubist manner. The choice of this pre-Revolutionary model was neither arbitrary nor accidental. Throughout the nineteenth and into the twentieth century the French *hôtel* had remained a quintessentially French institution. Julien Guadet's popular textbook written for Beaux-Arts students and first published in 1901 dated the birth of the 'modern dwelling' from the development of the eighteenth-century French *hôtel*.[160] So popular was its example that conservative French-speaking Swiss architects in the years immediately preceding World War I still used the model of the eighteenth-century French *hôtel* to establish the French cultural identity of their architecture.[161] Even Auguste Perret in his apartment building at 25 bis Rue Franklin (Paris, 1903), with its revolutionary expressed concrete frame, modeled the floor plans on the traditional *hôtel*.[162] Duchamp-Villon followed this tradition in the facade of his Maison Cubiste. So did Le Corbusier with the Maison Cook, for he was deeply concerned with French cultural identity.

At the time Duchamp-Villon presented his Maison Cubiste at the Salon d'Automne, Le Corbusier, at that time still Charles-Edouard Jeanneret, was seeking to assist peoples of French culture, especially France and his own French-speaking Switzerland, in developing their own, typically French decorative arts. The year 1912 saw the publication of Jeanneret's *Etude sur le mouvement d'art décoratif en Allemagne*, which had been commissioned by the Ecole d'Art in his home town of La Chaux-de-Fonds, and which was directed toward the French and the French Swiss. The next year Jeanneret was among the founding members of L'Oeuvre, the French Swiss counterpart to the Deutsche Werkbund. 'Throughout the early teens,' explains Nancy Troy,

and until he moved to Paris in 1917, Jeanneret supported himself primarily as a decorator for several wealthy families prominent in the watch-making industry of La Chaux-de-Fonds. In choosing objects for the interior ensembles he designed, Jeanneret looked to Paris, not only for the purchase of specific materials but also to study the most progressive French *décor*, which was shown each year at the Salon d'Automne.[163]

At this time, Jeanneret, as Troy demonstrates, was concerned with creating a modern French style in the decorative arts,[164] a field that, for progressives, was closely associated with reform in the domain of architecture. This interest in national cultural identity persisted at least into the mid-1920s, for in *La Peinture*

2.34
Raymond Duchamp-Villon. Maison
Cubiste, 1912

moderne (1925), Jeanneret and his co-author Amédée Ozenfant stressed that
national character would be apparent even among the international tendencies in
modern painting.[165] Le Corbusier then availed himself of the opportunity to design
the Maison Cook to invest the traditional French *hôtel* with modern form. Recipro-
cally, he gave national identity to the new Cubist architecture.

To understand Le Corbusier's intentions here it is important to recall the features
of the eighteenth-century *hôtel* as they were codified toward 1730. At this time, the
interior received its most variegated development of rooms of different sizes and
decor to serve varied functions. The building's facades, though, exhibited a neutral
regularity that in no way revealed the irregularity behind the exterior walls. Only
the entrance and the central salon were easily distinguishable. The floor plans and
facades of an ideal *hôtel* presented by Jacques-François Blondel in a treatise on the
subject prepared around this time demonstrate this dichotomy. In short, the
eighteenth-century *hôtel* presented a simple mask to the exterior and richly varied
forms to the interior.[166] The parallel with Le Corbusier's Maison Cook and Villa
Stein is self-evident.

The analogy, though, does not end here. As has been noted by several eminent
architectural writers, the interlocking spaces in Le Corbusier's Cubist villas present
marked analogies both to the varied geometrical shapes of adjacent rooms in the
eighteenth-century French *hôtel*, made possible by the use of *poché*, and to the use
of those interstitial spaces between rooms, the *dégagement*, for the circulation into
the more private realms of the home.[167]

The only important element of the eighteenth-century French hôtel missing
here is the axial procession through the principal public rooms arranged one after
the other, that is, *en enfilade*. It would appear, though, that Le Corbusier has
transformed the linear *enfilade* into his picturesque architectural promenade. Yet
even here he seems to have been following the lessons of Choisy who, in demonstrating the dominant role of the architectural promenade in world architecture,

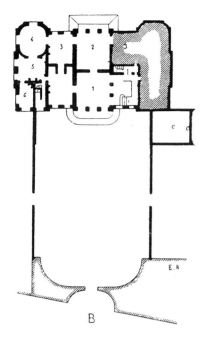

2.35
Jean Aubert and Jacques Gabriel. Hôtel
du Maine (later Hôtel de Biron, now
Musée Rodin), Paris, 1728–30.
Analytical plan by Choisy

had included a study of the important eighteenth-century Hôtel du Maine
(1728–30), now the Musée Rodin (figure 2.35).

Choisy presented the Hôtel du Maine, not in terms of axis and cross-axes, but
rather as organized into two suites of rooms to either side of a central axis, each
suite with an architectural promenade that circles around, passing from the
entrance to the most private rooms. The reader can follow this progression by
proceeding through the rooms numbered one through six in a counter-clockwise
manner along the left side of the *hôtel*. In the Maison Cook, Le Corbusier appears to
have combined Choisy's division of the French *hôtel* into two zones with the
synthetic Cubist procedure of simultaneously showing a face in profile and frontal
views. Translated into architecture, this meant presenting the two related facades
at right angles and linking them by an architectural promenade.

The problem of creating a modern national style, as the French Swiss architect
Camille Martin had recognized, was that it was seen as requiring the revival of past
styles.[168] At the Maison Cook, Le Corbusier resolved this dilemma by substituting
an abstraction of the French *hôtel* type for a revival of eighteenth-century French
architectural style. The attraction of eighteenth-century French interior design had
been especially powerful throughout the development of turn-of-the-century
French Art Nouveau.[169] Duchamp-Villon's subsequent Maison-Cubiste had relied
heavily upon a recognizable French style. At the Maison Cook, however, Le
Corbusier used an abstracted configuration of the eighteenth-century *hôtel* plan in
conjunction with the essential dichotomy between the impassive facade and the
highly variegated interior. In this way, he resolved the dilemma of creating a
modern architecture with national identity.

The ramp buildings

Le Corbusier's architectural promenade changed radically when he designed the
Villa Savoye around a central ramp (figures 1.8–1.10). This was followed by a series
of ramp buildings, extending through the remainder of the architect's career, in
which the ramp organizes the spatial ballet of successive and asymmetrically
balanced views. Whereas in some of these buildings it is still possible to weave
through variegated spaces, now the sloping element of the ramp, itself an active
sculptural component in the composition, provides the physical and conceptual
axis for the architectural promenade.

In creating a three-dimensional architectural equivalent to synthetic Cubist
aesthetics, Le Corbusier had already found a way to exploit the visual excitement of
diagonal views across the horizontal plane. With the ramp he introduced a diagonal
form into the vertical dimension as well. Its significance can be gauged largely from
his expression of wonder and awe in *Vers une Architecture* at the diagonal forms in
the interior of Santa Maria in Cosmedin (figure 2.36). One notes that all the
components of Le Corbusier's future Cubist architecture are here: the gridded
space with parallel planes established by the columns and the floor pattern, the
circular forms that are placed within this gridded volume, and the diagonal thrust
of the pulpit and lectern:

In the silent equilibrium of Santa Maria in Cosmedin, the oblique handrail of the pulpit rises,
the stone book rest of a lectern tilts at an angle in a silent conjugation like a gesture of assent.

NEF DE SAINTE-MARIE DE COSMÉDIN, an 790 et 1120 après J.-C.

2.36
Santa Maria in Cosmedin, Rome

From Le Corbusier, *Vers une Architecture* (1923)

These two modest obliques, which harmonize in the perfect movement of a spiritual mechanics, this is the pure and simple beauty of architecture.[170]

With his ramp buildings, Le Corbusier incorporated the gentle diagonal as an active element in the architectural promenade. It was not simply a sculptural form, nor merely the directing agent for movement, for it served a third function as well. The dynamism of gentle kinesthetic experience that Le Corbusier had anticipated in the Sittesque scenes of rising and descending streets for his unpublished *La Construction des villes* now became an integral feature of building design.

The ramp offered the perfect solution for the architectural promenade in a building designed according to the 'Five Points for a New Architecture.' On the one hand, it enabled a gentle, continuous movement from floor to floor. As the *Cahiers d'Art* explained in introducing the Villa Savoye, 'this communication between floors without the assistance of steps permits, when one has the requisite space, a passage from floor to floor that is hardly perceptible.' At the same time, the ramp offers the pedestrian equivalent to an airplane's take-off from the ground, a type of movement well suited to the building elevated on columns, which Le Corbusier termed *pilotis*. In the Villa Savoye (figures 1.9, 1.10), the ramp rises from the vestibule on the ground floor, passes through the interior of the house up to the main floor with living accommodations, then continues outside along the large elevated terrace and terminates on the next higher level, which is fashioned as a roof-garden with solarium. The ramp, then, makes the free-standing building elevated off the ground into a convincing statement about man's relationship to nature. As the *Cahiers d'Art* expressed it:

All of Le Corbusier's houses until this time were built on restricted sites; and the one in Garches had to take into account neighbors on the right and left. The Villa Savoye occupies among Le Corbusier's constructions a very special place, because it is completely isolated. The problem to solve here confronts every person who, after work, seeks to re-establish contact with organic nature, with plants, sky, and countryside. It is the problem that arises every time that one seeks to re-establish the link with nature, be it by the sea, in the mountains (for a sanatorium, a place of rest) or as here, on a vast undulation of the valley of the Seine, close to Paris. Just as over the course of the last years [Frank] Lloyd Wright used the slightest rock crevice to marry his houses as much as possible to the earth, it is exactly the opposite that is proposed here. Our attitude toward nature is completely different today. It is less a question of passively adapting oneself to the ground than of uniting with the country-side: with the sky, and especially with the air! The house rests on *pilotis* and the real living quarters are located on the first floor above the ground. The urban client for whom this construction is intended aspires to dominate the landscape rather than finding himself close to the trees and bushes. He wants to enjoy the panorama, the wind, the sun. He wants to feel the full liberty of nature, of which he is deprived in his profession. We know of no other house that expresses so clearly these imponderables.

The text then proceeds to explain the 'structure of the house': 'The house is a cube resting on *pilotis*. The cube is not a solid mass, but rather is cut out on the southeast and southwest sides such that the rising sun hits not only the exterior surfaces but also penetrates into the interior of the house.'[171] The large living room, measuring 5×14 meters, has two walls faced with sliding horizontal windows. The third wall facing the equally large outdoor terrace is surfaced with plate glass over two-thirds of its length. Half of this glass wall slides back to throw open the living room to the terrace.[172] And at the head of the composition is the ramp, which leads up from the ground to these main places before continuing up through the terrace to the top roof-garden.

In each successive building in which the ramp plays a central role in the architectural promenade, Le Corbusier used it as an integral component for a revised plastic treatment of the 'Five Points for a New Architecture.' In Dr Currutchet's house (La Plata, 1949) (figures 1.14–1.17), Le Corbusier fractured the volume in two and had the ramp join the two pieces across the garden between them. The ramp moves up through a complex interlocking composition of interior and exterior volumes of different sizes and heights, which becomes the distin-guishing spatial characteristic of the entire composition.

In the Villa Shodhan (Ahmedabad, 1952–56) (colour plate 2, figure 1.20), Le Corbusier explored once again the ramp that ascends through a cubical volume. 'This plan,' explains the *Oeuvre complète*, 'recalls the ingenuity of the Villa Savoye of 1929–30 at Poissy, placed here in a tropical and Indian setting.'[173] The difference in style derives largely from the abandonment of the closed box with thin facades in favor of the open box with deep sun-breaks and the concomitant switch from the smooth white stucco surfaces evocative of a machine aesthetic to the rough surfaces of 'raw concrete . . . showing the imprint of the wooden formwork . . . purposefully left unfinished.'[174]

In the Villa Shodhan the deep facades with sun-breaks are not isolated events but rather participate in a complete reformulation of the 'Five Points for a New Architecture.' Here then is a new version of the free facade, one that has been developing at least since Dr Currutchet's house. These deep wall fins, which form verandas on the ground level, also serve as a counterpoint to the free-standing piers of the free plan. In the Villa Shodhan, the vertical supports are not round columns but rather piers with a directionality at right angles to the sun-breaks. In effect, the

reinforce the sense of the home as the family's domain and its comforting refuge. We can trace the evolution of the architect's thought on this subject from the formal and ceremonial entrance sequence at the Winslow House (1893) (colour plate 12, figure 1.39) to the private and hidden entrance to the Robie House (1909) (figures 1.27, 1.30, 1.55). In each case the fireplace with massive chimney-stack serves as the symbolic center of the home as well as the compositional center of the design. The *mise en scène* is arranged to throw this central hearth into focus.

The entrance to the Winslow House is in the center of the front facade. Here Wright raised the line of the stone plinth to fashion a ceremonial stone frame around the front door and its related windows, which light the reception hall just behind it. This central bay is preceded by a paved 'esplanade' with a formally patterned pool and surrounding planted bed. At each transition point between one feature and the next Wright places a couple of steps, which heighten the sense of a progression away from the most public to a more private domain. The overall effect is of a stately ceremonial approach to the house, in general, and to the front door, in particular.

From the elevated platform in front of the central door of the Winslow House, one proceeds into the 'reception hall,' which is divided into two levels and three zones: a preliminary antechamber of about the same depth as the front exterior stoop with its steps, a transitional space reached by a couple of additional steps, and then an inner sanctum set off by a columnar screen. This inner sanctum contains the massive masonry wall with the 'integral fireplace,' as well as seating to either side. As mentioned above in chapter one, the wooden columnar screen is reminiscent of a rood screen in a church, which sets off the chancel from the nave. Perhaps Wright was taking a lesson here from the Tudor arch screen in Richard Upjohn's Kingscote (1839) in Newport, Rhode Island, which separates the front portion of the entrance hall from the stair hall just beyond.[180] In Wright's house, though, the religious connotation is developed even more effectively because the central hearth appears as a domestic altar at the end of this spatial sequence and at the virtual center of the house.[181]

If we move ahead to 1900 when Wright experimented with two different house plan types, we can see a radically different approach to the entrance sequence. Gone is the central door, with its ceremonial stone surround, as found in the Charnley, Winslow, and Heller houses. Instead Wright was developing a complicated sequence of movements, combining shifts, steps, and turns that make the arrival in front of the fireplace in the living-room seem as if one has reached a secluded inner sanctum much removed from the outer world. In all these instances, we find a perfect application of Viollet-le-Duc's notion of the *mise en scène*. At the same time, though, Wright doubled the goal of the *mise en scène* by creating a sheltered outdoor terrace as an alternative destination. This pairing of the fireplace and the exterior terrace corresponds to Bachelard's dialectic of shelter and expansiveness.

Wright's two plan types can be found in the two neighboring residences built in 1900 in Kankakee, Illinois: the Hickox and Bradley houses (figures 1.40–1.43). Although the houses are similar in massing, in the sense that the steeply sloped roofs project outward from the central chimney at right angles to each other, their plans are dramatically different. The Hickox House offers a formal, axial sequence of the public rooms — living-room in the center with semi-octagonal apse-like extensions that serve as the dining-room and the music room. This plan type, as

2.38, 2.39

Frank Lloyd Wright. Susan Lawrence Dana House, Springfield, Ill., 1902. View across the gallery

Frank Lloyd Wright. Avery Coonley House, Riverside, Ill., 1907. Living room with a view through the gallery toward the dining room

Hitchcock has observed, Wright had used earlier, as in the Emmond House of 1892 in La Grange, Illinois.[182] In the Emmond House, the central space is a library with double pocket doors on either side that open to the reception room on the left and the dining-room on the right.

In these houses Wright was working with an established plan type that Alexander Jackson Davis had popularized in his Gothic revival houses of the 1830s and 1840s, such as Donaldson's Gothic Villa (1834) and the Rotch House (1845) (figure 2.40).[183] Here the central space is a hall or saloon, which opens to either side to the living-room (drawing-room or parlor) and dining-room. This central hall, moreover, is situated behind the front door, placed in the middle of the front facade and behind a shallow porch.

In adapting this plan type, Wright brought his visitors and occupants into the house not through the central room of the axial sequence but rather through an entry room placed off to the side. Wright opened his central room to the exterior not for entry but rather as a way to reach an adjacent terrace from within the house. By the time he designed the Hickox House, he surrounded this terrace with the type of low wall that he would repeatedly use in his Prairie houses in order to extend the inside to the outside in the form of a private domain.

In addition, the entrance sequence in the Hickox House has become rather convoluted. We follow the arriving person who walks up several steps into the semi-octagonal porch where he or she shifts to the right side to pass into the entry before moving to the left side of the entrance hall in order to come into the long three-part living-, dining-, and music room. Even at this point one still has to turn to face the fireplace. The frontal arrangement of the Winslow House is no longer present.

The Bradley House (figures 1.42, 1.43) presents a T-plan which, as Hitchcock has noted, 'prepares the way for such a mature masterpiece as the Willits house two years later.'[184] Once again, the basic plan configuration derives from American domestic architecture, in this case, the T-plan that Bruce Price used in the Kent House (Tuxedo Park, New York, 1885) (figure 2.41), a building, along with Price's Chandler House, that Wright studied closely for the massing of the front facade in

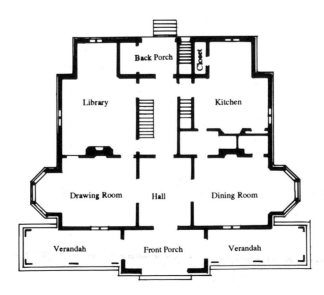

2.40
Alexander Jackson Davis. Rotch House, New Bedford, Mass., 1845

his own home constructed in 1889.[185] In the Bradley House, the living- and dining-rooms are arranged at right angles to the chimney stack, which faces the larger living-room. This configuration enabled Wright to break down the box, as he put it, by presenting adjacent rooms with a flow of space that nonetheless maintained discrete identity for each place. Entrance is effected through the other side of the T, which extends outward from the fireplace in a direction opposite to the dining-room. The 'box' is further broken down by the roof that projects beyond the entrance rooms to cover a porte-cochère and by the semi-octagonal bay that pushes the living-room out into its low-walled terrace.

In the Bradley House the *mise en scène* of the entry sequence is even more complicated than in the Hickox House. Although the porte-cochère has an axial arrangement, the projecting semi-octagonal bay of the reception room shifts the arriving person over to the right side where he or she is obliged to turn, climb several steps, and then turn again to open the door. Once in the entry one turns back again and is subsequently required to make one or two more turns before passing into the living-room where still another partial turn is needed in order to face the fireplace. A compressed transitional space separates the dining-room from the adjacent living-room.

In the Ward Willits House (Highland Park, 1902) (figures 1.44, 1.45) this spatial sequence of twists and turns and subtle changes of level is clarified and made more emphatic. This is the building that Henry-Russell Hitchcock has termed 'the first masterpiece among the Prairie houses' with its 'brilliant extension of the cruciform

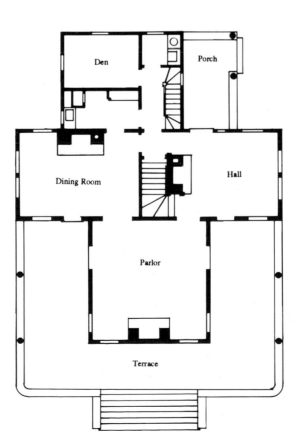

2.41
Bruce Price. William Kent House, Tuxedo Park, New York, 1885

plan,'[186] now more fully developed than the T-plan of the Bradley House. From the porte-cochère one ascends a few steps, walks forward to the door, enters into the left side of the entrance room, and moves over to the far right side where several more steps lead to a transitional space that faces the side of the fireplace as well as the wood-slatted back to the fireside seat. Here one turns to enter the living-room and then turns again to face the fireplace. Three more twists and turns are required to arrive at the center of the dining-room and still another turn to face the dining-room fireplace.

A large part of the effectiveness of Wright's *mise en scène* derives from the rich combination of adjacent rooms with views into various spaces, as well as the variation of ceiling heights. We have seen how Le Corbusier combined single-, double-, and even triple-height spaces as well, to great effect. Wright did the same, usually offering a double-height living-room with mezzanine or a raised ceiling for the living-room with lower spaces along the periphery, either in the same or adjoining rooms. The 'Home in a Prairie Town' project of 1901 features a double-height living-room with mezzanine gallery that extends outward over the fireplace to bring the ceiling height down at this point and adjacent single-height library and dining-room to either side. The high barrel-vaulted dining-room of the Dana house has a lowered ceiling on all four sides: at the entrance the ceiling is brought down while the wall above is opened to a second-story gallery; to the sides the lower ceiling forms side 'aisles'; and at the end it covers a semi-circular breakfast niche. The volumetrics of the gallery are even more complex. In the Isabel Roberts House (figure 2.42) the double-height living-room is made to seem as if it cuts into the second floor to fashion a projecting gallery that lowers the ceiling in front of the fireplace while giving the volume of the living-room a semi-octagonal projection into the mezzanine area that is defined not by full walls but rather by the parapet of the balcony. Finally, the Robie House (figure 1.55) drops the ceiling along the two long sides of the unbroken living- and dining-room, two zones that are separated by the chimney stack, which in turn is opened in the center to permit a continuous view down the length of this great double room. The ceiling also drops down at the far triangle bays that extend out under the deeply cantilevered roof. The combination of single- and double-height spaces or of raised and lowered ceilings, along with the compression and expansion of spaces between parallel walls, in the architecture of Frank Lloyd Wright as well as Le Corbusier, served the multiple purposes of the picturesque, ranging from the *mise en scène* to the desire to create variety that gave life to the architecture.

In the Robie House, Wright completed the logic of his increasingly complicated pathways into the home. In direct contrast to the ceremonial central entrance of the Winslow House, the Robie House displays no apparent entrance on either of its two street facades (figures 1.27, 1.30). Here it may be helpful to recall Louis Kahn's remark that the Pantheon was a perfect building except that it had a doorway. He meant that as soon as one enters this perfect cylindrical space one feels as if one is occupying the center under the round opening, or oculus, of the dome. The building's fault, so to speak, consisted in requiring the visitor to walk from the entrance to this central point. The Robie House presents an analogous experience. Viewed from the exterior the entire house appears to emanate from within, from the pivotal core of the massive chimney that anchors the perpendicular roof forms which appear to fly off into space at different levels. Unlike the Pantheon, the Robie House does not hide its interior space. Yet the numerous levels and planes created by the horizontal brick walls with stone base and coping, the elevated terrace, and

2.42
Frank Lloyd Wright. Isabel Roberts
House, River Forest, Ill., 1908. The
living room

the roofs impart a richly ambiguous impression of the house's domain. This keeps
the inwardly radiating building from appearing as an oppressive prison.

In addition, the *mise en scène* at the Robie House, which takes the arriving
person from the street into the house and up to the living room on the second level,
is the one of the most skillful in Wright's domestic architecture. In his masterful
book on this building, Donald Hoffmann diagrams this path, which takes a person
around to the rear of the house and through a dark and narrow passageway, then up
the stairs to the main floor. Hoffmann writes that Wright 'honors the living room by
an approach of great deference and subtlety,' which he explains as follows:

Through repeated counterclockwise turns, the way to the living room condenses and
reverses the long path from the south sidewalk to the entrance hall and stairwell: two
complete but opposite revolutions lie between a central position outside the house and a
central place indoors. The stairs rise toward the south front but turn twice to the left before
ending at a second and smaller hall; they fail to reach the living room.[187]

At this point the visitor must still proceed around the back of the wood-slatted
screen of the fireplace seat before arriving at the fireplace itself. From here one has
the option of proceeding out to the elevated terrace or, as Grant Hildebrand has
demonstrated, of enjoying simultaneously the experience of 'refuge' and 'prospect'
'without being seen,' thanks to the sight-lines created by the low parapet wall of the
terrace.[188] In the Robie House, Wright has combined his 'grammar' of the house
with the *mise en scène* of the arrival sequence to make one of the most powerful
statements about the sanctity of the home and the psychological sense of shelter
that a true home might convey.

This emphasis on the hidden entrance was also a distinguishing feature of many of Wright's institutional buildings where it reinforced the inward looking quality of the main space. In the Larkin Administration Building (figures 1.31–1.33) Wright established a pattern that he would continue throughout his career, of sliding the user into the building between the main atrium space and a subsidiary volume.[189] Although buildings such as the Larkin Administration Building, Unity Temple (colour plates 8, 9), Johnson Wax Administration Building (colour plate 5, figures 1.34, 1.35), and even the Guggenheim Museum (colour plate 11, figures 1.36, 1.37) have main spaces of strong regularity, Wright never establishes a central axis from the street into this space. As a result, the atrium space seems to emanate outward from within. In each of these buildings Wright has crafted a careful *mise en scène* to make the visitor feel as if he or she has left the outside world of ordinary space to enter a special, even sacred spatial realm. We have seen in chapter one how Vincent Scully has described the powerful effect of the dark, compressed cave-like entrance to the Johnson Wax Administration Building, which is a prelude to the tall, light-filled atrium. We can follow Scully profitably as he describes the entrance sequence into Wright's earlier institutional buildings:

Entrance [to the Larkin Company Administration Building] was at the side, under a portal set back between the main mass and the thin, subsidiary office block, from the end of which a metallic sheet of water sprang. Here Wright achieved one of the first of his monumental spatial sequences. The exterior is challenging and rather forbidding, but it tells us that something is contained inside. Entrance to it must be sought. It is finally found in the dark place behind the fountain. The block is thus penetrated surreptitiously, as it were, and essentially from below. The advance is from outer light toward interior dimness beyond which, to the left, somewhat more light could be perceived filtering down between the spatial piers. These then rise up toward their rich capitals in a climactic spatial expansion, lighted from above ... and creating ... an idealized interior space cut off from the world outside. ... Unity Church ... also creates an ideal interior space.... That space is again a hieratic progress: along a slightly raised platform at the side between two blocks, under a low entrance, into a dark place beyond which, after a tortuous passage, the main meeting place opens as an embracing room. ... The light is almost golden from the tinted skylights above.[190]

Like Le Corbusier, Wright also made powerful use of ramps in his sequencing of spaces. The most effective, and influential, is the Solomon R. Guggenheim Museum in New York, designed in 1944, but not built until 1956. Here the ramp is integral to the very concept and experience of the museum exhibition space. Upon entering the main atrium exhibition gallery, the visitor takes an elevator to the top level at which point he or she begins the winding descent down the spiraling ramp that leads from painting to painting along the outer walls. The relatively intimate size of the interior permits a panoramic view of the exhibition even across the other side of the room. In this building the ramp itself, as well as the other museum visitors, also become part of the spectacle.[191] As in Le Corbusier's Carpenter Center for the Visual Arts (figures 1.18, 1.19), the ramp in the Guggenheim Museum functions not as the preparatory agent of a *mise en scène*, but rather as an integral component of the architectural promenade.

Finally, even in the restricted spaces of the Usonian houses, Wright created a skillful *mise en scène* to heighten the feeling of a hidden inner sanctum as well as to surprise and delight the user and visitor. Beginning with the first Usonian home, the Jacobs House of 1937 (figures 1.62–1.64), Wright established his typical approach to these modest family dwellings: closed wall to the street, open window wall toward the rear garden and yard. A thin band of clerestory lighting just below the roofline along the outer wall not only allowed light to enter from this front side, but also strengthened the impression of a sheltering roof hovering above, while suggesting life, tantalizingly hidden from view, to the other side. In other words, Wright's closed exterior wall presented not the image of an unwelcoming fortress, but rather the suggestion of domestic pleasures discreetly hidden from view.

This arrangement, which gave physical and psychological privacy to the house, was seconded by the entrance sequence. In the Jacobs House, entrance is through a door at the far end of the carport created by the deeply projecting roof at the corner of the building. Upon entering one has only a partial view down the corridor of the bedroom wing, because a side wall of the second bedroom reaches outward to block the view as the corridor turns outward and out of view. To the right the visitor is afforded a partial view of the main interior spaces. The scene is a powerfully composed asymmetrical composition that is skillfully balanced in the manner of the 'ponderated' scenes of the Periclean Acropolis. The view is focused at the far end by two vertical slits of windows that rise from floor to ceiling. This long prospect serves as a visual fulcrum for two other paired views of spaces that are contained within the brick cross walls to either side. At the left side and close at hand is the cozy dining alcove with its lowered ceiling and recessed lighting; to the right and beyond the brick cross wall is a partial view of the living room with its tall ceiling reaching upward to 2.82 metres. The complex variety of horizontal and vertical lines created by the pattern of the brick and wooden surfaces, as well as the multi-paned windows, strengthens the dynamism of the scene. One must proceed further into the house beyond the cross walls to discover the battery of French doors with vertical accents to the left and the full living space with horizontal board and batten walls with built-in book shelves below the clerestory window to the right. Still another turn is required before facing the fireplace. Similarly, a second door from the carport offers an analogous *mis en scène* in the reverse direction. In either case, one has to proceed further into the house to glimpse the far side of the living room and then to turn around at this point to see the fireplace. Coming from either direction the visitor must pass through this carefully orchestrated sequencing of spaces before finally arriving at the physical and psychic core of the home.

Wright applied variations on this theme in his other L-shaped or 'polliwog' Usonian houses. He also created analogous effects in his other types of Usonian houses, such as those in which the bedrooms are 'in line' with the living and dining room spaces, those given a hexagonal plan, and those partially raised off the ground of a sloping site with masonry piers, the so-called 'in-line,' 'hexagonal,' and 'raised' houses.[192] One of the most complete sequences of movement occurs at the Pew House, built in 1940 along the sloping south shore of Lake Mendota in Madison, Wisconsin. Here Wright arranged not merely a *mise en scène* leading into the inner sanctum of the house, he also established a full-fledged architectural promenade through the entire home that joined with the other components of the nineteenth-century picturesque tradition to make this building a masterpiece. John Sergeant, in his study of Wright's Usonian houses was certainly correct when he explained:

The house has a simplicity and intimate scale that is immediately appreciated, yet it also has recesses and boundaries that are difficult to recall without actually sitting there. The brutal strength of its concept, the utility of the plan, the control of all sensations in an utterly ingenious way, and the delicate handling of its materials all make the Pew house, for me, the greatest of Wright's late career.[193]

Let us follow the path of the architectural promenade at the Pew House to see how this was accomplished.

The Pew House is perched over Lake Mendota part way down the sloping site (colour plate 18, figure 2.43). The building is turned diagonally not only 'to differentiate it from its neighbors and improve orientation and view,'[194] but also to introduce the theme of the diagonal that permeates the design. The architectural

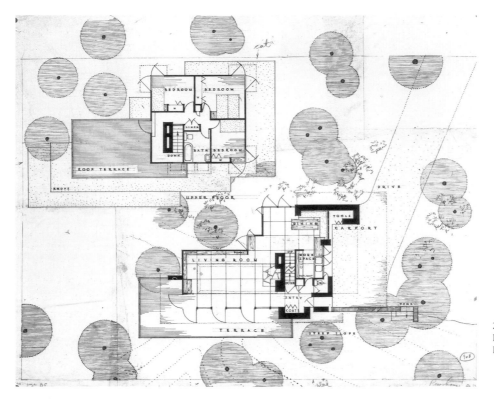

2.43
Frank Lloyd Wright. John C. Pew House, Madison, Wis., 1940. Plans

promenade begins as soon as one enters the site, for the house appears as a wedged-shaped box that establishes the sense of privacy and shelter that had become the hallmark of Wright's domestic architecture since the Prairie houses. How fussy the diagonal bastion-like wall in front of the entrance to the Heurtley House (colour plate 13) seems in retrospect when compared with this simple gesture of turning the closed side of the house diagonally toward the front of the site. As in the Robie House, the entrance is hidden from view.

A deeply projecting ledge over the ground floor creates not only a sheltered carport but also a dark shadowy place that imparts the feeling of a cave-like space along the side that extends to the entrance. The horizontal sliver of light-filled space, which frames a limited view of the lake between the ledge and a low stone wall, invites the visitor to turn the corner where he or she will discover the entrance. There is a sense of mystery, especially if one is walking down the slope rather than driving, which removes the kinestethic sense of descent, as the eye focuses upon the sliver of sky and lake with no view to the land beyond the low wall.

Before making that turn at the corner of the building, the visitor will be treated to four very small square windows, which function as peek-holes into the dining area, followed by a line of deeply recessed clerestory windows to the kitchen, but which offer no actual view at all. Both of these scenes occur under the sheltering projection of the carport's canopy. Then, as one turns the corner to face the entrance, the low stone wall stops and is followed, after a gap, by a stone wall that reaches to the soffit of the extending ledge. The gap creates a thin slot of vertical space that frames the body and now offers a full view of the land leading to the water, the lake itself, and the sky.

Immediately afterward the visitor proceeds into the dark and constricted space of the entry, made even more cave-like by the rough stone walls with their projecting courses and by the stone flooring. As the door opens (colour plate 19), the darkness and spatial compression is replaced by a burst of light and space provided by the row of glass French doors along the left side, which wrap around the adjacent wall to the far end of the living room directly in front of the viewer. The gaze focuses on this end bay not only because of its position and greater size, but also because within its frame a tree passes up through a hole in the terrace and then continues upward and out of sight beyond the level of the living room ceiling. This expansive view, both straight ahead and to the left, is similar to the first horizontal sliver of sky and water in that there is no indication of the land, which is hidden by the terrace's parapet. Only a hint of the closed portion of the living room with its higher ceiling to the right side is visible at this point.

Upon passing through the entrance and then closing the door, one discovers to the left still another vertical slot of space, now a floor-to-ceiling window located to the far side of the wall fragment that had created the dark and constricted entrance. This vertical slot of space re-stablishes an intimate sense of human scale not only through its configuration, but also by permitting once again a full vertical view of land, lake, and sky. To the right, one is given a view across the kitchen area into the dining room.

As one enters further into the house, the right side of the living room becomes visible with its lapped cypress boards, built-in bookshelves, raised cove ceiling at the center, and lower ceiling at the far side. Turning clockwise (colour plate 20) one sees the recessed space of the dining room diagonally opposite the corner of the glazed French doors and then the massive fireplace and chimney-stack, rising above the stone floor and built of the same thick, rock-faced limestone with projecting ledges as the walls around the entrance. This limestone presents a mixture of gray- and honey-toned accents. The overall effect is to provide a warm yellow aura that complements the golden color of the wooden walls. This aura of warmth is intensified at the fireplace where a massive sandstone lintel, irregular in shape and glowing golden in color, becomes the image incarnate of the hearth.

Frank Lloyd Wright, as Neil Levine demonstrated in a pioneering article, often used the diagonal to extend the architecture out into the landscape.[195] From within the Pew House the effect of the diagonal is extremely powerful. Seated in the cozy dining room area, which is contained within the solid wedge that had projected outward toward the arriving visitor, one looks diagonally across the living room and out through the glazed French doors at the opposite corner for a view to the lake and sky. Like the first-story bedroom windows perceived during the initial approach to the house, these glazed French doors without a corner mullion open outwards to dissolve the corner totally, as the eye follows the line of the flat ceiling that extends uninterrupted into the exterior. Once again here is a perfect example of the dialectics of refuge and prospect, which was a constant theme in Wright's domestic architecture.

As in many of Wright's other houses, the parapet of the terrace serves to mask a portion of the exterior.[196] In this case, it is the ground outside the house. When one is seated in the dining or living room, the land between the house and the lake is hidden from view. Looking out beyond the terrace one sees water and sky. The effect is like being on a houseboat, an impression strengthened by the intimate size of the rooms, the lapped cypress walls, the wooden 'deck' floor, the ship's portal-like windows in the dining room, and the detailing of the built-in storage. One is reminded of Wright's projects of 1922 for Lake Tahoe lakeside cabins and residential barges.

The architectural promenade continues from the living room upstairs after enjoying directed views toward the rear out the windows of the study and the dining area. To reach the stairs to the first floor one must walk all the way around the fireplace (or through the kitchen to the other side) and thus into the innermost part of the first level. This alone helps to remove the bedrooms psychologically from the public domain. The last sight before ascending the stairs are the four square portal windows, whose view takes you back to the beginning stages of the architectural promenade when these openings were first seen upon approaching the house. At this point one can commence the second stage of the journey, now to the upper level.

As one rises through this narrow stairway, a clerestory window at the far side of the landing directs the gaze outward to the sky and trees. From the landing one makes two more turns around the stone chimney core and then proceeds down the hall to reach glazed French doors that provide a view to the lake and access to the roof-terrace. One more ninety degree turn around the chimney-stack reveals the corridor with its entrances to the three bedrooms and one bathroom. A few more steps and still another turn places one by a parapet wall overlooking the flight of stairs from below with a second view of the clerestory window over the landing. The dynamic quality of this relatively small and tight space cannot be underestimated. Perhaps never have stairs been so completely integrated into the surroundings. Because all the walls step backward or forward with their lapped boards, the stairs themselves become an integral part of the form and space.

Proceeding into any of the bedrooms through the doorway located in each case at the corner of the room, one has an immediate diagonal view across the room and out of the double corner window, which, as previously mentioned, opens entirely to free the corner of any mass. The small canopy above each of these windows, when viewed from the inside, creates the illusion that the entire ceiling has been extended outward beyond the walls. These intimately scaled bedroom spaces, so cozy in dimension, materials, and form, nonetheless, share with the downstairs the dynamism of the diagonal view, albeit on a more modest scale and in an abbreviated fashion.

The complexity of the entire architectural promenade withing the limited area of the Pew House is amazing. The sense of compression and expansion, of shelter and prospect, or being on water and on land, and of darkness and light present an

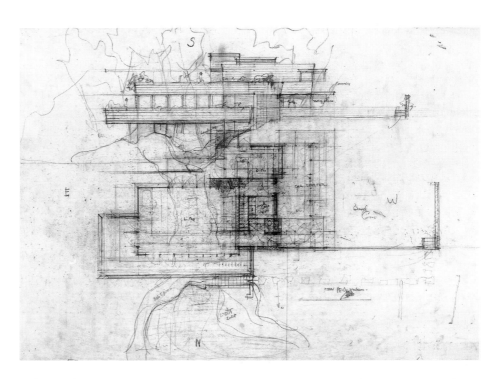

2.44
Frank Lloyd Wright. John C. Pew
House, Madison, Wis. Early project,
elevation and plan

experience within a limited space as rich as any sequencing that one might find in
the eighteenth-century landscape gardens that originally gave rise to the aesthetics
of the 'picturesque principle,' combining 'variety' and the 'path.' One of the most
striking features of this sequencing, fully consonant with Wright's use of the
chimney and fireplace as the symbolic core of the house, is the almost ritualized
encircling of this core before reaching the bedrooms. The question arises, did
Wright have to design the house this way? Is the journey around the chimney-stack
merely a felicitous by-product of the functional arrangement? The answer to both
questions appears to be no. The Pew House as built differs from Wright's earlier
project in important ways, which suggest the intentionality of all aspects of the
architectural promenade described above.

A cursory glance at the earlier project for the Pew House (figure 2.44) reveals
that it closely resembles the final version. Yet there are two significant differences,
in addition to the change from brick to stone walls. First, the fireplace and stairs
were to have been separate, hence with no possible circumambulation of the
former while ascending or descending the latter. Second, the stairs themselves
were to lead to the first floor directly from the entry. The logic of Wright's earlier
concept is apparent. He conceived the Pew House as a bridge over a ravine with
views out of two sides of the living room raised above the land that falls rapidly
beneath the house. In a series of sketches and drawings Wright showed a projected
water inlet coming up to the house from the lake, where it would end at the
ravine.[197]

In the initial scheme, the dialectical pairing of the windows looking out over the
chasm and the fireplace with chimney core would have had a powerful effect. The
Pew House has been likened to Fallingwater, because of the way its terraces
cantilever over a falling landform. Certainly that image was maintained on the
exterior in the executed building. In the earlier project, though, the interior was
also conceived to heighten the bridge-like quality of the form. In the final project,

Wright rotated the chimney core through ninety degrees to couple it with the stairs while closing the rear wall of the living room entirely. In the interior, the new design emphasized not the bridge but rather the experience of being on a boat. The circumambulating architectural promenade up and around the stairs was created by reversing the positions of the stair runs to the upper and lower floors.

The richness of the architectural promenade through buildings such as the Pew House was complemented by the picturesque variety contained within individual scenes. Whether in Prairie houses, in Usonian houses, or in transitional pieces, such as the Hollyhock House, Wright created all in one scene a combination of varied spaces, with a vista as the end goal, that encapsulated the workings of an architectural promenade. The overall effect of such vistas is a liveliness characteristic of the picturesque, which extends to the most subtle aspects of nineteenth-century picturesque thought, concerning the curved horizontal lines of the Parthenon and their complements, the inclination of the columns and walls, as well as of the contrapuntal stances of the Caryatids of the Erechtheion.

We have seen how the horizontal curvatures at the Acropolis were deemed to impart a feeling of life to building, just as the inclined vertical planes were thought to convey a sense of stability. The ramifications of these discoveries cannot be overestimated. I am not referring here simply to the subsequent use of curved horizontal lines in the architecture of practitioners as varied as Alexander 'Greek' Thomson and the firm of McKim, Meade and White, but also to the legacy of this thought to Art Nouveau which stressed the life-imparting force of the curved line.[198] The sense of life discovered by the nineteenth-century Romantic Hellenists in the Greek architecture of the Periclean Acropolis found its counterpart in progressive American architecture through the uncanny aesthetic sensibility of Henry Hobson Richardson, who, throughout his mature career, knew how to convey a sense of elasticity to his stone walls through an appropriately calibrated rock-faced finish to the masonry. This detailing, along with the sizing of the stones, the use of random ashlar, the simple and compact profile of the massing, and the gentle inward slope or battering of the walls also imparted a sense of power to his architecture. When Richardson abandoned his picturesque combination of brown sandstone trim with granite walls in favor of a single stone, he increased the intensity in his buildings of what Ruskin termed the lamps of life and power. This was achieved, as in the Allegheny County Courthouse (begun 1883), through the alternation of narrow and taller courses of rock-faced regular ashlar, whereby the narrow bands of stone create a cushion effect between the heavier layers.

At Wright's Pew House one encounters the worthy equivalent to the curved lines and inclined planes of the Periclean Acropolis and to the life-like walls of Richardson's architecture, as well as to their successor in Louis Sullivan's soaring, ornamented verticals of the Guaranty Building (Buffalo, 1894–96). In the Pew House, where all walls are picturesque in profile, either through the irregular outline of the rock-faced limestone or the overlapping cypress boards, the sense of life is omnipresent (colour plates 18–21, figures 2.43–2.45). The overlapped boards make the wooden walls project progressively in one direction or another; ends of walls even step outward in two directions, in a V-shaped manner. This lively movement is complemented by the stepped profile of the ceiling.

Looking back over Wright's earlier work, one finds a similar interest in the lessons of the subtle adjustments to horizontal and vertical surfaces as found, for example, at the Acropolis. Numerous Wright houses at the turn of the century use slightly inclined walls on the exterior to depart from strict rectangular form and to

Frank Lloyd Wright. Frank Thomas House

Frank Lloyd Wright. Second Herbert Jacobs
House. The solar hemicycle

Frank Lloyd Wright. 'Hollyhock' House

Frank Lloyd Wright. 'Fallingwater'

Frank Lloyd Wright. John C. Pew House

Frank Lloyd Wright. Pew House.
View to the living room

Frank Lloyd Wright. Pew House.
Living room with view to dining
alcove

Frank Lloyd Wright. Pew House.
View from the dining alcove toward
the living room

Le Corbusier. Monastery of La Tourette.
Detail of the cloister

Le Corbusier. Monastery of
La Tourette. Detail of the chapel

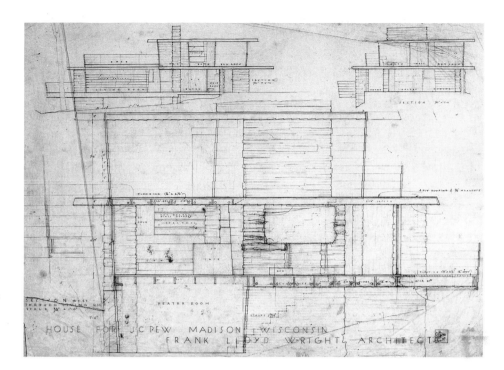

2.45
Frank Lloyd Wright. John C. Pew
House, Madison, Wis., 1940. Sections
showing irregular surface of stone
walls and lapped cypress walls

reinforce the sense of stability and hence shelter (figures 1.40, 1.42, colour plate 13). At the Bradley House, this technique is reinforced in the horizontal plane with the doubled layer of the projecting eaves (figure 1.42), made even livelier through the linear ornamentation. With time, the aesthetic lesson of such a doubled-layered hip roof was transformed into the triple-layered cantilevered flat roof, as in the Jacobs House (figures 1.62, 1.63). In describing the construction of this latter house, Wright explained that the offset layering of the roof permitted the required pitch, as well as the desired overhang that imparts a sense of 'gratifying' shelter.[199] Staggering forms, whether through the overlapping of the framing in the projecting roof, of the boards of a wall or ceiling, of the stepping profile of a wall adjacent to a fireplace (figure 1.47), or of the stepping profile to a plan (figure 1.64) were constant features of Wright's architecture.

The stepped profile of the plan was of particular importance to Wright's use of the picturesque. Of course, in the Usonian houses, this feature helped to stiffen the structure against collapsing. Its aesthetic use provided the opportunities for variety and vista. Yet its appearance in the design is not arbitrary but rather is joined with utility. It is precisely this conjunction of utility and beauty through the picturesque not only in Wright's but also in Le Corbusier's architecture that remains to be considered.

The reasoned picturesque

In the first part of this chapter we saw that the concept of the reasoned picturesque was widespread in the nineteenth century. Frank Lloyd Wright and Le Corbusier inherited this legacy, which they applied to their architecture in a variety of ways. We have already encountered repeated instances of picturesque arrangements in their buildings. Now we should consider the ways in which they were conceived as reasoned and reasonable architectural gestures.

We have already considered the purpose behind the complex twists and turns, coupled with subtle changes of level, that Wright employed to make the entrance into his homes seem like a journey into an inner sanctum. These irregular plan arrangements also satisfy the criterion of 'sufficient reason.' The same is true for Wright's departures from regularity of massing in his homes, where unequal wings seem to reach out into space from the massive chimney responsible for pinning the composition together.

In the Prairie houses, Wright assembled rooms with regular outlines into irregular patterns not only by rotating them around the chimney core but also by slipping volumes past each other and by establishing entry into rooms along the edges. Articulations in plan and volume create logical separations between rest spaces and movement spaces. One enters the formal spaces of the living and dining rooms of the Ward Willits House (figures 1.44, 1.45, 1.57), for example, along the edge of each space. At the end of the dining room, Wright introduces a circulation zone with a door to the rear garden to one side and a door to a wedge-shaped weather lock to the other. This circulation zone separates the dining table area from the triangular window seat with skylight that projects outward, with one side engaging the porch. The irregular and complex arrangement here makes a clear statement about the many possible relationships between interior zones of space and between inside and outside.

As for the weather lock, it establishes a buffer between access to the shallow dining room terrace to the right and to the large covered porch to the left, while providing entry to both spaces. Once again entrance to the large porch is confined to the edge of the space. This porch is one of those slipped forms that a Beaux-Arts architect would have aligned with the long axis of the dining room. Wright, though, has moved it down to create a complex network of interlocking and slipped spaces. The resulting picturesque composition displays a logic with respect to zoning different functions and to circulation, as well as to establishing interior and exterior relationships, that seems reasonable to the observer. One can apply this type of analysis to Wright's other homes of this period as well.

Later in Wright's career, in the Usonian house, he repeatedly used an irregular, step-like or echelon outline to the building's perimeter. The resultant picturesque form is yet another version of his breaking down the box and integrating the inside with the outside. We find this device in the Jacobs House of 1937 (figure 1.64), where it serves others ends in addition to stiffening the wooden walls. Around the entry, the brick walls step back to form a carport as well as to dramatize the cantilever of the roof. This technique is repeated to the far side of the living room, as well as at the end of the bedroom wing. Inside the house, the corridor of the bedroom wing is arranged according to an echelon that, as mentioned before, gives visual privacy and breaks up what might have been a long, monotonous hallway. Better sound privacy between the bedrooms is another benefit.

In the Usonian house Wright gives a further rationale to the stepped profile or echelon of the plan. He places table surfaces at the corners and even fashions small rooms from the resultant spaces. Thus, the broken line of the perimeter wall becomes an occasion for creating a place within a place, for situating an activity within a larger realm. In the Jacobs and Pew houses, for example, Wright provides a built-in study- or work-table at such corners (figure 2.43, colour plate 21). At the Rosenbaum House, to choose an additional example, Wright uses a three-part echelon to make a study, a living room, and a dining area, each with its own access to a shared terrace.

A similar approach to the reasoned picturesque can be found in Le Corbusier's architecture. Although the forms are different, the irregularities always have some easily discernible reason, often a functional reason that seconds the aesthetic impact. We have already seen that the curved walls, suggestive of organic shapes, are used to direct movement along the architectural promenade or to serve as metaphorical extensions of the human body that form a counterpoint to the gridded space and the straight walls. It appears that whenever possible Le Corbusier created a functional justification for these curves as well.

Consider, for example, the project for mass-produced artisans' houses of 1924 (figure 2.46). The building is an exercise in compact functional planning. A diagonal mezzanine zones the cubical interior into two parts – one with the living functions (kitchen and dining below the mezzanine with sleeping quarters), the other with the workshop or artist's studio space (large volume, large window, and full double-height wall). Le Corbusier engages the staircase in a rich composition with a variety of different forms and shapes, an abbreviated architectural promenade. With a metal railing on the inside and a low wall to the other side, like the parapet wall of the balcony, this staircase seems as if it has been pulled out from the balcony to descend down to the ground. In the reverse direction, this low balustrade wall appears to pivot at the landing to form a storage cabinet. The entire asymmetrical assemblage of forms in this scene clusters around the central column whose hollow core serves to evacuate the rain-water from the flat roof.

The picturesque composition is further balanced by the nearly equal rounded projecting balconies that are almost equidistant from this vertical shaft. The balcony to the left is slightly further away and is slightly larger than the one to the right. The left balcony requires this greater distance and larger size for aesthetic reasons, because it must join with the diagonal line of the stairs to balance the dense cluster of forms to the right of the column. Its size and position, though, also serve a functional purpose: without it, it would be impossible to pass round the end of the bed.

Le Corbusier was always getting himself out of these impossibly tight situations by curving a wall in a way that combined aesthetic appeal with functional justification. Consider, for example, the attenuated S-shaped wall on the bedroom floor of the Maison Cook (figure 1.5, bottom left). Straighten the wall from the bottom and the maid cannot get into her bedroom. Straighten the wall from the top and the maid has more than the necessary space while the adjacent room with the twin beds becomes too cramped. Here the curved wall solves the functional problems of entrance and appropriate allotment of space.

Le Corbusier's use of the reasoned picturesque also extended to the large-scale departures from regularity that were major compositional decisions and that effectively determined the overall form. In his project of 1933 for high-rise residential rental buildings along the cliffs of Algiers, for example, Le Corbusier proposed a new zoning regulation whereby all buildings on the cliffs would be raised off the ground so as to permit an unencumbered view of the sea. 'In Algiers,' commented Le Corbusier, 'a city famous for its magnificent panorama, not one inhabitant of the European city any longer knows this site: the houses . . . block the view from each other.' 'This is progress?', he asked rhetorically, 'This is Western culture?'[200] In response to this self-imposed requirement, Le Corbusier raised his tower off the ground. In this building there are four levels of two-story apartments in the elevated tower and two levels of two-story apartments in the lower section. No doubt this uneven distribution reflects the economies of construction, whereby the lesser number of floors below street level minimizes excavation costs. The section through the site shows how this uneven division in the massing has been co-ordinated between the terraces so that no building obstructs the views from another. Le Corbusier uses the leftover surface at street level for an elevator to lower the cars into the parking garage one level below, while simultaneously fashioning a loggia for viewing the panoramic site. As might be expected in Le Corbusier's domestic architecture, each apartment has single- and double-height spaces. The penthouse apartment even has an interior ramp and an exterior terrace that further breaks the regular prism of the facade.

One more example should suffice to demonstrate still another but related use of the reasoned picturesque. The High Court at the capital city of Chandigarh presents a powerful, asymmetrically balanced composition, that relates to the larger landscape (figure 1.68). The building proper is enclosed within an enframing megastructure that echoes the double range of mountains seen in the distance. Le Corbusier's drawing of the building rising along the mountain range and reflected in the adjacent monsoon-filled basins brings to mind the cosmic associations of

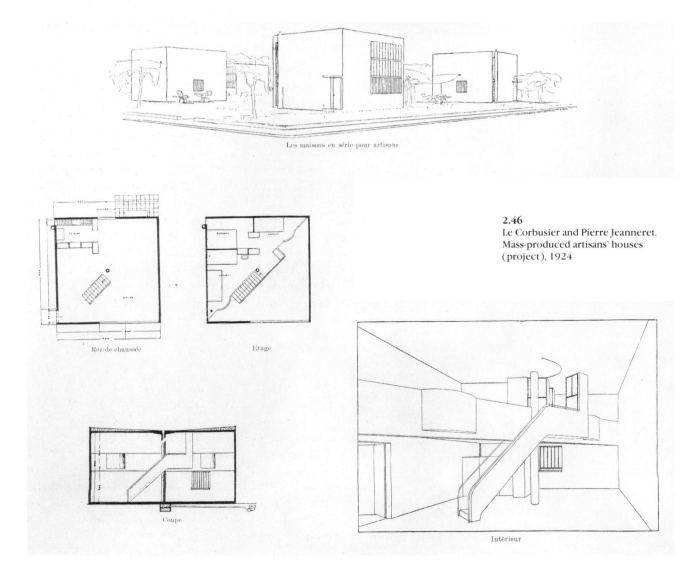

Les maisons en série pour artisans

Rez-de-chaussée

Etage

Coupe

Intérieur

2.46
Le Corbusier and Pierre Jeanneret. Mass-produced artisans' houses (project), 1924

2.47
Le Corbusier. Secretariat, Chandigarh, 1952–56. Partial view of south-west facade (in construction)

placid waters and surging mountains that had determined the choice of site for his aging parents' home in 1923.[201] The curved openings between the roof of the megastructure and the court building proper contribute to the poetry of the composition as they capture pockets of sky. The giant piers or 'pylons,' which interrupt the building, divide the building into two unequal parts while providing a 'grand entrance portico.' For a building viewed against the undulating outline of the double mountain range, the asymmetrical placement of this entrance portico gives a force to the entire composition that a central location could never have achieved. Once again, Le Corbusier combines this aesthetic decision with a functional and related symbolic rationale. The entrance portico separates the eight courtrooms placed on the right side from the single and larger High Court, located to the left. Not only is the composition balanced, but the High Court receives the isolation and prominence that its stature deserves. Its size and position satisfy the requirements of the principle of sufficient reason.

Whereas from the Swiss Dormitory (colour plate 1, figures 1.11–1.12) to the High Court in Chandigarh, Le Corbusier used the picturesque articulation of volumes to distinguish between different functions, he also changed the surface treatment of the facade for this purpose. Hence, at the Swiss Dormitory, the rooms with a view to the playing-field to the south are glazed, whereas the corridors to the north are given puncture windows. At the Secretariat in Chandigarh (figure 2.47), the governor's and ministers' offices are signaled on the facade by a break in the regular pattern of fenestration used for the workers' offices. The double-height spaces of the special offices and their hierarchical importance are also signaled through the use of loggias and, in the case of the governor's office, through the addition of a projecting balcony with canopy. At the Unité d'Habitation (figure 2.48), it is easy to identify the dwellings with their sun-breaks serving as loggias, the two levels of the shopping street with their vertical fins for sun protection, and the elevator shaft and stairs with small puncture windows. The Monastery of La Tourette (figure 2.49, colour plate 22) received analogous treatment. The facades of the monks' cells with their loggias, the communal spaces with one of two patterns of windows, either vertical strips or a grouping of squares and rectangles, and the corridors with their thin slit windows are all clearly indicated. In all of these cases, beginning with the Swiss Dormitory and continuing to the end of Le Corbusier's career, the 'mask' of the 1920s buildings has been abandoned in favor of the nineteenth-century ideal of articulating the facade according to the reasoned picturesque.

2.48
Le Corbusier. Unité d'Habitation, Marseille, 1946–52. East facade

2.49
Le Corbusier. Monastery of La Tourette, Eveux-sur-Arbresle, 1953-59

One could continue with an analysis of virtually every major building by Frank Lloyd Wright and Le Corbusier in which a departure from regularity provides aesthetic interest and satisfies some reasonable expectation related to functional, constructional, or symbolic concerns. The two architects disciplined their designs so that the picturesque would not seem arbitrary or whimsical. This was just one aspect of their adherence to the imperatives of the picturesque principle whose legacy they inherited from the nineteenth century. The concept of the picturesque, along with that of the architectural system, then, were the two guiding precepts in the design of their buildings. In applying these precepts, though, Wright and Le Corbusier found additional assistance in the notions of philosophical eclecticism, the engineer's aesthetic, and the spirit of the age, which are the subject of the next two chapters.

CHAPTER 3

Eclecticism and modern architecture

From the earliest years of the Romantic revolution through the triumphant days of avant-garde twentieth-century architecture, progressive architects and critics had a profound interest in the lessons of history. Camille Martin was voicing a widely shared conviction when he criticized the particular contingent of Art Nouveau architects who

> wrongly thought that the essential character of a modern art had to reside in the novelty of its forms. They followed to the letter the counsels of those who, in their disgust for the current anarchy, thought it possible to create entirely from scratch an absolutely new style that would not recall in the slightest degree those that had flourished in the past.[1]

To ascertain the common position taken by avant-garde architects, one should turn to *Stil i Epokha*, the 'first manifesto of Constructivist architecture,' by the Russian architect Moisei Ginzburg:

> Thus, the cycle of the 'classical' Greco-Italic and, in a certain sense, European system of thought appears, to us, to have been completed, and the path to a genuine modern architecture must surely lie beyond it. Does this mean that the whole complex path taken in the course of the centuries-long development of European architectural thought has proven to be 'superfluous,' and that we shall be forced to begin our own creative work at the very beginning, outside and beyond the completed cycle? Of course not. . . . The question thus remaining to be answered is this: which aspects of this completed cycle of architectural life can be regarded as possessing such value? Which parts of the whole artistic and historical baggage should we pursue with not only dispassionate appreciation, but the unrelenting perseverance of a modern, vitally concerned human being as well? Naturally, this question concerns neither the elements of any style nor their formal characteristics, but rather those basic *philosophical and architectural profundities* whose power has not yet abandoned us.[2]

The need to discern relevant 'philosophical and architectural profundities' to guide in the creation of a modern architecture was a leitmotif of this entire period, from the Romantic revolution onward. It arose as an integral component of the new cultural relativism that, in turn, fostered the notion that each age had its own characteristic architecture and that the contemporary world would have to develop its own.

In rejecting the elements of past styles, Ginzburg was repudiating the nineteenth-century tradition of stylistic eclecticism. Henry-Russell Hitchcock, in *Modern Architecture: Romanticism and Reintegration* (1929), made an important distinction between two types of stylistic eclecticism, which he termed 'eclecticism of taste' and 'eclecticism of style.' The former referred to 'different styles used contemporaneously but each building all in one style'; the latter designated those buildings in which 'features of different styles [were] used together on one building.'[3] What Ginzburg was advocating was actually a different type of eclecticism, one that might be termed 'philosophical eclecticism,' meaning the extraction of the principles of architecture from past cultures without borrowing stylistic features. The purpose of this chapter is to demonstrate how widespread this concept of philosophical eclecticism was in progressive architectural thought in the nineteenth and early twentieth centuries and how it informed the work of Frank Lloyd Wright and Le Corbusier.

The eclectic way

Since the opening years of the nineteenth century, eclecticism appeared to contemporaries as the mark of the times. The founders of a new literary review first published in January 1805, for example, could think of no better editorial approach than eclecticism and no better title than the *Eclectic Review*: 'Both the plan and the principles of our Review are indicated by its *Title*. No other than that of ECLECTIC, would have been equally appropriate.'[4] Throughout the century 'eclecticism' would re-appear in the title of various journals – *The Eclectic Museum of Foreign Literature* (1843), *The Eclectic Magazine* (1844), *The Eclectic* (1870).

Toward 1820 in France, eclecticism became an important concept in various fields. Victor Cousin popularized the notion in his courses on the history of philosophy and in subsequent publications. Cousin's method consisted in reviewing the history of philosophy not to distinguish between the true and the false but rather to consider each historical philosophical system as true in itself but incomplete from the vantage point of other philosophies. Thus the task of the contemporary philosopher was not to invent still another system but to gather together all the partial systems into a historical ensemble. In the age of cultural relativism, the history of philosophy became philosophy itself.[5] Similarly, after Pierre-Simon Ballanche published his *Essai sur les institutions sociales dans leur rapport avec les idées nouvelles* (1818), the *Revue des Deux Mondes* termed this work a 'type of political eclecticism' in which the author 'tried to reconcile doctrines that until that time had been seen as opposed, even contradictory.'[6]

Cousin's ideas were spread further by Théodore Jouffroy and then by Jouffroy's close associate Ludovic Vitet, who applied them to the realm of design.[7] Jouffroy's understanding of eclecticism recalls the cultural relativism of Herder's vision of the successive contributions made by the different cultures that constitute the entire human family over time. 'The reasonable man,' began Jouffroy in an article on 'modern eclecticism,'

does not declare himself either for or against any catechism, any code, any system; because he knows that all inevitably contain something true. . . . He would see how the human mind has successively reproduced, and under a thousand different forms, this invariable reality; always making it felt in the multiplicity of its forms, but deforming it always in a new way, showing always something of it but never all. . . . The reasonable man, then, would not belong to any school, to any sect, to any party; and yet, he would not be either a skeptic or indifferent. This way of envisaging human opinion is called *eclecticism*. . . . this conciliatory historical spirit . . . that visits the beliefs of all countries and ages . . . gleans from everywhere without stopping anywhere, because truth is to be found a little everywhere, but not entirely in any country, in any time, in any man.

This, Jouffroy explained, was the 'new spirit' – 'cet esprit nouveau' – that could be found in literature, in music, in politics, and in the natural sciences. 'It is to this new spirit that our century and especially our youth owe their physiognomy.'[8] As Sainte-Beuve observed, it was left to Ludovic Vitet to apply this approach first to landscape design and then to architecture.[9]

For his era, Vitet advocated what he termed the 'eclectic way.'[10] 'The critical spirit in architecture,' he explained, 'is the art of freeing oneself from all absolute systems . . . to choose courageously from among the traditions of all schools and all countries what can be appropriated to the conditions of climate under which we work and to the special destination of the monuments that we construct.'[11] In practice, the 'eclectic way' meant to Vitet the reconciliation of two opposing principles so that the result displayed the characteristics of each original component without permitting the attention to settle exclusively on either. Thus, in addressing garden design, Vitet admired Italian houses such as the Villa Aldobrandini in Frascati where the garden mediated between the formal architecture of the house and the natural landscape by a gradual metamorphosis of geometrical into vegetable and mineral forms. Vitet accordingly counseled contemporary designers to fuse the French formal garden and British landscape garden traditions in an analogous spirit.[12]

In architecture Vitet favored the Romanesque because to him it combined the grandeur of Roman construction with the dazzling spirit of Byzantine ornamentation. His choice of Notre-Dame de Noyen as the subject for extended study followed his proclivity for the reconciliation of opposites. This cathedral captured Vitet's imagination and affection because it succeeded in combining the 'nearly aerial and fragile' Gothic with the 'powerful solidity' of the Romanesque in a wondrous way that defied stylistic characterization.[13] Eclecticism, understood in this way, as a reconciliation of contrary principles in a dialectical manner, which maintained the integrity of each in an indissoluble union, was far from a superficial combination of diverse stylistic elements.

Eclecticism and the universal history of architecture

As might be imagined, the universal history – i.e., world history – of architecture was a principal source for stylistic and philosophical eclecticism. It provided the survey of different styles and architectural systems that made choice and combination possible. For advocates of the revival of a single national style, the universal history was sometimes perceived as a threat. For champions of the creation of a new and modern architecture, the universal history provided the opportunity to discern principles common to all styles as well as to derive an eclectic ensemble of useful principles particular to individual eras. In fact, from Thomas Hope's pioneering *An Historical Essay on Architecture*, published in 1835, four years after his death, to Auguste Choisy's *Histoire de l'architecture*, which first appeared in 1899, numerous authors hoped that the lessons of their histories of world architecture would serve the quest for a modern architecture.

How could conservatives, such as the pseudonymous 'Anglicanus,' who advocated the 'revival of our national Christian Architecture,' be satisfied with the effects of this new genre of architectural studies? In the pages of *The Ecclesiologist*, 'Anglicanus' lamented that Thomas Hope's history of world architecture had opened a Pandora's box of architectural confusion:

No book which has for many years been published, has done so much injury as Mr. Hope's on Architecture, replete as it is with interesting and instructive information. By following out the history of the early Italian, Lombardic, and Byzantine styles, it has given a terrific spur to that love of novelty and eccentricity, which is natural to an enquiring mind when devoid of a true principle on which to base its ideas, and has led to the introduction into England of architectural exotics of every imaginable variety. Every young architect has now his pet style of foreign architecture: one goes to Constantinople, and imports the domes and minarets of the Greek Church and the Turkish Mosque; another introduces the Arabesques of Morocco and Grenada; a third, the Classico-Gothic style of the Roman Basilica; and a fourth, the early architecture of Lombardy and Venice; all of which are alike unsuited to our climate, and unconnected with our traditions.[14]

In contrast, the mature Viollet-le-Duc of the *Entretiens sur l'architecture* welcomed the advantages of modern travel over the globe and wrote his book as a thematically organized universal history for the purpose of explaining first principles in architecture, as well as the different principles that could be gathered according to what Vitet had termed the 'eclectic way.' In the first volume of the *Entretiens* (1863), Viollet-le-Duc explained how he accepted the challenge posed by the nineteenth-century's expansion of cultural knowledge about the world:

We have seen, we see each day new things. It no longer takes six weeks to reach the Eternal City. Africa and Asia are at our door; photography floods us with reproductions of monuments of all countries and times.... What are we to do then? Forbid publications, photography, engraving? Prevent our students from taking the train or steamship?... It seems wiser to me to try to teach our students what they can take from the past and what they ought to leave aside. ... It is only by teaching the young how to reason about what they see, in educating them about the principles true for all the arts and in all times, that one can assist them to select what is good among the plethora of examples and to reject what is bad.[15]

It is only by understanding how in the past 'invariable principles' became 'translated into forms that were the expression of the mores of the times' that the architect would be able to escape from 'modern chaos.'[16] 'Every discussion on this subject,' explained Viollet in the second volume of the *Entretiens* (1872),

comes down to this; Is it the *letter* or the *spirit* that ought to be followed when it is a question of the arts of the past? It is very well to reason like Aristotle but to adopt his ideas is another matter. Now, why not extend from the domains of philosophy and science to that of art this distinction that modern times has established so well between the ancients' way of reasoning and their ideas, discoveries, or hypotheses?'[17]

The universal principles that Viollet-le-Duc found in the history of world architecture – a reasoned picturesque, the *mise en scène*, and the architectural system – have been reviewed above in chapters one and two. In addition to these general principles, which were given specific content in different cultures, Viollet-le-Duc also identified the particular principles developed by specific societies whose lesson could be separated from the stylistic features through which they had been historically manifested. For example, the ancient Roman combination of two different systems of construction – the masonry of the orders and the concrete of the arch and vault – without mixing the methods, seemed an admirable principle to be followed in the current age of iron and stone architecture. No doubt, Henri Labrouste's successful realization of such an approach in the Bibliothèque Sainte-Geneviève helped Viollet-le-Duc in retrospect to articulate this lesson from the past as a guide for the architecture of the future.

Viollet-le-Duc's *Entretiens* clarified the notion of philosophical eclecticism for which Hope had groped in his earlier universal history of architecture. In this book Hope showed himself to be an enemy of what Hitchcock would call 'eclecticism of taste' and 'eclecticism of style.' The former he dismissed as 'that species of variety in building which proceeds from an entire and general ignorance of what is suitable and appropriate to the age, nation, and localities.' Hence Hope rejected the current practice in house design to use the classical architecture of ancient public build-ings, Gothic ecclesiastical architecture, and even a style based on those 'rude and embattled castles' in the current 'times of profound peace.' These eclectic choices paled, though, before the quest 'for more striking novelty' achieved through an architecture taken from the 'ancient Egyptians, the Chinese, or the Moors.'

Hope reserved his strongest sarcasm for eclecticism of style whereby architects, 'by way of leaving no kind of beauty unattempted, have occasionally collected and knit together, as if they were the fragments of an [sic] universal chaos, portions of all these styles, without consideration of their original use and destination.'[18] Hope followed these condemnations with what appears to have been a groping approach to philosophical eclecticism in the book's closing paragraph, where the lessons of earlier architecture are conjured up to join with the achievements of contem-porary culture. If the appeal to history seems vague, then it is largely because it is quite difficult to articulate a concept that depends upon the extraction of abstract principles from visual artifacts for new forms not yet created.

No one seems yet to have conceived the smallest wish or idea of only borrowing of every former style of architecture whatever it might present of useful or ornamental, of scientific or tasteful; of adding thereto whatever other new dispositions or forms might afford conveniences or elegances not yet possessed; of making the new discoveries, the new conquests, of natural productions unknown to former ages, the models of new imitations more beautiful and varied; and thus of composing an architecture which, born in our country, grown on our soil, and in harmony with our climate, institutions, and habits, at once elegant, appropriate, and original, should truly deserve the appellation of '*Our Own.*'[19]

The authors of subsequent universal histories were clearer in their understand-ing of what was needed. We have already briefly considered Viollet-le-Duc's *Entretiens*. Between the publication of Hope's and Viollet-le-Duc's books, the British architect Thomas Leverton Donaldson and the French architect Daniel Ramée fashioned universal histories that illustrate this point. Donaldson's history was first presented in 1842 as a series of lectures at the University College of London. The current confusion in architecture, emphasized Donaldson, made it imperative that architects look to the history of world architecture to learn first principles rather than stylistic motifs:

There is no fixed style now prevalent here or at Paris, at Munich or Berlin. ... We are wandering in a labyrinth of experiments, and trying by an amalgamation of certain features in this or that style of each and every period and country to form a homogeneous whole. ... This movement has placed the Schools of all countries in a state of great uncertainty; as yet we have no fine leading principles as a guiding star.

The 'first principles' that Donaldson advocated as the subject of historical studies were 'the mutual relations of void and solid, loads and supports' and 'the laws of proportions, which guided the Freemasons of the Gothic ages in the conception of their wonder-producing edifices.' In addition, Donaldson counseled extracting the aesthetic spirit of historical styles: 'so the Architect is the more fitted for the emergencies of his difficult career, who can command the majesty of the classic style, the sublimity of the Gothic, the grace of the revival or the brilliant fancies of Arabic.'[20] In the introduction to his universal history published in 1843, Daniel Ramée expressed an analogous thought:

In the arts one should study the creations and the styles of all countries and all times, to ascertain that which they have that is beautiful, elevated, and natural, to draw inspiration from this and to invest new works with these qualities. But one must not copy servilely.

When one copies, it is because one lacks imagination, and when one lacks imagination, one is not an artist.[21]

So widespread and highly valued did the concept of abstracting principles rather than 'servilely' copying become that one finds it being offered as justification and praise of buildings that today clearly appear as stylistic revivals. Two examples will suffice to illustrate this point, one from the Greek revival, the other from a more broadly based stylistic eclecticism. Leo von Klenze, for example, did not consider himself to be copying when he designed the Walhalla (1830–42) as a memorial to German unity, which was also a German temple of fame honoring its great men. As the architect explained,

Although the schema of the Doric temple had been chosen . . . this did not at all mean the imitation or similarity of the individual forms and conditions of any particular temple of that type. . . . There was generally enough material in this architectural task of a monumental kind to meet the demand that art and artist have a right to make: free development of a poetic thought. . . . Because location, light, color of the material, ideas of the time, needs and circumstances here were entirely different from those of Doric Greek temples, it was neither possible nor permissible, in my opinion, to imitate slavishly . . . Greek forms, but rather only the very great teachings, which we have to abstract when viewing and comparing Greek monuments, have been followed.[22]

In 1845 an article in *The Builder* praised in the same manner the new church in Paris, Saint-Vincent-de-Paul begun by Jean-Baptiste Lepère and completed by Jacques-Ignace Hittorff. The following assessment is by a French author quoted approvingly by the British journal:

Although it fully recals [sic] the beautiful types of antique architecture and the primitive ages of Christianity, it is in no degree an imitation, except in the application of the principles which presided at the conception of the noble monuments of Greece and Rome. We find in it (the writer continues) no direct plagiarism; none of those counterfeits of ancient fragments.[23]

If today we fail to see the originality that these texts proclaimed as inherent to these buildings, it is because they had not attained that degree of abstraction and transformation in their use of history to make them into truly modern forms.

Greek and Gothic

Vitet's version of philosophical eclecticism, which relished the union of two opposing principles or styles, had its analogue in another theme of nineteenth-century architectural theory, which reached well into the twentieth century. This was the particular insistence placed upon the challenge to architecture to unite in some manner the radically different lessons of the Greek and the Gothic, seen as the two great systems of Western architecture. In France, the eighteenth-century theorists – such as Jean-Louis de Cordemoy and Marc-Antoine Laugier – and architects – such as Jacques-Germain Soufflot, Etienne-Louis Boullée, and Louis Combes – who helped promote and develop Neoclassicism combined an enthusiasm for the daring construction and impressive height of Gothic cathedrals with their allegiance to classical architecture.[24] If their repeated calls for a marriage between Greek and Gothic had not resulted in any buildings, then one could have said that the eighteenth-century Greco-Gothic ideal presented a true instance of philosophical eclecticism. Yet the major church designs conceived according to this notion – such as Soufflot's Eglise Sainte-Geneviève, Combes' Grand Prix of

1781, and Boullée's Métropole project – all clearly reveal that the lessons of Gothic architecture have been entirely subjugated to the classical idiom. One wonders how William Duff would have assessed these buildings after he too had expressed his hopes in 1767 that 'originality of Genius' in architecture might result 'from the union of the awful Gothic grandeur with the majestic simplicity and graceful elegance of the Grecian and Roman edifices.'[25]

In nineteenth-century architectural literature, one finds a reiteration of the eighteenth-century pairing of Gothic structural ingenuity with Greek beauty, as well as the conviction that some manner of union had actually taken place in Italy during the Middle Ages. That Italy had 'in fact, no genuine Gothic building,' seemed to Robert Willis in 1835 a particular advantage for the course of nineteenth-century architecture. Italian Gothic, Willis and others argued, had never abandoned its classical underpinnings. 'The curious result is a style in which the horizontal and vertical lines equally predominate, and which, while it wants alike the lateral extension and repose of the Grecian, and the lofty upward tendency and pyramidal majesty of the Gothic is yet replete with many an interesting and valuable architecture lesson.' Willis, though, was no more interested in creating a balanced integration of Greek and Gothic than had been his eighteenth-century predecessors. Whereas they had wished to assimilate certain lessons of Gothic to classical architecture, he hoped that the example of Italian Gothic would assist in the creation of a genuine nineteenth-century Gothic style: 'It is well worth examining, therefore, how it happens that these [i.e., Gothic] characteristics may be freely and exclusively used in a totally different style, and this enquiry may lead us to the discovery of some more certain principles by which we may be led to compose and invent Gothic buildings instead of copying them piecemeal.'[26]

The English Gothicist George Edmund Street was quite explicit in his *Brick and Marble in the Middle Ages: Notes of Tours in the North of Italy* (1855; second edition, 1874) about the parallel between the cultural situation of the medieval Italian and the nineteenth-century British architect:

There will ... always be much profit in the careful examination of such works as these in Italy, because the authors stood in the same position that we do now, and, conversant to some extent with the beauties of the best Gothic architecture of the North and the best Classic examples of Italy, took what they deemed best from each and endeavored to unite the perfection of both.

Yet in spite of the semblance of philosophical eclecticism that these lines convey, the entire thrust of Street's book clearly reveals that he was primarily interested in mining Italian Gothic for aesthetic features and principles that would enrich the new Gothic of his own day. Street explicitly rejected the eclectic approach of the Italian Gothic as a weakness and hence unsuitable as a model.[27]

The suggestiveness of the juxtaposition of Greek and Gothic architecture prompted at least one major theoretical statement in the twentieth century. For Moisei Ginzburg, the entire issue of what he termed the 'philosophical and architectural profundities' to be mined from the past revolved around this duality: 'At issue here are two contradictory sources of architectural thought, hurling us alternately into the currents of different stylistic tendencies.' Both ancient Greek and Italian Renaissance architecture yielded a 'purposive clarity of the spatial solution, which attained its formal expression in the form of longitudinally extended organisms' and which presented a 'harmonious coordination' of the parts. Gothic, and later, Baroque architecture revealed a 'predilection for dynamic aspects and for a pronounced sense of movement, investing perception not with a calming effect, but with the impulsive and unsettling feeling of pathos.'[28] The main points of this characterization had been a commonplace in architectural thought at least since Schopenhauer's reflections on this same subject.[29] Yet Ginzburg was not simply enunciating the characteristics of these two historical architectures. He was explaining the principles of his cultural heritage that he deemed worthy of guiding the creation of Russian Constructivism, one of the most radically new architectures of the twentieth century:

These two systems of architectural thought comprise that part of our cultural heritage which is still adequate to satisfy the needs of modernity. Which one is the more congenial to us? Both are. This constitutes the source of their generic significance, of their potential value for the present day. . . . The consolidation of this at first glance seemingly contradictory heritage – *the purposive clarity of the spatial problem, materialized and invigorated by the power of movement* – does this not constitute the legacy of modern creative work with which we too are now entering upon a new cycle in the development of European artistic thought?[30]

Ginzburg, like Willis and Street, was well aware that during the Middle Ages 'Italy did not for a minute sever its ties with the ancient traditions.'[31] Yet unlike Willis and Street, Ginzburg was not interested in reviving a historical style. Rather he was committed to creating a new, modern architecture. To this end, the methods of philosophical eclecticism that he applied to the Greek and Gothic heritage seemed to be the most natural and profitable strategy.

Imitation and inventive genius

The relationships between imitation and invention, as well as between copying and imagination, were at this time of particular concern to architects intent upon creating a characteristic modern architecture. In addressing these issues, architects appropriated both vocabulary and concepts from the outpouring of treatises on genius, originality, and imitation published between 1760 and 1780.[32] Two notions, in particular, merit attention, for they bear directly on attempts by mid-nineteenth-century architects to come to grips with the problems associated with the creation of a modern style in an age all too conscious of the plurality of styles. The first is the use of the term genius to mean not only people who create something original but also that component of human intelligence involved in creative acts. In the second sense, one could speak of 'original genius,' which, in effect, furnished the title for William Duff's *An Essay on Original Genius; and Its Various Modes of Exertion in Philosophy and the Fine Arts, Particularly in Poetry* (1767). Original genius, explained Duff in a passage assessing Gothic architecture, would 'shew the inventive power of the human mind in a striking light.'[33] It was in this sense that Hope, in his universal history of architecture, referred variably to 'inventive or imaginative genius' and to 'the genius that invents' and that John Claudius Loudon, in a series of articles on this subject published in his *Architectural Magazine* (1834) termed 'inventive or original genius.'

Such an understanding of the imagination required its obverse. If genius was not original or inventive then it was 'common or imitative.' It was felt that the problem for contemporary artists was that they lived in a world which had lost contact with a primal grace known only to primitive societies, deemed closer to nature and hence closer to original genius. As Duff explained, 'That original poetic genius will in general be displayed in its utmost vigour in the early and uncultivated periods of society, which are peculiarly favorable to it; and that it will seldom appear in a very high degree in cultivated life.'[34]

Loudon opened his essay 'On the Difference between Common, or Imitative, Genius, and Inventive, or Original, Genius, in Architecture' precisely in these terms:

In the infancy of all arts, the artist must have drawn his materials from nature and created an art by the exercise of his inventive powers; but in an advanced state of society, such as that to which we have now arrived, the artist derives his materials from the works of artists who have preceded him, and thus, as it were, works at second hand. In the former case, he must necessarily display inventive genius; and in the latter, imitative genius only.[35]

Thus, the architect's place within the historical development of culture made it difficult for him to have ready access to inventive genius. The architect could not easily escape from all that had been created before in order to touch nature directly.

To solve this dilemma, Loudon advocated going outside architecture for sources of inspiration 'by the application of architecture to a purpose to which it was never before applied; by the use of a material in construction, which was never before so used; and by the union of an art with architecture which never was before united with it.'[36] At this point, Loudon listed three recent developments of particular importance in Britain – greenhouses, cast iron construction, and suspension bridges – which entailed the first two of these categories, i.e., new purposes and new materials. All three we readily recognize as belonging to the realm of metal engineering structures that would become an increasingly popular source of inspiration for architects over the course of the next hundred years. The new utilitarian building types and the new engineering structures built with new materials not only offered an opportunity to regain 'inventive genius,' they also satisfied the perceived need to create a modern architecture characteristic of the times that would be grounded in a new way of building and would use the new building programs deemed most representative of contemporary culture. The importance of the new way of building was considered above in chapter one. The twin notions of representative architecture and the engineer's aesthetic will be the subject of the next chapter.

Frank Lloyd Wright and Le Corbusier following the eclectic way

The ways in which Wright and Le Corbusier derived lessons from historical architecture have been the subject of numerous studies: Vincent Scully's book on Wright, which points out possible precedents and influences for many of his buildings; Colin Rowe's analysis of the grid at the Villa Stein seen as a reformulation of Palladio's Villa Malcontenta; Kurt Forster's comparison between the La Roche-Jeanneret Houses and the Pompeiian House of the Tragic Poet; William Curtis's analogy between the Villa Savoye and the Parthenon, and so forth.[37] Furthermore, even the most cursory reading of *Vers une Architecture* reveals how important history is for the lessons of proportions, prismatic forms, the integral role of molding and related architectural details, and the architectural promenade. These and other examples of how Wright and Le Corbusier worked with history, without copying historical styles, are examples of the philosophical eclecticism imagined and advocated by progressives over the course of the nineteenth century. What Vitet termed the 'eclectic way' was integral to Wright's and Le Corbusier's approach to architecture.

Frank Lloyd Wright may well have inveighed against the trabeated system of Greek architecture, but when it came to defining what he termed the 'grammar' of his architecture, it was to the Greek temple that he turned. Simply put, the four-part division of Wright's Prairie houses is modeled upon the divisions of the Greek temple into stylobate, column, entablature, and pediment. This appears most clearly in the Winslow House (colour plate 12) where the projecting stone base corresponds to the classical stylobate, the walls that reach up to the first-floor windows take the place of the columnar shaft, the terracotta frieze with windows replaces the entablature, and the hip-roof corresponds to the pediment. In this building Wright has followed the classical prototype so closely that the terracotta band projects beyond the brick wall below, just as the entablature projects beyond the shaft of the end column of a Doric temple. Likewise, Wright joins the brick wall to the terracotta band with a projecting molding that serves the same aesthetic purpose as the projecting capital of the Doric order, whose form it echoes.

In the years following the construction of the Winslow House, we find ample written evidence that the Greek temple had indeed served as a model for Wright's grammar. A letter of 1904 by a young apprentice in Wright's office explains the architect's thinking at this time. The accompanying explanatory diagram (figure 3.1) presents the elements of Wright's grammar in a way that looks remarkably like an abstraction of a classical temple. In addition, both text and diagram label the terracotta band under the roof as a classical 'frieze.' The major difference between this drawing and the Winslow House is that it shows that now Wright, as in the Willits House (figure 1.44), was pulling back the 'frieze' rather than making it project beyond the wall. This makes sense from the point of view of giving an impression of shelter, for a recessed frieze strengthens the hovering and embracing effect of the roof. As this apprentice explained:

His tendency of the last two years has been to simplify and reduce to the 'lowest elements' (as he says) his designs. His grammar, which he may be said to have invented, is such as he used in the Winslow house, consisting of a base, a straight piece of wall up to the second story window sills, a frieze from this front to the roof, and a cornice with a wide overhang. He never cuts anything above the cornice line, like dormers. Here is his grammar, roughly sketched, and all his buildings today are built along these lines.[38]

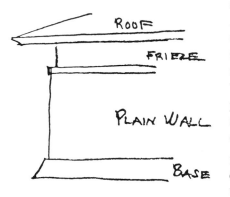

3.1
The 'grammar' of Frank Lloyd Wright's architecture

Just as this letter conveyed the lessons that Wright was giving in his office, so too had the article 'The Work of Frank Lloyd Wright' published in the *Architectural Review* in June 1900 and written by Robert C. Spencer, Jr, a Prairie school architect who shared office space with Wright in the same building.[39] Once again, we find the analogy with the Greek temple:

A careful study of his work will show that while Mr. Wright has an evident love for the horizontal dimension and the horizontal line, he seldom employs it except in sympathy with masses in which the horizontal dimension exceeds the vertical, and that whether the scheme of the wall treatment be horizontal or vertical there is almost invariably a base or stylobate of sufficient size to unify his masses and support the spring of the building from the ground with which it seems firmly and broadly associated. The simple matter of the scale and size of this stylobate, even on the small house, as compared to the weak and puny base of the average building, is a very pleasing departure from precedent and gives to these buildings a touch of the quiet dignity of the old Greek temples. In the treatment of his walls the ruling idea is that of a plain or subordinately treated surface between two terminals, the base or pedestal and the cornice or frieze; a beginning, an upward-growth and an ending.[40]

Not only does Spencer present Wright's grammar through analogy to the classical orders and the classical temple, he explains that Wright's stylobate represents a purposeful departure from normal architectural practice in favor of a lesson from ancient Greek architecture.

Finally, Wright himself addressed this issue in his famous essay, 'In the Cause of Architecture,' published in 1908 in *The Architectural Record*. Wright acknowledged his debt to the Greek temple in explaining the grammar of his architecture: 'There is good, substantial preparation at the ground for all the buildings [illustrated in the article] and it is the first grammatical expression of all the types. This preparation, or watertable, is to these buildings what the stylobate was to the ancient Greek temple.' In addition, Wright described the horizontal band with contrasting material at the top of the wall where the windows were placed as a 'frieze.'[41]

From the Winslow House to the Prairie houses and even to the Usonian houses, Wright adhered to this grammar that he had abstracted from the Doric temple. In the Prairie houses the exterior walls between the base and the roof became fragmented as the architect opened not one but two or three tiers of casement windows and French doors and as he exploded the enclosing envelope outward with projecting balconies and intermediary rooflines (figure 1.27). With the Usonian houses Wright further abstracted the elements of this architectural grammar (figures 1.62, 1.63). The wall now reached up to a thin band of clerestory windows and the roof was reduced in profile to a thin flat wafer that projected beyond the body of the house. At times Wright seemed intent on either evoking his classical prototype or at least availing himself of its effect through classicizing details, such as the line of small rectangular blocks called dentils that appeared under the projecting cornice of a classical entablature.[42] Toward the end of his life, in his Unity Temple and Cenotaph project of 1957–58, Wright chose the trabeated system of Greek architecture for the proposed mortuary chapel in which he hoped that he and his wife would be buried.[43]

The concrete block houses, as explained in chapter one, constituted Wright's next major step in domestic architecture after the Prairie houses in the creation of his architectural system (figures 1.46–1.52). They also drew heavily on the lessons of history. As as been often noted, the concrete block houses of the early 1920s used the decoratively patterned blocks in the way in which pre-Columbian architecture had used intricately carved or patterned stones.[44] Wright's genius had enabled him to look at pre-Columbian architecture in a way that enabled him to transform the new method of concrete block construction into a complete architectural system, yielding form and decoration from a mode of building, while creating an architecture that seemed to grow out of the earth even more forcefully than the earlier Prairie houses. To this end, Wright also adapted the pre-Columbian practice of raising buildings on vast terraces or placing them on pyramidal bases, which he achieved through greater abstraction in the Dr John Storer House (Hollywood, 1923) and through a more literal massing in the Charles Ennis House (Los Angeles, 1924).

In surveying the historical architecture that served as a source of inspiration for Wright's original work, we find that he favored those traditions that brought him closest to what he had termed 'earth-architecture,' whose 'mighty, primitive' forms evoked the same feelings as 'nature-masonry' of the natural world. These include the modern rendition of the ancient Egyptian hypostyle in the Johnson Wax Administration Building (figures 1.34, 1.35); the remains of the Great Gallery of Aké (figure 3.2) in the Yucatán, Mexico, whose forms seem to have inspired the Richard Lloyd Jones House (figure 1.52); the luminous mountain (Mt Sinai) of Beth

PILLARS OF THE GREAT GALLERY OF AKÉ.

3.2
The Great Gallery of Aké (detail),
Choaca, Yucatán, Mexico

Sholom Synagogue (figure 1.60); the Roman aqueduct building, like the Pont du Gard, of the Marin County Civic Center; and the inverted Near Eastern ziggurat of the Guggenheim Museum (colour plate 11).[45] In each case the earth-architecture of the prototype has served as inspiration for a thoroughly modern form, built from modern materials and fashioned into a new architectural system. In each case, the iconic image of the original remains visible, as if in watermark, under the bold transformation.

Le Corbusier's use of history to establish his unwavering approach to the 'Five Points for a New Architecture' was just as fundamental as was Wright's abstraction of the classical temple to create the grammar of the Prairie house. Basically, Le Corbusier applied his 'Five Points for a New Architecture' to the avant-garde villas of the late 1920s by extracting the principles of Egyptian and Greek architecture, which he then applied according to a Cubist aesthetic. In *Vers une Architecture*, as we have seen, Le Corbusier reiterated the principles of Egyptian and Greek architecture as they had been enunciated by Auguste Choisy: repetition of identical elements, primarily columns, for the former (figure 2.16), and picturesque movement of contraries in an architectural promenade, for the latter (figure 1.1). Egyptian architecture had special importance in French architectural theory outside of Choisy's *Histoire*. Both Léonce Reynaud and Anatole de Baudot pointed out that Egyptian architecture had presented one of the earliest trabeated systems. De Baudot even stressed the prototypical nature of the Egyptian pylon temple: 'Nothing could be simpler than such a system of construction and yet, nothing could be more characteristic or more monumental than such an arrangement whose effect derives primarily from the straightforward use of its elements and the repetition of the supports.'[46]

When Le Corbusier developed his Five Points in 1926 and applied them to the Maison Cook (figures 1.4, 1.5) and the Villa Stein (figures 1.6, 1.7, 2.31), he used the modern grid of concrete columns in a manner analogous to ancient Egyptian architecture. Writing about the Villa Stein, Le Corbusier explained: 'The independent arrangement of the columns spreads throughout the house a constant scale, a rhythm, a restful cadence.'[47] Within the area of this restful cadence, Le Corbusier set the free-standing walls and curved forms that furnished the other elements needed for his architectural promenade. As we have seen, this architectural promenade was conceived as a picturesque movement through the building, offering asymmetrically balanced scenes, like the movement of contraries in Greek architecture.

Of course, it is possible that Le Corbusier formulated his modern aesthetic without direct recourse to the principles of Egyptian architecture. After all, one did not need the Egyptian example to come up with a grid of concrete structural supports. Yet there are indications in Le Corbusier's work that he was purposefully making reference to the Egyptian prototype.

One indication concerns the design changes that Le Corbusier made between the nearly final projects of 13 November 1926, and 16–17 December, 1926.[48] In the December drawings, Le Corbusier introduced the continuous vertical strips of windows and doors on the side facades that, as Rowe and Slutzky have pointed out, have the effect of severing the taut surface of the front facade from the villa's box-like volume. In this way, the front facade becomes the first of a succession of frontally-layered planes that establish the conditions for the conceptual or 'phenomenal' transparency which Rowe and Slutzky have shown to be characteristic of Le Corbusier's aesthetic.

One could continue this argument by pointing out that when Le Corbusier made these changes in the December drawings, he also altered the front facade so that it appears as an abstract rendition of the ancient Egyptian pylon temple (figure 3.3). In other words, Le Corbusier appears to have been invoking the Egyptian prototype to show the historical lineage for his own achievement of creating a paradigmatic modern structural system in the trabeated tradition. Of course, the modern structural system was the reverse of the ancient. Whereas the Egyptian columns had been massive stone supports, Le Corbusier's columns were thin concrete shafts. As Le Corbusier explained, 'If one gathered these columns together, they would form a cluster measuring 1.1 by 0.8 meters.'[49] Similarly, just as the pylon, by virtue of its great thickness and height appeared to stand independently from the rows of

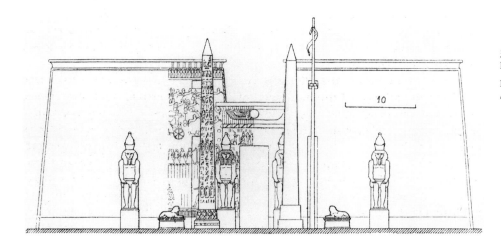

3.3
Egyptian pylon temple.

From Auguste Choisy, *Histoire de l'architecture* (1899)

columns behind it (figure 2.16), so too the thin pylon-like facade of the Villa Stein presents an example of the modern non-loading-bearing 'free facade.'

Another indication that Le Corbusier was purposefully creating a modern equivalent to Egyptian architecture in his free-standing columnar grid is seen in the highly differentiated shapes of the columns in the Maison Cook and the Villa Stein (figures 1.5, 1.7). Here Le Corbusier changed the column's profile according to the logic of its location. Free-standing columns are round, sometimes with an elongation related to directional movement. Columns engaged in a wall are square or rectangular, but are given partially rounded surfaces if one pivots around them or if the columns define an important plane of space. While it is possible that these subtle variations in column form are entirely Le Corbusier's invention, without any thought given to historical prototypes, this seems unlikely. He was already familiar with the discussion of irregularities in ancient Egyptian architecture by Georges Perrot and Charles Chipiez in their history of ancient art.[50]

Although the columnar grid in Egyptian architecture demonstrated an overall regularity and repetition of identical elements, there was, according to Chipiez and Perrot, a secondary system of differentiation that, through minor irregularities in the form, spacing, and placement of supports, imparted vitality to Egyptian architecture. These authors presented their discussion under the heading 'boredom [is] born from uniformity.'[51] In the seminal buildings of the Maison Cook and the Villa Stein, Le Corbusier appears to have created a comparable method of differentiating the shape of his columns, used here to impart variety, while emphasizing the logic of the column's relationship to stationary walls and human movement. With the Villa Savoye (figures 1.8–1.10), though, Le Corbusier abandoned this picturesque — some might say finicky — treatment of the column's shape in favor of regularity. By this time he had discovered more important historical themes to emphasize. One of the most crucial was the arrangement of forms comparable to the asymmetrically balanced scene in front of the Propylaia of the Periclean Acropolis (figure 2.12).

Upon entering the Villa Savoye, the visitor encounters a ponderated scene reminiscent of the view in front of the Propylaia. With the ramp in the center of the columnar field, a sculptural staircase to the left, and a table that engages a column to the right, Le Corbusier has created the same type of asymmetrically balanced configuration as in the entrance to the Acropolis. The full meaning of this reference only becomes clear when considered in conjunction with the image of the machine that the building presents and which is the subject of the next chapter. Suffice it to say at this time that in buildings such as the Villa Savoye, the Millowners' Building at Ahmedabad (figure 2.37), the High Court at Chandigarh, and the Carpenter Center for the Visual Arts at Harvard University (figure 1.18), Le Corbusier made recourse to an abstracted image of the Propylaia of the Acropolis to create a highly-charged symbolic entrance to his own buildings.

Even more important than the Propylaia for Le Corbusier was the Parthenon itself. His experience of the Parthenon placed him in contact with the type of primal and transcendent feelings that Wright found in 'nature-masonry' and 'earth-architectures.' Le Corbusier's response to the Parthenon recalls Charles Blanc's definition of the sublime: 'Issuing from the depths of nature, the sublime is absolute, imperishable. . . . The Sublime is like a sudden glimpse of infinity.'[52] We have seen that the early Hellenist Willey Reveley had reacted in this fashion. So too had the nineteenth-century French Hellenists, such as Emile Burnouf, who in 1847 had published in the *Revue des Deux Mondes* his observation that the oblique rays of the setting sun 'gild and set ablaze the Parthenon,' which at midday had in an analogous way shone 'like glowing metal.' Here was an architecture that 'elevates our soul by awakening the thought of divine power and infinite duration.'[53] Charles-Edouard Jeanneret (later Le Corbusier) had evidently heard that Ernest Renan had something powerful to say about the Parthenon because he asked a friend to direct him to Renan's 'Prière sur l'Acropole' (Prayer on the Acropolis) just before he embarked upon his *voyage à l'Orient*, his journey to the East.[54] In the 'Prière,' published in 1876, Renan had continued the tradition of the ardent spiritual response that had characterized nineteenth-century Hellenism: 'There is one place and only one where perfection exists. It is that one. I had never imagined anything like it. It was the ideal crystallized in Pentelic marble that showed itself to me. . . . When I saw the Acropolis, I had the revelation of the divine.'[55] When Le Corbusier reached the Acropolis in 1911 his reaction, as recorded in his travel notes, was fully in keeping with this Hellenist tradition. The Parthenon appeared to Le Corbusier like a monolithic natural outcrop: 'The eight columns obey a single law, surge from the earth, seeming not to have been posed there, as they had been, drum upon drum, but giving the impression that they had risen from below the earth.'[56] At noon, the marble of the Parthenon glowed with 'a gleam of newly cast bronze against the sky.'[57]

I had thought it possible to compare this marble with newly cast bronze, hoping that beside the color evoked in this way, this word would suggest the loud clamor of this formidable mass raised up with the inexorability of an oracle. In face of the inexplicable precision of this ruin, the abyss grows increasingly deeper between the soul that feels and the mind that measures.[58]

In short, Jeanneret (Le Corbusier) felt himself face to face with 'une fatalité extra-humaine.'

The sense of the absolute that Le Corbusier experienced at the Parthenon (figure 2.8) he certainly attempted to convey in the prismatic buildings such as the Villa Stein (figure 1.6), the Villa Savoye (figure 1.8), the Unité d'Habitation (figure 2.48), and the High Court at Chandigarh (figure 1.68). Toward the end of his career, he finally achieved this goal with a building whose spiritual impact far exceeds these others, the pilgrimage Chapel of Notre-Dame at Ronchamp (colour plate 4, figure 1.25). The look of this building could not be further from that of the Parthenon. Its siting on a hill, where it presents an oblique view to the pilgrims approaching on foot as they ascend to the top, though, is sufficiently analogous to the situation of the Parthenon on the Acropolis.[59] More importantly, the experience of this building, especially the interior, leaves the visitor with an understanding of the abyss between the soul that feels and the mind that measures. At the beginning of a long life in architecture, Jeanneret learned from the Parthenon the ultimate lesson about what architecture could offer. At the end of his long life, he was able to draw upon this experience of history to offer back to his fellows another opportunity to attain the same understanding and to have the same type of spiritual encounter. These were the ways, then, in which Frank Lloyd Wright and Le Corbusier, respectively, followed the charge of nineteenth-century philosophical eclecticism, to create an original modern architecture.

CHAPTER 4

The spirit of the age

The search for a new architecture between 1820 and 1940 was dominated by the conviction that culture acquired a distinctive character related both to national identity and to the tenor of the times. Since each historical period had created its own distinctive architecture, it was incumbent upon the artists of the present-day to create an architecture both suited to the era and expressive of its most widespread characteristics or its highest ideals. Not only was there to be a new style, but also certain building programs were favored as the 'representative architecture' of the times. For the nineteenth and early twentieth centuries, this meant an emphasis on utilitarian building types associated with the age of democracy and mass man. When architects looked for inspiration to create a modern style, they found sustenance in the marvels of civil and mechanical engineering, which offered the multiple lessons of belonging to the age, of using modern materials and methods of construction, of solving vital problems through clear reasoning, and of providing awe-inspiring forms admired for their force and beauty, as well as for the refreshing absence of historical styles. This chapter will first study the concept of the spirit of the age and then discuss the notion of representative architecture, followed by a consideration of the lessons of engineering structures. After a brief treatment of Le Corbusier's synthesis of these ideas in his highly influential and polemical *Vers une Architecture* (1923), the chapter ends with an explanation of how both Frank Lloyd Wright and Le Corbusier initiated the radically modern phase of their respective careers with buildings that evoked the machine.

Art reflects culture

The new view ushered in by the Romantic revolution that art was inseparably linked with culture, which it expressed, was felt so strongly that it was repeatedly emphasized throughout the nineteenth century. For example, in 1840 César Daly, architect and editor of the *Revue Générale de l'Architecture*, preceded an account of a recent visit to England with the epigram: 'Telle cause, tel effet. Telle société, telle architecture!!' Society and architecture were related like cause and effect. Daly explained:

Here is the expression of one of those laws that one finds demonstrated everywhere, in all places, in the ruins of the past as in the monuments of the present. It is to England that we will go this time to find confirmation. We will successively examine the general disposition of its cities and the various types of its domestic and public architecture, and always we will find verified the assertion placed at the head of this account.[1]

In such texts, the author's interest was as much to demonstrate the intimate relationship between art and culture as to study the art itself. In a similar vein, Viollet-le-Duc stressed in his *Entretiens sur l'architecture* (1863): 'I cannot repeat this too often, there is only art: it is the one that is in harmony with the mores, institutions, and genius of a people. If it assumes different forms, it is because this genius, these mores, and these institutions are different.[2] Hippolyte Taine, the influential cultural historian, based his *Philosophie de l'art* (1865) on the principle that neither the artist nor his work is an 'isolated' phenomenon. Both were inseparable from the 'general state of the spirit and mores' of society. Taine's widely read *Histoire de la littérature anglaise* (1863) had been conceived according to the same principle. The book opens:

History has been transformed for one hundred years now in Germany, for sixty years in France, by means of the study of literature. It has been discovered that a literary work is not a simple play of the imagination, the isolated caprice of an excited mind, but rather a copy of the reigning mores and the sign of a state of mind and feeling. From this it has been concluded that by studying literary monuments one can discern the way in which people felt and thought centuries ago. This has been tried with success.[3]

In 1897, Emile Boutmy, then a member of the prestigious Institut and director of the Ecole Libre des Sciences Politiques, could still recall 'the profound emotion' that Taine's approach to literature in the *Histoire* had aroused in young Frenchmen at the time of publication.[4] It was as if every nineteenth-century generation had to rediscover for itself the principle of the indissoluble link between art and culture that appeared again and again as a revelation and hence as the fundamental principle for any consideration about creating contemporary art.

Because of this principle, the contemporary architect needed more than ever before to study the past, for history taught that art must always reflect the current state of culture. This was the reason adduced by César Daly when the recently created chair in the history of architecture at the Ecole des Beaux-Arts fell vacant in 1840: 'Those who maintain that the study of history is of little value in architectural design are shortsighted: the history of architectural form, conceived according to its relationship with social forms, reveals the relationships that exist between human feelings and architectural forms, and hence offers a guide to the imagination' that creates architecture today.[5] In 1842 Thomas Leverton Donaldson proudly explained in a similar spirit that his course in the history of world architecture would address the relationship between style and culture: '. . . as no scholar can fully master a language, who is not familiar with the literature and manners and religion of the people, so no architect can fully appreciate any style of art, who knows not the history of the country, and the habits of thought, the intelligence, and customs of the nation.'[6]

What branch of human activity best reflected the physiognomy of a culture? Here opinions differed. Perhaps the most memorable lines written on the subject belong to John Ruskin: 'Great nations write their autobiographies in three manuscripts; – the book of their deeds, the book of their words, and the book of their art. No one of these books can be understood unless we read the two others; but of the three, the only quite trustworthy one is the last.[7] Of all the arts it appears that Ruskin considered painting the most important in this respect. Others, though, thought it was literature. 'M. de Bonald,' related the critic Pierre Leroux in 1833, 'has said that literature is the expression of an age: it is, in effect, the principal expression, the most direct, the most certain, the most evident, and the most complete expression of any age that has a literature.'[8]

Architecture too had its champions and they were numerous. According to the Reverend Thomas James, in a report of 1851 to the Architectural Society of the Archdeaconry of Northampton, nothing so expresses the character and genius of a nation [as its architecture]. Stern or frivolous, true or hollow-hearted, devoted to religion or to commerce, the ruling passion of a people is stamped on its architecture; and buildings will often give the true portrait of an age (unconsciously indeed, and therefore more faithfully), when historians flatter, and monuments lie, and records fail.[9]

As the Dutch architect Jan Wils expressed it in 1919: 'Religion, insight into life, and economic relations can be sensed, but when they belong to other times, they cannot be fully grasped. Art, however, immediately brings a completely clear image of the greatness of the age. And therefore its bounden duty is to inscribe its own signature.'[10] If art reflected the character of a civilization, then it was imperative that the current age create its own expressive architecture.

The call for a new style

Throughout this period, then, one heard the repeated call for a new architecture. 'Every major period has established its own architectural style,' wrote the great German architect Schinkel in 1830, 'so why do we not try to establish a style for ours? Why should we always build in the style of another period?'[11] As the new style was finally beginning to be created at the turn of the twentieth century, the members of the Austrian Secession inscribed over the entrance to their exhibition building the essentially Romantic motto: *Der Zeit ihre Kunst/Der Kunst ihre Freiheit* (To every age its art/to art its freedom).

Throughout this period, observers lamented the absence of a new and expressive style. In 1836 the Austrian architect Ludwig von Förster observed, 'The genius of the nineteenth-century is unable to proceed on its own road.... the century has no decisive color.'[12] The Frenchman Ludovic Vitet said the same in 1838.[13] Pieter Singelenberg informs us that in 1840 'the Dutch Society of Fine Arts and Science offered a prize for an essay "explaining why such little progress is taking place in the architecture of our fatherland." '[14] Montgomery Schuyler, the eminent American architecture critic, explained to his compatriots in 1894, 'But it is not American architecture alone, it is modern architecture in general that leaves a great deal to be desired as the expression in building of modern life. It is not only our country, but it is the time that is architecturally out of joint.'[15] We could continue this litany with quotations from the Italian architect Luca Beltrami in 1903, the Frenchman Emile Magne in 1908, the Belgian architect Antoine Pompe in 1913, and so forth.[16] Schuyler was correct in asserting that the problem was universal.

When people thought that they had been successful in giving identity to the intangibles of their culture, they often explained their sense of accomplishment as having achieved an adequate expression of the spirit of the age. As early as 1837, we find the Building Committee for Girard College confident that the design for their new central building had achieved this status: 'This beautiful work of art will form (when Complete) an object of the highest interest, especially to Philadelphia — inasmuch as no country on earth can boast a purer specimen of architecture, or a more substantial and elegantly wrought memorial, to convey to distant ages the "spirit of the time." '[17] Typical of this early date, the new building was designed in a historical style, in this case, Greek revival. Only later would a truly new architecture emerge. Yet over the course of the next hundred years, architects and critics continued to refer to the spirit of the age.

The spirit of the age: an 'elusive something'

The concept of the 'spirit of the age' is crucial to understanding the quest for a new architecture from the 1820s onward, at least until World War II, when this imperative began to weaken. Yet this notion is probably the most misunderstood and misrepresented of the period. Almost invariably invoked by historians and critics today in its German form as *Zeitgeist*, it has become an easy target of derision. When taken in its Hegelian form of an idealist World Spirit (*Weltgeist*) hovering over history and directing the course of human events through an inevitable sequence of ages, it is easy to ridicule. As Tom Wolfe knows, it makes a delightful title – 'The Spirit of the Age (and what it longs for).' [18]

Certainly Wolfe was not the first to mock its charge. The sarcasm began as soon as the phrase was first used. Hence, when a certain 'One of the Democracy' felt in 1830 that his political opponents were arrogantly claiming for their own cause an unapproachable and unopposable directing force behind the events of the times, he did not hesitate to expose the conceit:

Sir, That which, in the slang of faction, is called the Spirit of the Age, absorbs, at present, the attention of the world. All confess its omnipotence, advise submission to it, and proclaim that it will produce, at the least, a season of chaos and horrors; even its worshippers assert, that it must carry sweeping revolution into every quarter, which can only be prevented from taking the most fatal character by such concessions, as, in the nature of things, are impossible. . . . I have here this potent reason for opposing to the utmost the Spirit of the Age.[19]

Such texts make entertaining reading today, but a too exclusive attention to the German idealist variant of the concept of the spirit of the age offers a severely distorted picture of a popular concept given a wide variety of meanings throughout the West over the course of a hundred years. The recent use of the term *Zeitgeist*, understood in the Hegelian sense, to explain the writings of Augustus Welby Pugin and Viollet-le-Duc is to misrepresent their ideas.[20] To limit the 'search' for 'cultural history' to the Hegelian tradition[21] is to ignore important strands of nineteenth- and early twentieth-century thought that have sought to give meaning to the concept of the spirit of the age in a very different manner.

The notion of the 'spirit of the age' appears to have become popular toward 1830. As John Stuart Mill, in an essay of 1831 entitled 'The Spirit of the Age,' explained:

The 'Spirit of the Age' is in some measure a novel expression. I do not believe that it is to be met with in any work exceeding fifty years antiquity. The idea of comparing one's own age with former ages, or with our notion of those which are yet to come, had occurred to philosophers; but it never before was itself the dominant idea of any age. It is an idea essentially belonging to an age of change. Before men begin to think much and long on the peculiarities of their times, they must have begun to think that those times are, or are destined to be, distinguished in a very remarkable manner from the times which preceded them.[22]

In other words, the concept of the spirit of the age was closely tied to the Romantic revolution, which ushered in a sense of successive cultural periods, each with its own discrete identity.

In the 1830s people had the strong feeling that they were living in a new and distinctive era. As Mill observed, this was not the first time that such a notion had appeared. It had been largely prepared by Voltaire, who is credited by scholars today as having pioneered the genre of cultural history, although he was subject to the tendency to judge different cultures by his contemporary standard for civilized behavior rather than accept cultural differences.[23]

Herder, even more than Voltaire, had prepared the way for the ascendancy in the Romantic era of the concept of the spirit of the age. In his *Ideen zur Philosophie der Geschichte der Menschheit* (Reflections on the Philosophy of the History of Mankind) (1784–91), Herder presented an image of the human race as a panoply of cultures, each with a national basis and each with a distinctive character. The purpose of humankind, affirmed Herder, was to realize its *Humanität*, its humanity, which included not only becoming civilized, in the dual sense of being humane and creatively industrious, but also to realize its potential in the full variety of forms that customs, mores, laws, and arts and letters might assume. Each successive generation of each national culture was charged with adding to the heritage of the past its own particular contributions. This was not a theory of progress, in the sense of each age improving upon its predecessors, but rather of a fuller flowering of human potential through the creation of new cultural forms. Herder's ideas about different cultural ages received a powerful confirmation from the French Revolution, which demonstrated dramatically that the world order could be radically changed, and in fact had been. As Shelley put it in a letter of 8 September, 1816, to Lord Byron, the French Revolution 'may be called the master theme of the epoch in which we live.'[24]

Throughout the nineteenth and well into the twentieth century, the concept of the spirit of the age was employed to designate the common tenor of the times. As in any consideration of the workings of the human mind, it would be well to recall Joseph Warton's admonition about 'all those difficulties that await discussions relative to the productions of the human mind; and to the delicate and secret causes that influence them.'[25] The popularity of the concept of the spirit of the age reflects the great interest at the time in giving words, to borrow a phrase from Walter Jerrold, to 'that elusive something' in shared values and vision which, however difficult to characterize, people felt, nonetheless, was real and compelling.[26]

Shelley was certainly convinced of its reality, not only because of the French Revolution, but also because of the charge of lack of originality leveled against him. After being accused in a review of *The Revolt of Islam* of imitating Wordsworth, Shelley wrote:

It may as well be said that Lord Byron imitates Wordsworth, or that Wordsworth imitates Lord Byron, both being great poets, and deriving from the new springs of thought and feeling, which the great events of our age have exposed to view, a similar tone of sentiment, imagery, and expression. A certain similarity all the best writers of any particular age inevitably are marked with, from the spirit of that age acting on all.[27]

To forestall similar criticism of *Prometheus Unbound*, in 1820 he repeated this argument in the preface to his work, where one finds the famous lines: 'Poets, not otherwise than philosophers, painters, sculptors, and musicians, are, in one sense, the creators, and in another, the creations, of their age. From this subjection the loftiest do not escape.'[28]

The most popular figures or the greatest people seemed to epitomize the age in their person, works, or deeds. Hence, first William Hazlitt, with *The Spirit of the Age* (1825) and then Richard Horne, in *A New Spirit of the Age* (1844), presented a sequence of individual portraits of influential contemporaries. When the public sees its thoughts, feelings, or aspirations mirrored in such a person's life or art, that individual becomes the personification of the times. According to Edward Bulwer

Lytton, in *England and the English* (1833), this explains the popularity of the first two cantos of Lord Byron's *Childe Harold*: 'They touched the most sensitive chord in the public heart – they expressed what everyone felt.' Lord Byron, concluded Lytton,

became the Type, the Ideal of the state of mind he represented, and the world willingly associated his person with his works, because they thus seemed actually to incorporate, and in no undignified or ungraceful shape, the principle of their own long-nursed sentiments and most common emotions. Sir Philip Sidney represented the popular sentiments in Elizabeth's day – Byron that in our own. Each became the poetry of a particular age put into action – each, incorporated with the feelings he addressed, attracted towards himself an enthusiasm which his genius alone did not deserve.[29]

Lytton's observations have been confirmed on a larger scale by Jacques Barzun, who has demonstrated in his study of nineteenth-century 'cultural nationalism' that this was the era in which great artists – Shakespeare, Dante, Goethe, Cervantes, Wagner, and Berlioz – became 'symbols of national prestige, objects of national cults' and were seen 'as embodying the soul or spirit of a given people.'[30]

The spirit of a given people at a particular moment in time was not as uniform as some might imagine. Hence an artist might not always want to follow the spirit of his age. 'Should art,' queried the Belgian architect Antoine Pompe in 1913, 'reflect the physiognomy of the epoch in which it is born? As paradoxical as it may seem, I think that one can answer resolutely: no.' Art, explained Pompe, cannot follow the 'whims of the crowd without conviction' and should not be battered by the fluctuations of 'fashion.' Rather, art had to educate.[31] Thus the notion of the spirit of the age could be used to designate the paltriest and most frivolous tendencies as well as the highest.

One finds the full range of definitions in Hazlitt's *The Spirit of the Age*. Hazlitt subjected his contemporaries to his acerbic wit: 'Mr. Wordsworth's genius is a pure emanation of the Spirit of the Age. Had he lived in any other period of the world, he would never have been heard of.' In the essay on William Godwin, we learn that the current age is inconstant; in the essay on Coleridge, that it is filled with talkers, not doers; and so forth. Yet in the defense of the *Edinburgh Review*, Hazlitt identified the spirit of the age with the highest aspirations of the mind and spirit. The magazine's 'style of philosophical criticism' is

eminently characteristic of the Spirit of the Age. ... [I]t asserts the supremacy of intellect: the pre-eminence it claims is from an acknowledged superiority of talent and information and literary attainment, and it does not build one tittle of its influence on ignorance, or prejudice, or authority, or personal malevolence.[32]

For assessing the ridiculous to the sublime and in writings ranging from the satirical to the serious, the concept of the spirit of the age could and did serve a variety of purposes.

Zeitgeist: the 'mysterious genie'

At the opposite pole from Hazlitt's biting sarcasm one finds the tradition of German idealism that reaches from Kant to Hegel and, as Ernst Gombrich has demonstrated, that has exercised such an enormous influence on subsequent German art and cultural history through the work of Jacob Burckhardt, Heinrich Wölfflin, Alois Riegl, and Erwin Panofsky. Histories of this tradition usually begin with Immanuel Kant's *Idee zu einer allgemeinen Geschichte in weltbürgerlicher Absicht* (Idea for a Universal History with Cosmopolitan Intent) (1784). Here Kant rejects the view that history can be without a teleological purpose and answers that human history 'could be viewed on the whole as the realization of a hidden plan of nature in order to bring about an internally – and for this purpose also externally – perfect constitution,' in other words, a harmonious civic world order. Because he believed that actual history corroborated his theory, Kant felt confident in insisting that he was not rejecting empirical history in favor of 'this idea of a universal history which contains a principle *a priori.*'[33]

Friedrich Wilhelm Joseph von Schelling, in the *System des transscendentalen Idealismus* (System of Transcendental Idealism) (1800) had no such scruples. Repeating the Kantian principle that history is the 'gradual realization of the rule of law' and the establishment of a 'political world order,' Schelling insisted that this could not be shown empirically or even 'theoretically demonstrated *a priori.*' Rather, it had to be accepted as an 'article of faith.'[34] According to Schelling, 'History as a whole is a progressive, gradually self-disclosing revelation of the absolute.'[35] On this basis, Schelling postulated three successive periods of human history:

The first period is that wherein the ruling power still operates as destiny, *i.e.*, as a wholly blind force, which coldly and unwittingly destroys even what is greatest and most splendid. . . . The second period of history is that wherein what appears in the first as destiny, or a wholly blind power, reveals itself as nature, and the dark decree which formerly prevailed at least appears transformed into a manifest *natural law*, compelling freedom and wholly unbridled choice to subserve a *natural plan*, and thus gradually importing into history at least a mechanical conformity to law.

This age began with the 'expansion of the mighty republic of Rome.'

The third period of history will be that wherein the force which appeared in the earlier stages as destiny or nature has evolved itself as *providence*, and wherein it will become apparent that even what seemed to be simply the work of destiny or nature was already the beginning of a providence imperfectly revealing itself. When this period will begin, we are unable to tell. But whenever it comes into existence, God also will then *exist.*[36]

Schelling's *System des transscendentalen Idealismus* became the basis for Fichte's *Die Grundzüge des gegenwärtigen Zeitalters* (The Characteristics of the Present Age) (1804–05) in which history, as the progressive passage from instinct to full reason, was, according to the *Weltplan* (World Plan), divided into 'five main epochs of life on earth.'[37] The present time was located in the third of these five stages.[38] Like Schelling, Fichte had no need of empirical history to demonstrate the course of the *Weltplan*:

Without any instruction in history, the thinker can know that these epochs, as they have been characterized, have to follow each other. He is actually able to characterize in general also those epochs that have not yet come into factual being in history. . . . The philosopher, who as a philosopher deals with history, follows this *a priori* continuous thread of the World Plan, which is clear to him without any history; and he does not use history in order to prove anything because his principles were already proven earlier and independently of all history: but he uses history only to explain.[39]

In other words, the idealist philosopher will select from history only those occurrences that confirm his *a priori* system.[40]

Behind Fichte's *Weltplan* is *die Idee*, the Idea: 'The Idea is an *independent thought living in itself and giving life to matter.*'[41] 'The Idea,' Fichte further explains, 'is independent, is enough in itself, and evolves in itself. It will live and exist, just to exist, and it rejects every purpose of its existence that lies outside of itself.'[42] The Idea also has an original activity, an *Urthätigkeit*: Social organization, liberal arts, science, and divinity or religion are the four progressively higher emanations of the *Urthätigkeit*.[43]

In order to appreciate the great difference between the concept of the spirit of the age as used in most of the nineteenth- and early twentieth-century architectural literature throughout the West and the way in which the German idealist tradition developed its system of thought, it is necessary to consider the full flavor of these German texts that only the highly repetitive and abstract language of the following typical passage from Fichte's *Grundzüge* can convey:

So, I say, the eternal and self-encompassing, in itself living and from itself living Idea winds itself through the One stream of time. And, I add, in every moment of this stream of time, the Idea encompasses itself totally, penetrates itself totally, as it is in the entire limitless stream, eternal and always omnipresent for itself. What is present in the Idea in every moment *is* only in the respect of what *was*, what has passed, and because these *should be* what will be in all eternity. Nothing is lost in this system. Worlds give *birth* to worlds; epochs give birth to epochs. The latter ones being above the former and also enlighten the hidden connection between cause and effect in them.[44]

This is the idealist tradition in which Georg Wilhelm Friedrich Hegel delivered his lectures on the history of philosophy between 1805 and 1830, and then his lectures on the philosophy of history between 1822 and 1831. Hegel's thought, like Fichte's, was dominated by the *Weltgeist* (World Spirit), the *Volkgeist* (National Spirit), and the *Idee* (Idea). Hegel explained the relationship of these entities as follows:

On the one hand, the spirit of the nation is in essence particular, yet on the other, it is identical with the absolute universal spirit – for the latter is One. The *world spirit* is the spirit of the world as it reveals itself through the human consciousness; the relationship of men to it is that of single parts to the whole which is their substance. And this world spirit corresponds to the divine spirit, which is the absolute spirit.[45]

For Hegel the Spirit of the Age seems to be subordinate to the National Spirit. The latter occupies a more prominent place in his *Philosophy of History*. When Hegel defines universal history as the progressive 'development of the consciousness of Freedom on the part of Spirit, and of the consequent realization of that Freedom' over time, he explains the temporal factor as an 'idiosyncrasy of Spirit – peculiar National Genius.'[46] The spirit of the age then enters as a subordinate function to the unfurling of the *Volkgeist* over the course of time.

The German idealists did not have a monopoly on creating holistic systems for interpreting culture. Borrowing the analytical method developed by Baron Georges Cuvier for comparative anatomy in zoology and paleontology, Hippolyte Taine explained that all aspects of a civilization, its 'religion, philosophy, forms of family, literature, and arts' were so intimately interrelated that an 'experienced historian' could easily explain the whole by studying only a small part.[47] Since 'history is essentially a *problem of psychology*' and since the historian's task is to discern the living person behind the intellectual creations of the past, Taine also allowed himself all types of psychological generalizations: 'When his critical education is sufficient, [the historian] is capable of discerning under every architectural ornament, under every feature of a painting, under every sentence of a written piece, the particular sentiment from which the ornament, the feature, the sentence came forth.'[48]

Not everybody was as sanguine as Fichte and Hegel about the value of the philosophy of history conceived from on high. 'The philosophy of history in its current state,' wrote Pierre Leroux in 1833, was 'like that mysterious genie in the *Thousand and One Nights*, hidden in a little coffer hermetically sealed, and which, when the magic words are pronounced to call him forth, rises quickly toward the sky and presents in the twinkling of an eye the fantastic appearance of a giant; but it is a giant of smoke.'[49] Nor did everybody agree with Taine that all aspects of a culture developed together as a plant is determined by its seed, soil, and climate.[50] Viollet-le-Duc, for example, argued in the *Entretiens sur l'architecture* (1863) that the three principal domains of culture – thought, mores, and institutions – were not necessarily always in accord.[51] Culture was too complex a phenomenon to be reduced to a single law.

Empirical evidence and inductive reasoning

In general, the writers on architecture who were concerned with the themes that we have been studying – the architectural system, the picturesque, Romantic Hellenism, and eclecticism – adopted an empirically based approach to the notion of the spirit of the age. Their conclusions came not from *a priori* theorizing but rather through inductive reasoning. If we wish to understand the recurrence of the expression 'the spirit of the age' in the call for a modern architecture, then we must be aware of the empiricist and inductive tradition from which it drew sustenance. Rather than consult the oracle of the *Zeitgeist*, these thinkers saw themselves relying, to borrow a phrase from Francis Cranmer Penrose, on common sense. As readers of *An Investigation of the Principles of Athenian Architecture* (1851) know, Penrose was not given to flights of the imagination either in thought or prose. In the words of the man responsible for the definitive measurements of the Parthenon, the relationship between art and culture was a function of 'that universal rule of common sense, which requires that architecture shall be suited to the manners, habits, and wants of the people, and worthy of the science of the day.'[52]

Yet how was one to execute that common sense in undertaking historical studies? Thomas Leverton Donaldson, in his study of Pompeii, published in 1827, advised:

Before we proceed to the individual examination of the public edifices of the civil forum of Pompeii, it might be useful briefly to consider the manners and customs of the people in regard to their public life, upon which depended so materially not only the disposition and arrangement of the edifices themselves, but in effect their relation to one another.[53]

For the most complete realization of this approach, one must turn to a remarkable set of four essays by Auguste Choisy, dating from 1883–84 and assembled under the title *Etudes épigraphiques sur l'architecture grecque* (Studies of Greek Architecture through Inscriptions).

Choisy's study of inscriptions followed the example set by the German classical historian August Böckh, who has been credited with having first used weights, measures, and coins to reveal 'the relations of the nations from the Tiber to the Euphrates and the unity of civilisation of the Mediterranean states' and then for having used newly discovered inscriptions 'to explain the nature and administration of the Athenian marine.'[54] Similarly, Choisy examined ancient Greek building contracts and accounts to offer an imaginative interpretation of Greek building practice and social institutions. The task required the skills of the philologist to read and interpret the ancient Greek inscriptions filled with obscure technical and legal terms, the learning of a Hellenist familiar with classical texts as well as current scholarship written in German and French, and the extensive knowledge of both architectural history and of the history of methods of construction. Armed with these intellectual tools and the imagination needed to utilize them, Choisy was able to elucidate an entire legal, administrative, technical, and cultural apparatus that supported the creative vision of the Greek architects and that made the physical execution of their peerless work possible.

Choisy's study of the 'technical, administrative, and financial prescriptions' of the contract document for new construction around a temple in Livadia revealed important aspects of Greek culture that helped explain the society in which buildings such as the Parthenon and the Propylaia at Athens were created. The inscription that Choisy selected provided a detailed outline of how to extend the paving around the temple, which was located in a remote region. Out of this humble topic, Choisy demonstrated the 'extreme precision of workmanship that the Greeks imposed on all things,' thereby providing an empirical confirmation of the Greek attentiveness to the 'minutia of details.' These findings created a fuller picture of a cultural attitude in which a Parthenon could be designed with subtle adjustments to all surfaces, including the slight parabolic curvature to the horizontal lines and the slight inward inclination of the columns and walls. By studying the way in which the pavement was extended around a temple in Livadia, Choisy provided insight into both the frame of mind and technical abilities of a civilization that could conceive and execute so complex a work as the Parthenon.[55]

Choisy was able to throw even more light on the nature of Greek culture by studying the inscription ordering the restoration of the walls of Athens. This document contained a detailed account of the work to be undertaken and offered insights into the legal and cultural status of the entrepreneur in ancient Greek society. Faced with executing a given type of work, the contractor was free to improve upon the stipulated materials or method of construction. In this case, he was given the choice of substituting a finished rather than a rough appearance for the stone foundations and of providing a stone cornice in place of a less expensive pottery construction. If the builder upgraded the work at his own expense and if the popular assembly approved his zeal for the community, he would receive public honors. 'The undertaking of public works,' concluded Choisy,

was consequently less of a lucrative profession than an honorable but often burdensome charge: arming ships, equipping troops, everything down to set design for theater, was the subject of ruinous undertakings; and one felt himself amply compensated in hearing at the Pnyx or the Theater the proclamation of a decree recording the completed sacrifice.[56]

To reconstruct the Arsenal of Peiraieus, all Choisy had was a descriptive contract listing the dimensions of the building, the size and shape of the stones to be employed, and the thickness of the wood. This was a document, in effect, to be given to the contractor. Not the least of Choisy's accomplishments was the reconstruction of the building from this set of figures and technical terminology. Having hypothetically reconstituted the building as an elegant timber structure with large central nave and two side aisles, Choisy was able to explain its dual urban function. It served not only as an arsenal but also, by means of the central passageway through the building, it provided a 'public promenade' on the way between the agora and the harbor. Furthermore, Choisy found that this building combined the design principles that the Greeks had valued highly in all of their architecture: a 'daring' structure, in which the architect reduced the thickness of the walls and pillars to the utmost minimum, while still achieving a 'monumental appearance.'[57]

Choisy also addressed the question of how the Greeks built in wood. In addition to deducing an unfamiliar type of timber structure, which had been employed in the Arsenal of Peiraieus, Choisy was also able to conclude that the Greeks built in wood with the same logic that they applied when building in stone. Thus he was also able to throw light on the old controversy as to whether the Greek stone temple was an imitation of an antecedent wooden type or had developed directly out of the exigencies of stone construction, to which it responded so well. There was no contradiction here, explained Choisy, for in both wood and stone construction the Greeks proceeded by piling one piece upon another and thereby excluding oblique forces. Greek construction in both wood and stone relied primarily on compression and hence on the vertical transmission of forces. 'And if one allows that the Greeks inherited a civilization dominated by wood structures, one can see that they were able to build in stone without abandoning the forms consecrated by their traditional architecture.'[58]

Finally, the dimensions of the Arsenal 'proved' that the Greeks intended to impart 'an element of order and harmony' to their architecture. In this case it was a question of applying simple, numerical relationships of whole numbers in a modular relationship to all of the parts. Here, then, even in a modest utilitarian structure, was evidence of a desire for 'order and unity,' another instance of those *architectures rhythmées* that Choisy found in all cultures.[59]

With these empirically grounded essays, Choisy broadened the understanding not only of Greek architecture but of Greek society as a whole to demonstrate what his contemporaries termed the spirit of the age. He established the cultural context that made it possible to build the Parthenon, a building that since the mid-century had been considered, in the words of Emile Burnouf, 'not only the masterpiece of ancient temples, but also the most beautiful monument of religious architecture that Europe has ever produced.'[60] As Penrose, the man who measured the mathematical adjustments to the lines of the Parthenon, explained, this building was 'humanly speaking, perfect.'[61] With his *Etudes épigraphiques*, Choisy created a portrait of Greek civilization that made this type of achievement so much more comprehensible.

Harmony between life and art

In the nineteenth and early twentieth centuries, architects and critics used the concept of the spirit of the age to define the nature of their culture in the same way that Choisy studied the thoughts, mores, and institutions of ancient Greece; in order to explain the context in which their architecture had been created. Rather than accept the spirit of the age as a ready-made formula, these people attempted to give it definition to guide the creation of a modern art. In general, the spirit of the age was used to designate either the highest attributes of a culture or its most distinguishing characteristics. In this way, the Romantic cultural imperative of creating an art expressive of the age would be satisfied. Yet this perceived need did not exhaust the importance of designing according to the spirit of the age. Behind all these efforts was the conviction that a modern physical setting was crucial for a full and harmonious life. As a group of Turinese artists and their supporters who welcomed Art Nouveau explained:

By now it is no longer necessary to insist on the need for the modern age to have its own style. Nor is it rash, as it was a few years ago, to demonstrate that this is now possible. Modern man, busy until now with renewing his mind, has finally understood that his city, his house, and his person require equal care, without which his intellectual faculties cannot be given their full development. He has understood that if the material setting does not correspond to the spirituality of the person who inhabits it, it is not possible to have harmony either in life or in art, which is its highest expression.[62]

The times, it was felt, were different. So were people's sensibilities. In the 1830s, Lytton, for example, remarked about the 'revolutions in the *character* of nations': 'The English people of the present day are not the English of twenty years ago.'[63] This sense of an altered character was clearly expressed by Goethe when he explained in 1827 to his personal secretary Johann Peter Eckermann that he rejected the idea of making his home into a copy of either the German Renaissance or German Gothic style. To do so would be to create a ' "masquerade" ': ' "Such a fashion is in contradiction to the age in which we live, and will only confirm the empty and hollow way of thinking and feeling in which it originates." '[64]

The depth of feeling associated with this conviction can be gauged from Henry Van de Velde's assertion that the need to create 'a new art' was like a 'cry, coming from the very bowels of our century.'[65] Hermann Muthesius, in his essay 'Das Moderne in der Architektur,' talked about the mood or feeling that constituted the kernel of cultural identity during a given age: 'One only needs to compare a tool or weapon of the eighteenth century with one of the twentieth in order to recognize the great difference in the feeling of both times.'[66] Similarly, Van de Velde referred to 'l'état de l'âme que nous apportons,' utilizing that untranslatable French word *l'âme* that means our soul, referring here to the living person's psyche.[67]

This search for understanding is the opposite of the idealist pronouncement from afar. Rather, it represents an attempt to look at all aspects of the problem from within to ascertain what makes the times new. We are fortunate to have a clear articulation of this quest from a German-language speaker, for it shows that even *Zeitgeist* could be understood in an empirical and inductive, rather than idealist, sense. Hence we find the pioneering modernist German architect Erich Mendelsohn writing in 'Das Problem einer neuen Baukunst' (The Problem of a New Architecture) (1919): 'For the particular requirements of architecture, the shift in the mood of the age (*die zeitgeistige Umschichtung*) means: new tasks arise from changing building purposes as related to traffic, economics, and religion, and new possibilities for construction with the new building materials: glass, iron, and concrete.'[68] How does one determine the spirit of the age? Van de Velde advised, 'only by an extremely attentive scrutiny without preconceived ideas against anything that is being accomplished and that appears new in all realms of activity and of the social and moral evolution of the contemporary world.'[69] In 1912, the young Charles-Edouard Jeanneret (later Le Corbusier), on a study tour of the decorative arts in Germany, noted with approval the goal of contemporary German designers, as explained to him by the director of the Deutsches Museum für Kunst im Handel und Gewerbe in Hagen – to develop products 'that make the image of our age clearer.'[70] Virtually all observers were in agreement that by responding to new social needs, using new materials and methods of construction, and creating a new style in harmony with current sensibilities, the architect would succeed in fashioning an architecture that expressed the spirit of the age. Whereas this new style was to be applied to all tasks, it was believed that certain building types were more symbolically representative of contemporary culture than others and could reflect more fully the spirit of the age.

Representative architecture

The concept of representative architecture is probably as old as the history of human settlements. Since time immemorial distinctions have been made between monumental architecture and mere building. When the Renaissance architect and theoretician Alberti declared the church the most worthy building program and hence susceptible to distinction both through the use of the richest decoration and by its location, raised off the ground on a podium, he was making explicit what had been done for millennia.[71] Architects and critics of the modern period were fully cognizant of such hierarchical distinctions and sometimes employed the phrase 'representative architecture' to refer to the most elevated building types worthy of monumental treatment. The eminent German art critic Karl Scheffler, for example, contrasted *Nutzbauten* and *Profanarchitektur* with *Repräsentativbauten* and *die höheren Repräsentativformen der Monumentalbaukunst*. As Scheffler noted, 'temple, church, [and] palace,' were historically the pre-eminent representative building types.[72] In a similar spirit, the Italian Rationalist architect Giuseppe Terragni contrasted the 'utilitarian and functional' ends of an office building with the 'carattere di un edificio rappresentativo' such as a Casa del Fascio, a Fascist Party headquarters.[73]

In the modern era, though, the traditional hierarchy of representative buildings was undermined by a new importance accorded to the *Nutzbauten* and *Profanarchitektur* of the times. As Scheffler observed, the 'dualism' between utilitarian and monumental architecture had never seriously been questioned, 'never until our times, when we can watch the drama of a serious rivalry between apartment buildings and palaces, stock exchanges and temples, concert halls and churches.' The drama that Scheffler was chronicling was the nineteenth-century historicist practice of applying 'a dress of monumental representative forms' to the more practical building purposes.[74] Yet this enhanced visual dignity accorded to utilitarian and secular buildings reflected their heightened status in an age dominated by the conviction that art reflected culture and that therefore each society was most completely or typically represented by the building types most distinctive of that particular civilization. Richard Popplewell Pullan, in his *Elementary Lectures on Christian Architecture* (1879), was reflecting a widespread notion when he followed his opening remarks about buildings being 'the illustrations to the pages of the history of that country' with a rapid review of the building types most representative of the principal historical cultures: 'the mighty pyramids of Egypt and her vast temples . . . the chaste and elegant monuments of Greek art . . . the thermae, circi, and amphitheatres of the Romans . . . the cathedrals of the Middle Ages.'[75] Throughout the nineteenth and the early twentieth centuries, writers on architecture attempted to identify those building types that they deemed most representative of the current age.

In 1913, the Swiss architect Camille Martin, president of the Swiss Federation of Architects and editor of its new journal *L'Architecture Suisse*, encapsulated the full range of contemporary activity that was seen as meriting or yielding representative architecture:

What are, in effect, the most salient features of contemporary civilization? The extensive development of means of transportation; the intensity of commercial and industrial life, having as a consequence an ever-increasing concentration of people in cities; the concern with spreading the benefits of education to all classes of the nation, to relieve the misery and suffering of the people. All these factors translate into architectural creations that are, or rather that could be the true expressions of our modern life.

Martin then proceeded to enumerate the representative building types for the current times in a way that presented them as comparable to the representative building types of previous ages:

To the amphitheaters and aqueducts of the Roman period, to the châteaux and churches of the Middle Ages, we ought to put forward, with a legitimate pride, our hotels and train stations, our factories and our commercial buildings, our apartment buildings with their numerous floors, our schools and our museums, our hospitals and asylums. [76]

In the literature of this period, these building types were often separated according to two dominant themes. One was the representative value of works of modern civil and mechanical engineering – bridges, railroads, ocean liners, and later automobiles and airplanes – and of utilitarian buildings closely associated with engineering construction – markets, railroad stations, and exhibition halls. The second was the representative value of the new places of work and commerce – factories, office buildings, and department stores – as well as homes, both traditional – the single family house – and new – the large apartment building. In both instances, the value accorded to these new cultural types challenged the pre-eminence traditionally assigned to churches and royal palaces as the representative building types of Western societies, as well as the customary prestige to the monumental character of the architecture that such building types had been given.

Both the world of engineering structures and of modern places of work, commerce, and dwelling corresponded to the popular notion that the historical cycle of the modern age began after the French Revolution with the end of an aristocratic and the rise of a democratic culture, with its emphasis on the middle and working classes, along with accompanying developments in what we call the industrial revolution, known then primarily as the 'machine age' or the 'machine civilization.' As an anonymous letter to *L'Artiste* expressed it in 1833: 'An age is reflected in its monuments. It is impossible to escape the influence of one's times. Ours is that of utility and the reign of the bourgeoisie.'[77] Throughout this period, both engineering objects and buildings were deemed to partake of practicality, seen as a principal feature of the age. 'One of the characteristics of our age,' wrote the leading British Gothic revivalist architect George Gilbert Scott in 1857, 'or rather one of its vainglorious boasts, is its *practical character*.' This was a dominant theme throughout the entire period, from Thomas Carlyle's famous assessment in 1829 of the current 'Mechanical Age' to Hermann Muthesius's affirmation in 1902 that the current age 'thinks altogether in terms of functionality and straightforwardness,' and finally to the president of the 1939 New York World's Fair who reiterated that this was a 'mechanical civilization' whose 'keynote' should be 'simplicity.'[78]

The convention

This notion of representative architecture reflected what Scheffler termed a 'convention.' Conventions, explained Scheffler in 1902, enabled people to order the chaos of the world around them: 'No soul is capable of withstanding the mysteries of creation in unlimited freedom; conscious impressionable life needs the limitations of self-created form.' The convention provided a 'fixed pole' for thinking and feeling. Scheffler was primarily concerned with the primal convention (*Urkonvention*), which was religion, and with its relationship to art:

The unity of earlier epochs of art was almost exclusively based on the fact that people had agreed on religious conventions. The fragmentation in contemporary artistic production can be explained. . . . by the lack of a generally acknowledged concept of the world. . . . The times between two conventions (religions) are fruitless for the visual arts.

Scheffler's sentiment about the current times as a transitional period between eras of religious and consequently artistic unity was common in the nineteenth and early twentieth centuries. Yet his notion about the relationship of art to convention helps to explain the most salient aspect of representative architecture: 'There is no art that is not based upon a feeling about the world – whether expressed consciously as a system of knowledge or unconsciously as a directional instinct. . . .'[79] The idea of the representative building type was such a convention that served as a conveyor of cultural meaning. In this sense, the convention of representative architecture served purposes analogous to what Michael McKeon has recently attributed to the 'genres' of literature: 'Genres provide a conceptual framework for the mediation (if not the "solution") of intractable problems, a method for rendering such problems intelligible.'[80]

Like all conventions, the concept of representative architecture required focusing on certain building programs that were invested with meaning greater than that accorded to other building types deemed of lesser interest. In this sense, certain buildings became cultural icons, just as certain people came to be seen as embodying the pulse of the age. These building types did not exist as abstract notions but rather were realized in what came to be considered as representative forms. 'Each historical period, or rather each vital creative force,' explained the Russian Constructivist architect Moisei Ginzburg, 'is characterized by certain artistic organisms; each epoch in the plastic arts thus has its favorite types, which are especially characteristic of it.'[81] Ginzburg then cited from Greek art the frontal Archaic statue with a 'particular smile' and the Madonna in Renaissance art as examples of this phenomenon, which had its analogue in architecture: 'The temple, with its typical features, is thus most characteristic of Greece, the church and cathedral of the Middle Ages, and the palace of the Renaissance.' As Ginzburg's next lines reveal, he, like Scheffler, was aware that the representative building type and its characteristic form were both conventions:

This does not mean, however, that the aforementioned organisms exhaustively characterize the given epochs; it simply indicates that the artists' main energies were directed toward solving these particular problems, and that the forms created in the process assumed paramount importance in the minds of their contemporaries. . . .[82]

These representative forms might be thought of not only as cultural but also as aesthetic icons, at once representative of culture and its characteristic artistic creations. There is another sense, though, in which they became aesthetic icons. Required to exhibit an aesthetic integrity of such high quality, these buildings, when successful, could place the viewer in touch with that *Empfindungsleben* (feeling of life) and *Weltgefühl* (feeling of the world) that Scheffler considered basic to the conventions of art. On all three levels – cultural, aesthetic, and spiritual, – the representative building types served as 'formal signs in which the abstract fully materializes.'[83]

Engineering marvels

Works of engineering were cited as representative of the current age throughout the nineteenth and early twentieth centuries. As the industrial revolution developed, so did the opportunities for such observations multiply. Two events in particular – the Great Exhibition of 1851 at Hyde Park, London, with the Crystal Palace, and the Exposition Universelle of 1889 in Paris with the Galerie des Machines and the Eiffel Tower – prompted numerous expressions of optimism about the possibilities for the development of a modern architecture inspired by the lessons of contemporary engineering.

In each case, iron exhibition buildings were seen as a sign of the age. At the same time, though, they were deemed only a beginning that would have to be developed further and assimilated from the world of engineering into that of architecture. After the London exhibition and the reassembling of an enlarged Crystal Palace at the park in Sydenham, James Fergusson, for example, cited this structure as

at least one great building carried out wholly in the principles of Gothic or of any true style of art. . . . This, however, is only the second of the series. A third would probably as far surpass it as it is beyond the first; and if the series were carried to a hundred, with more leisure and a higher aim, we might perhaps learn to despise many things we now so servilely copy, and might create a style surpassing anything that ever went before. . . . Art, however, will not be generated by buildings so ephemeral as Crystal Palaces, or so prosaic as Manchester warehouses, nor by anything so essentially utilitarian as the works of our engineers.[84]

In a similar spirit, on the occasion of the 1889 Paris Exposition Universelle, the *Encyclopédie d'Architecture* sponsored a competition to design a building in a modern style inspired by the example of the great iron structures of the fair: 'The palaces raised on the Champ de Mars, with their new forms and new materials, have proven that people have been wrong in denying that nineteenth-century architecture has a style.' French architects were challenged to second this success by finding 'the forms appropriate to the state of today's civilization.'[85]

Among the numerous virtues of engineering structures was their status as new objects particular to the times and characteristic of modern society. By the 1840s, the railroad was seen, as Leo Marx has written, as 'a property of the general culture . . . the embodiment of the age.'[86] Hence one finds the architect Calvert Vaux referring in 1857 to his times as the 'locomotive age.'[87] By the early twentieth century the pre-eminence of the train had given way to newer forms of transportation, as reflected by Otto Wagner's encomium in the 1914 introduction to *Die Baukunst unserer Zeit* (The Art of Building of Our Times): 'an age characterized by automobiles, airplanes, Dreadnaughts.'[88]

The ability of the new means of transportation to acquire the status of what might be termed a cultural icon reflected, in part, the widespread appreciation of the changes in daily life that improved communications effects in any society and that revolutionary developments in this area were causing in the nineteenth and early twentieth centuries. This message was conveyed at the beginning of this period in an article published in April 1829 in the *Quarterly Review*:

In contrasting the present state of European society with the past, one of the first circum-stances which strikes us is the improvement which has taken place in its communications. . . . The combination of these discoveries and improved arrangements has produced an ease, certainty, and rapidity of intercourse, exceeding all past experience or imagination. We are, perhaps, not far enough removed from these changes to estimate them at their proper value. Though few in number and simple in their operation, they have yet done more to change the face and multiply the comforts of society, than all the inventions which have taken place from the earliest ages to the present day.[89]

Likewise, the new British periodical, *The Surveyor, Engineer, and Architect*, opened its first issue in February 1840 with a 'Preliminary Address' that echoed this same theme while suggesting a parallel between the contemporary steam engine and the Roman network of roads for the ability of new communications to make possible an entirely new life.[90] This appreciation of modern technology would find repeated expression over the course of the next hundred years.[91]

The new engineering products had lessons for architecture that went beyond the generalized notion of their status as cultural icons. Richard Horne had no idea how wrong he was with respect to all the arts when in his *New Spirit of the Age* (1844) he wrote that 'the spirit of railroads and ... steam' held 'no precedent for art.'[92] In architecture, the lessons of engineering structures were deemed to be numerous. The products of civil and mechanical engineering, because they both used and displayed new materials – iron and steel – were welcomed as artifacts of contemporary civilization and hence as bearing the mark of the times.[93]

The primacy of materials and methods of construction in the fabrication of engineering works reinforced the importance of the system of construction in the contemporary understanding of the 'architectural system.' This similarity reconfirmed the validity of the architectural system while conferring upon engineering works the status of role models for the development of a modern architecture. Furthermore, engineering works were also seen as healthy realizations of the true principles of design, because they were deemed to have been created out of inner necessity, governed by reason and logic, and guided by economy. The result was a form with integrity in the use and expression of its materials and with harmony in the shape and unity of its forms. For these reasons as well, the engineering work became a model for the proper way to create architecture. As the American sculptor Horatio Greenough counseled in the 1850s,

Let us now turn to a structure of our own, one which, from its nature and uses, commands us to reject authority, and we shall find the result of the manly use of plain good sense, so like that of taste, and genius too, as scarce to require a distinctive title. Observe a ship at sea! Mark the majestic form of her hull as she rushes through the water, observe the graceful bend of her body, the gentle transition [etc.]. Behold an organization second only to that of an animal, obedient as the horse, swift as the stag, and bearing the burden of a thousand camels from pole to pole! ... Could we carry into our civil architecture the responsibilities that weigh upon our shipbuilding, we should ere long have edifices as superior to the Parthenon, for the purposes that we require, as the *Constitution* or the *Pennsylvania* is to the galley of the Argonauts. Could our blunders on terra firma be put to the same dread test that those of shipbuilders are, little would be now left to say on this subject.[94]

Such thoughts would be repeated throughout the succeeding century. At times, the writer would emphasize the rational aspect of the lessons of engineering, while drawing a parallel to architecture, as did James Fergusson in his universal history of architecture:

In the ship the most suitable materials only are employed in every part, and neither below nor aloft is there one single timber nor spar nor one rope which is superfluous. Nor in the cathedral was ever any material used that was not believed to be the most suitable for its purpose; nor any form of construction adopted which did not seem the best to those who employed it; nor any detail added which did not seem necessary for the purpose it was put there to express; and the consequence is, that we can look on and contemplate both with the same unmitigated satisfaction.

This, explained Fergusson, was the 'proper spirit' to follow for the creation of a 'new style' in architecture.[95]

Just as Fergusson found satisfaction for the mind in the lesson of the machine, others found poetic inspiration: 'Not to perceive the poetry of the modern machine is not to perceive the poetry of modern life. I am convinced that in a time such as our own, so long as the Beaux-Arts disdain the mechanical arts, there will be no Beaux-Arts.'[96] The leading Dutch architect Hendrik Petrus Berlage quoted these lines approvingly to second his contention that 'the machine will be a powerful aid in the creation of an art.'[97]

Engineering works were deemed comparable to the works of great architecture for other reasons as well. The new engineering marvels evoked the same response of admiration and even awe in the viewer. 'It is necessary to have experienced the emotion,' explained Van de Velde,

that overcame us for the first time when we saw the line of that gigantic metal prow of an ocean liner exhibited by Krupp in 1902 at Düsseldorf to grasp the sense and the quality of the emotion that grips us when contemplating the profile of the colossal Ramses lying in the desert sands of Memphis. ... It is necessary also to experience the true, imperious and eternal beauty of the Parthenon and the perfect rhythm of the various parts of the Greek temple!

These were the types of aesthetic experiences that would 'reconnect the family ties broken between the art of antiquity to that of today.'[98] If the Greeks of the fifth century had known the trolleys, cable-cars, and locomotives of today, they would have loved and appreciated their beauty.[99]

Such an appreciation would not have been limited to the beauty of the new engineering works but would also have recognized the creative energies at work here, which were comparable to those that had realized the great architectural masterpieces of the past. Referring to the 'new class' of engineers who in the nineteenth century 'bridged rivers and deltas, built roads and vaulted spaces with enormous spans for train stations and markets, invented steam boats, locomotives, and the most amazing machines and scientific apparatus,' Muthesius affirmed, 'Here our times have developed such a high creative force that has nothing to fear through a comparison with the greatest times of building, the Greek and the Middle Ages. ... Here lies the constructive deed of modern times. It is congruent with the spiritual goals of the times, just as in other great epochs of building.'[100]

The machine and the Parthenon

Thus, in a seeming paradox, the same voices that were rejecting the use of historical styles were simultaneously affirming the deep affinity between the modern spirit as found in machine production and in the greatest productions of ancient architecture, most notably in the Doric temple. The analogy between the aesthetic perfection of the Doric temple and the machine was a popular theme from the mid-nineteenth-century onward. From these comparisons one senses that both the Doric temple and the machine were appreciated as much as aesthetic as cultural icons. Through this type of argument, the notion of representative architecture came to require a comparable combination of artistic perfection and cultural expression.

The status accorded the Parthenon as the supreme achievement in architectural beauty dates back to the turn of the nineteenth century when Willey Reveley rose to the defense of Greek architecture by responding to Sir William Chambers' attack upon Stuart and Revett's *The Antiquities of Athens*. With the subsequent development of Romantic Hellenism discussed above in chapter two, this appreciation continued throughout the century and entered into the literature of progressive architectural thought in the early twentieth century. Toward 1850 Horatio Greenough, drawing upon the combination of ineffable artistic unity and beauty seen by contemporaries in the Parthenon, was one of the first to describe the aesthetic achievement of the 'purer Doric temple' and the machine in the same terms. Each partook of a richly considered simplicity, 'not the simplicity of emptiness or of poverty,' but rather the simplicity 'of justness.'[101]

This parallel between Greek architecture and the machine was especially popular with the progressive architects of the early twentieth century. Van de Velde, for example, offered a variation on this theme in 1903 by reflecting upon the Greek theater at Syracuse:

The spirit from which Greek art was born is not dead. . . . It is palpitating in us as lively and as pure as three thousand years ago! . . . the spirit . . . that gave birth to this theater – whose admirably logical conception appears today, now that it has been stripped of all ornament, even more logical – is the same spirit that invented the electric light bulb. . . . The principle of its creation is that which guides our engineers in the construction of machines, of metal structural frames, and of ocean liners.[102]

In 1913 Camille Martin likewise observed that over the course of the nineteenth century architecture had lost 'its unity and its life,' while engineering had known vigorous success: 'I will simply note the following: everything new, daring, and original in the realm of construction in the nineteenth century has been the work of engineers.'[103] In his article 'L'Architecture du XXe siècle' (Architecture of the Twentieth Century), Martin repeatedly returned to the theme of the architect who was abandoning the related tasks of good design and appropriate cultural expression to the engineer:

Today the engineers speak a simple, comprehensible, modern language whereas the architects express themselves through outdated multiple idioms. The engineer resolves problems that he has been given by utilizing directly all the resources at his disposal. . . . The architect proceeds in a diametrically opposite way. Usually he disdains new materials and instead attempts to determine to what extent he can approach his task with the conventional signs of his cast: columns, cornices, domes or bell towers.[104]

Of all the architects and critics who reiterated these points during this period, it was Le Corbusier who made the most forceful argument in his *Vers une Architecture*, a book that became a rallying-point for the generation of architects responsible for creating what has come to be called the International Style.

Vers une Architecture and the modern architectural treatise

Le Corbusier's *Vers une Architecture* is a carefully balanced book, with its chapters nearly equally divided between the lessons of architectural history and the lessons of the machine and of engineering structures. For Le Corbusier, history provided examples of the harmony achieved through proportion, the aesthetic power of simple prismatic forms, the nature of the architectural promenade, the design principles that could be abstracted from different historical periods (figures 1.1, 2.16, 2.17), and the spiritual aura that architecture could provide (figure 2.8). Works of engineering complemented this list with parallel or separate lessons. Grain silos and factories taught the architect about volume and surface. Ocean liners, airplanes, and automobiles (figures 4.1–4.3) gave the example of the solution to well-posed problems that could inspire architects to achieve the same

DES YEUX QUI NE VOIENT PAS...

« AIR EXPRESS », le Goliath Farman.

4.1
'Eyes That Do Not See.' ' "Air Express" Goliath Farman'

degree of functional accommodation for the dwelling. 'The house,' quipped Le Corbusier, 'is a machine for dwelling.'

But these engineering marvels served still another function. They appear in Le Corbusier's illustrations as cultural icons. Although they carry this power when they are shown simply by themselves, Le Corbusier reinforced this point through the nature of his text, the selection of illustrations, and the relationships between the written and visual material. The book is filled with explanations such as:

A new era has just begun.
There exists a new spirit.
There exists a host of new works in the new spirit; they are found especially in industrial production.
Architecture suffocates in past customs.
The 'styles' are a lie.[105]

This message was also conveyed through illustrations. One sandwiched a page with six small photographs showing recent buildings in historical styles between two full pages, each filled with a photograph of one of the most modern airplanes, the Goliath Farman (figure 4.4). The two-page spread was captioned 'The problem

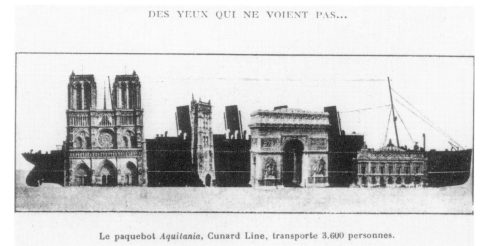

DES YEUX QUI NE VOIENT PAS...

Le paquebot *Aquitania*, Cunard Line, transporte 3.600 personnes.

4.2
'Eyes That Do Not See.' Architectural monuments compared in size to the ocean liner Aquitania

4.3
'Mass-produced houses'

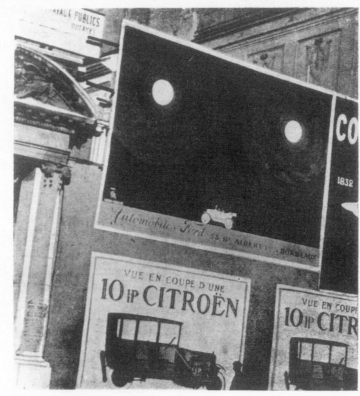

Cliché Hostache.

4.4
'The Goliath Farman, Paris–Prague in six hours. Paris–Warsaw in nine hours'

Le Goliath FARMAN. Paris-Prague en six heures, Paris-Varsovie en neuf heures.

poorly conceived: Eyes that do not see . . . Farman.' The implication is that the new style will be found in the engineering aesthetic that this airplane typifies. The aesthetic pedigree of engineering works Le Corbusier attempted to establish through text and illustrations, when he argued that the development of the car followed the pattern of development of the Doric temple from its primitive beginnings, through the perfecting of the type, to reach its culminating form in the Parthenon. For the automobile, this meant the successive perfecting of form and function resulting in the contemporary speedy and streamlined car. Finally (figure 4.2), by juxtaposing images of the great monuments of the past with that of the ocean liner Aquitania, Le Corbusier established the monumental character of this colossal construction. Other illustrations of the Aquitania presented the ocean liner as a lesson in modern architecture. One is even given the caption 'Architecture is the skillful, appropriate, and magnificent play of volumes assembled under light' – the aphorism that Le Corbusier repeated in his chapter on the Parthenon.

Le Corbusier's *Vers une Architecture* is a perfect illustration of Marshall McLuhan's point that the medium is the message. As the Swiss architect Hans Schmidt explained in 1927, 'The way in which [Le Corbusier] formulates his points and constructs his text in brief chapters, using particularly incisive phrases and illustrations, is a totally new way of writing, of convincing, closer to a living journalism, to daily life, than to literature or to science, which refers inward to itself.'[106] In Schmidt, Le Corbusier had found a perceptive reader who fully understood the architect's intentions. The publicity brochure for *Vers une Architecture*, which Le Corbusier wrote in May 1923, explained the author's goals:

This book draws its eloquence from new means; its magnificent illustrations present a powerful, parallel discourse alongside that of the written text. This new concept of the book with the explicit and revealing discourse of illustrations permits the author to avoid ineffective sentences and descriptions; things explode under the reader's eyes through the force of images; the book's text is no more than a guiding thread held out by a mind avid for clarity across the magnificent tumult of an age whose history begins to inscribe itself in the grandeur of mathematical calculation; the modesty, science, and lyricism of a century that advances beyond a hundred centuries before it.[107]

Le Corbusier, then, intended his book not simply as a polemical treatise, but as a creation consonant with the spirit of the age. It was a creation that gave form to the modern way of thinking and feeling. Its intention was to convey its contents through a medium that captured the pulse of modern life. To this end Le Corbusier applied the two modern methods of communication that had been identified as distinguishing features of the age – the poster or billboard and the short, aphoristic sentence.

The intense quality of Le Corbusier's imagery, carefully selected, sometimes altered, often cropped, and presented with a directed focus to achieve a forceful impact, reflects the aesthetic of the modern billboard. Le Corbusier mastered the technique to the point of capturing its fondness for visual puns and direct allusions. In the first case, the running header on top of the page – 'Eyes That Do Not See' – becomes the caption for the car in the photograph placed immediately below with its two round headlights 'staring' directly like eyes at the reader.

In the second case (figure 4.3), Le Corbusier has selected a photograph with publicity posters for automobiles to make the point about 'maisons en série,' mass-produced housing. The repeated posters for the Citroën car provide the lesson about creating mass-produced homes, which Le Corbusier designed and named, with the pun intended, 'maison en série "Citrohan" (pour ne pas dire

Citroën)' – 'mass-produced houses [called] "Citrohan" (so as not to say Citroën).' Le Corbusier also hoped that the automobile and airplane manufacturers would fabricate such homes.

The poster advertising the Ford automobiles serves a dual function, at once a reference to the highly admired American manufacturer, whom Europeans identified with 'standardization and mass-production,'[108] and a use of the poster's own visual pun that uses the automobile headlights peering through the night like two giant eyes staring, once again, at the viewer. It is significant that Le Corbusier substituted this photograph in the widely circulated third edition of *Vers une Architecture* for a less effective image that he had used in the first edition, which shows a cropped view of an automobile with the doors open to reveal the interior.

Since the turn of the century, *l'affiche*, the poster or billboard, had been widely regarded as a thoroughly modern phenomenon: 'L'affiche is essentially modern,' proclaimed Emile Magne in *L'Esthétique des villes* (1908). 'It did not exist in other times.'[109] The poster was also considered as partaking of the most characteristic aspects of contemporary life. As the eminent art critic and premier champion of *l'affiche* Roger Marx explained:

Understood by all ages, young and old, loved by the populace, the poster speaks directly to all. It has been developed to satisfy new aspirations. . . . It replaces the paintings once seen on palace walls, on the vaults of cloisters and churches; it is the temporary, moving picture called forth by an age taken with popularization and avid for change.[110]

Whereas Roger Marx belonged to the era of Art Nouveau and the movement for *l'art dans la rue* (art in the street), it was left to the painter Fernand Léger, whose aesthetic influenced Le Corbusier and whose canvases the architect hung in his buildings, to elucidate the relationship between the poster and modern means of transportation in ways that set the stage for the arguments presented in *Vers une Architecture* and in Le Corbusier's avant-garde houses:

If pictorial expression has changed, it is because modern life has made this necessary. . . . [T]he means of modern transportation have completely reversed the relationship known for all times. Before now, a countryside was a value in itself that a white and dead road traversed without changing the surroundings. Today, trains and cars with the cloud of smoke and dust take their dynamism with them, and the countryside becomes secondary and decorative. Posters on the walls, luminous advertisements are of the same order of ideas; it has given birth to the ridiculous formula: *Défense d'afficher* [post no bills]. It is the incomprehension of all that is new and alive that has prompted this policing of the walls. . . . The poster is the modern furnishing.[111]

Moreover, as Léger explained, abbreviated speech was as much a characteristic of contemporary life as the poster, with both issuing from the new pace of daily existence and from the altered experience of the world created by the machine.[112] In using short, aphoristic pronouncements, given as a list, Le Corbusier was joining other artists, such as Georges Bracque, whose 'Pensées et réflexions sur la peinture' (Thoughts and Reflections about Painting) appeared in this manner in the avant-garde journal *Nord-Sud* (December 1917).[113]

Whereas Le Corbusier had every right to proclaim proudly that his book 'is like no other,' it was not without pioneering precedents that had attempted to create a modern text in similar ways.[114] As Hans Schmidt observed, Le Corbusier belonged to the second generation of modernists, which had been preceded by architects like Van de Velde and Berlage, who had made important written contributions, the influence of which was at least as important as their buildings. In effect, Berlage, along with Otto Wagner, had pioneered a new form of architectural treatise that combined image and word in what Schmidt termed the propagandistic manner.[115]

As his polemical treatise calling for a modern architecture underwent four successive editions between 1896 and 1914, Otto Wagner perfected the visual and written format to make his presentation as forceful as possible. In the first edition of *Moderne Architektur*, Wagner used wider spacing between letters to emphasize his important points. The second edition, published two years later, gave greater visual prominence to these passages by printing them in capital letters (figure 4.5). Chapter titles, as well as the title of the book, were made to stand out visually by being printed in red ink. Each chapter title was now accompanied by a labeled photographic illustration of Wagner's own modern architecture, offered as a demonstration of the goals advocated throughout the whole book. Finally, the page was printed off-center as an example of modern typographic design.

The third edition of Wagner's book was published in 1902, a time when Art Nouveau was widely seen throughout the West as having succeeded in creating an international modern cultural expression. Like other avant-garde texts published at this time, the book was designed with Art Nouveau typography, ornamentation, and color. A pastel, caramel ink was used for chapter titles and decorative Art Nouveau vignettes. The text was centered again, now within wide margins of empty white space on all sides of the paper. Each page was provided with an illustration bordered by the caramel-colored Art Nouveau vignettes. The text itself was broken into brief visual arguments, established through tightly spaced text in

4.5
Sample page spread from Otto Wagner, *Moderne Architektur*, 1898 (2nd edition)

short paragraphs preceded and followed by small decorative boxes. With this third edition, Wagner succeeded in establishing parallel texts – written and visual – by grouping all the photographs at the top of the page. Since the illustrations did not correspond to the text below or even to the chapter, the written and visual arguments remained independent.

In the fourth edition, published with the new title *Die Baukunst unserer Zeit*, Wagner abandoned the decorative elements of the short-lived Art Nouveau style. The major innovation here was the addition of thematic 'decks' of titles printed at the top of each page that identified the subject matter discussed below. Once again, the illustrations of Wagner's work do not seem to have been organized systematically to correspond to the subject of each chapter. Main ideas are emphasized through capitalization.

Hendrik Petrus Berlage experimented with parallel visual and written texts in his *Grundlagen und Entwicklung der Architektur* (Foundations and Development of Architecture) (1908). Here Berlage adapted the example of Augustus Welby Pugin's *Contrasts: or, A Parallel between the Noble Edifices of the Middle Ages, and Corresponding Buildings of the Present Day Shewing the Present Decay of Taste* (1836; second edition 1841). Just as Pugin had juxtaposed drawings of Gothic architecture with contemporary classical counterparts to the advantage of the former, Berlage paired photographs of Roman and Renaissance buildings with modern imitations to demonstrate the aesthetic weakness of the latter. Berlage also provided his paired illustrations with aphoristic captions and co-ordinated their subject matter with the written text on the lower portion of the page.

Berlage developed this technique further in *L'Art et la société*, a book that surpasses Wagner's *Die Baukunst unserer Zeit* in its presentation of parallel written and visual arguments. *L'Art et la société* first appeared in installments between September 1913 and February 1914 in the avant-garde Belgian architectural journal *Art et Technique*. It was reissued as a book in 1921. The text reproduces three lectures delivered in February 1913 at the Université Nouvelle de Bruxelles where Berlage participated in a lecture series on modern decorative arts and architecture.[116] Berlage's book was a broad inquiry into the nature of culture and the dynamics of cultural change with a consideration of their relationship to artistic expression. Interspersed among the pages with the verbal argument, Berlage placed a second, pictorial 'text' consisting of entire pages of illustrations accompanied by their own page of identifying captions organized under a succinctly stated principle. In these captions we find the main themes of the nineteenth- and twentieth-century progressive tradition that have been the subject of this study:

In the great periods of art, artists, architects, painters, and sculptors collaborated in a great unity of style.

Material simplicity and the logical distribution of masses characterize every truly great architecture.

The purity of construction of Greek architecture is contrary to the tainted construction of the Romans. Roman architecture reduces the column to a decorative role and consequently becomes inferior to Greek architecture [figure 4.6, items 7, 8].

Several examples show the sublimity of Greek architecture as well as that of the Middle Ages. The Renaissance, incapable of attaining the sublime, only succeeds in achieving beauty.

Examples of Roman architecture and of Renaissance architecture placed in opposition to show the strength of one and the weakness of the other. The weakness being a result of imitation.

Figure 7   *Figure 8*

Figure 9

Figure 10   *Figure 11*

In the Renaissance painting and sculpture gradually separate from architecture to become separate arts. The contemporary period witnesses the absolute degeneration of art in the subjective sense.

From the relative simplicity of interiors in the middle of the nineteenth century came a chaotic period where one would search in vain for a trace of style.

The Ringstrasse of Vienna offers the proof of an absolute absence of unity in the architecture of the current era. One finds there, one after the other: the Parliament in Greek style, the new

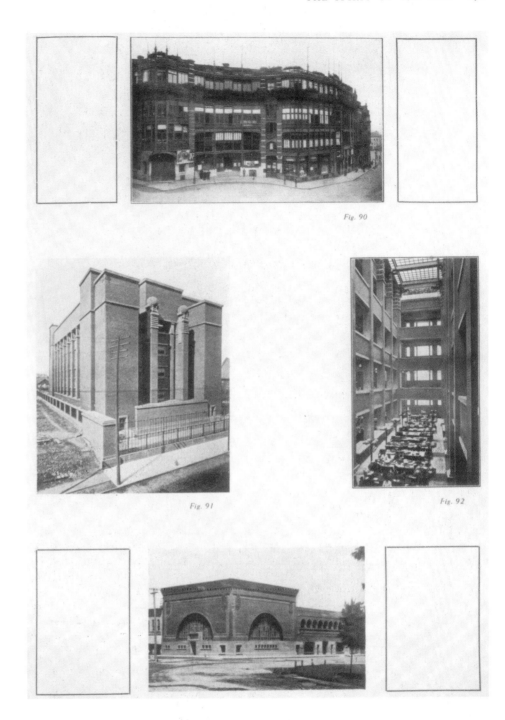

Fig. 90

Fig. 91

Fig. 92

4.6 [*facing*], **4.7**
Pages from Hendrik Petrus Berlage,
L'Art et la société

City Hall in pseudo-Gothic style, the new University in Italian Renaissance, the Votive Church in Gothic style.

Several examples will show the movement toward simplification that, toward 1890, began to manifest itself in furnishings. The reaction is characteristic.

The movement did not stop: soon the entire building becomes simpler. Note that the search for simplicity and the simple distribution of masses is international. A unity of style seems to be on the way toward realization.

Organization is the dominant characteristic of the modern epoch. Art, in particular, tends toward organization, toward simplification. Now, it seems that the ancients already took into account, in their buildings, linear and numerical relationships that were factors of beauty. The spirit of these laws is taken up again notably by modernist Dutch architects.

Modern architecture emphasizes the grouping of masses and the search for simplicity. It is the commercial building that best reflects modern social life. Commercial buildings in the Italian Renaissance style. The problem of large glass surfaces is given a rational solution thanks to the system of supports.

The final pair of pages (figure 4.7) with illustrations and aphorisms features Victor Horta's Maison du Peuple (Brussels, 1895–99) at the top, captioned 'an excellent example of a modern social building.' In the middle of the page are exterior and interior views of Wright's Larkin Administration Building (Buffalo, 1904) and at the bottom, Sullivan's National Farmers' Bank (Owatonna, Minnesota, 1906–08). The next pages were devoted to Berlage's Exchange (Amsterdam, 1897–1903). Under the Larkin Building, Berlage writes: 'It is a magnificent example of a modern commercial building with a grand simplicity and a beautiful daring.' The page concludes, 'These buildings remind us that strength is the essential quality of every work of art. This character, which the monuments of the nineteenth century utterly lacked, is expressed not through the absolute size of the edifice, but rather through the judicious grouping of masses.'

Many of these themes would reappear in *Vers une Architecture* where Le Corbusier learned to distill and focus the contents of his text, the accompanying illustrations and captions, the running headers that reiterated the chapter title, and the title-pages themselves of each chapter, followed by a page of aphorisms. As the reader ruminates on the arguments presented in the written text, he or she focuses on the striking images of the great monuments of ancient architecture, the dramatic forms of modern civil engineering, and the dynamic images of contemporary means of transport.

In considering Le Corbusier's avant-garde villas of the late 1920s, as well as Frank Lloyd Wright's earlier Prairie houses, we can see that they combined the lessons of the progressive Romantic tradition that Berlage had enumerated. Even more, they offered, in a polemical manner, an architecture that captured the spirit of the works of modern engineering. In certain buildings, such as Le Corbusier's Maison Cook, Villa Stein, and Villa Savoye, and Wright's Larkin Building and Robie House, the architect evoked the spaces or forms of the most modern means of transportation, those icons of the modern age.

'Eyes That Do Not See'

In three chapters in *Vers une Architecture* entitled 'Eyes That Do Not See,' Le Corbusier challenged the reader to observe a series of lessons taught by the example of ocean liners, airplanes, and automobiles. The most remarkable eye-opener is a page with two photographs of the ocean liner Aquitania (figure 4.8). The top photo, cropped to show only the rear deck, suggests designing a modern villa by the sea like an ocean liner rather than copying traditional regional styles: 'To Messieurs, the Architects: a villa on the dunes of Normandy, conceived like these ocean liners, would be more appropriate than the large "Norman roofs," so outmoded! But it might be claimed that this is not at all the maritime style!' The caption for the bottom photo extols the aesthetic virtue of the long promenade deck. Several years later, Le Corbusier would design the Villa Savoye with a form

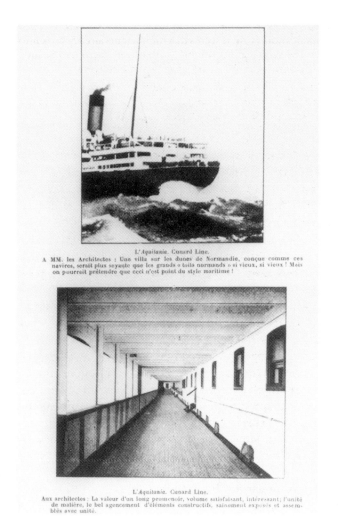

4.8
'Eyes That Do Not See. I. Ocean Liners'

that directly evokes the cubical mass of the rear deck of this ocean liner (figure 1.8). He also fashioned the facade of the main floor after the promenade deck of the lower photo. Presented in this manner, the Villa Savoye appears as more than a modern architectural creation conceived according to a machine-age aesthetic, it is offered as an icon of the times.

Similarly, at the turn of the century, Wright designed the Larkin Building (figures 1.31–1.33) according to the spirit of the marvels of modern mechanical engineering. As he explained in his article of March 1908, 'In the Cause of Architecture,' 'Here again most of the critic's "architecture" has been left out. Therefore the work may have the same claim to consideration as a "work of art" as an ocean liner, a locomotive or a battleship.'[117] Reflecting on this building, in particular, and on his Prairie houses of the same period, Wright, would remark in his *An Autobiography* (1932):

It now appears these values [i.e., simplicity and freedom] came into the architecture of the world. New sense of repose in quiet streamline effects arrived. The streamline and the plain surface seen as the flat plane, had then and there some thirty years ago, found their way into buildings as we see them in steamships, aeroplanes and motorcars, although still intimately related to building materials, environment and the human being.

In particular, Wright saw the Larkin Building as as a 'genuine and constructive affirmation of the new Order of the Machine Age.'[118]

The avant-garde Dutch architect J. J. P. Oud saw in Wright's Robie House (figures 1.27, 1.30, colour plate 10) both the evidence of a modern aesthetic and the embodiment of the modern machine-age spirit:

Instead of a stable and rigid compactness of the various parts, Wright *detaches the masses from the whole* and rearranges their composition. There is a direct relation here with the way the futurists have overcome rigidity in painting – which is by achieving movement of the planes. In this way Wright has created a new 'plastic' architecture. His masses slide back and forth and left and right; there are plastic effects in all directions. This movement, which one finds in his work, opens up entirely new aesthetic possibilities for architecture. . . . The effect that Wright achieves in the Robie House is partly due to his highly appropriate use of reinforced concrete, as seen in the long terrace. This expression is not absolutely pure, however, because brick conceals the concrete – with the result that the concrete shows its essence but not its characteristic appearance. Yet the function of reinforced concrete is clearly stated since such a span, made in such a way, cannot be conceived in any other material. In this house one completely feels the spirit of our age. One obtains a similar impression from a moving locomotive. One thinks of an automobile, rather than a horse-drawn carriage, as being appropriate for this home.[119]

Oud's reference to the automobile would certainly have pleased the client, Frederick C. Robie, who manufactured bicycles and who 'was especially interested in manufacturing motorcycles and his experimental cycle car.'[120] Robie, explains Donald Hoffmann, 'liked to ride around Chicago . . . in an experimental motorcar of his own making.'[121] Wright understood this well, for he too 'loved cars and had a Stoddard Dayton sportscar custom built to his own design (which included a cantilevered convertible roof).'[122]

Yet the similarity to mechanized transportation does not end with the harmonious feeling between the horizontal lines of the Robie House and the speed of the automobile and the locomotive. It can also be found in the main room of the interior, the long living and dining room with its lower ceiling along the periphery (figure 1.55). Visitors to this room in the years immediately following its construction would readily have recalled the similar spatial configuration of street-cars and river-boats, just as when viewing the exterior of the house they could easily have thought about the projecting eaves of suburban and small-town railroad stations. In street-cars and river-boats the higher central area enabled the provision of clerestory windows for further light and ventilation, a configuration that Wright would soon employ in the living room of the second Francis W. Little House 'overlooking Robinson Bay of Lake Minnetonka' (Deephaven, Minnesota, 1912).[123] If one wonders whether Wright had intended such references, then the answer might be found in still another question: where else could one have experienced such a spatial configuration at that time? Widely found in modern means of transportation, such spatial configurations would be understood readily in this manner.

As for Le Corbusier, he did not begin to design his avant-garde buildings as iconic analogues to the representative machine-productions of the day with the Villa Savoye, but rather with the Maison Cook, the first house constructed according to the 'Five Points for a New Architecture.' Here Le Corbusier used the nose of the Goliath Farman airplane (figures 4.1, 4.4) for the entry to the house (figure 4.9).[124] In a general way, the presence of the body of the airplane is intended to show that the aesthetics of the house fit the spirit of the modern machine.

On entre sous la maison

4.9
Le Corbusier and Pierre Jeanneret.
Maison Cook, Boulogne-sur-Seine,
1926. 'One enters under the house'

Le Corbusier conveys the same meaning when he publishes a view of the Villa
Stein with an automobile in the foreground (figure 4.10). The parallel between
house and machine is further emphasized by the similarity between the long
horizontal windows of the facade and the analogous configuration of the windows
of the car. Yet, at the Maison Cook (figures 1.4, 1.5) Le Corbusier was being even
more specific. He was asking his viewers to open their eyes once again and see the
analogy between the form of the airplane and the aesthetic that he had developed
with his 'Five Points for a New Architecture:' the wings have become the
cantilevered floors with the building elevated off the ground and provided with a

4.10
Le Corbusier and Pierre Jeanneret. Villa
Stein, Garches, 1927. 'Entrance to the
property'

flat-roof terrace, the vertical struts have become the free-standing concrete columns, and the rounded nose has become not simply the entry-hall but also, by extension, all the curved forms relating to movement and to the human body that Le Corbusier places in his building.

Just as the Maison Cook is the architectural equivalent to the Goliath Farman airplane, the Villa Stein (figures 1.6, 4.10) is the analogue to the front superstructure of the Aquitania ocean liner (figure 4.11). Le Corbusier, we recall, juxtaposed a photograph of an ocean liner with his definition of architecture, placed in quotation marks, as the play of volumes under light. Once again, he is asking his viewers, former readers of his chapters on the 'eyes that do not see,' to blink and see the Villa Stein as evoking this other icon of the machine civilization.

Le Corbusier's most complete statement of this theme occurs in the Villa Savoye. It is not merely an evocation of the rear deck of the Aquitania; it is also a consideration of the relationship between man and the machine by means of an architectural promenade that begins with the automobile leaving Paris to journey to this suburban villa. The machine, as we have seen Léger explain, revolutionized the experience of the landscape. Now the landscape is viewed as fleeting by rapidly while framed by the rectangle of the car window. When the car reaches the Villa Savoye (figure 1.8), it proceeds around the base, which, Le Corbusier explains, has been designed as a function of the tightest possible turning radius for a car passing under its elevated main floor.[125] Lest there be any doubt about the importance of this mechanized journey from Paris, Le Corbusier publishes two virtually identical photographs showing the straight passageway for the car under the house. One is labeled 'arrival of the cars under the *pilotis*'; the other 'the car returns to Paris.' Thus the automobile carrying its passengers from the city to the villa is a protagonist in this architectural promenade.

Automobile travel has been such an integral part of Western culture for over a half-century now that it is easy to forget the degree to which it was altering people's relationship to the natural world. It would be helpful to pause for a moment to consider the reflections of a keen observer in 1991 who, after a journey in an open carriage, shares with his readers the discovery of how the automobile has so profoundly changed this relationship:

To travel in this way is to make you regret the invention of the car. There is a different view of everything, more commanding and somehow more interesting. There is a comfortable, swaying rhythm as the suspension adjusts to the gait of the horse and the changes of camber and surface. There is a pleasant background of old-fashioned noises as the harness creaks and the hooves clop and the steel rims of the wheels crunch the grit on the road. There is the *parfum* – a blend of warm horse, saddle soap, wood varnish, and the smells of the fields that come to the nose unobstructed by windows. And there is the speed, or lack of it, which allows you time to *look*. In a car you're in a fast room. You see a blur, an impression; you're insulated from the countryside. In a carriage, you're part of it.[126]

Le Corbusier certainly did not regret the invention of the automobile. The Villa Savoye celebrates it. But it seeks to re-establish the equilibrium between man and nature after the exhilarating ride from the city to the villa. Upon leaving the car one enters the house and proceeds upward on the central ramp, which leads to the main floor and then to the upper level of the roof terrace with the solarium (figure 4.12). The ramp facilitates a smooth, gliding motion that continues the sense of movement of the automobile, but now at the slower pace of the pedestrian. Le Corbusier comments on the importance of this movement at the measured pace and rhythm of the human body.[127] At the top of the ramp, the promenade ends with

4.11, 4.12

The *Aquitania*

'Architectural Promenade.'
Le Corbusier and Pierre Jeanneret.
Villa Savoye, Poissy, 1928–31

a framed view of the landscape situated between the organic shapes of the solarium. This scene ritualistically re-enacts the initial, framed view through the car window that began the sequence when leaving Paris. With the Villa Savoye, the machine fully enters the garden. Through the architectural promenade, man and machine have become one, with the machine fully humanized.

This lesson reflects the crisis in Le Corbusier's thought that he expressed at an international symposium on the arts in contemporary life held in Venice in 1934. Here Le Corbusier warned against the dangers posed by a machine civilization that, with the advent of the railroad one hundred years earlier, had destroyed the traditional equilibrium between man and his social and physical milieu. He explained that 1930 had marked the opening of '*the second period of machine civilization*, this one consecrated to harmony – to harmonizing the new and revolutionary factors placed in the presence of the eternal and permanent desires and needs of the human mind and spirit.'[128] The Villa Savoye had been Le Corbusier's first polemical statement and architectural realization of that new harmony. We know that over the course of the next decade his domestic architecture would change radically to admit organic materials and imagery in his quest for an equilibrium between timeless needs and new technological possibilities.

There is still one further level of symbolic meaning that Le Corbusier invested in the Villa Savoye. In *Modern Architecture Since 1900* (1982), William J. R. Curtis juxtaposes photographs of the Villa Savoye and the Parthenon and comments:

Perhaps one may even go so far as to suggest a reminiscence of the Parthenon which had so obsessed Le Corbusier twenty years before. Surely the mechanized procession culminating in an entrance point at the opposite end of the building suggests affinities with the ceremonial route the artist had noted in the Acropolis. ... It is tempting to regard the *piloti*, the central element of Le Corbusier's architectural language ... as being a reinterpreted Classical column as well. ... Its individual elements – the *piloti*, the strip window, etc. – were elevated, like the columns and triglyphs of a Greek temple, to the level of timeless solutions: the abstraction of its forms implied a lofty and spiritual role for architecture.[129]

Curtis is certainly correct in drawing attention to the analogy between the Villa Savoye and the Parthenon that Le Corbusier seems to have intended. In the chapter on the picturesque, I mentioned that the configuration of the entrance hall with the ramp passing through the rows of free-standing columns and the asymmetrically balanced forms that flank the entrance door (figure 1.9) is analogous to the scene that Choisy described as the first view at the Acropolis, in front of the Propylaia (figure 2.12). The similarity, I believe, is intentional, for Le Corbusier appears to have cast what Curtis has termed the ritualized 'machine-age ceremony' of the architectural promenade as an analogue to the most important civic and religious festival in ancient Athens, the Panathenaia. The drive from Paris and back, signaled by the pair of captioned photos, substitutes for the Panathenaic procession that ascended on foot and in chariots from the main entrance of the city to the Acropolis. As a modern equivalent to the Parthenon, the Villa Savoye presents strip windows that capture the moving form of the automobile-window in an equivalent to the frieze, thought to depict the Panathenaic procession, which wraps around the cella of the Parthenon. The arrival into the forecourt of the Propylaia is ritualistically repeated in the analogous asymmetrically balanced scene encountered upon entering the main hall. There, a modern reinforced concrete ramp takes the place of the stepped ramp through the center of the columnar hall of the Propylaia. In this manner Le Corbusier has created a ritual for modern man that addressed his most important spiritual and material needs, namely to effect a harmonious relationship with both landscape and the machine.

In the 1930s, Le Corbusier and Frank Lloyd Wright each designed a building that made a clear and forceful statement about this relationship. At the Swiss Dormitory, Le Corbusier, as we have seen, designed the edifice as a dialogue between the elevated machine-like prism, which contains the repetitive cells for the student's rooms, and the low, curved rustic wall, representing nature, which forms the back to the space of sociability, the communal living room. The entire assemblage of gridded space and walls in the entrance hall provided a place of mediation between these two polar opposites. Likewise, in Fallingwater, Wright contrasted the daring cantilevered reinforced concrete balconies with the rusticated flagstone walls and chimney-stack built of local rock. Yet even here the balconies echoed the projecting stone ledges of Bear Run that had been created by the erosive forces of the stream. With Wright, the opposition between machine and nature could not be so direct. These are the types of thematic statements that Le Corbusier and Frank Lloyd Wright would continue to make with their architecture as they invested their forms not only with a style but also a symbolism that addressed what they and their contemporaries understood as the need to translate into building the essential challenges and dilemmas of the times. Whereas not all of their buildings were as explicitly narrative, they generally responded to the concept of giving form to current sensibilities and life-styles in ways that would harmonize with the universals of the human conditon. In pursuing this goal, both architects were guided by the tenets of the nineteenth-century progressive program for creating a modern architecture: the architectural system, the picturesque, and philosophical eclecticism. They believed that adherence to these values was the surest way to creating new and timeless works that their fellows and future generations would recognize as worthy testimonies to the age.

NOTES

PREFACE

1 Henri Matisse, 'Notes d'un peintre,' *La Grande Revue* 52 (25 December, 1908), in *Écrits et propos sur l'art*, ed. Dominique Fourcade (Paris, 1972), 53: 'Tous les artistes portent l'empreinte de leur époque, mais les grands artistes sont ceux en qui elle est marquée le plus profondément.'

2 John Louis Petit, *Architectural Studies in France* (London, 1854), vii.

3 Whereas aspects of the Romantic legacy can be found in various studies, including Henry-Russell Hitchcock's famous *Modern Architecture: Romanticism and Reintegration* (1929) and Reyner Banham's excellent *Theory and Design in the First Machine Age* (1960), there appear to be only two books that have addressed the issue directly. The first is Peter Collins' *Changing Ideals in Modern Architecture, 1750–1950* (London: Faber and Faber, 1965). A pioneering work, Professor Collins' book introduces many of the themes that I treat, but does not pursue them as systematically as I believe it should have. My book offers an alternative view of the subject as whole while also focusing on the architecture of Frank Lloyd Wright and Le Corbusier. The second is J. Mordaunt Crook, *The Dilemma of Style: Architectural Ideas from the Picturesque to the Post-Modern* (The University of Chicago Press, 1987). Crook's book is concerned primarily with England. He first focuses on stylistic revivals and then approaches twentieth-century modernism from the conceptual framework of historicism. Thus he generally ignores the progressive ideas that furnish the basis of my cross-cultural study.

4 For a further development of this idea, see Richard A. Etlin, 'Le Corbusier, Choisy, and French Hellenism: The Search for a New Architecture,' *The Art Bulletin* 69 (June 1987), 264–5, and Richard A. Etlin, *Modernism in Italian Architecture, 1890–1940* (Cambridge, Mass., 1991), xviii–xx ('The Romantic Legacy').

5 John Summerson, 'The Mischievous Analogy,' in *Heavenly Mansions and Other Essays on Architecture* (1948; New York, 1963), 195.

CHAPTER 1

1 Antoine-Chrysostôme Quatremère de Quincy, 'Style,' *Dictionnaire historique d'architecture* (Paris, 1832), II, 502.

2 Although the term 'architectural system' was used in the mid-eighteenth and early nineteenth centuries, it does not appear to have been given its first extended discussion until Quatremère de Quincy accorded it a full entry in the third volume on architecture in the *Encyclopédie Méthodique. Architecture* (Paris, 1825), 424. Quatremère de Quincy repeated this entry in his *Dictionnaire* (1832), II, 512–13. In the eighteenth and early nineteenth centuries several writers would apply the term to Gothic architecture. In the 'Introduction' to the *Essai sur l'architecture* (rev. edn, Paris, 1755), 3, the Abbé Marc-Antoine Laugier referred to Gothic architecture as 'un nouveau système d'architecture.' Francesco Milizia would follow his example in *Principi di architettura civile* (n.p., 1871), I, 10, in characterizing Gothic architecture as 'un sistema diverso' in comparison with Greek architecture. Augustus Wilhelm von Schlegel in lectures delivered in Vienna in 1808 and subsequently published in English as *A Course in Dramatic Art and Literature* (London, 1846), 23, observed of Gothic architecture 'that as well as the Grecian it constitutes in itself a complete and finished system.' J. B. L. G. Seroux d'Agincourt, in a history of art published in 1823, nearly a decade after his death, referred repeatedly to the 'Gothic System of Architecture' (*History of Art by Its Monuments, from Its Decline in the Fourth Century to Its Restoration in the Sixteenth*, vol. 1 (London, 1847), a translation of *Histoire de l'art par les monuments* (Paris, 1823). See the title to part 2 and plate XLII.). In addition to these, Quatremère de Quincy himself had occasionally used the word 'system' earlier, as in his entry 'Architecture,' in *Encyclopédie Méthodique. Architecture* (Paris and Liège, 1788), I, 109–27, as in 'le système général de l'architecture,' 'un système primitif de la cabane,' etc.

3 Quatremère de Quincy, 'Système,' in *Encyclopédie Méthodique. Architecture*, III, 424, and 'Système,' *Dictionnaire*, II, 512–13. For Quatremère de Quincy, the architectural system consisted of three parts: 'des systèmes locaux de construction, d'ordre, d'embellissement' (native systems of construction, form, and decoration). The *système d'ordre* refers both to the forms used and to the architectural orders with their rules for proportions that regulated not only the orders but also the forms employed. This system was often referred to simply as the 'system of proportion,' a notion that subsumed the reference to architectural forms within the controlling factor of proportions.

4 Quatremère de Quincy, 'Ordre,' *Dictionnaire*, II, 175, as quoted in Ludovic Vitet, 'Notre-Dame de Noyon' (1844) in *Études sur les Beaux-Arts. Essais d'archéologie et fragments littéraires*, 2 vols (Paris, 1846), II, 222–3. See also Quatremère de Quincy, 'Gothique (architecture),' *Dictionnaire*, I, 670–79.

5 Désiré Raoul-Rochette, 'Considérations sur la question de savoir s'il est convenable, au XIXe siècle, de bâtir des églises en style gothique,' Académie Royale des Beaux-Arts, Institut Royal de France, reprinted in Eugène-Emmanuel Viollet-le-Duc, 'Du Style gothique au XIXe siècle,' *Annales Archéologiques* 4 (June 1846), 326–33.

6 Charles Seymour, Jr, *Notre-Dame of Noyon in the Twelfth Century: A Study in the Early Development of Gothic Architecture* (New Haven, 1939; New York, 1968), 185.

7 For Lassus's works, see Barry Bergdoll, 'Jean-Baptiste-Antoine Lassus,' *Macmillan Encyclopedia of Architects* (New York, 1982), II, 611.

8 Ludovic Vitet, 'Rapport à M. le Ministre de l'Intérieur sur les monuments, les bibliothèques, les archives et les musées des Départements de l'Oise, de l'Aisne, de la Marne, du Nord et du Pas-de-Calais' (1831) and 'Notre-Dame de Noyon,' in *Études*, II, 63–4, 224–5, 232–3.

9 Viollet-le-Duc, 'Du Style gothique,' *Annales Archéologiques* 4 (June 1846), 333–53. See also J.-B.-A. Lassus, 'De l'art et de l'archéologie,' *Annales Archéologiques* 2 (February 1845), 61–3.

10 Thomas Hope, *An Historical Essay on Architecture by the Late Thomas Hope, Illustrated from Drawings Made by Him in Italy and Germany* (London, 1835), 364.

11 Vitet, 'Rapport,' in *Études*, II, 46 n. 1.

12 On the popularity of Garbett's *Rudimentary Treatise* in the United States, see Robert W. Winter, 'Fergusson and Garbett in American Architectural Theory,' *Journal of the Society of Architectural Historians* 17 (Winter 1958), 25–9.

13 Léonce Reynaud, 'Architecture,' *Encyclopédie Nouvelle* (1836), I., 772.

14 Vitet, 'Des Monuments de Paris' (March 1838), in *Études*, I, 279.

15 Ugo Ojetti, 'L'Arte Nuova a Torino,' *Corriere della Sera* (20–1

June, 1902), in Francesca R. Fratini, ed., *Torino 1902, polemiche in Italia sull'Arte Nuova* (Turin, 1970), 194.

16 John Claudius Loudon, 'On the Difference between Common, or Imitative Genius, and Inventive, or Original Genius, in Architecture,' *The Architectural Magazine* 1 (July 1834), 185.

17 George Edmund Street, 'The True Principles of Architecture, and the Possibility of Development,' *The Ecclesiologist* (1852), as quoted in David B. Brownlee, *The Law Courts: The Architecture of George Edmund Street* (New York and Cambridge, Mass., 1984), 22.

18 Richard Popplewell Pullan, *Elementary Lectures on Christian Architecture* (1879), 65–6.

19 H. A. Caparn, 'The Riddle of the Tall Building: Has the Skyscraper a Place in American Architecture?', *The Craftsman* 10 (July 1906), 483.

20 Karl Scheffler, *Moderne Baukunst* (Berlin, 1907), 11: 'Die Technik war immer die Mutter der Stilgedanken.' Cf. also: 'die Konstruktion ist dort immer schon die Grundlage eines Stilgedankens' (ibid.), and 'Every primary architectural style can easily be traced back to a particular constructive principle (*Konstruktionsprinzip*),' (Karl Scheffler, 'Der neue Stil,' in *Die Architektur der Großstadt* [Berlin, 1913], 65).

21 Scheffler, 'Der neue Stil,' in *Die Architektur der Großstadt*, 66.

22 Le Corbusier, 'Barcelone 15 mai' (lecture in Barcelona in 1927), Fondation Le Corbusier, Paris, C3–8, fol. 89: 'Comment parler d'architecture présente ou future si ce n'est en n'ayant présent toujours, le passé, la tradition? ... le passé nous montre des architectures qui sont toutes basées sur des systèmes de structure. Ces systèmes des structure = la totalité des moyens techniques disponibles ...'

23 Montgomery Schuyler, 'Modern Architecture,' *The Architectural Record* 4 (July/September 1894), now in *American Architecture and Other Writings by Montgomery Schuyler*, eds. William H. Jordy and Ralph Coe, 2 vols (Cambridge, Mass., 1961), I, 110–15; Henry Van Brunt, 'Architecture in the West,' *The Atlantic Monthly* 64 (December 1889), 777, and now in *Architecture and Society: Selected Essays of Henry Van Brunt*, ed. William A. Coles (Cambridge, Mass., 1969), 186.

24 Eugène-Emmanuel Viollet-le-Duc, *Entretiens sur l'architecture*, 2 vols (Paris, 1863–72; Ridgewood, N. J., 1965 reprint), I, 102.

25 Otto Wagner, *Moderne Architektur: Seinen Schülern ein Führer auf diesem Kunstgebiete* (Vienna, 1896), 56, and *Die Baukunst unserer Zeit* (Vienna, 1914), 60. This latter book is the fourth edition of Wagner's *Moderne Architektur*, which was also published in 1898 and 1902. For an English translation, see Otto Wagner, *Modern Architecture: A Guidebook for His Students to this Field of Art*, tr. Harry Francis Mallgrave (Santa Monica, 1988). The translation here is my own.

26 Angiolo Mazzoni, 'Appunti autobiografici' (September 9, 1976), 2: 'Mi rivelò come dovesse essere l'architettura: costruzione divenuta poesia.' This thirty-six page typewritten manuscript is conserved in the Archivio Angiolo Mazzoni-Galleria Museo Depero, Rovereto.

27 Hans Poelzig, 'Der neuzeitliche Fabrikbau,' *Der Industriebau* 2 no. 5 (1911), in *Gesammelte Schriften und Werke*, ed. Julius Posener (Schriftenreihe der Akademie der Künste, Band 6, Berlin, Gebr. Mann Verlag, 1970), 39.

28 Anatole De Baudot, *L'Architecture: le passé, le présent* (Paris, 1916), 132.

29 Albert Lenoir, 'De l'Architecture byzantine. Article 1er,' *Revue Générale de l'Architecture et des Travaux Publics* 1 (1840), cols 7–17; Eugène-Emmanuel Viollet-le-Duc, 'De la Construction des édifices religieux en France depuis le commencement du Christianisme jusqu'au XVIe siècle' and 'Du Style gothique au XIXe siècle,' *Annales Archéologiques* 1 (October 1844), 334–47, 2 (February, March, June 1845), 69–76, 134–41, 319–30, 3 (December 1845), 316–36, 4 (May, June 1846), 266–83, 325–53; Paul-Emile

Botta, *Monument de Ninive découvert et décrit par M. P.-E. Botta, mesuré et dessiné par M. E. Flandin. Ouvrage publié sous les auspices de M. le Ministre de l'Intérieur et sous la direction d'une commission de l'Institut* 5 vols (Paris, 1849–50); J[ules] Quicherat, 'De l'Architecture romane,' *Revue Archéologique* 8 (15 April – 15 September), 1851), 145–58; Charles-Edouard Isabelle, *Les Edifices circulaires et les dômes, classés par ordre chronologique et considérés sous le rapport de leur disposition, de leur construction et de leur décoration. Publiés sous les auspices du Ministre de l'Intérieur et du Ministre d'Etat* (Paris, 1855); Anatole de Baudot, *Eglises de bourgs et villages*, vol. 1 (Paris, 1867).

30 Eugène-Emmanuel Viollet-le-Duc, *Lectures on Architecture*, tr. Benjamin Bucknall (London, 1877–81; New York, 1987 reprint), II, 1; *Entretiens sur l'architecture*, II, 1.

31 See Auguste Choisy, *Etudes épigraphiques sur l'architecture grecque* (Paris, 1884) discussed below in 'Empirical Evidence and Inductive Reasoning' in chapter 4.

32 Arthur Schopenhauer, *The World As Will and Idea*, trs. R. B. Haldane and J. Kemp (London, 1883; 1964 reprint), I, 277.

33 Ibid., III, 189.

34 Ibid.

35 Ibid., III, 190–1.

36 Edward Lacy Garbett, *Rudimentary Treatise on the Principles of Design in Architecture as Deducible from Nature and Exemplified in the Works of the Greek and Gothic Architects* (London, 1867), 131, 135.

37 Karl Boetticher, 'The Principles of Hellenic and Germanic Ways of Building with Regard to Their Application to Our Present Way of Building,' translation by Wolgang Herrmann of 'Das Prinzip der hellenischen und germanischen Bauweise hinsichtlich der Übertragung in die Bauweise unserer Tage,' *Allgemeine Bauzeitung* 11 (1846), in Wolfgang Hermann, *In What Style Should We Build? The German Debate on Architectural Style* (Santa Monica, 1992), especially 153–9. On Boetticher see also 33–4, 193.

38 Karl Boetticher, *Die Tektonik der Hellenen* 2nd rev. edn. Berlin, 1874), I, 19–27, 182, 185.

39 Hendrik Petrus Berlage, 'Gottfried Semper' (1903), in *Architettura, urbanistica, estetica: scritti*, ed. Herman van Bergijk (Bologna, 1985), 87–8.

40 As reported in French in the *Bollettino della Società degli Ingegneri e degli Architetti Italiani* 12 (8 May, 1904), 557 I have translated *le ciment armé* as reinforced concrete.

41 Reynaud, 'Architecture,' in *Encyclopédie Nouvelle*, I, 771.

42 Léonce Reynaud, *Traité d'architecture. Première partie: Art de bâtir* (2nd ed, Paris, 1860). See especially the preface to the first edition, reprinted here as pp. vii–ix, and then the introduction, pp. 1–16. On the popularity of this book, which underwent three editions between 1850 and 1878, see Robin Middleton, 'The Rationalist Interpretations of Léonce Reynaud and Viollet-le-Duc,' *AA Files* (Spring 1986), 47.

43 Gottfried Semper, 'Ueber architektonische Symbole' (1854), in *Kleine Schriften* (Berlin and Stuttgart, 1884), 295; Hermann Muthesius, *Stilarchitektur und Baukunst* (Mülheim-Ruhr, 1902), 52.

44 Fritz Stahl, 'Hans Poelzig' (1919), in Hans Poelzig, *Gesammelte Schriften und Werke*, ed. Julius Posener, 107.

45 See especially Viollet-le-Duc's letters of 23 and 25 May, 1836, and the accompanying drawings in *Le voyage d'Italie d'Eugène Viollet-le-Duc 1836–1837*. Exhibition Catalogue, Ecole nationale supérieure des Beaux-Arts, Paris, and Accademia delle Arti del Disegno, Florence, January–June 1980 (Florence, 1980), 110–11.

46 Viollet-le-Duc, *Entretiens*, I, 293, 55.

47 For example, see Auguste Choisy, *L'Art de bâtir chez les Byzantins* (Paris, 1883), 4–5, on the differences between Roman and Byzantine architecture and culture.

48 Ibid., 3.

49 See chapter 2 below.

50 Auguste Choisy, *Histoire de l'architecture*, 2 vols (Paris, 1899), I, 317–18. See also I, 290–2.

51 I am translating 'l'esprit' as 'mind and spirit.'

52 Le Corbusier, 'Modénature,' in *Almanach d'architecture moderne* (Paris, 1925; Turin, 1975 reprint), 116. I have translated 'l'esprit' as 'mind and spirit.'

53 James Fergusson, *An Historical Inquiry into the True Principles of Beauty in Art, More Especially with Reference to Architecture. Part the First* (London, 1849), xv.

54 James Fergusson, *A History of Architecture in All Countries from the Earliest Times to the Present Day, in Three Volumes* (London, 1865), I, xiii.

55 Montgomery Schuyler, 'Architecture,' *The Inland Architect and News Record* 17 (February 1891), 5, and now in Schuyler, *American Architecture*, eds. Jordy and Coe, I, 96–7, with the title 'The Point of View.'

56 Ernest Renan, *Voyages: Italie (1849) – Norvège (1870)* (Paris: Editions Montaigne, n.d.), 118.

57 Charles Plumet, 'Le Mensonge de l'architecture contemporaine,' *Les Arts de la Vie* 1 (January 1904), 36–7.

58 Hendrik Petrus Berlage, *Grundlagen und Entwicklung der Architektur* (Berlin, 1908), 16.

59 Le Corbusier, *Vers une Architecture* (Paris, 1923; 3rd edn, 1928; 1958 reprint), xxiv, 25.

60 Le Corbusier, *Précisions sur un état présent de l'architecture et de l'urbanisme* (Paris, 1930; 1960 reprint), 70.

61 Frank Lloyd Wright, 'In the Cause of Architecture. II. What "Styles" Mean to the Architect,' *The Architectural Record* (February 1928), now in Frank Lloyd Wright, *In the Cause of Architecture: Essays by Frank Lloyd Wright for 'Architectural Record,' 1908–1952, with a Symposium on Architecture with and without Wright by Eight Who Knew Him*, ed. Frederick Gutheim (New York, 1975), 166.

62 H. Toler Booraem, 'Architectural Expression in a New Material: Practical and Ethical Problems of Design in Reinforced Concrete,' *The Architectural Record* 23 (April 1908), 263.

63 James Fergusson, *The Illustrated Handbook of Architecture: Being a Concise and Popular Account of the Different Styles of Architecture Prevailing in All Ages and All Countries* (2nd edn., London 1859), lvi.

64 Reynaud, *Traité d'architecture*, vi.

65 Joris-Karl Huysmans, 'Le Salon de 1879,' in *L'Art moderne* (Paris, 1883), 75–6.

66 See 'Engineering Marvels' in chapter 3 below.

67 Schuyler, 'Architecture' ('A Point of View'), 6, and 'Last Words about the World's Fair,' *The Architectural Record* 3 (January–March 1894), 295, and now in Schuyler, *American Architecture*, eds Jordy and Coe, I, 98 (with editors' identification and description of the Casino Theater); II, 564.

68 For Borrmann, Behrendt, and Meyer, see Walter Curt Behrendt, 'Backstein als Baumaterial,' *Die Kunst* 18 (1908), 405–6. On brick see also Louis Sullivan, 'Artistic Brick,' foreword to *Suggestions in Artistic Brick* (St Louis: Hydraulic-Press Brick Co., c. 1910), now in Louis Sullivan, *The Public Papers*, ed. Robert Twombly (Chicago, 1988), 200–5.

69 Booraem, 'Architectural Expression,' *The Architectural Record* 23 (April 1908), 263.

70 Letter of 22 November 1908, from Charles-Edouard Jeanneret to his former teacher and master Charles l'Eplattenier, in Jean Petit, *Le Corbusier lui-même* (Geneva, 1970), 34.

71 Quatremère de Quincy, 'Gothique (architecture),' *Dictionnaire*, I, 672. The text in the *Encyclopédie Méthodique. Architecture* (Paris, 1820), II, 458, differs slightly.

72 Le Corbusier, 'Calendrier d'architecture,' in *Almanach*, 6–7.

73 Ibid.

74 Book contract for *L'Architecture Nouvelle* from Editions G. Crès et Cie, signed and dated 21 December by the company and countersigned 'Ch E Jeanneret,' with accompanying letter of 12 December 1922 from the publisher to Jeanneret, which expresses the desire to have the book appear in April. Fondation Le Corbusier, Paris, A1-3, fol. 255 (the letter), 256 (the contract).

75 This illustration was first published by Mary McLeod in Joan Ockman, Deborah Berke, and Mary McLeod, eds, *Architecture Criticism Ideology* (Princeton, 1985), 48. See also the undated letter in the Fondation Le Corbusier, Paris, A1-3, fol. 258, addressed to 'Monsieur Le Corbusier-Saugnier,' about the cost for the illustrations (3233.80 francs) in 'la maquette de votre ouvrage: "Architecture et Révolution."'

76 The text for 'Les 5 points d'une architecture nouvelle' is signed Le Corbusier and Pierre Jeanneret, the engineer who was Le Corbusier's cousin and collaborator. Volumes 1–3 of the *Oeuvre complète*, with works extending into 1938, were published under the dual authorship of these two men.

77 Le Corbusier and Pierre Jeanneret, 'Le Maisons "Dom-ino,"' *Oeuvre complète 1900–1929* (1930; 9th edn, Zurich, 1967), 23.

78 Le Corbusier, *Précisions*, 93, 95.

79 In the foreword to the 1966 edition of *The International Style: Architecture since 1922* (New York, 1932), vii, Henry-Russell Hitchcock explains that the book was prepared concurrently with the 1932 exhibition that he and Philip Johnson organized at the recently established Museum of Modern Art in New York.

80 See Le Corbusier's remarks made at the international symposium 'Les Arts et la réalité contemporaine – L'Art et l'état, Venice, 25–28 July, 1934, in *L'Art et la réalité. L'Art et l'état* (Paris: Société des Nations, Institut International de Coopération Intellectuelle, n.d.), 76, 79.

81 On the subject of the changing relationship between columns and walls in Le Corbusier's architecture of the late 1920s and early 1930s I am indebted to Barry Maitland's pioneering study 'The Grid,' *Oppositions* no. 15/16 (Winter/Spring 1979), 91–117.

82 On Charlotte Perriand's contributions to the furniture designed in Le Corbusier's *atelier*, see Mary McLeod, 'Furniture and Femininity,' *The Architectural Review* 181 (January 1979), 43–6.

83 Le Corbusier, *Vers une Architecture* (3rd. edn, 1928; 1958 reprint), 178. For the translation of this passage I have used Le Corbusier, *Towards a New Architecture*, tr. Frederick Etchells (1927; New York, 1960, 4th printing, 1970), 202.

84 The weekend house outside Paris at La Celle Saint-Cloud (1935) was constructed with rubble stone bearing walls (as well as several free-standing concrete piers) carrying shallow concrete vaults finished with thin wood surfacing, which shows the natural grain. The Villa Sarabhai (Ahmedabad, 1955) and the Jaoul Houses (1954–56) use traditional Catalonian vaults carried by rough concrete beams that, in turn, rest on brick walls.

85 Willy Boesiger, ed., *Le Corbusier* (New York, 1972), 124.

86 Semper, 'Ueber architektonische Symbole,' in *Kleine Schriften*, 297.

87 Gottfried Semper, *The Four Elements of Architecture: A Contribution to the Comparative Study of Architecture* (1851), in *The Four Elements of Architecture and Other Writings*, trs. Harry Francis Mallgrave and Wolfgang Hermann (Cambridge, 1989), 103–4.

88 Gottfried Semper, ' "Development of Architectural Style," translated and arranged by John W. Root, Architect,' *The Inland Architect and News Record* 14 (December 1889), 77. For the original text, see Gottfried Semper, *Ueber Baustyle. Ein Vortrag gehalten auf dem*

Rathaus in Zürich am 4. März 1869 (Zurich, 1869), 13–14. See also, Frederick Baumann, FAIA, 'Thoughts on Architecture,' *The Inland Architect and News Record* 16 (November 1890), 59: 'Architectural construction, according to Semper, bases on four constitutent parts: The fireside as center; the protecting roof; the circumvallation; the substruction.' Root's article, beginning with the second installment, is accompanied by the following clarification: 'In your publication of Professor Semper's essay, I alone am credited with the translation. No one well acquainted with my linguistic accomplishments will believe any such statement. The fact is, that but for the assistance of my friend, Mr. Fritz Wagner, the translation would never have seen the light. [signed] J. W. Root.' In *The Architecture of John Wellborn Root* (Baltimore, 1973), 91, 93, Donald Hoffmann explains that Baumann's use of a sentence from Semper about style during a symposium held by the Illinois State Association of Architects on 5 March 1887, at which Root was the principal speaker, prompted Root to undertake this translation. (For this symposium, see 'Illinois State Association,' *The Inland Architect and News Record* 9 [March 1887], 23–6.) Root had delivered an address on 'Style' to the Chicago Architectural Sketch Club the preceding 3 January (Harriet Monroe, *John Wellborn Root: A Study of His Life and Work* [1896; 1966 reprint, Park Forest, Ill., 76]). From Root's clarification quoted above, it would appear that Stern did the actual translating with Root assisting in the choice of phrasing and arrangement of the text. In other words, Semper's thoughts were deemed of sufficient importance that Root initiated a translation of material that he himself could not have undertaken without Wagner's linguistic assistance.

89 Grant Carpenter Manson, 'Frank Lloyd Wright and the Fair of '93,' *Art Quarterly* 16 (Summer 1953), 117.

90 Irving K. Pond, 'The Home,' *The Inland Architect and News Record* 10 (November 1887), 64. On Ruskin, see Gwendolyn Wright, *Moralism and the Model Home: Domestic Architecture and Cultural Conflict in Chicago, 1873–1913* (Chicago, 1980), 12–13.

91 Frank Lloyd Wright, *The Natural House* (New York, 1954; 1982 reprint), 16, 33. This text restates ideas that Wright had published in 'In the Cause of Architecture,' *The Architectural Record* (March 1908), in *In the Cause of Architecture*, ed. Gutheim, 55, 57–8.

92 Frank Lloyd Wright, *An Autobiography* (New York and London, 1932), 138–9, and reutilized in *The Natural House*, 32. The clause about the large chimney comes from the earlier version of this passage published in *Modern Architecture* (1931), now in Frank Lloyd Wright, *Writings and Buildings*, eds Edgar Kaufmann and Ben Raeburn (Cleveland and New York, 1960), 42.

93 Wright, *The Natural House*, 16.

94 Ibid.

95 Gaston Bachelard, *La Psychanalyse du feu* (Paris, 1938) [The Psychoanalysis of Fire (Boston, 1964)], *L'Eau et les rêves: essai sur l'imagination de la matière* (Paris, 1942), *L'Air et les songes: essai sur l'imagination du mouvement* (Paris, 1943), *La Terre et les rêveries de la volonté* (Paris, 1948), *La Terre et les rêveries du repos* (Paris, 1948), *La flamme d'une chandelle* (Paris, 1961), *La poétique de l'espace* (Paris, 1957) [The Poetics of Space (1964; paperback edn, Boston, 1969)]. For a definition of the 'material imagination,' as well as a discussion of its relaltionship to aesthetic experience, see *L'Eau et les rêves*, 5–7.

96 Edward T. Hall, *The Silent Language* (New York, 1966), especially 160–4, and *The Hidden Dimension* (Greenwich, Conn., 1959), especially 95–122.

97 Bachelard, *La Poétique de l'espace*, 51–2.

98 For an analysis of Wright's Prairie houses according to the poetics of space, see Grant Hildebrand toward the end of his excellent article 'The Wright Space: The Parti of the Prairie House,' in Richard Guy Wilson and Sidney K. Robinson, eds, *Modern Architecture in America: Visions and Revisions* (Ames, Iowa, 1991), 112–43. Although Hildebrand refers briefly to Bachelard's book, he preferred to cast his argument according to the terms of Jay Appleton's 'prospect-refuge theory.' This article has been followed by a more extensive treatment in Hildebrand's *The Wright Space: Pattern and Meaning in Frank Lloyd Wright's Houses* (Seattle, 1991).

99 See the excellent analysis in Dominique Rouillard, 'Logiques de la pente à Los Angeles. Quelques figures de F.L. Wright et R.M. Schindler,' *Les Cahiers de la recherche architecturale* no. 14 (1984), 12–13.

100 Frank Lloyd Wright, 'Some Aspects of the Past and Present of Architecture,' in Baker Brownell and Frank Lloyd Wright, *Architecture and Modern Life* (New York, 1928), 20, and reprinted in Frank Lloyd Wright, *The Future of Architecture* (New York, 1953), 36.

101 Frank Lloyd Wright, 'In the Cause of Architecture. III. The Meaning of Materials – Stone,' *The Architectural Record* (April 1928), in *In the Cause of Architecture*, ed. Gutheim, 177.

102 Frank Lloyd Wright, *A Testament* (n.p., 1957), 111.

103 Grant Carpenter Manson, *Frank Lloyd Wright to 1910: The First Golden Age* (New York, 1958), 3. Cf. also Edgar Tafel's account of his first drive out to Taliesin from Spring Green, recorded in *Years with Frank Lloyd Wright: Apprentice to Genius* (New York, 1979), 19: 'I climbed into the rumble seat and we drove off directly, out of Spring Green through the river valley and rolling countryside, very beautiful with its strange, rough outcroppings of stone.'

104 Thomas Beeby, 'Wright and Landscape: A Mythical Interpretation,' in Carol R. Bolon, et al., eds, *The Nature of Frank Lloyd Wright* (Chicago, 1988), 156, 160.

105 Iovanna Lloyd Wright, 'Biography,' in Frank Lloyd Wright, *Architecture: Man in Possession of His Earth* (New York, 1962), 17 (text), 18 (photograph of 'rock strata and pool'). See also Wright, *An Autobiography* 18–19, where Wright describes the 'soft, white sandrock cropped out in long, thin ledges . . . Fascinated by whatever there is in sand that bewitches boys, [young Wright] scraped away at it with his knife . . .

106 Neil Levine, 'Frank Lloyd Wright's Own Houses and His Changing Concept of Representation,' in Bolon et al., eds, *The Nature of Frank Lloyd Wright*, 21. Levine's thesis is faulty in two ways. First, it assumes that there was a singular and unified classical meaning to the notion of architecture as an art of representation that presented an imitation of nature. Second, it defines this notion in a mistaken manner.

By classical, I assume that Levine means the architecture of the Greco-Roman tradition which reached through the Renaissance and has continued to this day in the form of Beaux-Arts classicism. At different times aspects of this classical tradition can be said to have been concerned with imitating nature. Perhaps the most long-standing concept of representation can be found in the classical orders, which were considered as representations of the proportions and of the degree of force or grace of the human body. This is discussed in Vitruvius and appears to have been a constant feature of architecture in all subsequent classical periods. At times, especially in the Renaissance, the geometrical ordering and proportioning of architectural forms were seen as reflections of the divine order of the cosmos reflected in the microcosm of building. A third type of representation of nature can be found in the adherence to bilateral symmetry, seen as adhering to the order that nature had established.

These three types of representation, related to the architectural orders, to geometry and proportions, and to bilateral symmetry, involve a level of abstraction that differs radically from Frank Lloyd Wright's imitative approach to nature. As for bilateral symmetry, Wright used it when it suited his purposes and abandoned it in favor of asymmetry on other occasions. If we are to find a classical notion of representation that corresponds in some manner to Wright's approach to architecture, then it would be through the use of rustication in Renaissance and post-Renaissance architecture whereby rustication often, but not always, signified the world of rough nature, as opposed to the man-made world, and by extension, the realm of culture and civilization. Thus, the ground floor of urban palaces was often rusticated to signify the realm of nature, whereas the floors above, starting with the *piano nobile*, might be given a surface treatment of smooth ashlar and provided with elaborate ornamentation. Similarly, rusticated surfaces or rusticated columnar shafts would be used in garden architecture to signal that it belonged to the world of nature in which it was situated.

Curiously, Levine mentions none of these four examples from the classical tradition of architecture as an art of representation that imitates nature. Rather he uses the example of the primitive hut as found in the writing of the eighteenth-century French Neoclassical theorist Marc-Antoine Laugier. The problem with Levine's explanation, though, is that it misrepresents the Abbé Laugier's text and misinterprets its meaning, which he presents as follows:

> In his *Essay on Architecture* of 1753 the French theorist Marc-Antoine Laugier used the example of the primitive hut to testify to architecture's natural origins. He explained how the primitive hut was not merely the first example of built form, but the natural prototype for the conventional forms of classical architecture. Imagining four trees growing out of the ground joined at the tops of their trunks by horizontal branches and supporting others set at an angle to one another, Laugier pictured in the celebrated frontispiece of the second edition (1755) of his book what he considered to be the most rational, and therefore natural, form of construction. He claimed that the Greeks first understood this and took the hut as the natural model for their temples. They transformed the various parts of the hut into stone. . . . Thus, the Greek temple imitated in permanent materials the forms of nature and could therefore be considered the representation of the natural prototype of the hut.

Contrary to Levine's account, Laugier did not present the primitive hut as the 'first example of built form.' Just as importantly, the hut that he described in the unillustrated first edition of his *Essay* was not identical to the famous illustration by Charles Eisen that accompanied the second edition. This illustration was an allegorical, not a literal depiction of Laugier's text. Let us consider these matters one at a time.

Laugier's story of the natural hut was a secular parable, not an exercise in the history of primitive architecture. It belongs to the same realm of discourse as Jean-Jacques Rousseau's account of primitive man in his *Discours sur l'origine et les fondements de l'inégalité parmi les hommes* (Discourse on the Origin and Causes of Inequality among Men) (1754). Rousseau's was not an anthropological account but rather an inquiry into the basic nature of humankind undertaken by postulating a hypothetical first human. Similarly, Laugier's was an inquiry into the fundamentals of architecture presented through a fable of the conception and construction of a primitive hut. All subsequent architecture was to adhere to the principles embodied in this model. The model belonged to the world of nature in the same way that the Founding Fathers of the American republic based their Declaration of Independence on the natural rights of humankind.

The figurative as opposed to literal nature of Laugier's account is evident from his text:

> It is for architecture as for the other arts: its principles are founded in simple nature, and in the proceedings of nature are found clearly marked the rules of architecture. Let us consider man in his first state without any assistance, without any guide other than the natural instinct of his needs. He needs a place to rest. At the bank of a tranquil stream he spies a lawn; its young grass pleases his eyes, its softness invites him; he approaches, and languidly stretched out on this lawn, he thinks only of enjoying in peace the gifts of nature: he lacks nothing, he desires nothing. But soon the heat of the sun burns him and forces him to seek shelter. He spies a forest that offers him the freshness of its shade; he runs to hide himself in its thickness, and there he is content. However, evaporating water gathers into thick clouds that cover the sky; a frightful rain falls like a torrent on this delightful forest. Man, poorly covered by the shelter of the leaves, does not know how to protect himself from this bothersome rain that completely soaks him. He finds a cave,

slips inside, and finds himself out of the rain; he congratulates himself on his discovery. But new troubles bother him even in this domain. He is left in the dark, he breathes unhealthy air. He leaves resolved to rectify, through his own work, the inattention and negligence of nature. Man wants to make for himself a lodging that covers him without burying him. Several downed branches in the forest are the materials appropriate to his project. He selects four of the strongest, which he raises vertically and which he arranges in a square. Above he places four others horizontally across them; and on top of these last branches he raises still others on an incline such that the two sides meet together in a point. This type of roof is covered with leaves thick enough to keep out both sun and rain; and now man is housed. It is true that cold and heat will bother him inside his house, which is open on all sides; but he will fill in the space between the pillars and find himself secure. Such is the way of simple nature: art owes its birth to the imitation of these proceedings. The small rustic hut that I have just described is the model on which all the great creations of architecture have been conceived. It is by staying close to the simplicity of this first model that one will avoid the essential defaults and that one will achieve true perfection.

Laugier continues by explaining that his first model consists of three elements: the free-standing round column, which is a means of support; the entablature, which signifies the level of a ceiling or floor; and the pediment, which signifies a roof. He then proceeds to criticize all those Baroque departures from his idealized model; engaged columns, pilasters, broken entablatures, rounded pediments, stacked pediments, pediments placed in the center of a facade as a decorative feature, and so forth. Throughout Laugier's text it is clear that he is postulating the logic of the forms and arrangements of the parts of the Greek temple as the prototype for all future architecture and that he has used the secular parable of the creation of the primitive hut as a way to present his case. Laugier's parable, which remains the same in both the 1753 and 1755 editions of his *Essay*, is rendered symbolically by the allegorical frontispiece in the latter edition. In this drawing a female figure representing Architecture (or perhaps Nature) points, for the benefit of a winged cherub (her young charge, presumably humankind) to the primitive hut in which the four vertical posts are not branches that have been erected in the ground but rather trees that grew according to Nature's direction straight upward and in a square arrangement. This hut has not been constructed by human hands; it exists in the same imaginary world as the goddess and the cherub. It is, to reiterate, part of an allegorical depiction of Laugier's secular parable. Laugier's story is definitely not about the 'first example of built form.' Levine's contention that Frank Lloyd Wright's architecture is an art of representation that imitates nature in the manner of this model is untenable. Wright's architecture certainly was a representative art that imitated nature, but not through the model that Laugier established. Wright himself recognized the difference between his organic approach and the classical paradigm for architecture: 'The first great integrity is a deeper, more intimate sense of reality in building than was ever pagan – that is to say, than was ever "classic" ' (*The Natural House*, 43). Wright found this 'deeper, more intimate sense of reality' through the various degrees of imitation or abstraction of natural forms that are studied in this chapter.

107 Hildebrand, 'The Wright Space,' in Wilson and Robinson, eds, *Modern Architecture in America: Visions and Revisions*, 121.

108 Bachelard, *La Poétique de l'espace*, chapters 2 and 8 and *La Terre et les rêveries du repos*, chapter 6.

109 Wright, *An Autobiography* (1932), 137, 139–40; *The Natural House*, 34, 80; *A Testament*, 219.

110 See below.

111 See 'Winslow House: The Sacramental Home,' in Norris Kelly Smith, *Frank Lloyd Wright: A Study in Architectural Content* (Watkins Glen, N.Y., rev. edn, 1979), 85, especially the paragraph that begins, 'It is particularly in the design of the reception hall [of the Winslow House] that Wright affirms the sacredness of home and hearth.'

112 In discussing this destroyed building, I am relying on the description given in William Allin Storrer, *The Architecture of Frank Lloyd Wright: A Complete Catalog* (Cambridge, Mass., 2nd rev. edn, 1978), item 62 (with photograph of the building before the addition of 1901). In *Frank Lloyd Wright to 1910: The First Golden Age* (New York, 1958), 94, Grant Carpenter Manson, who publishes a view of the building after the enlargement of 1901, describes the cladding as shingle siding. Yet even the shingle siding of this later covering is arranged to create an effect analogous to that of the earlier horizontal board and batten.

113 John Lloyd Wright, *My Father Who Is on Earth* (New York, 1946), 136.

114 Wright, *An Autobiography* (1977 edn.), 178–80. Cf. also Edgar Tafel in *Years with Frank Lloyd Wright*, 71–2, who explains this building in terms that precisely define an architectural system:

> Unity Temple was Mr. Wright's first building in which the material became one with the basic design concept. The methods and materials of construction grow out of the design, from overall massing of the building down to ornament. It was conceived in concrete. It was the first all-concrete building. . . . The beauty of the building is the appearance of one material doing everything – reinforced concrete for walls, roof slab, ornament. In an integrated chorus, subservient materials add their voice: stained glass, lighting fixtures designed in wood, and the wooden organ pipe screens inside.

115 Wright, *An Autobiography* (1932), 241.

116 Wright, *The Natural House*, 197–210; John Sergeant, *Frank Lloyd Wright's Usonian Houses: The Case for an Organic Architecture* (New York, 1976), 144–5.

117 Pamela H. Simpson, 'Cheap, Quick, and Easy: The Early History of Rockfaced Concrete Block Building,' in Thomas Carter and Bernard L. Herman, *Perspectives in Vernacular Architecture, III* (Columbia, Mo., 1989), 108–18. See also, Ronald L. M. Ramsey, 'Frank Lloyd Wright's Textile Block Construction System: A Technological and Architectural Evaluation,' read at the 39th Annual Meeting of the Society of Architectural Historians, Washington, D.C., 4 April, 1986; Donald Leslie Johnson, *The Architecture of Walter Burley Griffin* (South Melbourne, 1977), 56–62; Brendan Gill, *Many Masks: A Life of Frank Lloyd Wright* (New York, 1987), 267.

118 See also Edgar's Tafel's assessment of the textile block houses in *Years with Frank Lloyd Wright*, 125: 'The architecture had to grow out of the construction system, unforced and unfancied.'

119 Wright, *An Autobiography* (1970 edn), 270.

120 Wright, *An Autobiography* (1932), 245.

121 Ibid., 244, 248.

122 Ibid., 268.

123 Gill, *Many Masks*, 268.

124 Wright, *An Autobiography* (1932), 309:

> Every straight horizontal line in San Marcos In the Desert is a dotted line. Every flat plane grosgrained like the sahuaro itself. The building itself an abstraction of cactus life in masonry shells made more cactus than any cactus. . . . The Arizona desert itself was architectural inspiration and actually the architect's workshop in this endeavor. Is this not what we mean by an 'indigenous architecture?'

125 Wright, *An Autobiography* (1977 edn), 191–2.

126 'In his conversation with Hugh Downs, Wright spoke of the wooded site and protruding rock ledges in Wisconsin and commented that "the same thought applied to Taliesin that applied later to Bear Run." ' Donald Hoffmann, *Frank Lloyd Wright's Fallingwater: The House and Its History* (New York, 1978), 18 n. 24.

127 Ibid., 35.

128 This was not the first time that Wright had presented the four elements together in a symbolic manner. At the Hollyhock House (Los Angeles, 1920–21), in front of the living room chinmey-stack, he created a pool of water, lit from above by a glass skylight. This arrangement is discussed in Neil Levine, 'Landscape into Architecture: Frank Lloyd Wright's Hollyhock House and the Romance of Southern California,' *AA Files* no. 3 (January 1983), 35.

129 Hoffmann, *Fallingwater*, 49–50, using Edgar Kaufmann, Jr, 'Twenty-Five Years of the House on the Waterfall,' *L'Architettura-Cronache e Storia* no. 82 (August 1962), 41.

130 Wright, *The Natural House*, 40–1.

131 Wright, 'In the Cause of Architecture,' *The Architectural Record* (March 1908), in *In the Cause of Architecture*, ed. Gutheim, 61.

132 Wright, 'In the Cause of Architecture, Second Paper' (May 1914), ibid., 122.

133 Ibid., 124. See also Wright, *An Autobiography* (1932), 25, where Wright refers to 'all the architectures of the world.'

134 Wright, 'In the Cause of Architecture. 1. The Architect and Machine,' *The Architectural Record* (May 1927), in *In the Cause of Architecture*, ed. Gutheim, 131.

135 The title is taken from Wright's phrase, 'the nature of materials,' which he repeatedly used in his writings. See, for example, *An Autobiography* (1932), 148, where it is used as a heading, or 'In the Cause of Architecture. II. Standardization, The Soul of the Machine,' *The Architectural Record* [June 1927], in *In the Cause of Architecture*, ed. Gutheim, 136, and *The Natural House*, 59.

136 Wright, 'In the Cause of Architecture. Part III. Steel,' *The Architectural Record* (August 1927), in *In the Cause of Architecture*, ed. Gutheim, 141–2.

137 In publishing these figures, Wright would sometimes crop the photograph so as to emphasize certain characteristics, such as the long span shown in 'In the Cause of Architecture. V. The Meaning of Materials,' *The Architectural Record* (June 1928), in *In the Cause of Architecture*, ed. Gutheim, 195.

138 Wright, 'In the Cause of Architecture. 1. The Logic of the Plan,' *The Architectural Record* (January 1928), in *In the Cause of Architecture*, ed. Gutheim, 154.

139 Arthur C. David, 'The Architecture of Ideas,' *The Architectural Record* 15 (April 1904), 364.

140 The long terrace merely gives the appearance of a long span without intermediary support. In *The Robie House of Frank Lloyd Wright* (Chicago, 1984), 25, Joseph Connors explains, 'the long balcony that runs along the side of the house is in fact supported by metal beams that protrude at regular intervals from the living and dining room floors. But with the stone copings above and below, the balcony itself looks like one giant I-beam, supported by a brick post at either end.' Figure 13 in Connors's book is a photograph that shows the construction of a true brick wall, hence not a brick veneer, above the bottom coping of this balcony.

141 See Richard A. Etlin, *Modernism in Italian Architecture, 1890–1940* (Cambridge, Mass., 1991), 250–1.

142 Frank Lloyd Wright, 'The Art and Craft of the Machine' (March 1901), in Wright, *Writings and Buildings*, eds Kaufmann and Raeburn, 65–6, with a variant published earlier in the first of Wright's 1931 Princeton Lectures ('Modern Architecture') as reproduced in Frank Lloyd Wright, *The Future of Architecture* (New York, 1953), 83; 'In the Cause of Architecture,' *The Architectural Record* (March 1908), in *In the Cause of Architecture*, ed. Gutheim, 56, 60–1; *An Autobiography* (1977 edn), 167.

143 Ford, *The Details of Modern Architecture*, 161–3.

144 Reyner Banham, *The Architecture of the Well-Tempered Environment* (London, 1969), 117–21 (with analytical drawings). Banham's analysis, briefly summarized here, has been taken up by numerous distinguished authors, including William H. Jordy, *American Buildings and Their Architects: Progressive and Academic*

Ideals at the Turn of the Twentieth Century (New York, 1972; 1976), 212–14.

145 Jonathan Lipman, *Frank Lloyd Wright and the Johnson Wax Buildings* (New York, 1986), 65–8, 151–7; Gill, *Many Masks*, 366–7, 370.

146 Kenneth Frampton, 'The Johnson Wax Buildings and the Angel of History,' introduction to Lipman, *Frank Lloyd Wright and the Johnson Wax Buildings*, xii.

147 Lipman, *Frank Lloyd Wright and the Johnson Wax Buildings*, ix.

148 Henry-Russell Hitchcock, *In the Nature of Materials: The Buildings of Frank Lloyd Wright, 1887–1941* (New York, 1942; 1975 reprint), 92; Leonard K. Eaton, 'Frank Lloyd Wright and the Evolution of the Lily-Pad Column,' read at the 41st Annual Meeting of the Society of Architectural Historians, Chicago, 16 April 1988.

149 Hitchcock, *In the Nature of Materials*, 92.

150 Lipman, *Frank Lloyd Wright and the Johnson Wax Buildings*, 62.

151 Hitchcock, *In the Nature of Materials*, 92; Frampton, 'The Johnson Wax Buildings,' in Lipman, *Frank Lloyd Wright and the Johnson Wax Buildings*, xiv.

152 Vincent Scully, Jr, *Frank Lloyd Wright* (New York, 1960), 29.

153 In 'Technology in the Design of Modern Masterpieces,' a public lecture delivered at the School of Architecture, University of Maryland, on 15 February, 1989, the architect David Guise questioned whether the Price Company Tower actually was built with floors simply cantilevered from the central core. The important issue here is that Wright wanted his building to function in this manner and that he portrayed it this way to the public.

154 Frank Lloyd Wright to Roy S. Thurman, letter of 27 August 1940, as reproduced in Bruce Brooks Pfeiffer, *Frank Lloyd Wright: Treasures of Taliesin: Seventy-Six Unbuilt Designs* (Fresno, Cal.; Carbondale and Edwardsville, Ill., 1985).

155 'Frank Lloyd Wright,' *Architectural Forum* (June 1959), 123; Scully, *Wright*, 31–2. Wright attributes both phrases in quotation marks to Rabbi Mortimer J. Cohen, whom Wright listed on the plans as codesigner.

156 Scully, *Wright*, 30.

157 Wright, *The Natural House*, 69–77.

158 Ibid., 73.

159 Ibid., 78–9.

160 Ibid., 77, 80, 88–90.

161 Ibid., 141.

162 Ibid., 73, 80–1.

163 Ibid., 157.

164 Le Corbusier, *Une Petite maison, 1923* (Zurich, 1954; 2nd edn, 1968), 15.

165 Bachelard, *La Terre et les rêveries du repos*, 186.

166 Ibid., 162.

167 Le Corbusier, *Une Petite maison, 1923*, 22–4.

168 Jules Supervielle, *Boire à la source* (1933), in James A. Hiddleston, *L'Univers de Jules Supervielle* (Paris, 1965), 26.

169 Jules Supervielle, *Gravitations* (1925 edn), ibid., 25.

170 Henri Bosco, *Hyacinthe* (Paris, 1940), 20.

171 Etienne-Louis Boullée, *L'architecture, essai sur l'art*, ed. Jean-Marie Pérouse de Montclos (Paris, 1968), 82–5 (fol. 89–91). For an English translation, see Etienne-Louis Boullée, 'Architecture, Essay on Art,' in Helen Rosenau, *Boullée and Visionary Architecture, Including Boullée's 'Architecture, Essay on Art'*, tr. Sheila de Vallée (London and New York, 1976), 91–2.

172 Jules Supervielle, *Le Voleur d'enfants* (1926), in Hiddleston, *L'Univers de Jules Supervielle*, 59.

173 Bachelard, *La Terre et les rêveries du repos*, 185–6.

174 Le Corbusier, *Une Petite maison, 1923*, 27, 29.

175 Gaston Bachelard, 'Les nymphéas ou les surprises d'une aube d'été,' *Verve* 7 (1952), now in G. Bachelard, *Le droit de rêver* (Paris, 1970), 11–12.

176 Le Corbusier writes that the 'Open Hand' as a symbol dates from 1948. See Le Corbusier, *Modulor 2* (1958), trs. Peter de Francia and Anna Bostock (Cambridge, Mass., 1968), 254–61; Norma Evanson, *Chandigarh* (Berkeley and Los Angeles, 1966), 86–7.

177 Le Corbusier, *Précisions*, 76.

178 Le Corbusier, *Une Petite maison, 1923*, 41, 46–7.

179 Marcel Proust, *Jean Santeuil*, ed. Pierre Clarac (Paris: Gallimard, 1971), 306.

180 Le Corbusier, *La Ville radieuse* (Paris, 1933; 1964 reprint), 53–5.

181 Ibid., 51.

182 Ibid., 54.

183 Le Corbusier, *Le Modulor. Essai sur une mesure harmonique à l'échelle humaine applicable universellement à l'architecture et à la mécanique* (Boulogne-sur-Seine, 1948), 28. See also Le Corbusier, *La Ville radieuse*, 52.

184 Le Corbusier, *La Ville radieuse*, 52.

185 It should be pointed out that Le Corbusier's Villa Schwob (La Chaux-de-Fonds, 1916), was built around a double-height living room.

CHAPTER 2

1 Richard Payne Knight, *The Landscape, A Didactic Poem in Three Books, Addressed to Uvedale Price, Esq.* (London, 2nd edn, 1795), notes on pp. 17–18.

2 William Burgh, in William Mason, *The English Garden: A Poem in Four Books . . . New Edition . . . to Which Are Added a Commentary and Notes by W. Burgh, Esq., LL.D.* (York, 1783; 1971 reprint), 133, 135, for example, mentions the first two (133, 135); Peter Collins, in *Changing Ideals in Modern Architecture, 1750–1950* (London, 1965), 56, the last two.

3 John Claudius Loudon, *A Treatise on Farming, Improving, and Managing Country Residences . . . So As To Combine Architectural Fitness with Picturesque Effect*, 2 vols (London, 1806), I, 40. See also p. 14

4 For Vitet, see the preface above.

5 Loudon, *A Treatise on Farming*, I, 34–5.

6 Burgh in Mason, *The English Garden*, 134.

7 Loudon, *A Treatise on Farming*, I, 147–8.

8 Knight, *The Landscape*, 12.

9 Stewart thought that he was the first to apply Leibnitz's term to aesthetics. Dugald Stewart, *Philosophical Essays. With Many New and Important Additions* (1816 edn) in *The Collected Works of Dugald Stewart, Esq., F.R.SS.*, ed. Sir William Hamilton, vol. 5 (Edinburgh and Boston, 1855; 1971 reprint), 209.

10 Ibid., 222.

11 Ibid., 209, 226.

12 Ibid., 226.

13 Ibid., 210.

14 Ibid., 211.

15 Loudon, *Encyclopedia of Cottage, Farm, and Villa Architecture and Furniture*, 54. On the popularity of this book, see John Steegman,

Victorian Taste: A Study of the Arts and Architecture from 1830 to 1870 (1950; Cambridge, Mass., 1970), 116–17.

16 In *The Gothic Revival: An Essay in the History of Taste* (New York, 1962), 114, 117, Kenneth Clark remarks that until the Houses of Parliament competition of 1835, 'no one had ever suggested that a large secular public building should be designed in [the Gothic] style.' The Gothic 'was still a non-professional style. . . . Gothic had no rules, no principles, no professional standing.'

17 Augustus Welby Pugin, *On the Present State of Ecclesiastical Architecture in England* (London, 1843; 1969 reprint), 61.

18 Augustus Welby Pugin, *The True Principles of Pointed or Christian Architecture: Set Forth in Two Lectures Delivered at St. Marie's, Oscott* (London, 1841; London and New York, 1973 reprint), 71–2.

19 Ibid., 69–70.

20 Pugin, *On the Present State*, passim.

21 Francis Goodwin, *Rural Architecture* (London, 1835), II, xi. This text also appeared in the second and third editions of this book, published in 1843 and 1850 with the title *Domestic Architecture*.

22 Andrew Jackson Downing, *Cottage Residences* (New York and London, 1842), 28. In the reprint issued by the Library of Victorian Culture (Watkins Glen, 1967), this passage occurs on pp. 18–19.

23 Ibid. (1967 reprint), 18–20.

24 Andrew Jackson Downing, *The Architecture of Country Houses* (1850; New York, 1969 reprint), 12–15.

25 Downing, *Cottage Residences* (1967 reprint), 19–20, 113.

26 Eugène-Emmanuel Viollet-le-Duc, *Entretiens sur l'architecture*, 2 vols. (Paris, 1863–72; Ridgewood, N.J., 1965 reprint), I, 56.

27 Ibid., I, 478–9.

28 Ibid., I, 163.

29 Ibid., I, 86–7, 478–83.

30 Ernest Beulé, *L'Acropole d'Athènes*, 2 vols. (Paris, 1853–54) I, 265.

31 This assessment is by the architect Joseph Gwilt in his preface to William Chambers, *A Treatise on the Decorative Part of Civil Architecture* (London, 1825 edn), xxvii–xxviii.

32 Charles Blanc, *Grammaire des arts du dessin* (Paris, 1867), 7–8.

33 Willey Reveley, preface to James Stuart and Nicholas Revett, *The Antiquities of Athens* (London, 1794), III, xiv.

34 Ibid., xiii. On this last point, see, for example, William M. Leake, *The Topography of Athens with Some Remarks on Its Antiquities* (London, 1821), 212.

35 Leake, *The Topography of Athens*, 422–3. As English ambassador to the Ottoman Porte, Thomas Bruce, 7th Earl of Elgin, acquired the sculpture from the Parthenon and the Erechtheion between 1799 and 1803. For a drawing of 1808 by Charles Robert Cockerell of Lord Elgin's Museum at Park Lane, see Fani-Maria Tsigakou, *The Rediscovery of Greece: Travellers and Painters of the Romantic Era* (New Rochelle, N.Y., 1981), 25. For an account of Elgin's activity, see Adolf Michaelis, *A Century of Archaeological Discoveries*, tr. Bettina Kahnweiler (London, 1908), 28–31, 38–45.

36 Leake, *The Topography of Athens*, 212 n. 2, 423–4, 211–12.

37 John Papworth in William Chambers, *A Treatise on the Decorative Part of Civil Architecture . . . Fourth Edition, to Which Are Added Copious Notes, and An Essay on the Principles of Design in Architecture by John B. Papworth* (London, 1826), xvi, xxvii.

38 Ibid., xxii–xxiii.

39 Michaelis, *A Century of Archaeological Discoveries*, 53 (Ross); William Henry Goodyear, *Greek Refinements: Studies in Temperamental Architecture* (London, 1912), 3 (Hoffer).

40 The history of these discoveries is recounted in Goodyear, *Greek*

Refinements. The following discussion of this matter is an expanded version of my 'Le Corbusier, Choisy, and French Hellenism: The Search for a New Architecture,' *The Art Bulletin* 69 (June 1987), 264–78. More recently, József Sisa has published an article on Joseph Hoffer, which reviews this material from the perspective of the contributions made by this German-speaking Hungarian architect ('Joseph Hoffer and the Study of Ancient Architecture,' *Journal of the Society of Architectural Historians* 49 [December 1990], 430–9).

41 John Pennethorne, *The Elements and Mathematical Principles of the Greek Architects and Artists, Recovered by an Analysis and Study of the Remaining Works of Architecture Designed and Executed in the Age of Pericles* (London: Printed for Private Circulation by William Clowes and Sons, 1844), 30.

42 Ibid.

43 Francis Cranmer Penrose, *Two Letters from F.C. Penrose, Esq., Associate R.I.B.A., on Certain Anomalies in the Construction of the Parthenon* (London: The Society of Dilettanti, n.d.), 8, 10. The letters are dated 6 November 1846, and 6 February 1847.

44 Francis Cranmer Penrose, *An Investigation of the Principles of Athenian Architecture* (London, 1851), 78–80.

45 Penrose, *Two Letters*, 3.

46 Penrose, *An Investigation*, 82.

47 Goodyear, *Greek Refinements*, 83, 87 for all these German texts.

48 Neil Levine, 'The Romantic Idea of Architectural Legibility: Henri Labrouste and the Neo-Grec,' in Arthur Drexler, ed., *The Architecture of the Ecole des Beaux-Arts* (New York, 1977), 358–67.

49 Georges Radet, *L'Histoire et l'oeuvre de l'Ecole française d'Athènes* (Paris, 1901), 18–19.

50 Désiré Raoul-Rochette, 'Rapport fait au nom de la commission chargée de préparer les propositions destinées à régulariser les travaux de l'Ecole française d'Athènes, le 8 mars 1850,' *Archives des Missions Scientifiques et Littéraires* 1 (1850), 186. For accounts of this collaboration and close influence as recorded by members of the Ecole française d'Athènes, see Emile Burnouf, 'Le Parthénon,' *Revue des Deux Mondes* (1847), 836 n. 1, 839, 847, 849 n. 1, and 'Les Propylées' (June 1848), *Archives des Missions Scientifiques et Littéraires* 1 (1850), 27 n. 1, 29–30; Beulé, *L'Acropole d'Athènes*, II, 218; Olivier Picard, 'Archéologues et architectes,' in *Paris, Rome, Athènes: le voyage en Grèce des architectes français aux XIXe et XXe siècles*. Exhibition Catalogue, Ecole nationale supérieure des Beaux-Arts, Paris; Ecole française d'Athènes; and the Museum of Fine Arts, Houston, May 1982–March 1984 (Paris, 1982; 2nd edn 1983), 18. Beulé also illustrated his book on the Acropolis with drawings by Prix-de-Rome architects, whose observations he cited or utilized throughout both volumes.

51 James Fergusson, *The Illustrated Handbook of Architecture: Being a Concise and Popular Account of the Different Styles of Architecture Prevailing in All Ages and All Countries* (London, 2nd edn, 1859), 131.

52 James Fergusson, *Picturesque Illustrations of Ancient Architecture in Hindostan* (London, 1848), 13, 24.

53 James Fergusson, *An Historical Inquiry into the True Principles of Beauty in Art, More Especially with Reference to Architecture. Part the First* (London, 1849), *The Illustrated Handbook of Architecture: Being a Concise and Popular Account of the Different Styles of Architecture Prevailing in All Ages and All Countries* (London, 1855; 2nd edn, 1859). These were followed by *A History of Architecture in All Countries from the Earliest Times to the Present Day, in Three Volumes* (London, 1865–7).

54 John Ruskin, *The Seven Lamps of Architecture* (1848; New York, 1986 reprint), 148–9.

55 Fergusson, *The Illustrated Handbook of Architecture* (1859 edn.), 239, 251.

56 Fergusson, *An Historical Inquiry*, 284.

57 Ibid., 397, 398.

58 Ibid., 398–9.

59 Fergusson, *The Illustrated Handbook of Architecture* (1859 edn), 280.

60 Ibid., 281.

61 Fergusson, *An Historical Inquiry*, 251. See also p. 284.

62 Ibid., 399.

63 See, for example, ibid., 398–9; *The Illustrated Handbook of Architecture* (1859 edn), 280.

64 Leake, *The Topography of Athens*, 177. See also p. 408. In the second edition (1841, I, 315), the word 'equalled' is replaced by 'rivalled.'

65 Beulé, *L'Acropole d'Athènes*, I, 165.

66 For another early use of this notion, see Francesco Milizia, *Vita del Bernini*: 'l'abilità dell'architetto si conosce principalmente in convertire i difetti del luogo in bellezze.' As quoted in Crescentino Caselli, *Tempio Israelitico in Torino* (Turin, 1875), 10.

67 Beulé, *L'Acropole d'Athènes*, I, 165.

68 Jacques-Martin Tetaz, 'Mémoire explicatif de la restauration de l'Erechtheion (Acropole d'Athènes) par M. J.-M. Tétaz, architecte pensionnaire de l'Académie de France à Rome. Restauration à Rome en 1847,' fol. 1; Mémoire explicatif et justificatif de la restauration de l'Erechtheion d'Athènes. Présenté à l'Institut (Académie des Beaux-Arts) en 1850),' *Revue Archéologique* 8 (15 April – 15 September, 1851), 3. I am grateful to Annie Jacques, librarian at the Ecole nationale supérieure des Beaux-Arts, for assisting me in acquiring a microfilm of the *mémoires* written by the Prix-de-Rome architects who worked in Athens.

69 Beulé, *L'Acropole d'Athènes*, II, 277–82.

70 Ibid., II, 279–80.

71 Ibid., II, 281–2.

72 Ibid., II, 265–6.

73 Viollet-le-Duc, *Entretiens*, I, 7, 101–2. This last statement should not be confused with an apparently similar one by the architect Jacques-Ignace Hittorff: 'Mais les principes de l'architecture des Hellènes sont les seuls vrais, les seuls applicables dans tous les temps, chez tous les peuples, pour tous les pays' in J.-I. Hittorff, *Recueil des monuments de Ségeste et de Sélinonte mesurés et dessinés par J.-I. Hittorff et L. Zanth, suivi de recherches sur l'origine et le développement de l'architecture religieuse chez les Grecs* (Paris, 1870), xiii. Viollet-le-Duc was referring to basic principles of design that can be discerned in Greek architecture and then found in an analogous way in very different architectural styles, including the Gothic. Hittorff, on the other hand, literally meant that the contemporary architect should work within the Greco-Roman tradition, which he saw as capable of yielding new works, just as it had in the Renaissance.

74 Eugène-Emmanuel Viollet-le-Duc, 'De la Construction des édifices religieux en France depuis le commencement du christianisme jusqu'au XVIe siècle,' *Annales Archéologiques* 4 (May 1846), 267.

75 Viollet-le-Duc, *Entretiens*, I, 55.

76 Ibid., I, 293.

77 Ibid., I, 86.

78 Ibid., I, 101.

79 Ibid., I, 61.

80 The *Entretiens* 'did not offer a coherent theory of architecture but rather an array of essays and commentaries outlining his pre-occupations and prejudices' (Robin Middleton, 'Eugène-Emmanuel Viollet-le-Duc,' *Macmillan Encyclopedia of Architects* (New York, 1982), IV, 329.

81 Viollet-le-Duc, *Entretiens*, I, 52–3.

82 Ibid., I, 104.

83 Ibid.

84 Ibid., I, 61.

85 Ibid., I, 293–4.

86 Alexis Paccard, 'Mémoire explicatif de la restauration du Parthénon' (1845), in *Paris, Rome, Athènes*, 351.

87 Viollet-le-Duc, *Entretiens*, I, 256.

88 Ibid., I, 67, 256.

89 Ibid. I, 253–6.

90 Auguste Choisy, 'Note sur la courbure dissymétrique des degrés qui limitent au couchant la plate-forme du Parthénon,' in *Académie des Inscriptions et Belles-Lettres. Comptes rendus des séances de l'année 1865*, Nouvelle série (Paris, 1865), I, 413–17. Choisy's lecture was reprinted separately, without the Académie's introduction (p. 413) and discussion (p. 417), as an 'Extrait des comptes rendus . . .,' Paris, n.d.

91 Choisy appears to have taken advantage of his being in southern France on a *mission*, for he crossed the Alps and then made his first visit to Greek architectural sites. See Paris, Archives Nationales, F.[14] 11469; Choisy, 'Note,' in *Académie des Inscriptions et Belles-Lettres . . . 1865*, 413; and Maurice d'Ocagne, *Auguste Choisy et l'art de bâtir chez les anciens* (Vannes, 1930), 4. I am grateful to Robin Middleton for sharing his transcription of F.[14] 11469 with me. Middleton is the author of 'Auguste Choisy Historian: 1841–1909,' *International Architect* vol. 1 no. 5 (1981), 37–42.

92 Karl Boetticher, 'Meine Untersuchungen auf der Akropolis von Athen im Frühjahre 1862,' *Zeitschrift für Bauwesen* 12 (1863), cols. 195–224, 405–70, 557–608. This text was reprinted as *Bericht über die Untersuchungen auf der Akropolis von Athen im Frühjahre 1862* (Berlin, 1863). See especially pp. 86–8, 103–6, 112–15. Choisy refers briefly to Boetticher's work in 'Note,' in *Académie des Inscriptions et Belles-Lettres . . . 1865*, 413 n. 1.

93 Leake, *The Topography of Athens*, 2 vols (London, 2nd edn, 1841), I, 516.

94 Penrose, *An Investigation*, 4. This text can be found in both editions.

95 Auguste Choisy, *Histoire de l'architecture*, 2 vols (Paris, 1899), I, 414. This is a variation of 'Rien n'est dissymétrique comme la disposition générale des Propylées: la masse toutefois, de part et d'autre, s'équilibre. . . .' ('Note,' in *Académie des Inscriptions et Belles-Lettres . . . 1865*, 414–15).

96 Choisy, 'Note,' in *Académie des Inscriptions et Belles-Lettres . . . 1865*, 415. See also Choisy, *Histoire*, I, 418–19.

97 Thomas Leverton Donaldson, *Preliminary Discourse Pronounced before the University College of London, upon the Commencement of a Series of Lectures on Architecture, 17th October, 1842* (London, 1842), 6 n. 2, 7, 11–13. See also Thomas Leverton Donaldson, *Pompeii, Illustrated with Picturesque Views*, 2 vols (London, 1827), I, 52. On Donaldson, who was awarded the RIBA Gold Medal in 1851 and who served as president of the RIBA in 1863–64, see Sandra Blutman, 'The Father of the Profession,' *Journal of the Royal Institute of British Architects* 74 (December 1967), 542–4.

98 'Mr. Cockerell's Fourth Lecture on Architecture,' *The Builder* 3 (February 8, 1845), 63.

99 Choisy, *Histoire*, I, 60, 64, 84.

100 Ibid., I, 174–5.

101 Ibid., I, 100, 104.

102 Paul-Emile Botta, *Monument de Ninive découvert et décrit par M. P.-E. Botta, mesuré et dessiné par M. E. Flandin. Ouvrage publié par ordre du gouvernement sous les auspices de M. le Ministre de l'Intérieur et sous la direction d'une commission de l'Institut*, 5 vols (Paris, 1849–50), V, especially 34–6, 39, 63–5; Victor Place, *Ninive et l'Assyrie par Victor Place consul général avec des essais de restauration par Félix Thomas. Ouvrage publié d'Après les ordres de l'Empereur*, 3 vols. (Paris, 1867–70), I, especially iii, vi, 41, 51, 109–11, 116, 134.

103 Choisy, *Histoire*, I, 100–6.

104 Ibid., I, 570–4.

105 Choisy's general approach has recently been confirmed by Professor Jerome J. Pollitt, classical archaeologist and art historian at Yale University, who, in a Smithsonian Institution lecture of 1 May 1985, 'The Design of the Athenian Acropolis,' cosponsored by the Museum of Natural History and the Archaeological Institute of America, argued that there was a conscious planning tradition in Greek architecture that differed radically from Hippodamian grid planning. This alternative tradition, which he termed 'kinetic planning,' is basically the same as the 'picturesque' planning described by Choisy. After reviewing a couple of illustrative sites, Pollitt turned to the subject of the Periclean Acropolis where his discussion of the kinetic principle of moving through the site to consider buildings arranged to be seen in certain ways within delimited precincts presented marked similarities to Choisy's earlier analysis. Working with a reconstruction of the Acropolis established after Choisy's death, which presented the site as slightly more subdivided by precinct walls, Pollitt nonetheless offered an analogous interpretation. The similarities are all the more striking since Pollitt made no mention of Choisy and hence appears to have come to his conclusions independently.

106 The phrase comes from Michaelis, *A Century of Archaeological Discoveries*, 216.

107 Choisy, *Histoire*, I, 240.

108 Ibid., I, 409–22.

109 Ibid., II, 762–4.

110 Victor Laloux and Paul Monceaux, *Restauration d'Olympe* (Paris, 1889), 49. See also Victor Laloux, *L'Architecture grecque* (Paris, [1888]), 217–18.

111 On these excavations, see Michaelis, *A Century of Archaeological Discoveries*, 238–41.

112 Choisy, *Histoire*, I, 413.

113 See George R. and Christiane Crasemann Collins, *Camillo Sitte: The Birth of Modern City Planning: With a Translation of the 1889 Austrian edition of his 'City Planning According to Artistic Principles,'* (New York, 1986), 91–9 ('The Influence of Sitte and German Planning Abroad'). On pp. 134–5 the Collinses discuss the rationale behind their translation of the title *Der Städte-Bau nach seinen künstlerischen Grundsätzen*. I have chosen a translation that I consider closer to the original meaning of the words and to the author's intentions. On this subject see also below, including note 131.

114 Ibid., 100–7 ('The Influence of Sitte and German Planning Abroad'). For the Italians, See Richard A. Etlin, *Modernism in Italian Architecture, 1890–1940* (Cambridge, Mass., 1991), 106–28, 142–50.

115 Camillo Sitte, *Der Städte-Bau nach seinen künstlerischen Grundsätzen*, English translation in Collins and Collins, *Camillo Sitte*, 222. The ( ) brackets are mine, the [ ] brackets are the Collinses'.

116 Ibid., 243–9.

117 Ibid., 154.

118 Ibid., 150.

119 Ibid., 248.

120 Ibid., 142.

121 Ibid., 270.

122 Ibid., 166.

123 Ibid., 160.

124 Ibid., 186.

125 Ibid., 188.

126 Ibid., 267.

127 Ibid., 197. As Sitte explained elsewhere in this book (pp. 267–8), narrow, winding streets broke the wind, whereas wide, straight modern streets assaulted the health of passers-by with chilling blasts of wind and 'clouds of dust.'

128 Ibid., 199.

129 Theodor Goecke and Camillo Sitte, 'To Our Readers,' *Der Städtebau* (1904), in Collins and Collins, *Camillo Sitte*, 325–6.

130 Camille Martin 'Streets,' in Sitte, *Der Städte-Bau*, 201.

131 The Collinses proceed to explain their translation of the title as 'City Planning According to Artistic Principles': 'But since *Städtebau* nowadays has come to mean 'city planning' in German as well, we have usually translated it as such, e.g., in the title of the book' (p. 134).

132 As quoted in translation in H. Allen Brooks, 'Jeanneret and Sitte: Le Corbusier's Earliest Ideas on Urban Design,' in Helen Searing, ed., *In Search of Modern Architecture: A Tribute to Henry-Russell Hitchcock* (New York and Cambridge, Mass., 1982), 282.

133 On Henrici, see Collins and Collins, *Camillo Sitte*, 91–2, passim.

134 Karl Henrici, 'Langweilige und kurzweilige Strassen,' *Deutsche Bauzeitung* 27 (3 June 1893), 272. For Jeanneret's copies of many of these figures, see Brooks, 'Jeanneret and Sitte,' in Searing, ed., *In Search of Modern Architecture*, 284–5 (figs. 7–9). Brooks points out that Jeanneret cites Henrici, but neglects to mention that he also uses Henrici's drawings. These 'visual demonstrations' Brooks believes were 'contributed on his own' by Jeanneret (pp. 284–5). It is not certain whether the other illustrations reproduced by Brooks are original designs by Jeanneret.

135 Ibid., 284.

136 Ibid. (Jeanneret as quoted in translation by Brooks.)

137 'Les architectures se classent en mortes et en vivantes selon que la règle du *cheminement* n'a pas été observée, ou qu'au contraire la voilà exploitée brillament.' In this disucussion, 'cheminement' refers to 'le déroulement des faits architecturaux apparus à la suite l'un de l'autre,' which causes 'l'émoi, fruit de commotions successives.' (Le Corbusier, *Entretien avec les étudiants des écoles d'architecture* (Paris, [1943]), no pagination). Le Corbusier uses the phrase 'les architectures,' which refer to the distinct architectures of different historical periods. On this subject see 'Le Corbusier and the Architectural System' in chapter 1 above.

138 Le Corbusier, *Le Voyage d'Orient* (Meaux, 1966), 5. Several articles from Le Corbusier's travel journal had previously appeared in the local newspaper of La-Chaux-de-Fonds. One section of Le Corbusier's book was published in his *Almanch d'architecture moderne* (Paris, 1925), 62–71, under the title 'Sur l'Acropole (Extrait du carnet de route d'étudiant, 1910).' On the dating of these texts as well as their variants, see Etlin, 'Le Corbusier,' *The Art Bulletin* (June 1987), 274 n. 51. For Le Corbusier's journey, see Giuliano Gresleri, *Le Corbusier, viaggio in Oriente: Gli inediti di Charles Edouard Jeanneret fotografo e scrittore* (Paris and Venice, 1984).

139 Le Corbusier, *Vers une Architecture* (3rd edn, Paris, 1928; 1958 reprint), 37.

140 Ibid., 37–8. The first edition (pp. 37–8) read: 'compensation (contrasts).' By changing this in the third edition of 1928 to read 'compensation (movement of contraries)' Le Corbusier clarified his summary of Choisy's principles.

141 Le Corbusier, *Vers une Architecture* (3rd edn, 1928, 1958 reprint), 31, 39. In these two captions, I have modified the translation in *Towards a New Architecture*, tr. Frederick Etchells (London, 1931; New York: Dover Publications, Inc., 1986 reprint), 43, 52. Vincent Scully observes that Le Corbusier was the first to note 'the visual importance of the central axis from sea to mountain in the architecture of the Acropolis,' while pointing out that 'he confused the place names.' Scully sees the axis as extending from Salamis to the sacred mountain of Hymettos. Elsewhere, though, he explains, 'From the Piraeus [the Parthenon] stands bright upon the Acropolis within the V of the higher mountains behind it.' Vincent Scully, *The Earth, The Temple, and The Gods: Greek Sacred Architecture* (rev. edn, New Haven, 1979), 177, 181, 247 n. 53.

142 Le Corbusier, *Vers une Architecture*. For this text I have used the English version, *Towards a New Architecture*, tr. Frederick Etchells (London, 1931; New York: Dover Publications, Inc., 1986 reprint), 181–4, 187, 189–90.

143 Le Corbusier and Pierre Jeanneret, *Oeuvre complète 1910–1929* (1930; 9th edn, Zurich, 1967), 189. The following discussion is adapted from my 'A Paradoxical Avant-Garde: Le Corbusier's Villas of the 1920s,' *The Architectural Review* 181 (January 1987), 21–32.

144 Le Corbusier and Pierre Jeanneret, 'Deux hôtels particuliers à Auteuil,' *Oeuvre complète 1910–1929*, 60.

145 Kurt Forster, 'Antiquity and Modernity in the La Roche-Jeanneret Houses of 1923,' *Oppositions* nos. 15–16 (Winter/Spring 1979), 139.

146 Ibid., 143, 146.

147 Sitte, *Der Städte-Bau*, in Collins and Collins, *Camillo Sitte*, 246.

148 Ibid.

149 For American examples, see Vincent Scully, Jr, *The Shingle Style: Architectural theory and Design from Richardson to the Origin of Wright* (New Haven, 1955), figs. 73, 96, 98, 128.

150 Forster, 'Antiquity and Modernity,' *Oppositions* (Winter/Spring 1979), 139.

151 Le Corbusier, 'L'Esprit nouveau en architecture' (1924), *Almanach*, 28.

152 Pierre Reverdy, for example, was considered a Cubist poet. Paul Dermée, poet and co-editor of *L'Esprit Nouveau*, readily embraced the term 'Cubist poet' both for himself and for his colleagues. See André Malraux, 'Des origines de la poésie cubiste' (January 1920), Stanislaus Fumet, 'La "poésie plastique" de Pierre Reverdy' (March 1924), Odysseus Elytis, 'Pierre Reverdy entre la Grèce et Solesmes,' *Mercure de France* (January 1962), 27, 31, 75. Dermée's autographic dedication to Léonce Rosenberg in Dermée's book, *Spirale* (1917), which had been illustrated by Henri Laurens, read in part: 'Vous aimez les peintres, les sculpteurs, les poètes cubistes' (as quoted in Donna Stein, *Cubist Prints, Cubist Books* [New York, 1983], 63). On the 'Cubist' nature of Igor Stravinsky's music and of James Joyce's and Virginia Woolf's novels, see Robert Rosenblum, *Cubism and Twentieth-Century Art* (New York, 1976 edn), 43.

153 Le Corbusier, 'L'Esprit nouveau in architecture' (1924), *Almanach*, 28.

154 Amédée Ozenfant and Charles-Edouard Jeanneret, *La Peinture moderne* (Paris, 1925), 164. See also Amédée Ozenfant, *Mémoires 1886–1962* (Paris, 1968), 99: 'Sans Cubisme il n'y aurait pas eu de Purisme: le Cubisme cézannien, puis le cubisme "cristallin" suscitèrent le Purisme originel . . .'; Forster, 'Antiquity and Modernity,' *Oppositions* (Winter/Spring 1979), 140.

155 Colin Rowe and Robert Slutzky, 'Transparency: Literal and Phenomenal,' *Perspecta* (1963), now in Colin Rowe, *The Mathematics of the Ideal Villa and Other Essays* (Cambridge, Mass., 1976), 159–83.

156 Forster, 'Antiquity and Modernity,'

157 Marcel Proust, 'Le Côté de Guermantes I' (1920) in *A la Recherche du temps perdu*, eds. Pierre Clarac and André Ferré, 3 vols (Paris: Gallimard, 1954) II, 82.

158 Le Corbusier, 'L'Exposition de l'Ecole Spéciale d'Architecture' (1924), *L'Esprit Nouveau* no. 23 [May 1924], and reprinted in French, with an English translation, in *Rob Mallet-Stevens Architecte* (Brussels 1980), 379–84, where it is mistakenly identified as an unpublished manuscript. I am following 'Datation des numéros de *L'Esprit Nouveau*,' Fondation Le Corbusier, Paris, for the dating of the articles in this journal.

159 Le Corbusier and Pierre Jeanneret, letter of October 1925 to Mme Meyer, in *Oeuvre complète 1910–1929*, 89.

160 Julien Guadet, *Eléments et théorie de l'architecture: cours professé à l'Ecole nationale et spéciale des Beaux-Arts*, 4 vols (Paris, 1901–4; 5th edn, n.d.), II, 37ff.

161 See, for example, Edwin Strub, 'A quelques oeuvres d'architectes bâlois,' *L'Architecture Suisse* (September 1912), 17–20. See also Hermann Röthlisberger, 'Art Français et art allemand,' *L'Architecture Suisse* (April 1913), 98, 100, 109–10, (May 1913), 115–17, which emphasizes the distinct cultural identities and rivalries between the French- and German-speaking parts of Switzerland and which praises Charles-Edouard Jeanneret's (Le Corbusier's) *Etude sur le mouvement d'art décoratif en Allemagne* (1912) as offering '. . . d'excellents principes dont l'application contribuerait certainement à améliorer la qualité des oeuvres d'art appliqué, dans la Suisse française' (116).

162 Pierre Saddy, 'Perret et les idées reçues,' *Architecture Mouvement Continuité* no. 37 (November 1975), 22.

163 Nancy J. Troy, 'Le Corbusier and Art Deco: Reconstructing the Context.' I am grateful to Nancy Troy for permitting me to quote from this unpublished manuscript, which was subsequently integrated into Troy's *Modernism and the Decorative Arts in France: Art Nouveau to Le Corbusier* (New Haven, 1991).

164 Nancy J. Troy, 'Le Corbusier, Nationalism, and the Decorative Arts in France, 1900–1918,' in Richard A. Etlin, ed., *Nationalism in the Visual Arts*, proceedings of the symposium jointly sponsored by the Center for Advanced Study in the Visual Arts, National Gallery of Art, and the Department of the History of Art, the Johns Hopkins University, 16–17 October, 1987, in *Studies in the History of Art* 29 (1991), 64–87.

165 Charles-Edouard Jeanneret and Amédée Ozenfant, *La Peinture moderne* (Paris, 1925), 119, 163–4.

166 Richard A. Etlin, ' "Les dedans," ' Jacques-François Blondel and the System of the Home, c. 1740' *Gazette des Beaux-Arts* 91 (April 1978), 137–47.

167 Michael Dennis, *Court and Garden: From the French Hôtel to the City of Modern Architecture* (Chicago and Cambridge, Mass., 1986), 190–204.

168 Camille Martin, 'Réflexions sur l'architecture locale.' *L'Architecture Suisse* 1 (July 1912), 14–16.

169 See Debora L. Silverman, *Art Nouveau in Fin-de-Siècle France: Politics, Psychology, and Style* (Berkeley and Los Angeles, 1989), 17–32, 109–71, passim.

170 Le Corbusier, *Vers une Architecture* (3rd edn, 1928; 1958 reprint), 131.

171 'La Maison Savoye à Poissy, 1928–1930,' *Cahiers d'Art* year 5, no. 4 (1930), 212.

172 Ibid.

173 Le Corbusier and Atelier, 'Villa Shodhan,' *Oeuvre complète 1952–1957*, ed. Willy Boesiger (Zurich, 1957; 4th edn, 1966), 134.

174 Ibid.

175 Le Corbusier, *Précisions sur un état présent de l'architecture et de l'urbanisme* (Paris, 1930; 1960 reprint), 138–9 (illustration).

176 Mary McLeod, 'Urbanism and Utopia: Le Corbusier from Regional Syndicalism to Vichy' (Ph.D. Dissertation, Princeton University, June 1985), vol. 1.

177 Le Corbusier, *Vers une Architecture* (3rd edn, 1928; 1958 reprint), 178.

178 Wright, *An Autobiography* (1932), 147.

179 Bruce Brooks Pfeiffer, *Treasures of Taliesin: Seventy-Six Unbuilt Designs* (Carbondale and Edwardsville, 1985), 5.

180 For an illustration of the entrance hall of Kingscote, see William H. Pierson, Jr, *American Buildings and Their Architects: Technology and the Picturesque, The Corporate and the Early Gothic Styles* (Garden City, 1980), 377.

181 See chapter 1, note 111.

182 Henry-Russell Hitchcock, *In the Nature of Materials: The Buildings of Frank Lloyd Wright, 1887–1941* (New York, 1942; 1975 reprint), p. 31 and fig. 18 (plan).

183 For the plan of Donaldson's Gothic Villa, see Pierson, *American Buildings and Their Architects: Technology and the Picturesque*, 299.

184 Hitchcock, *In the Nature of Materials*, caption to figures 55–6.

185 On the influence of the Kent House for the design of Wright's home in Oak Park, see Vincent Scully, Jr, *Frank Lloyd Wright* (New York, 1960), 15.

186 Hitchcock, *In the Nature of Materials*, caption to figures 73–4.

187 Donald Hoffmann, *Frank Lloyd Wright's Robie House: The Illustrated Story of an Architectural Masterpiece* (New York, 1984), 60–1.

188 Hildebrand, 'The Wright Space,' 121, 132–5, and *The Wright Space*, 53, 55.

189 For a recent study of this phenomenon, see Jonathan Lipman, 'Consecrated Space: The Public Buildings of Frank Lloyd Wright,' in Robert McCarter, ed., *Frank Lloyd Wright: A Primer on Architectural Principles* (New York, 1991), 193–217.

190 Scully, *Wright*, 20.

191 With this design Wright effectively redefined the nature of the modern museum. When The National Gallery of Art in Washington, D.C. decided to add another building, the architect I. M. Pei adapted Wright's prototype by designing an atrium building with various mezzanine galleries. In Atlanta Richard Meier designed the High Museum with a ramp that spirals around a central atrium.

192 These labels come from John Sergeant, *Frank Lloyd Wright's Usonian Houses: The Case for an Organic Architecture* (New York, 1976).

193 Ibid., 68.

194 Ibid.

195 Neil Levine, 'Frank Lloyd Wright's Diagonal Planning,' in Helen Searing, ed., *In Search of Modern Architecture: A Tribute to Henry-Russell Hitchcock* (New York and Cambridge, Mass., 1982), 245–77 (268 on the Pew House).

196 See note 188 above.

197 For additional illustrations related to the ideas presented in this and the subsequent paragraph, see the following drawings in the Frank Lloyd Wright Archives at the Frank Lloyd Wright Foundation, Taliesin West, Scottsdale, Ariz.: 4012.001 (perspective view), 4012.038 (*esquisse*-like sketch of plan and elevation), 4012.22 (plans of the initial scheme).

198 See, in particular, Henry Van de Velde's discussion of the line as a 'force' in *Les Formules de la beauté architectonique moderne* (Weimar, 1916–17; Brussels, 1978 reprint), 61–7, as well as his 'Suite d'idées sur une conférence' (1903), also included in this reprint, which opens with a quotation from Hippolyte Taine that extols the 'imperceptible inflexion of the swelling horizontals and the converging perpendiculars that give to [the Greeks'] most beautiful temple its supreme beauty.' See also, Ronald McFadzean, *The Life and Works of Alexander Thomson* (London, 1979), 83, 88, and Leland M. Roth, *McKim, Mead & White, Architects* (New York, 1983), 195.

199 Wright, *The Natural House*, 77.

200 Le Corbusier and Pierre Jeanneret, *Oeuvre complète de 1929–1934* (1935; 7th edn, Zurich, 1964), 173.

201 I am referring to the sketch that Le Corbusier labels, 'show, by *reflection*, the double square,' reproduced in Le Cobusier, *Oeuvre complète 1952–1957*, 57. For the discussion of his parents' house, see the section 'Oh "excuse-me," Vignola!' in chapter 1 above.

CHAPTER 3

1 Camille Martin, 'L'Architecture du XXe siècle. (Suite),' *L'Architecture Suisse* (April 1913), 94.

2 Moisei Ginzburg, *Style and Epoch*, tr. Anatole Senkevitch, Jr (New York and Cambridge, Mass., 1982), 70–1. Anatole Kopp, who translates the title as *The Style and the Age*, explains the fundamental role of this book in helping to crystallize the nascent Russian Constructivist movement (*Constructivist Architecture in the USSR* [London and New York, 1985], 22).

3 Henry-Russell Hitchcock, *Modern Architecture: Romanticism and Reintegration* (New York, 1929), 6.

4 'Preface,' *Eclectic Review* 1 (January 1805), ii.

5 Victor Cousin, *Fragmens philosophiques* (Paris, 1826), xlviii:

... that is to say: that each system expresses an order of phenomena and ideas that is real in itself, but is not alone in human consciousness, and yet which in the system plays a nearly exclusive role; from which it follows that each system is not false, but incomplete; from which it then follows that by uniting all the incomplete systems, one would have a complete philosophy, adequate to the totality of human consciousness.

6 Aug. Barchou, 'Essai d'une formule générale de l'histoire de l'humanité, d'après les idées de M. Ballanche,' *Revue des Deux Mondes* 2 (1831), 525.

7 Vitet publically acknowledged his debt to Jouffroy on the occasion of his reception into the Académie Française. See Charles-Augustin Sainte-Beuve, 'Académie Française. Réception de M. Vitet par M. le comte Molé,' *Revue des Deux Mondes* 14 (1846), 130.

8 T[héodore] J[ouffroy], 'De la Philosophie morale de M. Droz, ou De l'Eclectisme moderne,' *Le Globe* (9 April, 1825), 457–8.

9 Sainte-Beuve, 'Académie Française. Réception de M. Vitet,' *Revue des Deux Mondes* 14 (1846), 130–2.

10 Ludovic Vitet, 'De la Théorie des jardins' (1828), in *Etudes sur les Beaux-Arts. Essais d'archéologie et fragments littéraires*, 2 vols (Paris, 1846), I, 322.

11 Ludovic Vitet, 'Monuments de Paris' (March 1838), in *Etudes*, I, 281.

12 Vitet, 'De la Théorie des jardins,' in *Etudes*, I, 323, passim.

13 Vitet, 'Notre-Dame de Noyon' (1844), in *Etudes*, II, 183–4. See also, 179–80.

14 Anglicanus (pseud.), 'Letter to the editor,' *The Ecclesiologist*, (July 1842), 161–2.

15 Viollet-le-Duc, *Entretiens sur l'architecture*, 2 vols (Paris, 1863–72; Ridgewood, N. J., 1965 reprint), I, 144–5.

16 Ibid., I, 32.

17 Ibid., II, 15.

18 Thomas Hope, *An Historical Essay on Architecture by the Late Thomas Hope, Illustrated from Drawings Made by Him in Italy and Germany* (London, 1835), 559–60.

19 Ibid., 561.

20 Thomas Leverton Donaldson, *Preliminary Discourse Pronounced before the University College of London, upon the Commencement of a Series of Lectures on Architecture, 17th October, 1842* (London, 1842), 28–9.

21 Daniel Ramée, *Manuel de l'histoire générale de l'architecture chez tous les peuples, et particulièrement de l'architecture en France au Moyen-Age*, vol. 1 (Paris, 1843), ix.

22 Leo Von Klenze, from the text that accompanies the publication of the plates 'Die Walhalla bei Regensburg,' in Oswald Hederer, *Leo von Klenze: Persönlichkeit und Werk* (Munich: Verlag Georg D. W. Callwey, 1964), 309, 313. Hederer gives the date as 1843.

23 'Church Architecture in Paris,' *The Builder* 3 (4 January 1845), 3.

24 Jacques-Germain Soufflot, 'Mémoire sur l'architecture gothique' read at the Académie des Beaux Arts, Lyons (12 April, 1741), in Michael Petzet, *Soufflots Sainte-Geneviève und der französische Kirchenbau des 18. Jahrhunderts* (Berlin, 1961), 135–42; Jean-Marie Pérouse de Montclos, *Etienne-Louis Boullée, 1728–1799: de l'architecture classique à l'architecture révolutionnaire* (Paris, 1969), 156–61; Jean-Louis de Cordemoy, *Nouveau traité de toute l'architecture* (Paris, 1714), 110; and Marc-Antoine Laugier, *Essai sur l'architecture* (2nd rev. edn, Paris, 1755), 4, 177; Etienne-Louis Boullée, *Architecture, essai sur l'art*, ed. Jean-Marie Pérouse de Montclos (Paris, 1968), 89–94; Louis Combes, 'Paralelle (*sic*) de l'architecture gotique (*sic*) avec l'architecture greque (*sic*) et moderne,' Bibliothèque Municipale de Bordeaux, Ms. 48, no. 2 and no. 3. See also François-Georges Pariset, 'Les Théories artistiques d'un architecte du néo-classicisme, Louis Combes, de Bordeaux,' *Annales du Midi* no. 68–9 (July–October 1964), 543–55; Wolfgang Herrmann, 'Gothic through Classical Eyes' (chapter 5), in *Laugier and Eigtheenth Century French Theory* (London, 1962), 68–90.

25 William Duff, *An Essay on Original Genius; and Its Various Modes of Exertion in Philosophy and the Fine Arts, Particularly in Poetry* (London, 1767; Gainesville, Fla., 1964 reprint), 258.

26 Robert Willis, *Remarks on the Architecture of the Middle Ages, Especially of Italy* (Cambridge, 1835), 3.

27 George Edmond Street, *Brick and Marble in the Middle Ages: Notes of Tours in the North of Italy* (2nd edn, London, 1874), 363–70. See also p. 252 in the 1855 edition.

28 Ginzburg, *Style and Epoch*, 71–2.

29 See 'The System of Construction' in chapter 1 above.

30 Ginzburg, *Style and Epoch*, 72.

31 Ibid., 62.

32 On this literature, see Logan Pearsall Smith, *Four Words: Romantic, Originality, Creative, Genius*. S.P.E. Tract No. XVII (Oxford, 1924), 26.

33 Duff, *An Essay on Original Genius*, 257–8.

34 Ibid., 260. This is the title for Section V, pp. 260–96.

35 John Claudius Loudon, 'On the Difference between Common, or Imitative, Genius, and Inventive, or Original, Genius, in Architecture,' *The Architectural Magazine*, 1 (July 1834), 185.

36 Ibid., 186.

37 Vincent Scully, Jr, *Frank Lloyd Wright* (New York, 1960); Colin Rowe, 'The Mathematics of the Ideal Villa,' in *The Mathematics of the Ideal Villa and Other Essays* (Cambridge, Mass., 1976, 1982), 1–27; Kurt W. Forster, 'Antiquity and Modernity in the La Roche-Jeanneret Houses of 1923,' *Oppositions* nos. 15/16 (Winter/Spring 1979), 131–53; William J. R. Curtis, *Modern Architecture since 1900* (Englewood Cliffs, N.J., 1983), 193–5.

38 Charles E. White, Jr, letter of 13 May, 1904, in H. Allen Brooks, ed., *Writings on Wright: Selected Commentary on Wright* (Cambridge, Mass., 1981), 86.

39 Brooks, ed., *Writings on Wright*, 105 (editor's note): 'Thus Wright probably furnished some of these ideas' expressed in Spencer's article.

40 Robert C. Spencer, Jr, 'The Work of Frank Lloyd Wright,' *Architectural Review* 7 (June 1900), in Brooks, ed., *Writings on Wright*, 106.

41 Frank Lloyd Wright, 'In the Cause of Architecture,' *The Architectural Record* 22 (March 1908), in Frank Lloyd Wright, *In the Cause of Architecture: Essays by Frank Lloyd Wright for 'Architectural Record,' 1908–1952, with a Symposium on Architecture with and without Wright by Eight Who Knew Him*, ed. Frederick Gutheim (New York, 1975), 57–8.

42 This was a recurrent feature of Wright's houses in the 1950s.

43 For an illustration of this project, see Bruce Brooks Pfeiffer, *Frank Lloyd Wright Monograph 1951–1959* (Tokyo, 1988), 304. On the evolution of this design, which became more explicitly classical in its final variants, see Richard A. Etlin, 'The Space of Absence,' in Francisco Javier Rodríguez Barberán, ed., *Una Arquitectura para la Muerte. 1 Encuentro internacional sobre los cementerios contemporaneos. Actas* (Seville, 1993), 179–80, 595–6, and *Symbolic Space: French Enlightenment Architecture and Its Legacy* (Chicago, 1994), chapter 7.

44 Henry-Russell Hitchcock, *In the Nature of Materials: The Buildings of Frank Lloyd Wright, 1887–1941* (1942, 1978), 77; Dimitri Tselos, 'Exotic Influences in the Architecture of Frank Lloyd Wright,' *Magazine of Art* 47 (April 1953), 163–84; Scully, *Frank Lloyd Wright*, 24–7; Majorie I. Ingle, *The Mayan Revival Style: Art Deco Mayan Fantasy* (Salt Lake City, 1984), 13–19.

45 'On the first concept section of the Guggenheim Museum – one of the most remarkable drawings ever made in the realm of architecture – [Wright] penciled in the word 'ziggurat' (Bruce Brooks Pfeiffer, ed., *Frank Lloyd Wright: The Guggenheim Correspondence* [Fresno, Cal., and Carbondale, Ill., 1986], 27). Wright, upon unveiling his model for the Guggenheim Museum ('The Modern Gallery of Non-Objective Art'), explained to the press that he had derived the idea for the design from the Assyrian ziggurat ('Optimistic Ziggurat,' *Time* [1 October 1945], 74). See also Frank Lloyd Wright, *Architecture: Man in Possession of His Earth* (New York, 1962), 52–3. In *Wright*, 31, Scully relates that Wright called his 'Golden Triangle' project for Pittsburgh a 'ziggurat.'

46 Léonce Reynaud, *Traité d'architecture. Première partie: Art de bâtir* (2nd edn, Paris, 1860), 11; Anatole de Baudot, *L'Architecture: le passé, le présent* (Paris, 1916), 16. Le Corbusier had this latter book in his library. Paul Venable Turner believes that it was acquired in 1916 (Turner, *The Education of Le Corbusier* [New York and London, 1977], 243).

47 Le Corbusier and Pierre Jeanneret, 'Villa à Garches,' *Oeuvre complète 1910–1929* (1930; 9th edn, Zurich), 140.

48 For illustrations, see Tim Benton, *Les Villas de Le Corbusier, 1920–1930* (Paris, 1984), 174–5.

49 Ibid.

50 Le Corbusier owned a copy of this book and repeatedly referred to the section on ancient Egyptian architecture in his 1915 sketchbook (A2).

51 Georges Perrot and Charles Chipiez, *Histoire de l'art dans l'antiquité* vol. 1 (Paris, 1882), 'L'ennui naquit un jour de l'uniformité,' 587–600.

52 Charles Blanc, *Grammaire des arts du dessin* (Paris, 1867), 8.

53 Emile Burnouf, 'Le Parthénon,' *Revue des Deux Mondes* (1847), 838, 841. The article ends: 'Seulement il faut reconnaître comme une vérité que le Parthénon est non-seulement le chef-d'oeuvre des temples antiques, mais aussi le plus beau monument d'architecture religieuse que l'Europe ait produit jamais' (853).

54 It is not clear whether Jeanneret was able to acquire a copy before his visit.

55 Ernest Renan, *'Prière sur l'Acropole' with Readings from the Original Manuscript*, ed. Eugène Vinaver and T. B. L. Webster (Manchester, 1934), 23.

56 Le Corbusier, 'Le Parthénon,' undated manuscript in the Fondation Le Corbusier, Paris. This manuscript, developed from Jeanneret's (Le Corbusier's) travel notes of 1911, was published in part as 'Sur l'Acropole (Extrait du carnet de route d'étudiant, 1910),' in Le Corbusier, *Almanach d'architecture moderne* (Paris, 1925),

62–71, and then as a chapter in Le Corbusier, *Le Voyage d'Orient* (Meaux, 1966), 152–68. According to the introduction to this latter book, *Le Voyage d'Orient* was to have been published in 1914 by *Mercure de France*, but did not appear because of the War. Later, 'en juillet 1965, [Le Corbusier] en corrige le manuscrit . . .' (p. 5).

There are slight variants between the three texts. Anthony Eardley, who has studied this matter closely, believes that the handwritten manuscript dates from around 1914. It is written on the same type of paper and in the same ink as the chapter entitled 'Athos,' which is dated at the end: '24 juin 1914.' I am grateful to Dean Eardley for sharing his thoughts with me as well as for providing me with a copy of the manuscript. The sentence quoted here appears in the manuscript and in *Almanach* (p. 63) with the words 'obéissant' and 'très fond' in place of the later 'obéissent' and 'tréfond' as found in *Voyage* (p. 162).

57 Le Corbusier, 'Le Parthénon,' and *Voyage*, 154. This part of the text was not included in *Almanach*.

58 Le Corbusier, 'Le Parthénon,' and *Voyage*, 162. The text in *Almanach*, 65, presents several minor variants in wording.

59 See Stuart Cohen and Steven Hurtt, 'The Pilgrimage Chapel at Ronchamp: Its Architectonic Structure and Typological Antecedents,' *Oppositions* nos. 19/20 (Winter/Spring 1980), 150.

CHAPTER 4

1 César Daly, 'Résumé du voyage d'un architecte en Angleterre,' *Revue Générale de l'Architecture et des Travaux Publics* 1 (1840), col. 157.

2 Eugène-Emmanuel Viollet-le-Duc, *Entretiens sur l'architecture*, 2 vols (Paris, 1863–72; 1965 reprint, Ridgewood, N.J.). I, 96.

3 Hippolyte Taine, *Histoire de la littérature anglaise*, 3 vols (Paris, 1863), I, iii.

4 Emile Boutmy, *Le Parthénon et le génie grec* (Paris, 1897), xii–xiii.

5 César Daly, 'Vacance de la chaire d'histoire de l'architecture. L'Ecole des Beaux-Arts,' *Revue Générale de l'Architecture et des Travaux Publics* 1 (1840), col. 488.

6 Thomas Leverton Donaldson, *Preliminary Discourse Pronounced before the University College of London, upon the Commencement of a Series of Lectures on Architecture, 17th October, 1842* (London, 1842), 26–8.

7 John Ruskin, *Saint Mark's Rest. The History of Venice . . .* (Kent: George Allen, 1884), in *The Works of John Ruskin*, eds E. T. Cook and Alexander Wedderburn (London: George Allen, 1906), XXIV, 203.

8 Pierre Leroux, 'Philosophie de l'histoire. De la loi de continuité qui unit le dix-huitième siècle au dix-septième,' *Revue Encyclopédique* (March 1833), 469.

9 Quoted in George L. Hersey, *High Victorian Gothic: A Study in Associationism* (Baltimore, 1972), 44–5.

10 Jan Wils, 'De nieuwe tijd. Eenige gedachten bij het werk van Frank Lloyd Wright,' *Wendingen* 2 (June 1919), 14.

11 Karl Friedrich Schinkel as cited in Georg Germann, *Gothic Revival in Europe and Britain: Sources, Influences and Ideas*, tr. Gerald Onn (London, 1972), 9.

12 As quoted in Carl E. Schorske, *Fin-de-Siècle Vienna: Politics and Culture* (New York, 1980; 1981 ed.), 36.

13 Ludovic Vitet, 'Des Monuments de Paris' (March 1838), in *Etudes sur les Beaux-Arts. Essais d'archéologie et fragments littéraires*, 2 vols (Paris, 1846), I, 279: 'I do not believe that it is possible to expect our century to have its own architecture. . . . Architecture is an art that reproduces too faithfully contemporary mores and social conditions for a distinctive identity to issue forth from our bland and undistinguished era.'

14 Pieter Singelenberg, *H. P. Berlage: Idea and Style, The Quest for a Modern Architecture* (Utrecht, 1972) 5.

15 Montgomery Schuyler, 'Modern Architecture,' *The Architectural Record* 4 (July–September 1894), now in *American Architecture and Other Writings by Montgomery Schuyler*, eds William H. Jordy and Ralph Coe (Cambridge, Mass., 1961), I, 104.

16 Luca Beltrami, 'La Mostra della Ditta Ceruti (Architetto Gaetano Moretti) all'Esposizione d'Arte Decorativa Moderna in Torino,' *Edilizia Moderna* 12 (May 1903), now in Francesca R. Fratini, ed., *Torino 1902, polemiche in Italia sull'Arte Nuova* (Turin, 1970), 103–4; Emile Magne, *L'Esthétique des Villes* (Paris, 1908), 11–13 (Magne also quotes Vitet's lines of 1838 given in note 13 above); Antoine Pompe, 'L'Art Moderne et la Tradition,' *Tekhné* 2 (1 March, 1913), 1025–6, (8 March, 1913), 1029–30, (15 March, 1913), 1041–2. See also Lucien Magne, 'L'Architecture moderne,' *Art et Décoration* (February 1898), 45; Ugo Ojetti, 'L'Arte Nuova a Torino,' *Corriere della Sera* (20–1 June 1902), in Fratini, ed., *Torino 1902*, 194.

17 As quoted in Agnes Addison Gilchrist, 'Girard College: An Example of the Layman's Influence on Architecture,' *Journal of the Society of Architectural Historians* 16 (May 1957), 24.

18 Section title in Tom Wolfe, *Mauve Gloves, Madmen, Clutter & Vine, and Other Stories, Sketches, and Essays* (New York, 1976), 105.

19 One of the Democracy (pseud.), 'Letter to Christopher North, Esquire, on the Spirit of the Age,' *Blackwood's Edinburgh Magazine* 28 (1830), 900–1.

20 See David Watkin, *Architecture and Morality: The Development of a Theme in Architectural History and Theory from the Gothic Revival to the Modern Movement* (Oxford, 1977).

21 Ernst H. Gombrich, 'In Search of Cultural History,' in *Ideas and Idols: Essays on Values in History and in Art* (Oxford and New York), 28.

22 John Stuart Mill, 'The Spirit of the Age,' *Examiner* (6 January, 29 May. 1831), now in *Essays on Politics and Culture*, ed. Gertrude Himmelfarb (New York, 1962), 3.

23 See Ernst Cassirer, *The Philosophy of the Enlightenment*, trs. Fritz C.A. Koelln and James P. Pettegrove (1932; English tr. Princeton, 1951; Boston, 1955), 216–22; Karl J. Weintraub, *Visions of Culture: Voltaire, Guizot, Burckhardt, Lamprecht, Huizinga, Ortega y Gasset* (Chicago, 1966), 19–74; John Barker, *The Super Historians: Makers of Our Past* (New York, 1982), 107–10.

24 Percy Bysshe Shelley, letter of 8 September, 1816 to Lord Byron, in *Lord Byron's Correspondence*, ed. John Murray, 2 vols (London, 1922), II, 15.

25 Joseph Warton, *An Essay on the Genius and Writings of Pope in Two Volumes* (London, 1782; 1970 reprint, New York), I, 209.

26 Richard Hengist Horne, *A New Spirit of the Age* (1844), introduction by Walter Jerrold (London, 1907), vi: 'that elusive something which we denominate the spirit of the age.'

27 Percy Bysshe Shelley, letter of 15 October 1819, to Charles and James Ollier, in *The Works of Percy Bysshe Shelley*, eds Roger Ingpen and Walter E. Peck, (New York and London, 1965 reprint), X, 95–6. See also 'Shelley's *Revolt of Islam*,' *Quarterly Review* 21 (April 1819), 461.

28 Percy Bysshe Shelley, 'Preface,' *Prometheus Unbound*, in *Works*, II, 174.

29 Edward Bulwer Lytton, *England and the English*, 2 vols (London, 2nd edn, 1833), II, 71.

30 Jacques Barzun, 'Cultural Nationalism and the Makings of Fame,' in Edward Mead Earle, ed., *Nationalism and Internationalism: Essays Inscribed to Carlton J. H. Hayes* (New York, 1950), 3.

31 Pompe, 'L'Art Moderne et la Tradition,' *Tekhné* 2 (15 March 1913), 1042.

32 William Hazlitt, *The Spirit of the Age: or, Contemporary Portraits* (1825), in *The Complete Works of William Hazlitt*, ed. P. P. Howe (London and Toronto, 1932), XI, 86, 16, 28, 127–8.

33 Immanuel Kant, 'Idea for a Universal History with Cosmopolitan Intent' (1784), in *The Philosophy of Kant: Immanuel Kant's Moral and Political Writings*, ed. Carl J. Friedrich (New York, 1949), 127–30; See also R. G. Collingwood, *The Idea of History* (1946; New York, 1956), 93–104.

34 Friedrich Wilhelm Joseph von Schelling, *System of Transcendental Idealism (1800)*, tr. Peter Heath (Charlottesville: University Press of Virginia, 1978), 202–3.

35 Ibid., 211.

36 Ibid., 211–12.

37 Johann Gottlieb Fichte, *Die Grundzüge des gegenwärtigen Zeitalters. Dargestellt von Johann Gottlieb Fichte in Vorlesungen gehalten zu Berlin, im Jahre 1804–1805* (Berlin, 1806), in *Fichte's sämmtliche Werke* (Berlin: Verlag von Veit und Comp., 1846) VII, 6, 11, 65.

38 Ibid., 18.

39 Ibid., 139–40.

40 Ibid.

41 Ibid., 55.

42 Ibid., 57.

43 Ibid., 59–60.

44 Ibid., 62.

45 Georg Wilhelm Friedrich Hegel, 'The Philosophical History of the World' (Second Draft, 1830) in Hegel, *Lectures on the Philosophy of World History*, tr. H. B. Nisbet (Cambridge: Cambridge University Press, 1975), 52.

46 Georg Wilhelm Friedrich Hegel, *The Philosophy of History*, tr. J. Sibree (New York: Dover Publications, Inc., 1966), 63–4.

47 Taine, *Histoire de la littérature anglaise*, I, xxxix.

48 Ibid., xliii, iv–v, x–xi, respectively.

49 Pierre Leroux, 'Philosophie de l'histoire. De la loi de continuité . . .,' *Revue Encyclopédique* (March 1833), 465.

50 Hippolyte Taine, *Philosophie de l'art. Leçons professées à l'Ecole des Beaux-Arts*, 2 vols (Paris, 1865), II, 11, 55.

51 Viollet-le-Duc, *Entretiens*, I, 97.

52 Francis Cranmer Penrose, *An Investigation of the Principles of Athenian Architecture* (London, 1851), 83.

53 Thomas Leverton Donaldson, *Pompeii, Illustrated with Picturesque Views*, 2 vols (London, 1827), I, 51.

54 George Peabody Gooch, *History and Historians in the Nineteenth Century* (London and New York, 1913), 32.

55 Auguste Choisy, 'Un Devis de travaux publics à Livadie' (Paris, 1884), now in Choisy, *Etudes épigraphiques sur l'architecture grecque* (Paris, 1884), 173–208.

56 Auguste Choisy, 'Les Murs d'Athènes d'après le devis de leur restauration' (Paris, 1883), now in Choisy, *Etudes épigraphiques*, 80.

57 Choisy, 'L'Arsenal du Pirée d'après le devis original des travaux' (Paris, 1883), now in Choisy, *Etudes épigraphiques*, 15, 19.

58 Choisy, 'Préface,' *Etudes épigraphiques*, v.

59 Ibid., vi.

60 Emile Burnouf, 'Le Parthénon,' *Revue des Deux Mondes* (1847), 853.

61 Penrose, *An Investigation of the Principles of Athenian Architecture* (1851), 82.

62 Ernesto di Sambuy, Leonardo Bistolfi, Giovanni Angelo Reycend, Enrico Thovez, Davide Calandra, Lorenzo Delleani, Giorgio Ceragioli, Mario Vicari, Enrico Marchesi, Giuseppe Lavini, Guido Rey, Edoardo di Sambuy, 'Manifesto del Comitato Torinese' (January 1901) announcing the coming Prima Esposizione Internazionale d'Arte Moderna Decorativa that would be held the following year in Turin.

This 'Manifesto' was published in *Arte Italiana Decorativa e Industriale* 10 (February 1910), 15. The passage quoted here was repeated in the opening editorial of *L'Arte Decorativa Moderna* 1 (January 1902), 1, entitled 'Lo scopo,' and signed by this avant-garde journal's five founders: Bistolfi, Calandra, Ceragioli, Reycend, and Thovez. On this subject, see Richard A. Etlin, *Modernism in Italian Architecture, 1890–1940* (Cambridge, Mass., 1991), chapter 2.

63 Lytton, *England and the English*, I, 4.

64 Johann Wolfgang von Goethe, *Conversations with Eckermann: Being Appreciations and Criticisms on Many Subjects with a Preface by Eckermann*, tr. John Oxenford (Washington and London: M. Walter Dunne, 1901), 156.

65 Henry Van de Velde, *Déblaiement d'art* (2nd edn, Brussels, 1895) in *Déblaiement d'art, suivi de La Triple offense à la beauté . . .* (Brussels, 1979), 4, 14.

66 Hermann Muthesius, 'Das Moderne in der Architektur,' in *Kunstgewerbe und Architektur* (Jena, 1907), 33.

67 Van de Velde, *Déblaiement*, 21.

68 Erich Mendelsohn, 'Das Problem einer neuen Baukunst,' lecture delivered to the Arbeitsrat für Kunst, Berlin, 1919, and published in *Erich Mendelsohn: Das Gesamtschaffen des Architekten: Skizzen, Entwürfe, Bauten* (Berlin, 1930), 8. English translations of excerpts of this talk can be found in Erich Mendelsohn, *Letters of an Architect*, ed. Oskar Beyer, tr. Geoffrey Strachan (London, 1967), 45–50, and Ulrich Conrads, *Programs and Manifestoes on 20th-Century Architecture*, tr. Michael Bullock (Cambridge, Mass., 1970), 54–5.

69 Henry Van de Velde, 'La Triple offense à la beauté' (1917–18), in *Déblaiement d'art, suivi de La Triple offense à la beauté . . .* (1979), 32.

70 Charles-Edouard Jeanneret, *Etude sur le mouvement d'art décoratif en Allemagne* (1912; 1968 reprint), 25, 28.

71 Leon Battista Alberti, *On the Art of Building in Ten Books*, trs. Joseph Rykwert, Neil Leach, and Robert Tavernor (Cambridge, Mass., 1988), 194, 199.

72 Karl Scheffler, *Moderne Baukunst* (2nd edn, Berlin, 1907), 8.

73 Giuseppe Terragni, 'La costruzione della Casa del Fascio di Como,' *Quadrante* nos. 35/36 (October 1936), 6.

74 Scheffler, *Moderne Baukunst*, 9.

75 Richard Popplewell Pullan, *Elementary Lectures on Christian Architecture* (London, 1879), v–vi.

76 Camille Martin, 'L'Architecture du XX siècle,' *L'Architecture Suisse* (April 1913), 95–6.

77 'Au Directeur de *l'Artiste*,' *L'Artiste* 5 (1833), 278.

78 George Gilbert Scott, 'The Architecture of the Future,' in *Remarks on Secular and Domestic Architecture, Present and Future* (London, 1857), 270; Thomas Carlyle, ' 'Signs of the Times' (1829), in *Carlyle: Selected Works, Reminiscences and Letters*, ed. Julian Symons (London, 1955), 19–44; Hermann Muthesius, *Stilarchitektur und Baukunst* (Mülheim–Ruhr, 1902), 59. The quotation from Grover A. Whalen, president of the fair, was part of the exhibition 'The Machine Age in America, 1918–1941,' The Brooklyn Museum, 1986.

79 Karl Scheffler, 'Die Konventionen der Kunst (Aphoristisch),' *Die Kunst* 8 (1903), 301, 304.

80 Michael McKeon, *The Origins of the English Novel 1600–1740* (Baltimore, 1987), 20.

81 Moisei Ginzburg, *Style and Epoch*, tr. Anatole Senkevitch, Jr (New York and Cambridge, Mass., 1982), 78.

82 Ibid.

83 Scheffler, 'Die Konventionen der Kunst (Aphoristisch),' *Die Kunst* 8 (1903), 308.

84 James Fergusson, *The Illustrated Handbook of Architecture:*

Being a Concise and Popular Account of the Different Styles of Architecture Prevailing in All Ages and All Countries (2nd edn, London, 1859), lvi–lvii. See also Sigfried Giedion, *Space, Time and Architecture: The Growth of a New Tradition* (5th rev. edn, Cambridge, Mass., 1967), 251–4.

85 'Concours de *L'Encyclopédie*,' *Encyclopédie d'Architecture* (1889–90), 184. This competition announcement was published in other journals as well. See, for example, 'Appel à tous les architectes français. Un Concours sans programme,' *L'Architecte-Constructeur* 5 (31 August 1890), 123–4. For other articles related to this competition, see Anatole de Baudot, 'Le Concours de *l'Encyclopédie*'; Félix Narjoux, reporter, 'Concours de *L'Encyclopédie*. Rapport du jury'; 'Concours de *L'Encyclopédie*. Prorogation du concours,' *Encyclopédie d'Architecture* (1889–90), 169, (1890–91), 49, 65. For the resonance of this competition in Italy as well as the excitement generated there by the iron monuments at the 1889 Paris Exposition Universelle, see Etlin, *Modernism in Italian Architecture*, 3, 10–14, 20. For other expressions of enthusiasm for these iron monuments, see Meredith L. Clausen, *Frantz Jourdain and the Samaritaine: Art Nouveau Theory and Criticism* (Leiden, 1987), 84–8; Debora L. Silverman, *Art Nouveau in Fin-de-Siècle France: Politics, Psychology, and Style* (Berkeley and Los Angeles, 1989), 2–5.

86 Leo Marx, *The Machine in the Garden: Technology and the Pastoral Ideal in America* (Oxford and New York, 1964; 1968 reprint), 191.

87 Calvert Vaux, *Villas and Cottages: A Series of Designs Prepared for Execution in the United States* (New York: Harper & Brothers, 1857), 33.

88 Otto Wagner, *Die Baukunst unserer Zeit: Dem Baukunstjünger ein Führer auf diesem Kunstgebiete* (Vienna, 1914; 1979 reprint), 3: 'in der Zeit der Kraftwagen, Luftfahrzeuge, Überdreadnoughts.' The Dreadnought was an armored British battleship built in 1906.

89 Review of *On the Rise, Progress, and Present State of Public Opinion, in Great Britain and Other Parts of the World* (London, 1828), *Quarterly Review* 39 (April 1829), 490, 492.

90 'Preliminary Address,' *The Surveyor, Engineer, and Architect; or London Monthly Journal of the Physical and Practical Sciences in All Their Departments. By a Committee of Practical Surveyors, Engineers and Architects, of Much Experience and in Active Employment. Robert Mudie, Literary Conductor* 1 (1 February 1840), 1–3.

91 On this subject, see my discussion of the future street and modern apartment building popularized by Mario Morasso and their relationship to the architecture of Antonio Sant'Elia, in Etlin, *Modernism in Italian Architecture*, 79–88.

92 Horne, *A New Spirit of the Age*, 358.

93 On this theme see 'New Materials and Methods of Construction' in chapter 1.

94 Horatio Greenough, *Form and Function: Remarks on Art, Design, and Architecture*, ed. Harold A. Small (Berkeley and Los Angeles, 1947), 60–1.

95 Fergusson, *The Illustrated Handbook of Architecture* (1859), liv.

96 As quoted in French by Hendrik Petrus Berlage, *L'Art et la Société. Tirés à part de la revue 'Art et Technique' septembre 1913-février 1914* (Brussels, [1921]), 38–9. Berlage identifies this text as part of 'La voix des machines' by 'l'écrivain Lee.'

97 Ibid., 38

98 Henry Van de Velde, *Les Formules de la beauté architectonique moderne* (Weimar, 1917; 1978 reprint, Brussels), 22.

99 Lee, as quoted in Berlage, *L'Art et la société*, 39.

100 Muthesius, 'Das Moderne in der Architektur,' in *Kunstgewerbe und Architektur*, 31–2.

101 Greenough, *Form and Function*, 128. Greenough is describing the machine in this passage. For the comparable characterization of the Doric temple in general and the Parthenon in particular, see the preceding pages.

102 Van de Velde, 'Suite d'idées pour une conférence' (1903) in *Les Formules*, 86.

103 Camille Martin, 'L'Architecture du XXe siècle,' *L'Architecture Suisse* (February 1913), 48.

104 Martin, 'L'Architecture du XXe siècle (suite),' (April 1913) *L'Architecture Suisse*, 94.

105 Le Corbusier, *Vers une Architecture* (Paris, 1923; 3rd edn, 1928; 1958 reprint), xxiv.

106 Hans Schmidt, 'Le Corbusier als Architekt und Schriftsteller' (manuscript, 1927), in Hans Schmidt, *Beiträge zur Architektur 1924–1964*, ed. Bruno Flierl (Berlin, 1965), 29–30.

107 Four-page publicity brochure for Le Corbusier–Saugnier, *Vers une Architecture*, [p. 4]. Fondation Le Corbusier, Paris, B2(15).7.

108 The characterization is from Lewis Mumford, 'Frank Lloyd Wright and the New Pioneers,' *The Architectural Record* 65 (April 1929), 415. On this subject, see also Mary McLeod, ' "Architecture or Revolution": Taylorism, Technocracy, and Social Change,' *Art Journal* 43 (Summer 1983), 132–47.

109 Emile Magne, *L'Esthétique des villes* (Paris, 1908), 69.

110 Roger Marx, 'Préface' (10 November, 1897), *Les Maîtres de l'affiche* (Paris, 1898), III, iv. (These lines were later quoted in Gustave Kahn, *L'Esthétique de la rue* [Paris, 1901], 219.) Between 1896 and 1900, Marx published five volumes of this 'publication mensuelle contenant la reproduction des plus belles affiches illustrées des grands artistes, français et étrangers.'

111 Fernand Léger, 'Les Réalisations picturales actuelles' (1914), in Fernand Léger, *Fonctions de la peinture* (Paris, 1965), 20–2. For the entire text in English translation, see Fernand Léger, 'Contemporary Achievements in Painting,' in *Functions of Painting*, ed. Edward F. Fry, tr. Alexandra Anderson (New York, 1973). The translation here is my own.

112 Ibid., 20.

113 Georges Braques, 'Pensées et réflexions sur la peinture,' *Nord–Sud* no. 10 (December 1917), 3–5. *Nord–Sud* was edited by Paul Dermée, who would later co-edit *L'Esprit Nouveau* with Amédée Ozenfant and Le Corbusier.

114 Four-page publicity brochure for Le Corbusier–Saugnier, *Vers une Architecture*, [p. 3]. Fondation Le Corbusier, Paris, B2(15).7.

115 In 'Le Corbusier als Architekt und Schriftsteller,' Hans Schmidt uses the word 'propaganda' to refer to Le Corbusier's writings (Schmidt, *Beiträge zur Architektur 1924–1964*, 29).

116 R. V., 'Berlage a Bruxelles' *Tekhné* 2 (25 January 1913), 965–6; 'Art et Société,' *Tekhné* 2 (8 February 1913), 989; A. T., 'Biographie,' in Berlage, *L'Art et la société* (1921), 2.

117 Frank Lloyd Wright, 'In the Cause of Architecture,' *The Architectural Record* 23 (March 1908), now in Frank Lloyd Wright, *In the Cause of Architecture: Essays by Frank Lloyd Wright for 'Architectural Record,' 1908–52, with a Symposium on Architecture with and without Wright by Eight Who Knew Him*, ed. Frederick Gutheim (New York, 1960), 65.

118 Frank Lloyd Wright, *An Autobiography* (London and New York, 1932), 145, 152.

119 J. J. P. Oud, 'Architectural Observations Concerning Wright and the Robie House,' *De Stijl* no. 4 (1918), as published in translation by Elsa Scharbach in H. Allen Brooks, ed., *Writings on Wright: Selected Comment on Frank Lloyd Wright* (Cambridge, Mass., 1981), 136. Oud's reference to the south terrace as constructed out of concrete and then partially hidden with a brick veneer appears to be mistaken. On this subject, see chapter 1, note 140.

120 Donald Hoffmann, *Frank Lloyd Wright's Robie House: The*

Illustrated Story of an Architectural Masterpiece (New York, 1984), 5.

121 Ibid., 3.

122 Connors, *The Robie House*, 6.

123 William Allin Storrer, *The Architecture of Frank Lloyd Wright: A Complete Catalog* (2nd edn, Cambridge, Mass., 1979), item 173. This living room was reconstructed in the Metropolitan Museum of Art, New York, after its demolition in 1972.

124 Michael Graves, ed., *Le Corbusier: Selected Drawings* (New York, 1981), 12, 24 n. 2. Graves credits Anthony Eardley for first making this observation.

125 Le Corbusier and Pierre Jeanneret, *Oeuvre complète de 1929–1934* (1935; 7th edn, Zurich, 1964), 24.

126 Peter Mayle, *Toujours Provence* (New York: Vintage Books/ Random House, 1991), 41–2.

127 Le Corbusier and Pierre Jeanneret, *Oeuvre complète de 1929–1934*, 24: 'Mais on continue la promenade. Depuis le jardin à l'étage, on monte par la rampe sur le toit de la maison où est le solarium. L'architecture arabe nous donne un enseignement précieux. Elle s'apprécie *à la marche*, avec le pied. . . .'

128 Remarks by Le Corbusier at the international symposium 'Les Arts et la réalité contemporaine – L'Art et l'état,' Venice, 25–8 July 1934, in *L'Art et la réalité. L'Art et l'état* (Paris: Société des Nations, Institut international de coopération intellectuelle, n.d.), 76, 79. In *Modern Architecture Since 1900* (Englewood Cliffs, N.J., 1982), 187–92, William J. R. Curtis characterizes the nature of the architectural promenade of the Villa Savoye as 'some Corbusian machine-age ceremony' with a 'curious quality of ritual.' My own account is based on the remark made to me in the later 1970s by a former architect from Le Corbusier's *atelier* who explained that his colleagues there were fond of pointing out that the rectangular opening in the wall at the end of the promenade was a purposeful recollection of the view from the automobile window.

129 Curtis, *Modern Architecture Since 1900*, 193–5.

INDEX

Page numbers with illustrations are italicised.
Individual buildings and projects are generally listed under
placenames.

Ahmedabad
    Millowners' Association Building, *128*, 128–9, 163
    Villa Shodhan, 22, *26*, 127–8
Alberti, Leon Battista, 177
Algiers, high-rise buildings (project), 145–6
Amsterdam Exchange, 192
Appleton, Jay, 35, 39
Architectural Magazine, 3, 157
Arizona (San-Marcos-in-the-Desert)
    Owen D. Young House, 48, *50*
    Wellington and Ralph Cudney House, 48, *50*
Art et Technique, 189
artisans' houses (project), 145, *146*
Athens
    Acropolis, 9, 83–90, 92–101, 104–5, *106*, 107, 111–14, 137, 142,
            164, 198
        Ecole Française d'Athènes, 83, 88–9, 92–3
        Erechtheion, 8, *84*, 90, 92–3, 95, *96*, *98*, 99, 101, 113–14, 142
        Panathenaia, 198
        Parthenon, *84*, 85–8, 90, *98*, 99, *100*, 113–14, 142, 158, 163–4,
            174–5, 181–3, *190*, 198
        Propylaia, *84*, 90, 92–3, *98*, 99, 101, 113–14, 116, 163, 174, 198
        Statue of Athena Promachos, 101, 113
        Temple of Athena Nike, 87, 90, *100*

Bachelard, Gaston, 32, 35, 39, 72, 74, 130
Ballanche, Pierre-Simon, 151
Banham, Reyner, 59
Barzun, Jacques, 170
Baudelaire, Charles, 32
Baudot, Anatole de, 5, 161
Baumann, Frederick, 27
Baumeister, Reinhard, 107
Beltrami, Luca, 167
Berlage, Hendrik Petrus, 6–7, 11–12, 182, 187, 189, *190–1*, 192
Beulé, Ernest, 83, 92–3, 96, 101
Blanc, Charles, 85, 163
Blondel, Jacques-François, 124
Böckh, August, 173
Boetticher, Karl, 6, 99
Bosco, Henri, 71
Botta, Paul Emile, 5, 103
Boullée, Etienne-Louis, 155–6
Boulogne-sur-Seine
    Hôtel Collinet, *120*, 121
    Maison Cook, 15, 17, *18–19*, 119, 121, *122*, 123–5, 145, 161, 163,
            192, 194, *195*, 196
Boutmy, Emile, 166
Bracque, Georges, 187
Brooks, H. Allen, 111–12
Broussa
    Green Mosque, 113
Brussels
    Maison du Peuple, *191*, 192
    Philips Pavilion, 23
    Université Nouvelle, 189

Buffalo
    Larkin Company Administration Building, *36–7*, 39, 59, 61, 136,
            191, 192–3
    Darwin D. Martin House, *32*, 57–8, 129
Buls, Charles, 106
Burgh, William, 77
Burckhardt, Jacob, 170
Burnouf, Emile, 163, 175
Byron, George Gordon, Lord, 169–70

California
    Los Angeles
        Charles Ennis House, 57, 160
        Dr. John Storer House, 160
        Samuel Freeman House, *49*, 51
    Pasadena
        Alice Millard House ('La Miniatura'), *46*, 50–1
    San Raphael
        Marin County Civic Center, 160
Carlyle, Thomas, 178
Chambers, William, 85, 182
Chipiez, Charles, 163
Choisy, Auguste, 5, 8–9, *10*, 27, 47, 76, 93, 96–7, *98*, *103–4*, 105, *106*,
            107, 109, 112–16, 124, *125*, 152, 161, *162*, 173–5, 198
Cockerell, Charles Robert, 102
Coleridge, Samuel, 170
Collins, George R. and Christianne Crasemann, 110–11
Combes, Louis, 155
Cordemoy, Jean-Louis de, 155
Cousin, Victor, 151
Craftsman, 4
Crystal Palace, *see* London
Curtis, William, J. R., 158, 198
Cuvier, Georges, 172

Daly, César, 165–6
Davis, Alexander Jackson, *132*
Dr Currutchet's House, *see* La Plata
Dom-ino, *15*
Donaldson, Thomas Leverton, 102, 154, 166, 173
Dörpfeld, Wilhelm, 105
Downing, Andrew Jackson, 80, *81*, 82, 109
Duchamp-Villon, Raymond, 123, *124*, 125
Duff, William, 156–7

Eckermann, Johann Peter, 176
Edinburgh Review, 170
Encyclopédie d'Architecture, 13, 180
Etchells, Frederick, 14
Eveux-sur-Arbresle (Monastery of La Tourette), 147, *148*

Fallingwater, *see* Pennsylvania
Fergusson, James, 11, 89–90, *91*, 92, 95, 100, 105, 180–1
Fichte, Johann Gottlieb, 171–3
Five Points for a New Architecture, 15, *16*, 17, 22–3, 119, 121, 126–7,
            161, 194–5
Ford, Edward R., 58–9
Forster, Kurt, 115–16, *117*, 119, 158
Förster, Ludwig von, 167
Frampton, Kenneth, 60

Garbett, Edward Lacy, 2–3, 6
Garches (Villa Stein), 15, 17, *20*, *119*, 124, 127–9, 161–4, 192, *195*, 196
Gill, Brendan, 51
Ginzburg, Moisei, 150, 156–7, 179
Godwin, William, 170
Goecke, Theodor, 110
Goethe, Johann Wolfgang von, 176
Gombrich, Ernst, 170
Goodwin, Francis, 80
Great Exhibition, *see* London
Greenough, Horatio, 181, 183
Gris, Juan, *118*, 119, 121–2
Guadet, Julien, 123

Hall, Edward T., 32
Hazlitt, William, 169–70
Hegel, Georg Wilhelm Friedrich, 170, 172–3
Henrici, Karl, *111*
Herder, Johann Gottfried, 151, 169
Hildebrand, Grant, 34, 135
Hitchcock, Henry-Russell, 17, 55, 61, 132–3, 150, 153
Hoffer, Joseph, 87–8
Hoffmann, Donald, 53, 135
Hoffmann, Josef, 4
Home in a prairie town (project), 134
Hope, Thomas, 2, 152–4
Horne, Richard, 169, 181
Horta, Victor, *191*, 192
Huysmans, Joris-Karl, 12 3

Illinois
  Chicago
    Frederick C. Robie House, *31*, *35*, 42, 57, 58–60, 130, 134–5, 192, 194
    Isidore Heller House, 130
    James Charnley House, 130
    World's Columbian Exposition (1893), 13
      Ho-o-Den, 27, *31*
  Highland Park
    Ward W. Willits House, *45*, 58, *59*, 133, 143, 159
  Kankakee
    B. Harley Bradley House, 40, *44*, 47, 58, 130, 132–4, 143
    Warren R. Hickcox House, 40, *43*, 47, 130, 132–3
  La Grange
    Emmond House, 132
  Oak Park
    Frank Lloyd Wright House, 133
    Frank Thomas House, 40, 47, 129
    Arthur Heurtley House, 47, *58*, 129
    Ullman House, 57
    Unity Temple, 39, 47, 48, 57, 59, 61, 136
  River Forest
    Golf Club, 40, 42
    Isabel Roberts House, 134, *135*
    Winslow House, 39, *42*, 47, 130, 134, 160
  Riverside
    Avery Coonley House, 56, 129, *131*
  Springfield
    Susan Lawrence Dana House, *131*, 134
India (Chandigarh)
  High Court, *72*, 146–7, 163–4
  Open Hand, *72*, 73
  Secretariat, 147
Inland Architect and Record News, 27
International Style, 17
Isabelle, Charles-Edouard, 5

Jerrold, Walter, 169

Johnson, Philip, 17
Jouffroy, Théodore, 151

Kahn, Louis, 134
Kant, Immanuel, 170–1
Kawerau, Georg, 105
Khorsabad (King Sargon's summer palace), 103, *104*
Klenze, Leo von, 155
Knight, Richard Payne, 76, 78
Kugler, Franz, 88

Labrouste, Henri, 89, 153
La Celle Saint-Cloud (Weekend House), 23, *28*
Lake Léman (*Une Petite maison*), 69, 70–4, 147
Lake Tahoe cabins and residential barges (projects), 140
Laloux, Victor, 105
La Plata (Dr Currutchet's House,) 22, *24*, 127–8
Lassus, Jean-Baptiste-Antoine, 2
La Tourette, *see* Eveux-sur-Arbresle
Laugier, Marc-Antoine, 155, 205
Layard, Austen Henry, 103
Leake, James, 85–6, 100
Léger, Fernand, 187
Lenoir, Albert, 5
Leroux, Pierre, 166, 173
Les Mathes (Vacation House), 23, *29*
Levine, Neil, 139, 204–5
Lipman, Jonathan, 60–1
Livadia, 174
Liverpool (Saint Oswald's), *80*
London, Great Exhibition of 1851 (Crystal Palace), 13, 180
Loudon, John Claudius, 3, 77, 79, 157–8
Lytton, Edward Bulwer, 169–70, 176

Madrid (Sixth International Congress of Architects, 1904), 7
Magne, Emile, 167, 187
Maillart, Robert, 61
Mallet-Stevens, Robert, *120*, 121
Manson, Grant Carpenter, 34
Marseille (Unité d'Habitation), 147, *148*, 164
Martin, Camille, 106, *109*, 110–11, 125, 150, 177–8, 183
Marx, Leo, 180
Marx, Roger, 187
Mason, William, 77
Massachusetts
  Cambridge (Carpenter Center for the Visual Arts), 22, *25*, 129, 136, 163
  New Bedford (Rotch House), *132*
Mazzoni, Angiolo, 4
McKim, Meade and White, 142
McLeod, Mary, 128
McLuhan, Marshall, 186
Mendelsohn, Erich, 176
Mill, John Stuart, 168
Minnesota (Deephaven, Second Francis W. Little House), 194; *see also* Owatonna
Monceaux, Paul, 105
Muthesius, Hermann, 8, 11, *118*, 176, 178, 182

Nash, John, 77
Neuilly (Jaoul Houses), 23, *29*
Newport (Kingscote), 130
New York
  Buffalo (Guaranty Building), 142
  New York City (Solomon R. Guggenheim Museum), 39, *40*, 51, 64, 136, 160
  Tuxedo Park
    Chandler House, 132
    Kent House, 132, *133*

Ojetti, Ugo, 3
Oklahoma
    Bartlesville (Price Company Tower), 62, *63*
    Tulsa (Richard Lloyd Jones House), *52*, 160
Oud, J. J. P., 194
Owatonna, Minn. (National Farmers' Bank), *191*, 192
Ozenfant, Amédée, 118, 124

Paccard, Alexis, 96–7, 107
Panofsky, Erwin, 170
Papworth, John, 85–7
Paris
    Académie des Beaux Arts, 1, 83, 89, 99
    Bibliothèque Sainte-Geneviève, 153
    Ecole des Beaux-Arts, 89
    Eglise Sainte-Geneviève, 155
    Exposition Universelle, 1889 (Eiffel Tower and Galerie des
        Machines), 13, 180
    Hôtel du Maine (later Hôtel de Biron, now Musée Rodin), *125*
    La Roche-Jeanneret Houses, 111, 115–18, *117*, 122, 129, 158
    Saint Vincent-de-Paul, 155
    Salon d'Automne, 1912 (Maison Cubiste), 123, *124*
    Swiss Dormitory (Pavillon Suisse), 18, 21, *22*, 147–8, 199
Peiraieus (Arsenal), 174–5
Pennethorne, John, 9, 87–8
Pennsylvania
    Bear Run
        Edgar J. Kaufmann House (Fallingwater), 52–3, *54*, 61, 141
    Elkins Park
        Beth Sholom Synagogue, *64*–5, 160
    Philadelphia
        Girard College Building Committee, 167
    Pittsburgh
        Allegheny County Courthouse, 142
Penrose, Francis Cranmer, 87–8, 100, 173, 175
Perret, Auguste, 13
Perriand, Charlotte, 21
Perrot, Georges, 163
Pfeiffer, Bruce Brooks, 129
Place of all measures, 73, *74*
Place, Victor, 103
Plumet, Charles, 11
Poelzig, Hans, 4–5, 8
Poissy (Villa Savoye), 15, 17, *21*, 125–9, 158, 163–4, 192–4, 196, *197*,
    198
Pompe, Antoine, 167, 170
Pompeii, 173
    Casa del Noce, 114
    House of the Tragic Poet, 114–15, 158
Pond, Irving K., 29
Price, Bruce, 132, *133*
Proust, Marcel, 120
Pugin, Augustus Welby, 5, 79, *80*, 92, 168
Pullan, Richard Popplewell, 4, 177

Quarterly Review, 180
Quatremère de Quincy, Antoine-Chrysostôme, 1–3, 8, 14, 47, 48, 92
Quicherat, Jules, 5

Ramée, Daniel, 154
Raoul-Rochette, Désiré, 1–2, 8
Renan, Ernst, 11, 92, 164
Reveley, Willey, 85, 163, 182
Revett, Nicholas, 85, 183
Reynaud, Léonce, 3, 7, 12, 161
Richardson, Henry Hobson, 142
Riegl, Alois, 170

Rome
    Associazione Artistica fra i Cultori di Architettura, 106
    Baths of Caracalla, *104*
    Baths of Diocletian, 102
    Pantheon, 134
    Santa Maria in Cosmedin, 125, *126*
Ronchamp (Notre-Dame-du-Haut), 23, *30*, 164
Root, John Wellborn, 27
Ross, Ludwig, 87
Rowe, Colin, 119, 158, 162
Ruskin, John, 30, 89, 142, 166

Sainte-Beuve, Charles-Augustin, 151
St Oswald's, *see* Liverpool
Scheffler, Karl, 4, 177–9
Schelling, Friedrich Wilhlem Joseph von, 171
Schinkel, Karl Friedrich, 167
Schliemann, Heinrich, 105
Schmidt, Hans, 186–7
Schnaase, Carl, 88
Schopenhauer, Arthur, 5–6
Schuyler, Montgomery, 11, 13, 167
Scott, George Gilbert, 178
Scully, Vincent, 61, 64, 136
Semper, Gottfried, 6, 8, 27–8, 33, 47, 51, 53
Shaubert, Edward, 87
Shelley, Percy Bysshe, 169
Singelenberg, Pieter, 167
Sitte, Camillo, 77, 106–7, *108–9*, 110–12, 115
Slutsky, Robert, 119, 162
Soufflot, Jacques-Germain, 155
Spencer, Robert C., Jr, 159
Stahl, Fritz, 8
Street, George Edmund, 4, 156–7
Stewart, Dugald, 77–9
Stuart, James, 85, 183
Sullivan, Louis, 13, 142, *191*, 192
Supervielle, Jules, 71
Surveyor, Engineer, and Architect, 181
Sydenham (Crystal Palace), 180

Taine, Hippolyte, 166, 172–3
Taliesin, *see* Wisconsin
Terragni, Giuseppe, 177
Tetaz, Jacques-Martin, 92–3
Thomson, Alexander, 142
Tokyo (Imperial Hotel), 56
Troy, Nancy, 123
Turin (Prima Esposizione Internazionale d'Arte Decorativa Moderna,
    1902), 3, 175–6

Upjohn, Richard, 130

Van de Velde, Henry, 176, 182–3, 187
Vaux, Calvert, 180
Venice (International symposium, Les Arts et la réalité
    contemporaine – L'Art et l'état, 1934), 198
Vienna
    Ringstrasse, 107, 190–1
    Secession Building, 167
Vignola, Giacomo Barozzi da, 70, 73
Villa Stein, *see* Garches
Viollet-le-Duc, Eugène-Emmanuel, 2, 4–5, 8, 27, 47, 80, 105, 109,
    129–30, 168
    Entretiens sur l'architecture (Discourses on Architecture), 4–5,
        8–10, 47, 50, 76, *82*, 83, 93, 95, *96*, 97, 153–4, 165, 173
Vitet, Ludovic, 1–3, 77, 151–2, 155, 167
Voltaire, 168–9

Wagner, Otto
  Moderne Architektur (Die Baukunst unserer Zeit), 4, 11, 180, *188*,
    189
Walhalla, 155
Warton, Joseph, 169
Washington, D. C.
  Crystal Heights (project), 63
White, Charles E., Jr, *159*
Willis, Robert, 156–7
Wils, Jans, 167
Wisconsin
  Driftless Area, 33–4
  Madison
    First Herbert Jacobs House, 65, *66–7*, 68, 136, 143–4
    John C. Pew House, 137, *138*, 139–40, *141*, 142, *143*, 144

Middleton
  Second Herbert Jacobs House, 40, *41*
Racine
  Johnson Wax Administration Building, *38*, 39, 60–1, 62, 68, 136
  Johnson Wax Research Tower, *62*
Spring Green
  Taliesin, 34, 52
  Unity Temple and Cenotaph (project), 160
Wolfe, Tom, 168
Wölfflin, Heinrich, 170
Wordsworth, William, 169–70
Wright, Iovanna Lloyd, 34
Wright, John Lloyd, 48

Yucatán, Mexico
  Great Gallery of Aké, 160, *161*